Embroidery Stitches
STEP BY STEP

· · · · · · · · · · ◆ · · · · · · · · · · ·

Embroidery Stitches
STEP BY STEP

Lucinda Ganderton

DK

Dedicated to the memory of
Mary Josephine Ganderton,
my mother and my inspiration

Senior Editor: Mary Lindsay
Senior Art Editor: Sarah Hall
Production Controller: Michelle Thomas
DTP Designer: Jason Little
Managing Editors: Stephanie Jackson, Jonathan Metcalf
Managing Art Editor: Nigel Duffield
Jacket Designer: Nicola Powling

Produced by
C&B Packaging Ltd
London House, Great Eastern Wharf
Parkgate Road, London SW11 4NQ

Managing Editor: Kate Yeates
Editor: Heather Dewhurst
Art Director: Roger Bristow
Art Editor: Helen Collins
Designers: Suzanne Metcalfe-Megginson, Bill Mason
Photography: Sampson Lloyd

First published in Great Britain in 1999
This edition published in Great Britain in 2015 by
Dorling Kindersley Limited,
80 Strand, London, WC2R 0RL

Copyright © 1999, 2015 Dorling Kindersley Limited
A Penguin Random House Company
Text copyright © 1999, 2015 Lucinda Ganderton
The moral right of Lucinda Ganderton to be
identified as the author of this book has
been asserted.
10 9 8 7 6 5 4 3 2 1
001-280243-June/2015

All rights reserved.
No part of this publication may be reproduced,
stored in or introduced into a retrieval system, or
transmitted, in any form, or by any means
(electronic, mechanical, photocopying, recording, or
otherwise) without the prior written permission of
the copyright owner.

A CIP catalogue record for this book
is available from the British Library.

ISBN: 978-0-2412-0139-8

Printed and bound in China.
Colour reproduction by Altaimage UK.

All images © Dorling Kindersley Limited
For further information see: www.dkimages.com

A WORLD OF IDEAS:
SEE ALL THERE IS TO KNOW

CONTENTS

INTRODUCTION 6

· · · · · · · · · ◆ · · · · · · · ·

HOW TO USE THIS BOOK
9

· · · · · · · · · ◆ · · · · · · · ·

MATERIALS, TOOLS, AND TECHNIQUES 10

· · · · · · · · · ◆ · · · · · · · ·

TOOLS, FABRICS, THREADS, AND FRAMES
12

MOUNTING TECHNIQUES
17

STITCHING TECHNIQUES
18

· · · · · · · · · ◆ · · · · · · · ·

GALLERY OF STITCHES 22

· · · · · · · · · ◆ · · · · · · · ·

Line and Border Stitches 36

..........◆..........

Outline Stitches
38
Border Stitches
47
Composite Border Stitches
62

..........◆..........

Filling Stitches 70

..........◆..........

Powdered Filling and Isolated Stitches
72
Open and Solid Filling Stitches
84

..........◆..........

Openwork Stitches 94

..........◆..........

Pulled Fabric Stitches
96
Drawn Thread and Insertion Stitches
104
Cutwork and Edging Stitches
111

..........◆..........

Needlepoint Stitches 116

..........◆..........

Straight Needlepoint Stitches
118
Diagonal Needlepoint Stitches
128
Cross and Star Needlepoint Stitches
138
Looped and Tied Needlepoint Stitches
150

..........◆..........

Index and Acknowledgments
156

..........◆..........

Introduction

THE ART OF embroidery has been defined simply as the ornamentation of textiles with decorative stitchery. It is an ancient craft which encompasses a wealth of history, and the same stitches are used by embroiderers throughout the world. They provide an international vocabulary that crosses the boundaries of land and time. Local patterns, designs, and ways of working vary from place to place, but the actual stitch techniques do not. The language of stitches is infinitely adaptable. It is being constantly reinterpreted by contemporary stitchers, who produce their new work as part of a continuing tradition.

INTERNATIONAL HERITAGE

Sewing was once an essential part of daily life for most women, and some men. Before mass production, many clothes and items of domestic furnishing had to be made at home and embroidery evolved as a means of decorating and personalising the plain needlework used for household linens and garments.

People in different countries concentrated on their own particular aspects of embroidery and names such as Bokhara couching, Antwerp edging, Portuguese border, and Algerian eye reflect the international aspect of the stitches they worked with. Creative concepts are always interchanged; patterns and ideas have travelled and developed throughout the world. German immigrants in Pennsylvania, for example, had to adapt their own traditional dense cross stitch patterns to outline-based designs, because of the shortage of embroidery threads in the New World.

PORTRAIT OF A LADY
Fine silk threads in a subtle range of natural dyes were used to embroider this eighteenth century picture. Layers of straight stitches have been worked in many directions to build up the image.

FLORAL BORDER
Long decorative bands, like this tent stitch pattern in bright Berlin wools, were worked by Victorian ladies and used to adorn cushions and throws.

Types of Stitch

Embroidery stitches are worked on fabric, while needlepoint stitches are sewn on to canvas. Although there are hundreds of individual stitches used for both these techniques, they can be classified into just four groups, according to the way they are constructed: flat stitches which lie on the surface of the fabric; looped stitches, where one stitch is anchored by another; knotted stitches in which the thread is twisted back on itself to form a raised stitch, and openwork stitches which create a regular pattern of spaces, integrating the thread with the background fabric.

Using Stitches

The various stitches within these four groups are endlessly adaptable and can be used in many ways, depending on the effect required. They can outline a design, be worked closely together so that they conceal the fabric completely, or be spaced further apart to allow the background to show through. Others may be used singly, repeated in rows, or stitched in a solid line.

Certain stitches were developed for particular reasons. Gold thread is costly and too thick to pass easily through the fabric, so couching stitch was used to anchor it to the fabric with small stitches in fine thread. Turkey stitch evolved as an imitation of the cut pile of a rug, and insertion stitches were used as a means of joining two pieces of fabric.

One single stitch may be used throughout a piece of work. Rows of tent and cross stitches are used to create both samplers and embroidered pictures, while straight stitch can be used randomly like a painter's brushstrokes to build up a textured, three-dimensional surface. It is when the patterns and shapes of the various stitches are combined, however, that their full potential is realised.

Stitch Names

For many centuries, knowledge of embroidery stitches was handed down as part of the wider folk tradition of needlecraft. It was not until 1631, when *The Needle's Excellency* was printed, that their names began to be formalised in Europe. This was a book of patterns,

Country Garden
This characteristic transfer design from the 1930s features plants worked with French knots, link, fly, and buttonhole stitches, and outlines in stem stitch.

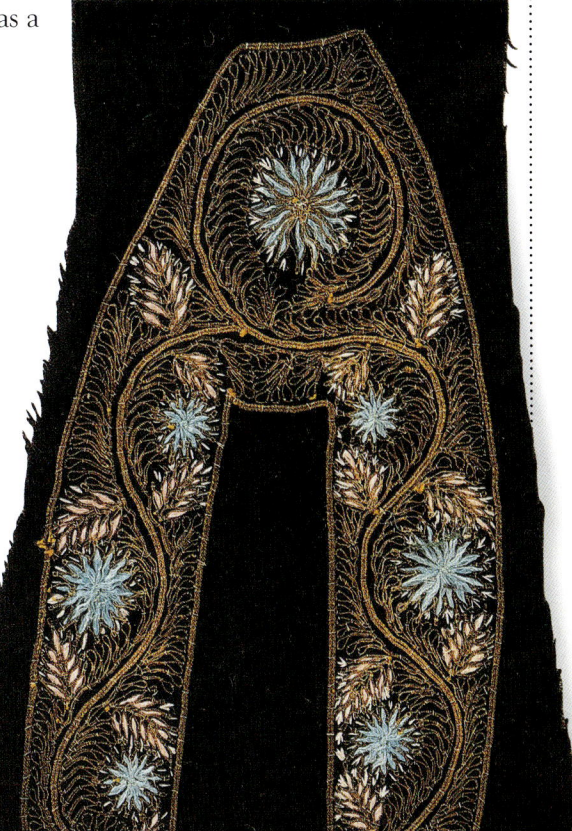

Gold Slipper
Straight stitch flowers in silk floss have been combined with gold thread couched in a swirling pattern to decorate this beautiful nineteenth century slipper top.

not a practical manual, and there were no working diagrams or stitch illustrations. Some of the stitches listed – Fern-stitch, Chain-stitch, Back-stitch and the Crosse-stitch – are still in general use. Various other names were adopted over the following centuries. Some described the way in which the actual stitches were made, for example, twisted insertion and back stitch trellis. Others, such as cushion stitch, ladder stitch, window filling, and rope stitch, were named after the objects of daily life that they resembled. Still more were inspired by the surroundings of the natural world: star, wave, cloud, feather, coral, leaf, petal, and wheatear stitches.

Needlework was not valued as a separate area of study until the late nineteenth century. Under the influence of the Arts and Crafts Movement, designers interested in the history of stitching set about examining embroidered fabrics, and even unpicked old examples from across the world to discover how they had been worked. New historical texts and instruction books were written, and the format and names of stitches were standardised for the first time.

MIRROR, MIRROR
Shisha stitch, using tiny mirrors, highlights the traditional chain stitch design of a contemporary Indian embroidery in silk rayon.

INDIAN PATCHWORK
Fragments of antique fabrics in metallic threads were salvaged and stitched together to make this hanging.

How to Use This Book

The book is divided into six chapters. The first deals with the equipment, threads, and fabrics used for stitchery, and the various techniques involved. This is followed by the Gallery of stitches, which is a visual library of the 234 stitches featured. The stitch instructions are grouped into four chapters – Lines and Borders, Filling Stitches, Openwork, and Needlepoint – each of which has several sub-sections showing the different types of stitches within the group.

Gallery of Stitches
These pages provide a quick visual reference to all the stitches featured in the book. The name of each one is given, followed by the number of the page where the instructions for working it can be found.

28 Gallery of Stitches

Bullion Knot (p.76) · Sorbello (p.79) · Tulip (p.81)
Danish Knot (p.77) · Palestrina Knot (p.79) · Woven Spider Web (p.82)
Four-legged Knot (p.77) · Link (p.80) · Ribbon Rose (p.82)
Sword (p.77) · Lazy Daisy (p.80) · Ribbed Web (p.82)
Fly (p.78) · Berry (p.80) · Buttonhole Wheel (p.82)
Sheaf Filling (p.78) · Picot (p.80)
Crown (p.78) · Detached Wheatear (p.81) · Shisha (p.83)

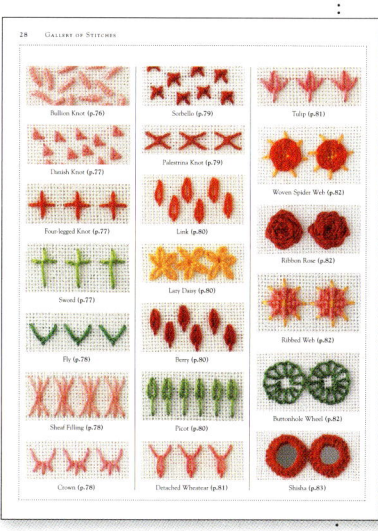

Stitch Instruction Chapters

Stitch Example
Illustrates finished appearance of stitch

Other Name
Shows most common alternatives for stitches with two or more names

Level
Indicates the skill level required to make the stitch – easy, intermediate, or advanced

Uses
Suggests practical ways in which each stitch can be used or adapted

Method
Describes the way in which the stitch is constructed

Materials
Lists type of fabric, thread, and any other equipment needed

Letter Annotation
Shows points at which needle enters and exits fabric, in alphabetical order

80 Powdered Filling and Isolated Stitches

Link

Other Name: Detached chain stitch
Level: Easy
Uses: Scattered as light filling; leaves and flower petals
Method: Single looped stitch
Materials: Any fabric; any thread

1 Start at A. Make a loop and take the needle down at A. Come out at B and pull the needle through over the working thread.

2 Insert the needle directly below B, at C, making a tie stitch (see p.20) to complete.

Berry

Level: Intermediate
Uses: Powdered filling; flowers and leaves
Method: Double link stitch
Materials: Any fabric; any thread

Make a small link stitch (see above). Bring the needle out at A and slide it under the tie stitch between B and C. Take the needle back up and insert at A to complete the stitch.

Picot

Other Name: Long-tailed daisy stitch
Level: Easy
Uses: Powdered filling; in circles as floral motif
Method: Link variation with long tie stitch
Materials: Any fabric; any thread

Start at A and follow link stitch (see above) the needle down belo[w] C, to make a long tie

Stitch Variation
Trammed tent stitch is s[…] over long straight stitch[…] worked through the sma[…] a double canvas. Thi[…] [e]dged effect and beca[…] [har]dwearing, this stitch […] for seat covers.

Technique Variation
Make a slanting straight stitch on either side of the picot stitch, instead of a single one passing beneath the tie stitch (see step 2 above). This creates the effect of two separate leaves at the base of the flower.

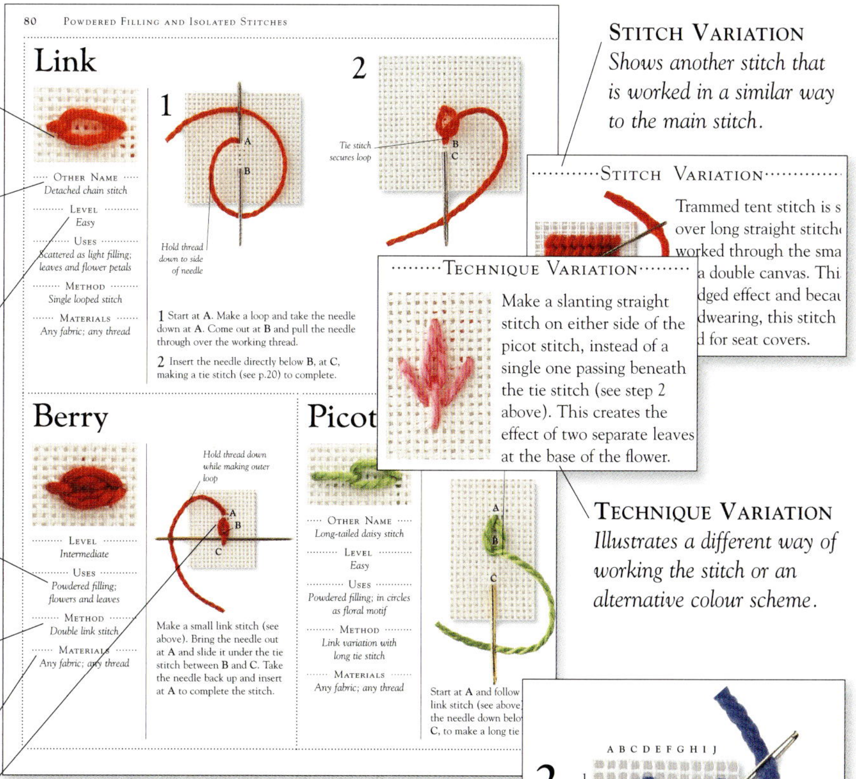

Stitch Variation
Shows another stitch that is worked in a similar way to the main stitch.

Technique Variation
Illustrates a different way of working the stitch or an alternative colour scheme.

Grid System on Needlepoint Pages
Every hole on the canvas can be located by using the grid system. The horizontal rows are labelled with numbers at one side and the vertical rows with letters along the top or bottom edge. The start and end points for each stitch are referred to by a number (indicating the horizontal row) and a letter (indicating the vertical row), eg 9F to 7F.

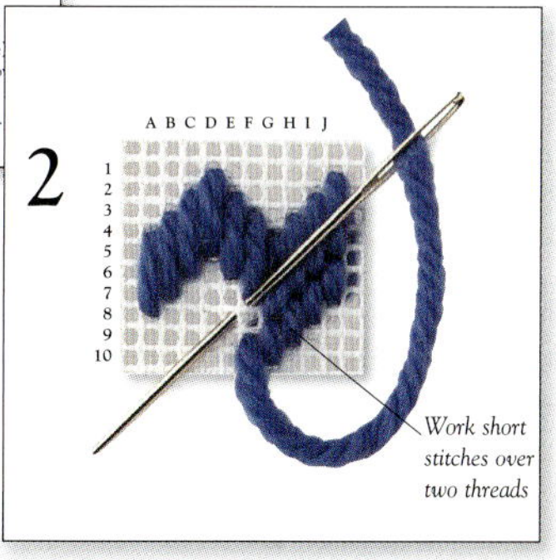

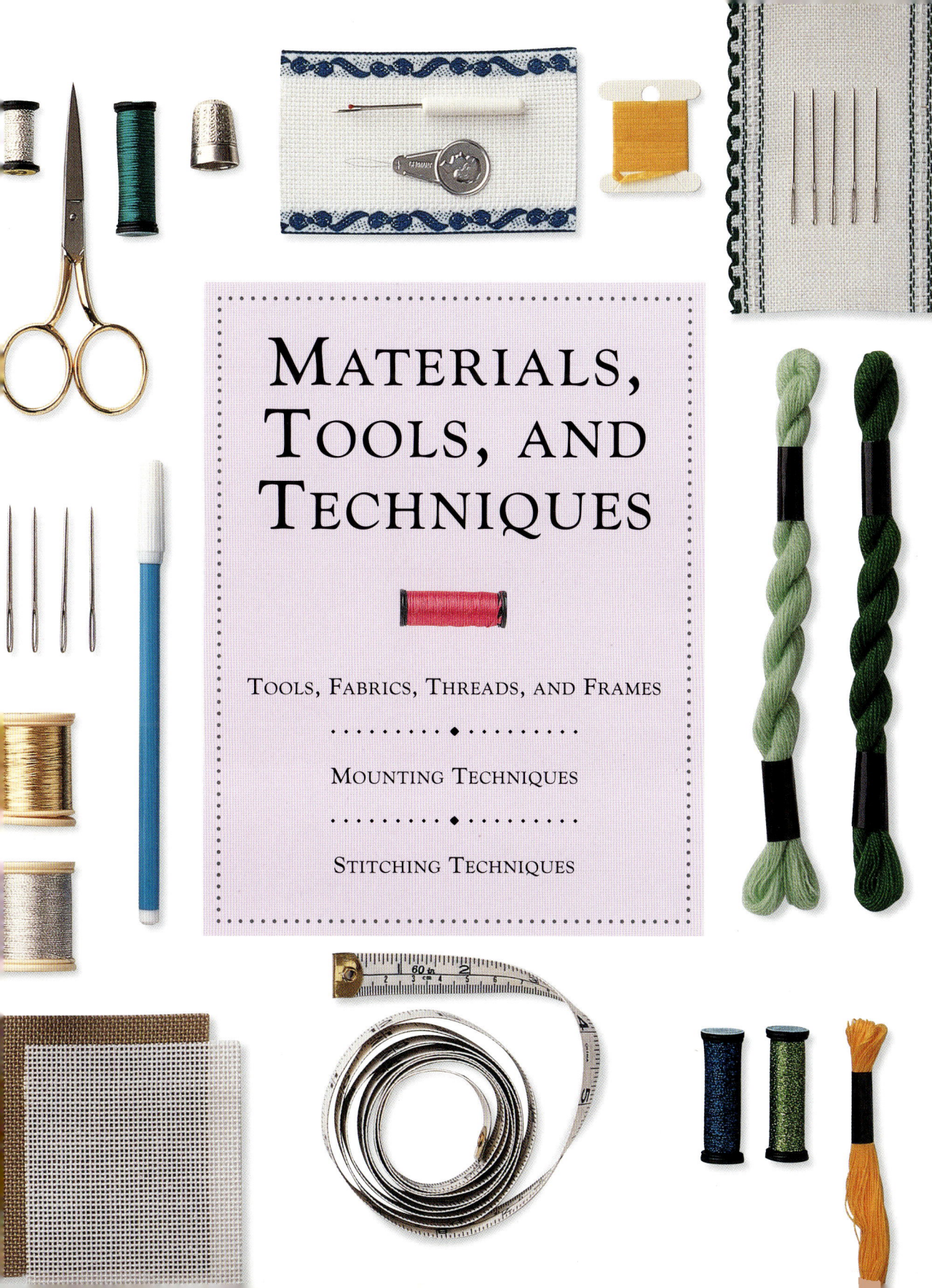

Materials, Tools, and Techniques

Tools, Fabrics, Threads, and Frames

· · · · · · · · · ◆ · · · · · · · · ·

Mounting Techniques

· · · · · · · · · ◆ · · · · · · · · ·

Stitching Techniques

Tools, Fabrics, Threads, and Frames

The basic equipment required for embroidery is minimal; as with many other sewing crafts, all that is necessary to start stitching is a needle, a length of thread, a piece of cloth, and a pair of scissors. Much time and care will be invested in creating a finished piece of needlework, so the choice of materials at the outset is important. In order to achieve a professional and long-lasting result it is worth investing in the best quality tools, threads, and fabric, and in taking time over their selection.

> **Handy Tip**
>
> Purpose-made sewing boxes and fabric-lined wicker baskets are the traditional way, to keep embroidery equipment together in one place. Art storage cases and plastic tool boxes from hardware suppliers provide practical alternatives: they are easy to transport and have many individual compartments in which to store threads, needles, and scissors.

Workbox Tools

Every workbox should be equipped with two pairs of sharp, steel-bladed scissors: large shears for cutting out cloth or canvas, and pointed embroidery scissors to clip threads and knots. A stitch ripper is convenient for unpicking mistakes and removing tacking. Dressmaker's pencils or pens are used to draw motifs and guidelines directly on to fabric. Choose a pen with fading ink for any items that cannot be washed, or a watersoluble version for those that will be laundered. Chalk leaves a fine powdered line which can easily be brushed away. A ruler and tape measure may also prove helpful when marking up designs. A needle threader, pins, and thimble are also useful tools.

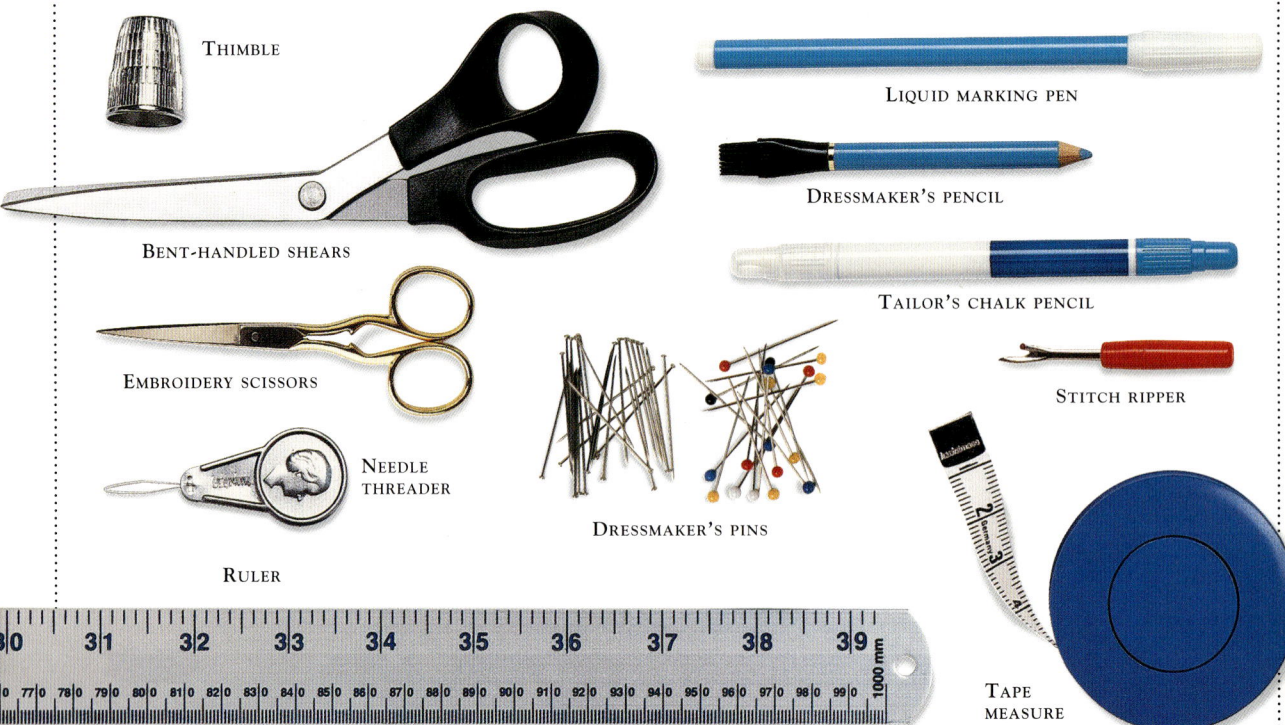

THIMBLE

BENT-HANDLED SHEARS

EMBROIDERY SCISSORS

NEEDLE THREADER

RULER

DRESSMAKER'S PINS

LIQUID MARKING PEN

DRESSMAKER'S PENCIL

TAILOR'S CHALK PENCIL

STITCH RIPPER

TAPE MEASURE

Fabric and Canvas

Stitches can be worked on to any fabric, but there is a wide range designed especially for embroidery. Woven from cotton or linen, the square mesh produces regular, even stitches. They are gauged by the count or number of threads to every 2.5cm (1in): the more threads, the finer the fabric. Use soft, single thread evenweave for counted thread, pulled fabric, and drawn thread work; double thread (Aida, Binca or Hardanger) for geometric patterns and cross stitch; and canvas for needlepoint.

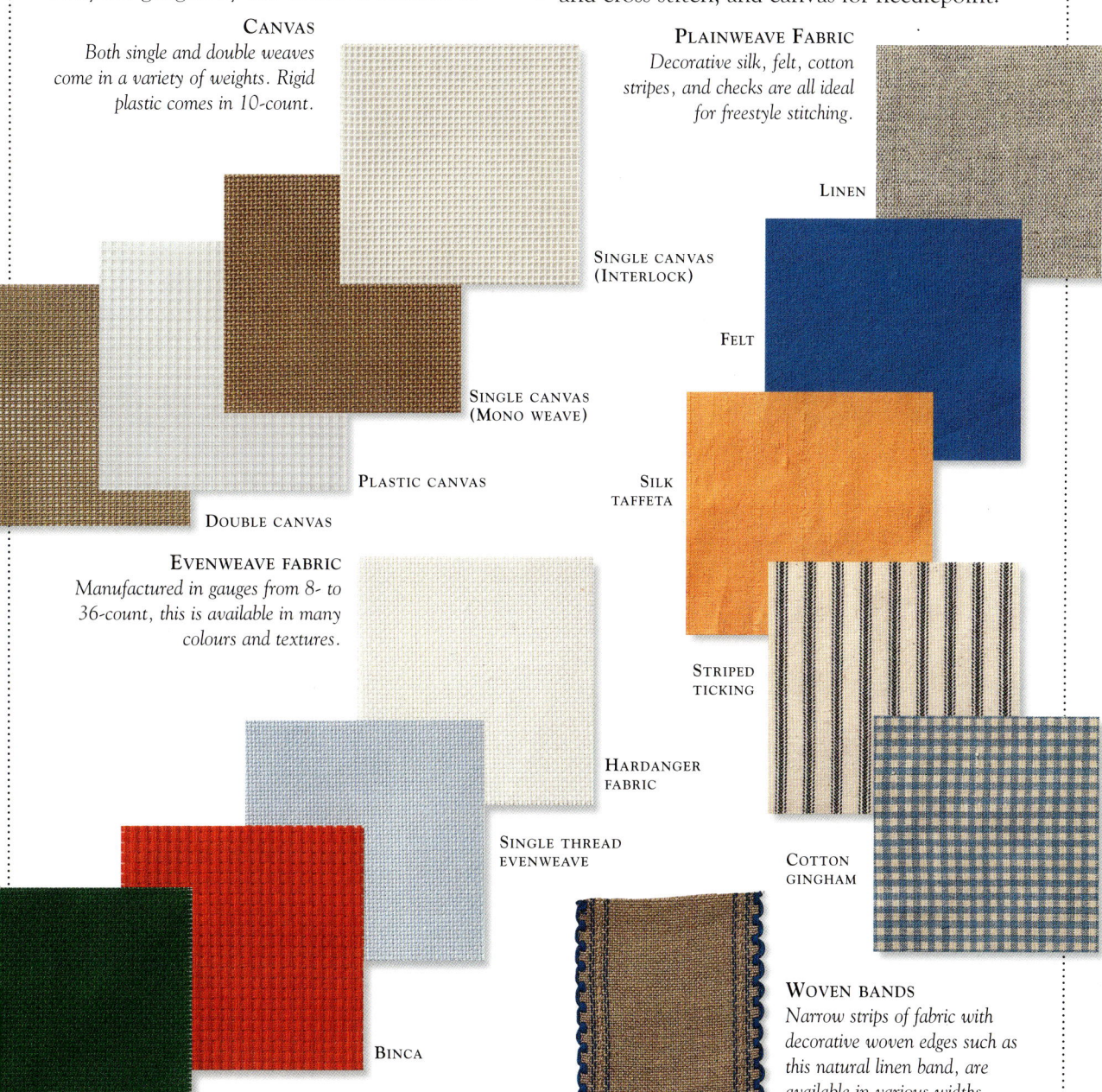

CANVAS
Both single and double weaves come in a variety of weights. Rigid plastic comes in 10-count.

- SINGLE CANVAS (INTERLOCK)
- SINGLE CANVAS (MONO WEAVE)
- PLASTIC CANVAS
- DOUBLE CANVAS

PLAINWEAVE FABRIC
Decorative silk, felt, cotton stripes, and checks are all ideal for freestyle stitching.

- LINEN
- FELT
- SILK TAFFETA
- STRIPED TICKING
- COTTON GINGHAM

EVENWEAVE FABRIC
Manufactured in gauges from 8- to 36-count, this is available in many colours and textures.

- HARDANGER FABRIC
- SINGLE THREAD EVENWEAVE
- BINCA
- AIDA CLOTH

WOVEN BANDS
Narrow strips of fabric with decorative woven edges such as this natural linen band, are available in various widths.

THREADS

Embroidery threads come in myriad colours and a broad spectrum of textures and weights. The thickness of the thread dictates the size and shape of the stitch, which will have a very different appearance if worked in a fine matt yarn or a lustrous pearl cotton. Certain wools and threads are spun in a single strand, whilst others consist of up to six fine strands which are loosely twisted together. These can be separated out and re-combined, depending on the effect or line width required. The needle can be threaded with strands of two or more colours to create subtle shaded effects. Manufacturer's sample books and shade cards show the full range of different threads that are available and can be a good source of inspiration when planning a new project.

SILKS AND COTTONS

Silks and cottons are made in both single and stranded skeins. Silk, rayon, and twisted pearl cotton all have a high sheen, whilst stranded cotton gives a smooth finish. Use fine flower thread or the thicker soft cotton for a more matt appearance. Metallic threads add textural interest, and silk ribbon is used for embroidering naturalistic roses and flowers.

FLOWER THREAD

STRANDED COTTON

SILK RIBBON   METALLIC THREAD

SOFT COTTON

SILK THREAD   SILK THREAD

CREWEL WOOL

SILK RAYON

STRANDED SILK

PEARL COTTON

WOOLS

The thickest wool is 4-ply tapestry, used on 10- to 14-count canvas. Use several strands of fine 2-ply crewel on canvas or a single strand on fabric. Persian has three easily separated medium-weight strands: use two or three for needlepoint and one to stitch on fabric.

TAPESTRY WOOL

PERSIAN WOOL

NEEDLES

The correct choice of needle is essential for any piece of embroidery or needlepoint. There are five different types used for decorative stitching, each with a particular purpose. All come in a range of thicknesses and lengths; select one that can be threaded easily and that passes smoothly through the fabric without snagging the thread.

Types of Needle

Chenille needles have sharp points, designed for working on heavy plainweave fabrics with thick threads. Blunt tapestry needles with long oval eyes are used with evenweave fabric and canvas, interlacing, and for all pulled fabric and drawn thread work. Versatile crewel needles are used for most embroidery stitches. They are long with easily-threaded eyes which take one or more strands. Sharps are mainly used for hand-sewing but, like betweens, they are ideal for fine stitching and French knots.

NEEDLES
There are five types of needle used for decorative embroidery. Each needle has a specific purpose.

- CHENILLE
- TAPESTRY
- CREWEL (EMBROIDERY)
- SHARP
- BETWEEN (QUILTING)

PREPARING THE THREAD

A length of thread can be easily unwound from a reel, but care must be taken when working with cotton or wools that come in individual skeins. Twisted skeins have to be undone before they can be used, but the paper bands should not be removed from looped skeins or they will become tangled. To prevent the thread becoming damaged as it passes repeatedly through the fabric, cut off a working length of no more than 50cm (20in). Use a needle threader with fine cotton and silk or the loop method of threading (see below) for stranded and pearl threads or wool.

Keep slip knot loose

UNTYING A TWISTED SKEIN
Remove the paper bands. Untwist the skein and cut through the threads, then tie them together with a loose slip knot.

Pull thread out gently

USING A LOOPED SKEIN
Leave the bands in place. Hold one end of the skein firmly and draw out the loose thread to the required length.

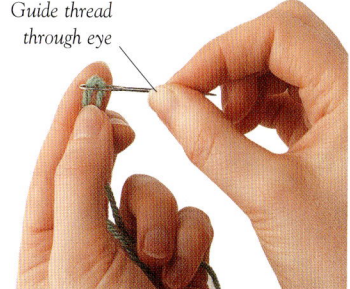

Guide thread through eye

THREADING A NEEDLE
Fold thread over needle and hold the loop between thumb and finger. Slide the loop off; pass it through the eye.

Frames

Small-scale projects and some needlepoint can be stitched in the hand, but most embroidery has to be worked on a frame to achieve the best result. The frame maintains the fabric at an even tension and holds the grain straight, which keeps the stitches regular and even, and protects the work by reducing the amount of handling it undergoes. The choice of frame depends on both the scale of a project and the fabric being used, but is very often a personal preference. There are three basic types: fixed stretchers and adjustable scroll frames which are used for embroidery fabrics and all weights of canvas, and round hoops for cotton and linen. All of these are available with integral or additional stand attachments, which give the advantage of freeing up both hands for stitching. Larger embroideries in particular are manageable if worked on a free-standing frame. Any frame should be large enough to accommodate the whole design area; moving fabric within a frame can damage the stitches.

Square and Rectangular Frames
These can be used for canvas or embroidery fabric. Stretcher frames are sold as two pairs of struts which can be chosen and assembled to fit a particular piece of work. Scroll frames come in several widths, depending on the roller length.

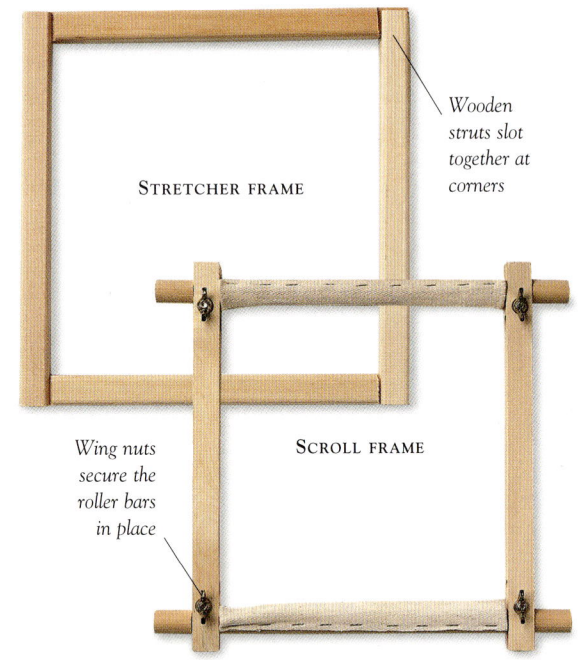

STRETCHER FRAME

Wooden struts slot together at corners

Wing nuts secure the roller bars in place

SCROLL FRAME

Round Frames
Wooden hoop frames range in diameter from 12 to 32cm (4⅘ to 13in) and are ideal for smaller pieces of embroidery worked on fabric. They are light, portable, and easily held in one hand, but free-standing versions, which can be clamped on to a table, are also available.

Preparing the Inner Ring
To prevent delicate fabrics from becoming damaged and to stop them slipping within the hoop, bind the inner ring tightly with narrow cotton tape or bias binding. Stitch the two ends together to secure.

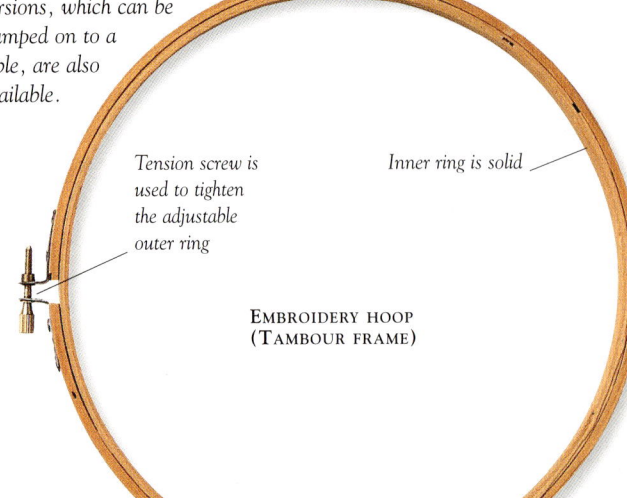

Tension screw is used to tighten the adjustable outer ring

Inner ring is solid

EMBROIDERY HOOP (TAMBOUR FRAME)

Mounting Techniques

It is worth taking time at the outset of a project to prepare and mount the fabric properly. Neaten the edges to prevent them fraying or snagging by working a narrow hem or a machine zigzag stitch around linen and cotton fabrics, or by binding canvas with masking tape. Use a steam iron to press the fabric and remove any creases.

> .... **Handy Tip** ....
>
> Before mounting the fabric, fold it into quarters and work two rows of tacking along the creases, following the weave. Keep these lines straight to ensure that the grain of the fabric does not become distorted when stretched in the frame.

Using an Embroidery Hoop
The fabric should be at least 8cm (3in) larger all round than the diameter of the hoop. Loosen the screw slightly before mounting.

Mounting the Fabric
Centre the fabric over the inner ring, then gently push the outer ring over the fabric, keeping the grain straight. Tighten the screw to hold the frame together.

Setting up a Scroll Frame
Cut the fabric or canvas to the same width as the webbing. If it is longer than the struts, any surplus can be wrapped round the bottom roller and adjusted as work progresses.

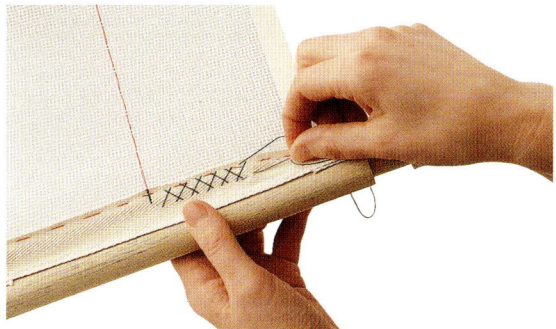

1 *Neaten the side edges. Match the midpoints of the canvas and webbing, then tack together. Sewing outwards from the centre, work herringbone stitch (see p.52) over the join.*

Preparing a Stretcher Frame
The neatened fabric or canvas should be the same size as the frame. Use drawing pins or a staple gun to fix the fabric in place.

Pinning Canvas
Mark the middle of each strut; line the canvas up to these four points. Pin from the centre out towards each corner, spacing the pins at regular intervals.

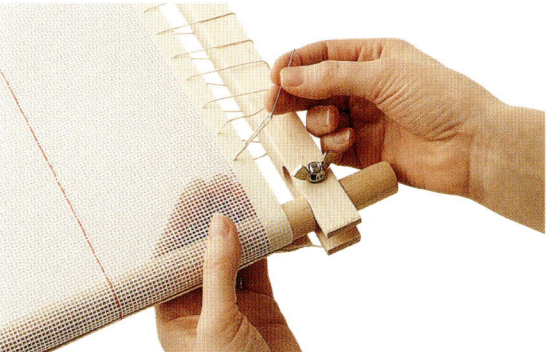

2 *Slot the rollers into the spaces in the struts. Tighten the two top screws, then turn the bottom roller to stretch the fabric. Secure the other screws, then lace the fabric tightly over the edges using thin string and a tapestry needle.*

Stitching Techniques

The key to a professional finish for any piece of needlework is to keep the length of the stitches regular and to maintain even tension throughout, whether or not the fabric is mounted on a frame. Take time to sew a small sample piece before embarking on any new project, to become familiar with the stitches and to establish a rhythmic pattern of working. Embroidery stitches are constructed either vertically, usually from top to bottom, or horizontally towards the left or right, although they may appear at any angle in the finished piece. Needlepoint fillings, which form all-over patterns, are worked in diagonal, horizontal, or vertical rows.

> ··· **Left-Handed Workers** ···
>
> *All the illustrations in the following chapters show how the stitches would be sewn by a right-handed worker, but most left-handed stitchers will prefer to sew in the opposite direction. Hold a small mirror in front of the page to turn the step-by-step diagrams the other way round and to reverse the direction of the needle.*

Beginning to Stitch
Follow one of the two techniques shown below to start off or to join a new length of thread. Both will help to ensure that the reverse side of the stitching is as neat as the front.

Fastening Off a Thread
Fasten off the thread when it is no less than 10cm (4in) long. Try not to finish too many threads in the same area as this can create an uneven surface, especially in needlepoint.

Lost Knot Method
Use this technique for needlepoint and open embroidery stitches. Knot one end of the thread and insert the needle from the front, a short distance along the line to be worked. Continue stitching so the thread is held down at the back by the first stitches. Cut off the knot.

Running Stitch Method
Use when working embroidery stitches which are spaced closely together and for needlepoint. Leaving a loose end of thread at the back, work a few small running stitches, and stitch over them. The end can then be darned through the reverse of the stitches.

Fastening Off
Take the needle through to the wrong side of the fabric and turn the work over. Pass the needle under the loops at the back of the final few stitches for a distance of about 2.5cm (1in), then clip the end of the thread close to the fabric surface.

Ways of Working

Holding the fabric in the hand is a familiar sewing technique and some stitches, including looped embroidery stitches, are best worked this way. When the fabric is mounted in a frame, a special two-handed technique is used.

Embroidering in the Hand

Support the area being worked over the forefinger. Hold the needle in the other hand and slide it in and out in a single movement.

LOOPED STITCHES

Loop the thread from one side to the other and use the free thumb to hold it down. Pull the needle through over the working thread. The step-by-step diagrams will indicate the point where the thread should be held.

Using Both Hands

Working with a free-standing frame may prove awkward at first but, with practice, both right- and left-handed workers will find that they can stitch quickly and evenly with two hands.

STABBING TECHNIQUE

Keep one hand on either side of the frame. Push the needle down into the fabric from the top and pull it through from below. Pass it back up with this hand, and draw it through from above.

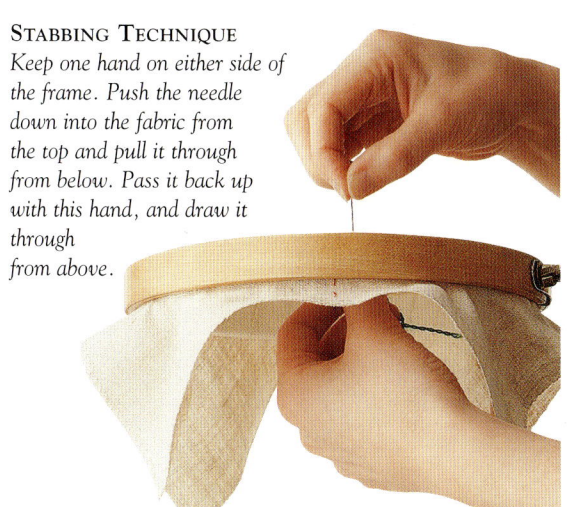

Hand-held Needlepoint

Straight, and some crossed, stitches can be worked in the hand without any problems, but diagonal stitches will cause some distortion.

STITCHING ON CANVAS

Bind the edges of the canvas and start at the far side. Keep the unworked part rolled in one hand, while stitching with the other. Be sure to keep the tension even.

Working Needlepoint Stitches

Stitches on canvas are worked into the square holes between the woven threads. To avoid splitting the stitches, always try to bring the needle up through an unworked space and take it down into an already worked hole. Do not pull the yarn too tightly or the holes will become enlarged so the canvas shows through.

1 *Work the first row, then fill in the bottom corner. Start each stitch from an unworked hole and insert the needle in to the base of the stitches in the previous row.*

2 *Fill the top corner with stitches worked in the opposite direction, ending each one at the top of the last row. Use this method with the stabbing technique.*

Working Filling Stitches

Powdered, open, and solid fillings, along with most needlepoint stitches, are worked within a specific area of a design, which may be a naturalistic leaf or petal, or a more regular geometric form. The size and shape of the individual stitches have to be altered to fill the given shape. For open and solid embroidered fillings, this means that the stitches must be worked at different lengths to fit within a curved or zigzag line, or all at the same length to complete a rectangular or square motif. Powdered fillings are worked singly within an outline: their size may be varied to add extra visual interest. Diagonal needlepoint stitches, which have a regular, all-over surface pattern, require part stitches to be worked at the edges of the shape.

NEEDLEPOINT FILLINGS
Straight, cross, and star stitches fit easily within a square, but diagonal stitches have to be adapted. Count the intersections carefully, and make part stitches to square off the edges of the area being worked.

Counted Thread and Freestyle

Embroidery stitches can be worked on either evenweave or plainweave fabric. A regularly spaced effect can easily be created by counting the threads on evenweave; work between guidelines to achieve the same result with freestyle stitching on finer plainweave fabric.

OPEN AND SOLID FILLINGS
Start a leaf at the top with a short straight stitch to fill in the point, then work downwards, first increasing, then reducing the length of the stitches. Insert the needle just beyond the edge of the shape so the stitches hide the line.

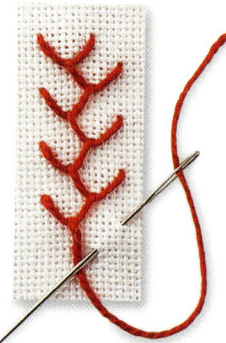 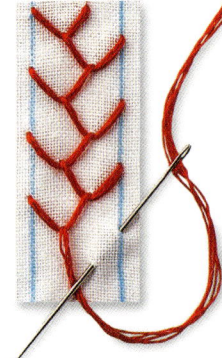

EVENWEAVE FABRIC
Make each stitch over the same number of threads or thread intersections.

PLAINWEAVE FABRIC
Stitch between two parallel lines drawn on to the fabric with a dressmaker's pen.

Tie Stitches

These short stitches are used to anchor looped stitches such as chain stitch, in couching, and to bunch together groups of straight stitches.

POWDERED FILLINGS
Work a fine outline stitch over the guideline to define the motif, then fill the shape with individual stitches. These can be arranged in a regular pattern or scattered randomly within the leaf.

MAKING A TIE STITCH
Bring the needle up above the long stitch or inside the loop and insert it just below the thread.

Working Openwork Stitches

In all types of openwork the background fabric is as important as the stitches themselves, and forms an integral part of the finished piece. It has to be carefully prepared for drawn thread work and for insertion (faggoting) stitches.

Drawn Thread Stitches

The open spaces that give drawn thread work its characteristic lacy appearance are formed by removing some of the woven threads that make up the fabric.

Pulling Out the Threads
Evenweave cotton or linen are the best fabrics to work with. Use the point of a needle to lift up the threads and pull out enough to make an open band or bands of the required width.

Insertion Stitches

To ensure that the space between the two hems remains constant and the stitches are worked regularly, the fabric being joined has to be stitched on to paper before starting.

Mounting the Fabric
Stitch a narrow hem along each long edge. Draw two parallel lines, 6mm (¼in) apart on to a strip of heavy paper. With the right sides facing, tack one piece of fabric along each line.

Finishing Off

When the final stitches have been completed, take the work off the frame. Press embroidery lightly on the wrong side before mounting.

Blocking

A piece of needlepoint which incorporates diagonal stitches will inevitably become pulled out of shape as it is worked. Any distortion can be remedied by blocking the canvas.

How to Block
Make a template of the finished piece and mark into quarters. Tape to a board and cover with polythene. Place the dampened work face down. Match the centre top edge to the template and pin. Stretch and pin the bottom edge and two sides. Insert more pins at 2.5cm (1in) intervals. Allow to dry.

Mounting

If a project is to be framed it should first be mounted on to board to keep it in shape, whether it is worked on fabric or canvas.

1 *Cut the board to size and mark into quarters. Centre it on the wrong side of the fabric and fold back long edges. Pin them to the card from the centre out.*

2 *Using strong thread, lace the edges together. Do the same with the other two sides. Check the fabric is centred, then tighten up and secure the threads.*

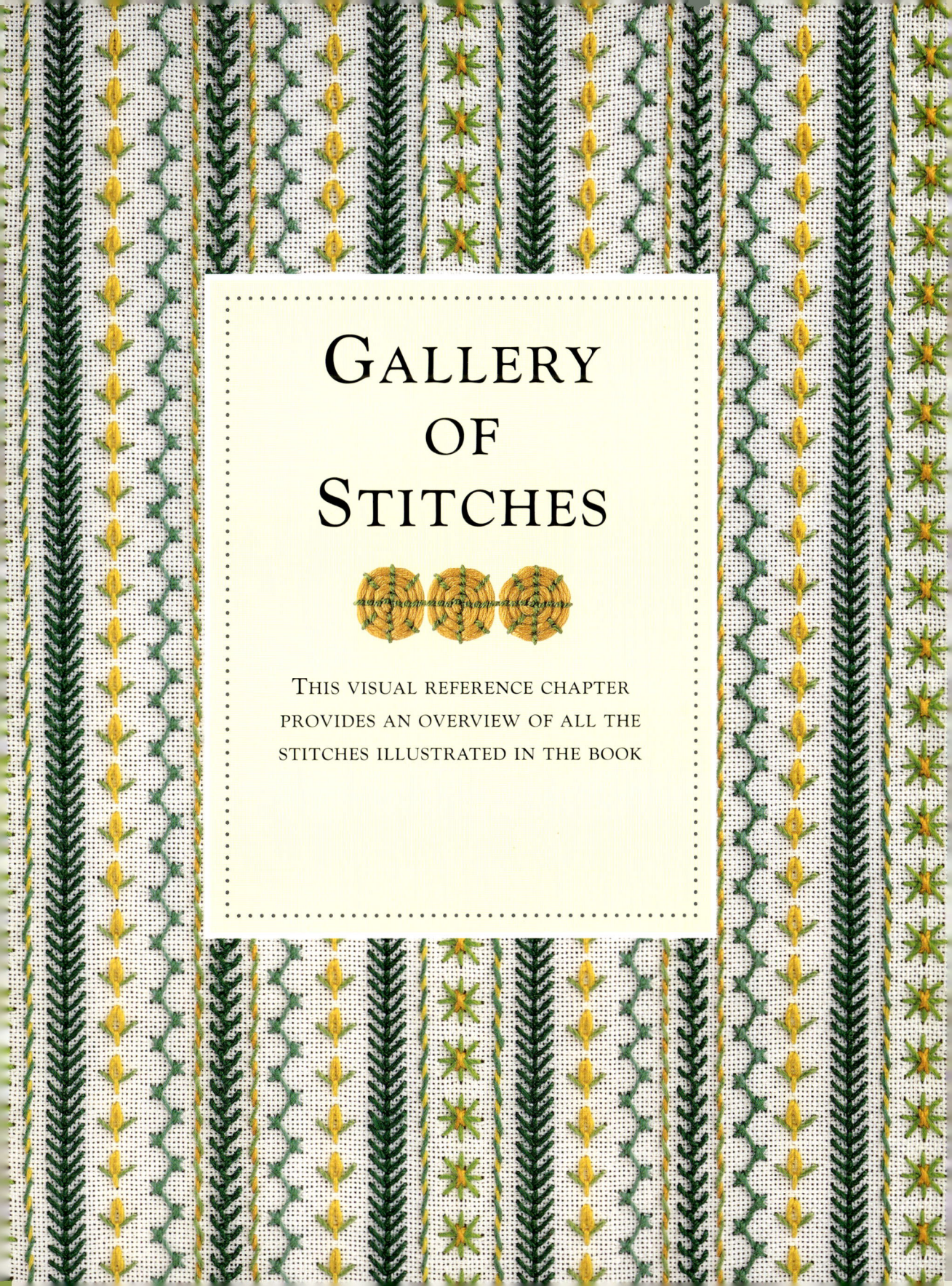

Gallery of Stitches

This visual reference chapter provides an overview of all the stitches illustrated in the book.

24 Gallery of Stitches

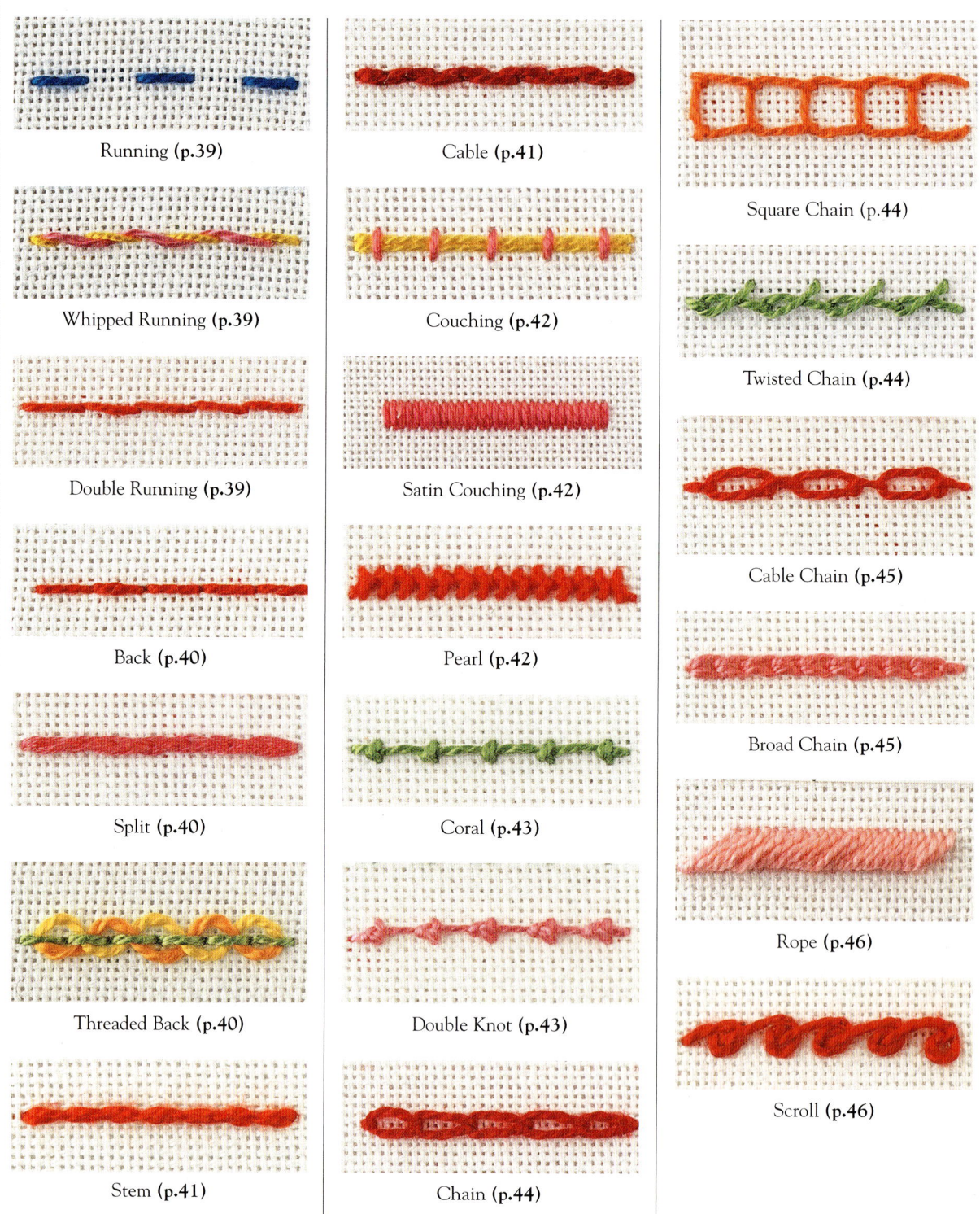

Gallery of Stitches

Gallery of Stitches

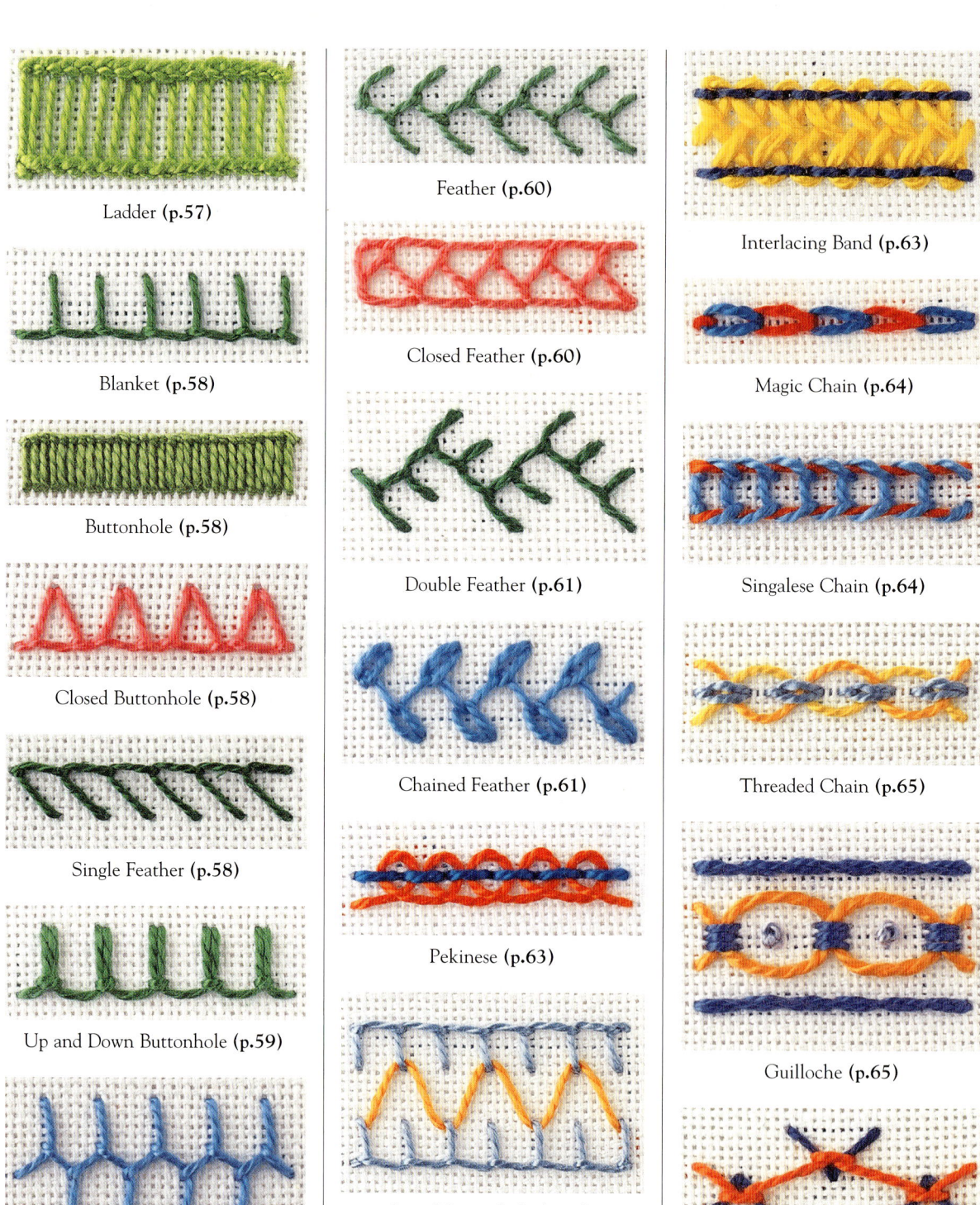

Gallery of Stitches

Gallery of Stitches

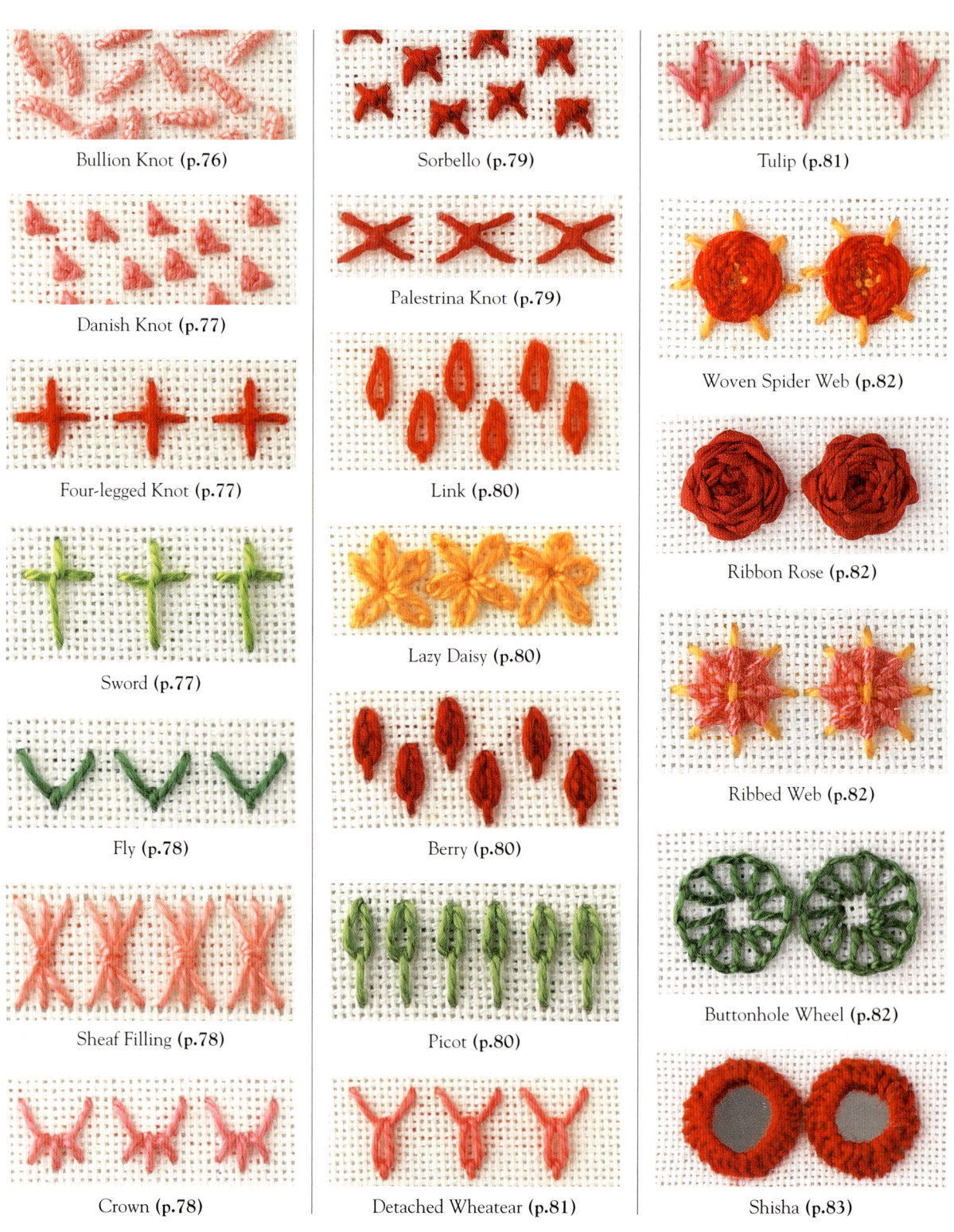

Gallery of Stitches

Gallery of Stitches

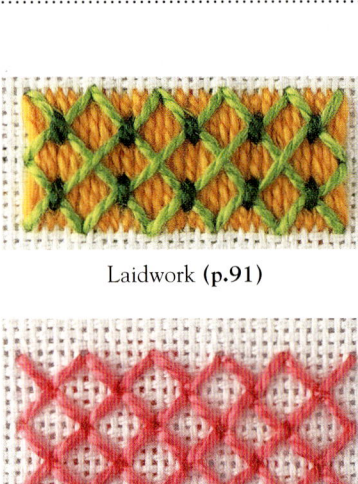
Laidwork (p.91)

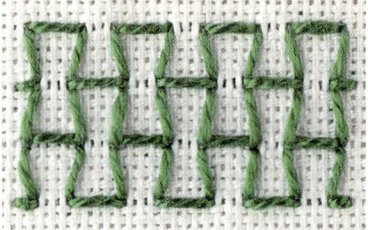
Back Stitch Trellis (p.92)

Japanese Darning (p.92)

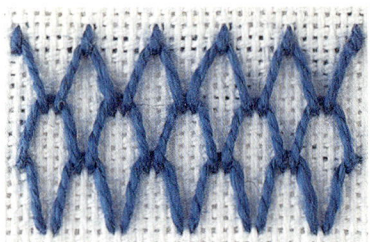
Cloud Filling (p.93)

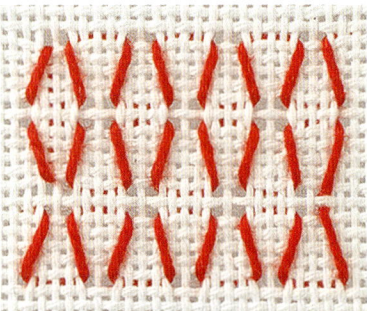
Wave Filling (p.93)

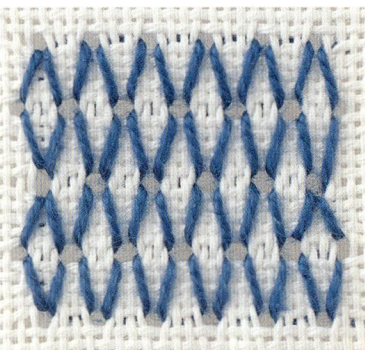
Window Filling (p.97)

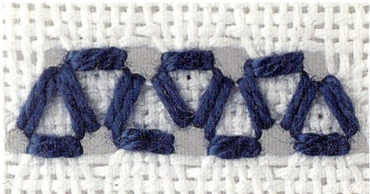
Pulled Wave Filling (p.97)

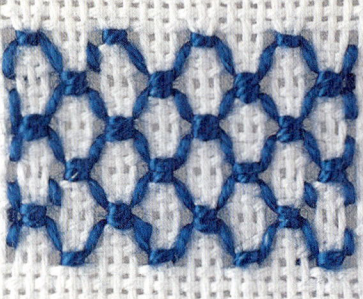
Three-sided (p.97)

Honeycomb Filling (p.98)

Russian Filling (p.98)

Diagonal Raised Band (p.99)

Ridged Filling (p.99)

Punch (p.99)

Cobbler Filling (p.100)

Gallery of Stitches 31

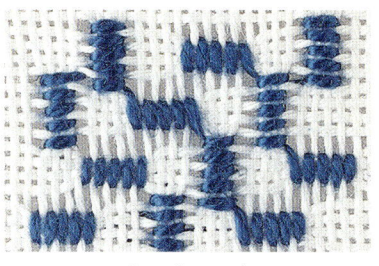
Step (p.100)

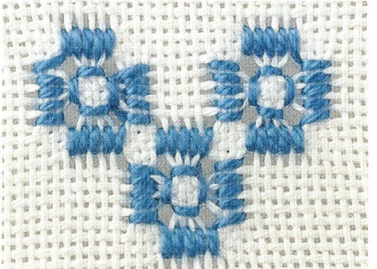
Mosaic Filling (p.101)

Diagonal Satin Filling (p.101)

Back Stitch Rings (p.102)

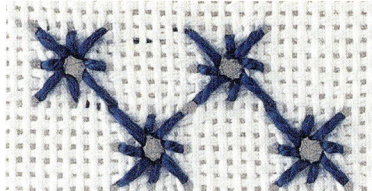
Algerian Eye (p.102)

Outlined Diamond Eyelet (p.103)

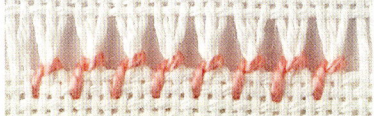
Single Hem (p.105)

Ladder Hem (p.105)

Serpentine Hem (p.105)

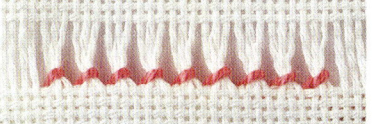
Antique Hem (p.105)

Italian Border (p.106)

Four-sided (p.106)

Chevron Border (p.107)

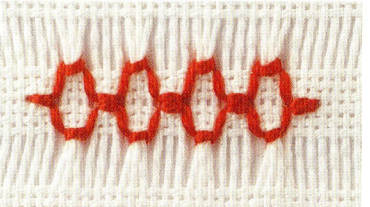
Diamond Border (p.107)

Laced Insertion (p.108)

Faggot Bundles (p.108)

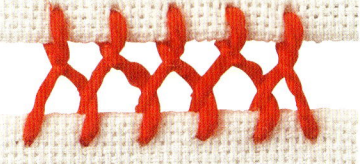
Cretan Insertion (p.108)

32 GALLERY OF STITCHES

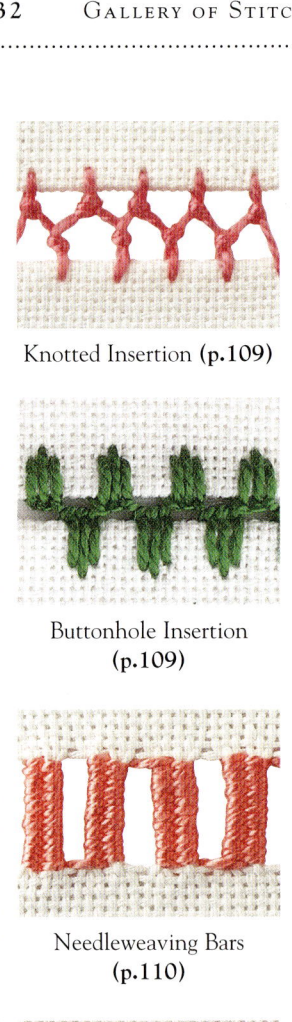

Knotted Insertion (p.109)

Buttonhole Insertion (p.109)

Needleweaving Bars (p.110)

Zigzag Clusters (p.110)

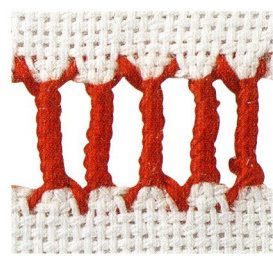

Corded Clusters (p.110)

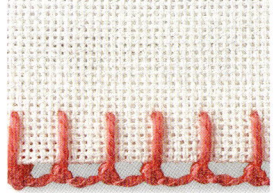

Antwerp Edging (p.112)

Sailor Edging (p.112)

Looped Edge (p.113)

Half Chevron (p.113)

Scalloped Edge (p.114)

Ring Picot Edge (p.114)

Buttonhole Eyelet (p.115)

Overcast Eyelet (p.115)

Square Eyelet (p.115)

Upright Gobelin (p.119)

Gobelin Filling (p.119)

Parisian (p.119)

Hungarian (p.120)

Hungarian Diamond (p.120)

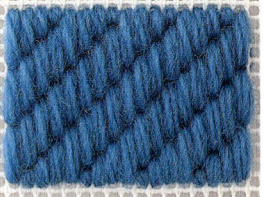

Single Twill (p.121)

Double Twill (p.121)

Gallery of Stitches

34 Gallery of Stitches

Cashmere (p.132)

Diagonal (p.133)

Byzantine (p.133)

Jacquard (p.134)

Moorish (p.135)

Milanese (p.135)

Mosaic (p.136)

Cushion (p.136)

Scottish (p.137)

Chequer (p.137)

Cross (p.139)

Diagonal Cross (p.139)

Double Cross (p.139)

Upright Cross (p.140)

Diamond Cross (p.140)

Smyrna Cross (p.140)

Double Leviathan (p.141)

Diagonal Tweed (p.141)

Broad Cross (p.142)

Cross-corner Cushion (p.142)

Brighton (p.143)

Gallery of Stitches

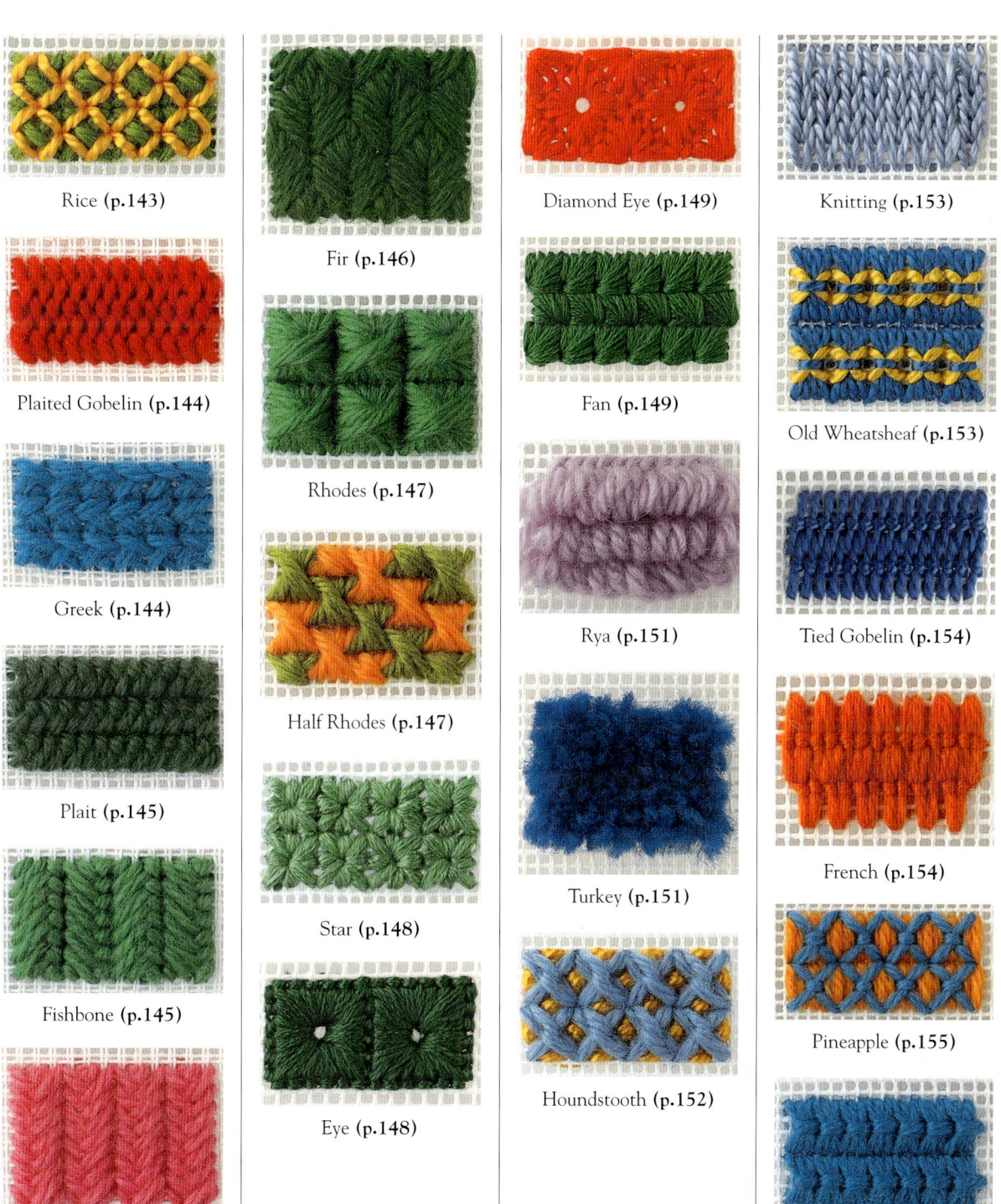

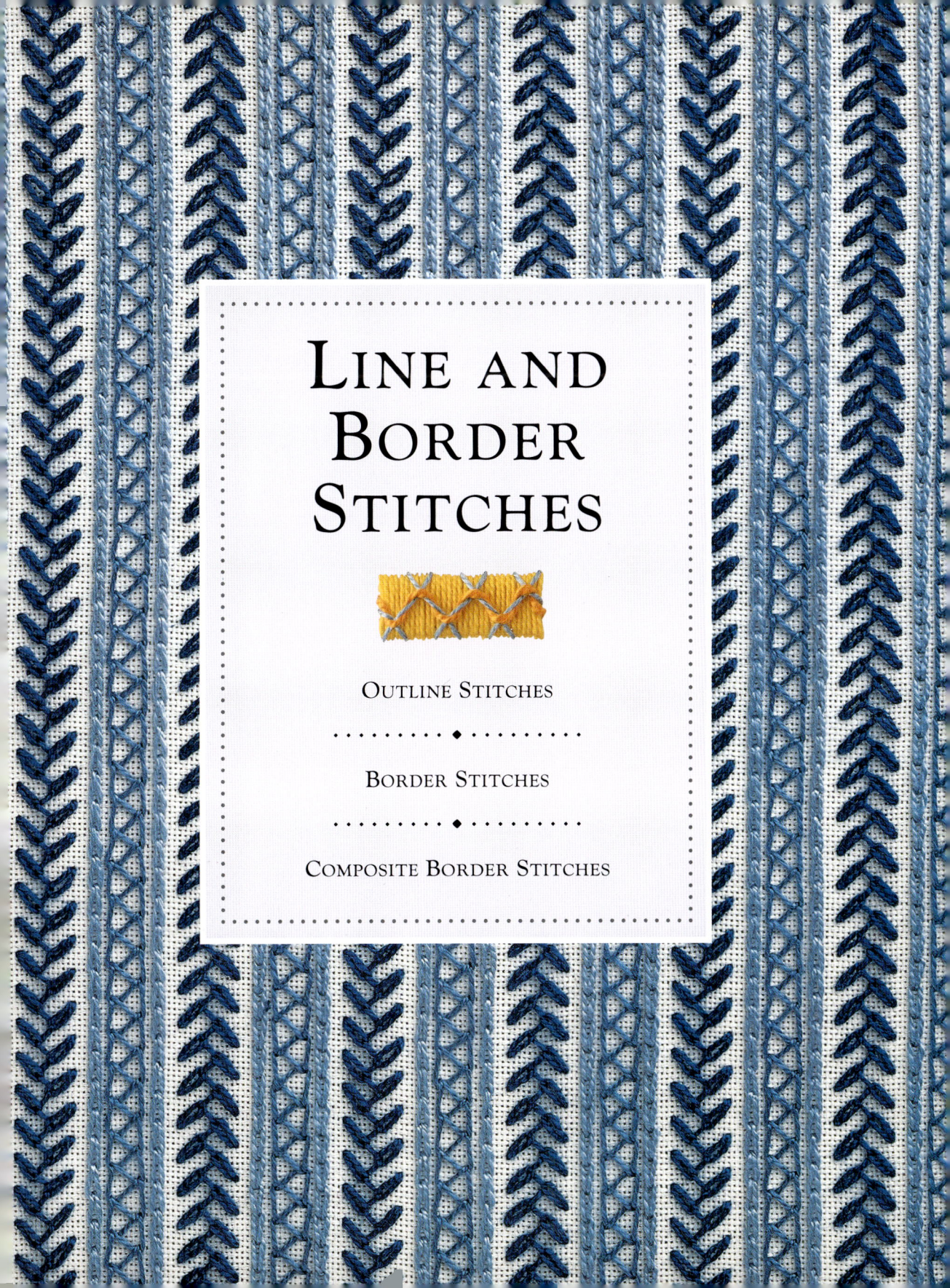

Line and Border Stitches

Outline Stitches

• • • • • • • ◆ • • • • • • •

Border Stitches

• • • • • • • ◆ • • • • • • •

Composite Border Stitches

Outline Stitches

T‍HIS GROUP INCLUDES some of the most basic and versatile embroidery stitches, which are all worked continuously in a curved or straight row. They can be sewn in any thread on any fabric, depending on the effect required, and are employed whenever fine lines and details are needed. Use these stitches to 'draw' designs and motifs, for monograms and lettering, or to define shapes which will be completed with filling stitches. Running and back stitches provide the foundation for some composite stitches and can be interlaced with contrasting threads.

Running 39	Pearl 42
Whipped Running 39	Coral 43
Double Running 39	Double Knot 43
Back 40	Chain 44
Split 40	Square Chain 44
Threaded Back 40	Twisted Chain 44
Stem 41	Cable Chain 45
Cable 41	Broad Chain 45
Couching 42	Rope 46
Satin Couching 42	Scroll 46

Running

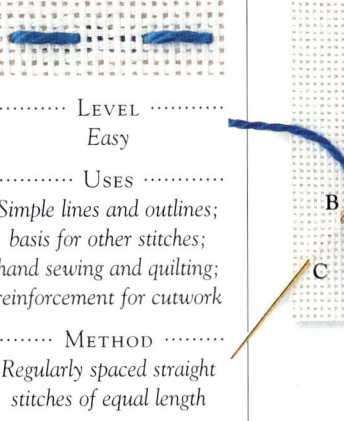

- **Level**
  Easy
- **Uses**
  Simple lines and outlines; basis for other stitches; hand sewing and quilting; reinforcement for cutwork
- **Method**
  Regularly spaced straight stitches of equal length
- **Materials**
  Any fabric; any thread

Work stitches at equal intervals

Come up at **A**, then insert the needle at **B**. Bring it out again at **C**. Continue, spacing the stitches evenly and making them all the same length.

Whipped Running

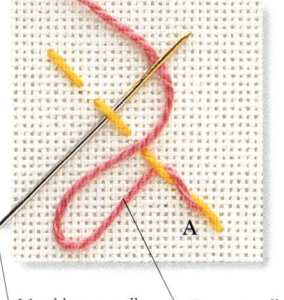

- **Other Name**
  Cordonnet stitch
- **Level**
  Easy
- **Uses**
  Straight or curved outlines
- **Method**
  Laced running stitch
- **Materials**
  Any fabric; any two threads – contrasting colours and thicknesses for greater effect; blunt needle for whipping

Use blunt needle to avoid catching threads

Do not pull lacing thread tightly

Work a foundation of closely spaced running stitch (see left). Using a blunt needle, bring the second thread up at **A**. Slide the needle under the next stitch from right to left and pull through gently. Continue whipping to the end of the line.

Double Running

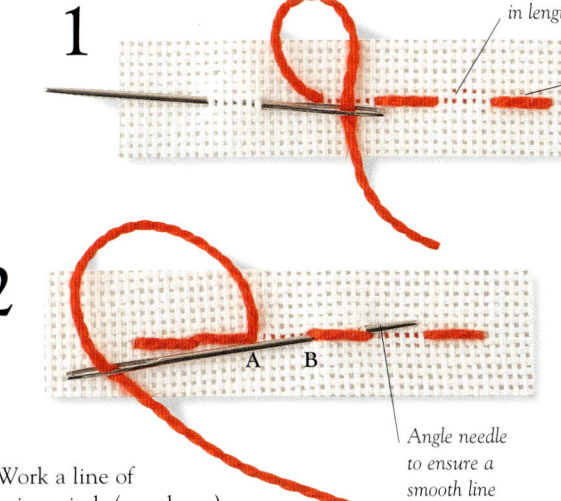

- **Other Names**
  Holbein stitch; Assisi stitch
- **Level**
  Easy
- **Uses**
  With cross stitch; in Assisi and blackwork
- **Method**
  Counted thread stitch worked with two rows of running stitch
- **Materials**
  Evenweave fabric; any embroidery thread

Ensure spaces are equal in length to stitches

Make stitches all same length

Angle needle to ensure a smooth line

1 Work a line of running stitch (see above). Make sure the stitches are all the same length and equal in length to the spaces.

2 Fill in the spaces on the return journey. Come out at the top of the previous stitch, at **A**. Insert the needle just below the start of the next stitch at **B**. Repeat to the end of the row.

Technique Variation

Double running stitch can be used to create intricate geometric bands and filling patterns. Chart the design on squared paper. Stitch along the line, working every other stitch. On the return journey, fill in the spaces with a second row of running stitch worked in the opposite direction.

Back

.... Level ....
Easy

.... Uses ....
Details and fine outlines, lettering, basis for other composite stitches

.... Materials ....
Any fabric; any thread – untwisted threads give smooth effect

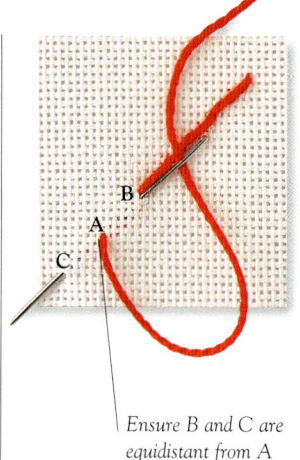

Ensure B and C are equidistant from A

Come up at **A**. Insert the needle at **B**, then bring it out again one stitch length ahead of **A** at **C**. Insert the needle again at **A** and continue making regular backward stitches in the same way.

Split

.... Level ....
Easy

.... Uses ....
Outlines; in close rows as filling; padded edge for solid filling stitches

.... Materials ....
Any fabric; soft, untwisted thread such as stranded cotton or silk floss; sharp needle

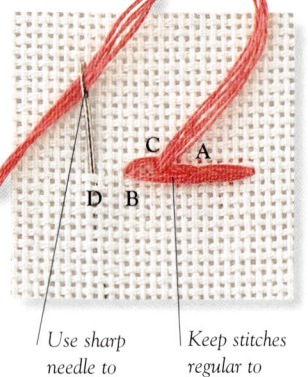

Use sharp needle to divide thread easily

Keep stitches regular to create smooth surface

Come up at **A** and work a straight stitch across to **B**. Bring the needle up at **C**, halfway along the stitch, so that it splits the thread. Pull through. Insert the needle at **D** and repeat to continue.

Threaded Back

.... Level ....
Easy

.... Uses ....
Flexible, decorative outlines and borders

.... Method ....
Row of back stitch interlaced with one or two threads

.... Materials ....
Any fabric; two or three colours of any thick embroidery thread; blunt needle

1

Do not pull thread too tightly

Use blunt needle to avoid catching threads

2

Keep loops even on both sides

1 Work a foundation of back stitch (see above). Bring the second thread up at **A**. Slide the needle under the next stitch, then pass it back under the following stitch. Continue weaving from side to side.

2 Take the thread down at **B** and finish off. For a double-threaded variation bring another thread up at **C** and weave in the same way as before, filling in the gaps.

Outline Stitches   41

Stem

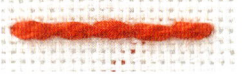

···· Other Names ····
*Outline stitch;
crewel stitch*

········ Level ········
Easy

········· Uses ·········
*Outlines; flower stems;
worked in rows as filling*

······· Materials ·······
*Any fabric;
any embroidery thread
or crewel wool*

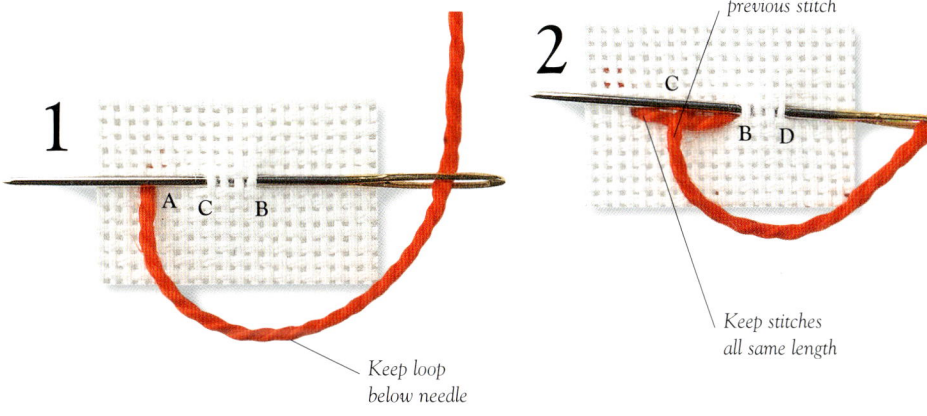

Keep loop below needle

Ensure thread comes up above previous stitch

Keep stitches all same length

1 Start at **A**, then insert the needle at **B**. Bring the needle up in the centre at **C**.

2 Insert the needle at **D** and bring it out at the end of the previous stitch, at **B**. Continue making a row of overlapping stitches.

········ Technique Variation ········

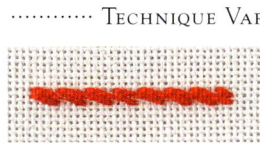

For a more solid, rope-like effect, work the stitches at an angle.

Cable

···· Other Names ····
*Alternating stem stitch;
side-to-side stem stitch*

········ Level ········
Easy

········· Uses ·········
*Straight and curved
outlines; narrow border*

······· Materials ·······
*Any fabric;
any embroidery thread*

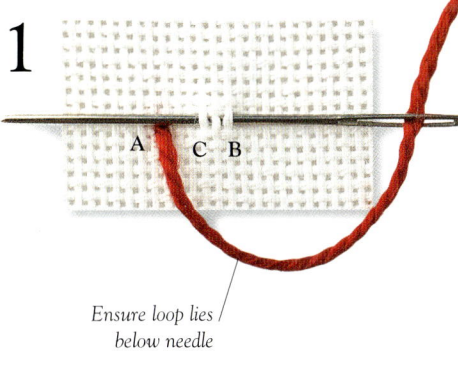

Ensure loop lies below needle

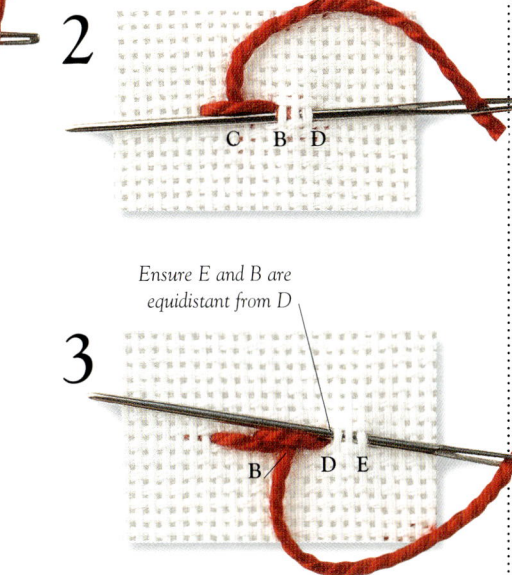

Keep loop above needle

Ensure E and B are equidistant from D

1 Start at **A**, then insert the needle at **B**. Bring the needle up in the centre at **C** and pull through.

2 Insert the needle at **D** and bring it back up at **B**.

3 Keeping the loop below the needle, insert at **E** and come up again at **D**. Repeat steps 2 and 3 to continue stitching.

Couching

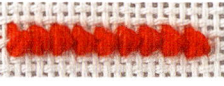

- **Level**
  Easy
- **Uses**
  Straight and curved outlines; metal thread work; in rows as filling
- **Method**
  Laid threads held down with small tie stitches
- **Materials**
  Any closely woven fabric; thick or delicate embroidery threads; finer thread for couching; frame

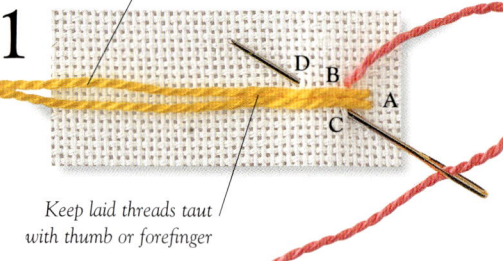

Vary number of laid threads depending on thickness of line required

Keep laid threads taut with thumb or forefinger

Work tie stitches in same or contrasting colour

1 Bring the main threads out at **A** and lay them along the line to be worked. To make the tie stitches (see p.20), come up at **B** using the couching thread. Insert the needle at **C**, over the laid threads, and bring it out at **D** to start the next stitch.

2 Continue working evenly spaced tie stitches over the laid thread to the end of the line. Finish off all threads at the back.

·········· **Stitch Variation** ··········

Satin couching, known also as trailing stitch, is a variation of couching, in which the tie stitches are worked very closely together so that the laid thread is completely covered.

Pearl

- **Level**
  Intermediate
- **Uses**
  Intricate or straight outlines; monograms
- **Method**
  Knotted stitch, worked in continuous line
- **Materials**
  Any fabric; thick, non-stranded embroidery thread

Ensure needle emerges directly below B

Do not pull stitch too tightly

Use thick thread to create raised knot

1 Start at **A** and make a diagonal stitch up to **B**. Bring the needle out at **C**.

2 Pull the thread to form a loop. Slide the needle under the stitch from right to left.

3 Tighten the knot by pulling the thread gently downwards. Take the needle up to the left and insert at **D** to form the loop for the next stitch. Come out at **E**. Repeat steps 2 and 3 to continue along the row.

OUTLINE STITCHES   43

Coral

····· OTHER NAMES ·····
Knotted stitch; snail trail; beaded stitch

········· LEVEL ·········
Easy

·········· USES ··········
Straight and curved outlines; in rows as textured filling

········ METHOD ········
Series of closely or widely spaced single knots

······· MATERIALS ·······
Any fabric; thick, non-stranded thread

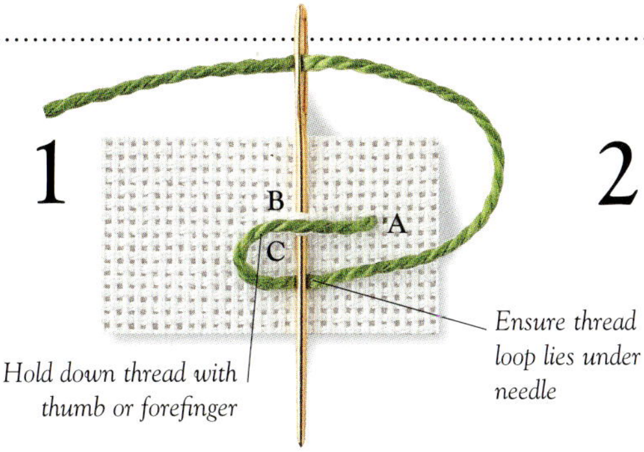

1 *Hold down thread with thumb or forefinger*
Ensure thread loop lies under needle

3 *Keep needle at right angle to line*

1 Start at **A** and hold the thread down along the stitching line. Insert the needle at **B** and loop the thread from left to right. Bring the point out over the loop at **C**.

2 Pull the needle gently through the loop so that the thread tightens into a knot.

3 Take the needle across to the left and insert it at **D**. Bring it out at **E**, ready for the next knot. Repeat steps 1 and 2 to continue.

Double Knot

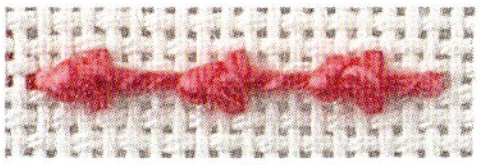

····· OTHER NAMES ·····
Old English knot stitch; Palestrina stitch; Smyrna stitch

········· LEVEL ·········
Intermediate

········ METHOD ········
Knotted stitch, worked in continuous line

·········· USES ··········
Outlines and borders

······· MATERIALS ·······
Any fabric; thick, non-stranded embroidery thread

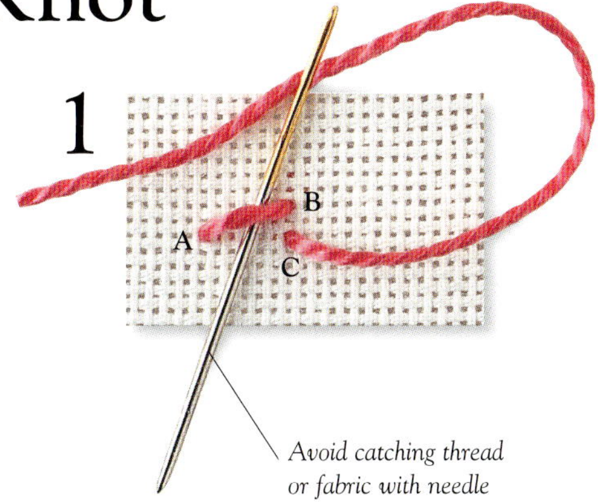

1 *Avoid catching thread or fabric with needle*

2 *Pass needle over looped thread*

3 *Space knots at regular intervals: for more texture, place closer together*

1 Start at **A** and make a diagonal stitch across to **B**. Bring the needle out at **C**, then slide it under the stitch from top to bottom.

2 Take the needle to the right of the loop and pass it under the diagonal stitch again. Bring it through over the working thread.

3 Pull the thread up to form a knot. Insert the needle at **D** and bring it out in line with **C** at **E**, ready to work the next stitch.

Chain

····· Other Names ·····
*point de chainette;
Tambour stitch*

········ Level ········
Easy

········ Uses ········
*Straight lines and curves;
lettering; in rows
or spiral as filling*

······· Method ·······
*Looped stitch, worked
from top to bottom*

······ Materials ······
Any fabric; any thread

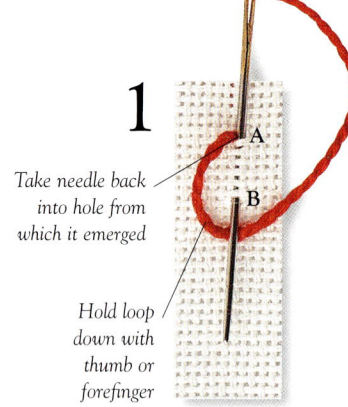

1 Start at **A**. Loop the thread from left to right and insert the needle again at **A**. Bring it through over the working thread at **B**.

2 Repeat step 1 to make the second stitch. Insert the needle inside the first loop at **B** and bring it out at **C**.

3 When the final stitch has been made, finish off by anchoring the last loop down with a small tie stitch (see p.20) from **D** to **E**.

Square Chain

····· Other Names ·····
*Ladder stitch; Roman
chain; open chain stitch*

········ Level ········
Easy

········ Uses ········
*Broad outlines; couching
stitch; foundation for
ribbon decoration;
traditional Indian
embroidery*

······· Method ·······
*Looped stitch, worked
from top to bottom*

······ Materials ······
Any fabric; any thread

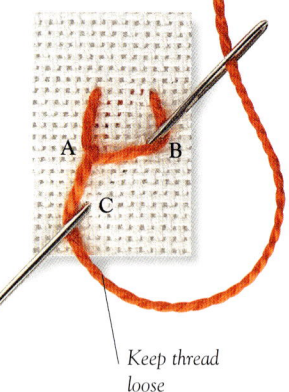

Come out at **A**. Insert the needle inside the previous loop at **B**. Bring it through over the working thread at **C**, leaving an open loop. Repeat to continue. Anchor the final loop with a tie stitch (see p.20) at each corner.

Twisted Chain

········ Level ········
Easy

········ Uses ········
*Curved and textured
outlines*

······· Method ·······
*Chain stitch variation
with crossed loop*

······ Materials ······
*Any fabric; any thread –
non-stranded threads
give best effect*

Come up at **A**. Loop thread from left to right, insert the needle at **B**. Come up at **C**, pull through over the working thread. Repeat to continue. Finish with a tie stitch (see p.20) over the final loop.

Cable Chain

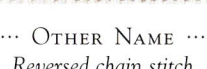

- **Level**
  Intermediate
- **Method**
  Looped and twisted stitch, worked from top to bottom
- **Uses**
  Decorative straight or curved outlines
- **Materials**
  Any fabric; any thick embroidery thread

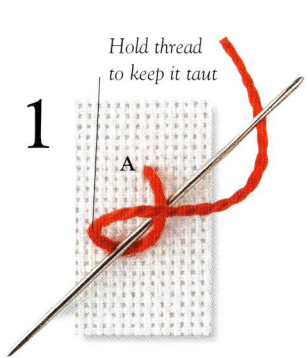

1 Start at **A**. Wrap the thread over and under the needle from left to right.

2 Insert the needle at **B**. Bring the point out at **C** over the working thread. Pull the needle through to form the first two links.

3 Twist the thread around the needle again and work the next stitch from **D** to **E**. Repeat steps 1 and 2 to continue stitching downwards.

Broad Chain

- **Other Name**
  Reversed chain stitch
- **Level**
  Intermediate
- **Method**
  Looped stitch, worked from top to bottom
- **Uses**
  Solid, flexible outline
- **Materials**
  Any fabric; firm embroidery thread

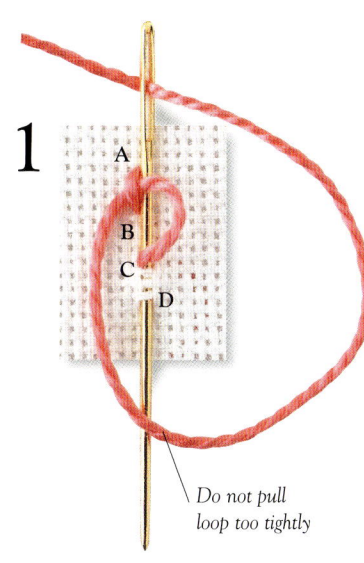

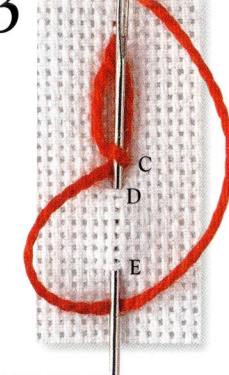

1 Start at **A** and make a short upright stitch to **B**. Come out directly below **B** at **C**, and slide the needle under the upright stitch from right to left. Take it down at **C**, pulling the thread gently to form the first loop. Bring the needle out again at **D**.

2 Pass the needle under both sides of the loop, then take it down at **D**. Repeat from **C** to continue.

Rope

- **Level**
  Advanced
- **Uses**
  Straight, curved or spiral outlines
- **Materials**
  Any fabric; any thick thread – stranded cotton gives a smooth effect; frame
- **Tip**
  Vary the angle of the stitches to work around a curve

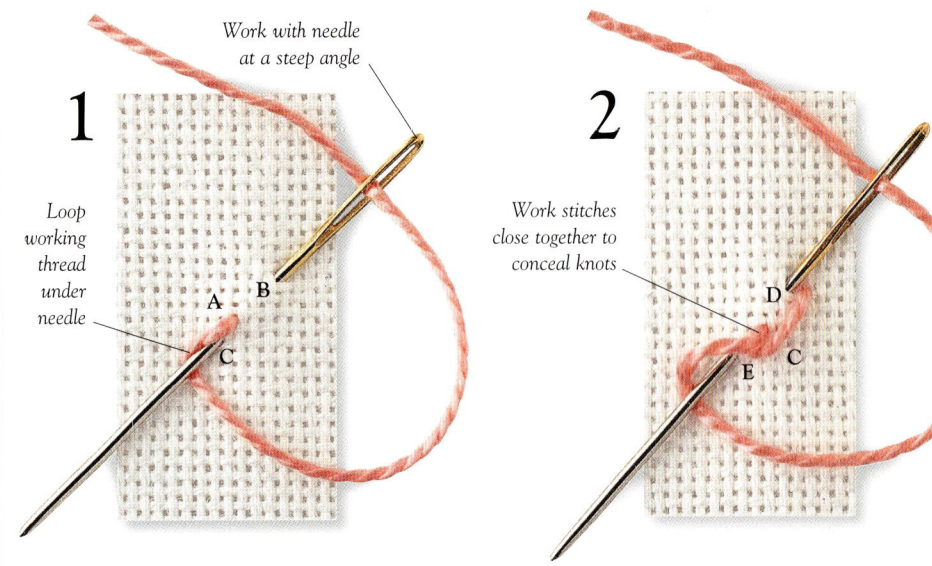

1 Start at **A**. Take the needle diagonally across and insert at **B**, then bring it up below and to the left of **A**, at **C**.

2 Pull the needle over the working thread to form a small knot at the base of the stitch. Insert the needle at **D** and bring it up at **E** to make the next stitch. Repeat this step to continue.

Scroll

- **Other Name**
  Single knotted line stitch
- **Level**
  Intermediate
- **Uses**
  Decorative outlines
- **Method**
  Looped knot stitch
- **Materials**
  Any fabric; firm, non-stranded embroidery thread; frame

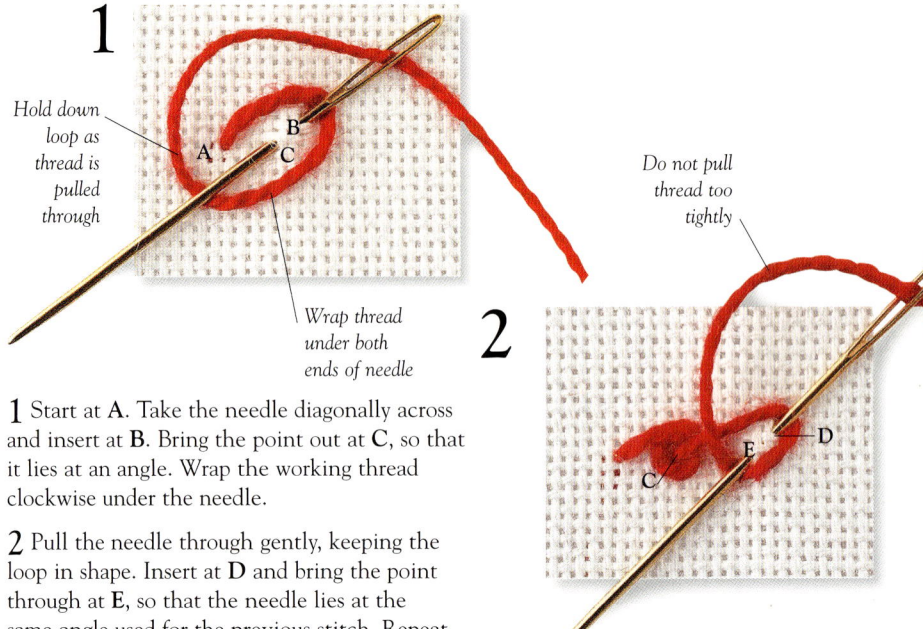

1 Start at **A**. Take the needle diagonally across and insert at **B**. Bring the point out at **C**, so that it lies at an angle. Wrap the working thread clockwise under the needle.

2 Pull the needle through gently, keeping the loop in shape. Insert at **D** and bring the point through at **E**, so that the needle lies at the same angle used for the previous stitch. Repeat the sequence to continue.

Border Stitches

This is the largest, most widely used group of stitches and includes flat, looped and knotted techniques. Border stitches are used to create broad, decorative straight lines, frames, and edgings. They can be worked in straight or curved rows, singly as outlines or repeated to form a filling to cover a larger area. Use plainweave fabric for freestyle stitching or evenweave to produce the more regular stitches of counted thread work. Mount the fabric in a frame to prevent it puckering and to keep the stitches even, especially those such as herringbone which are made up of long straight stitches.

Paris 48	Zigzag Chain 55
Fern 48	Rosette Chain 55
Bosnian 49	Loop 56
Chevron 49	Flat Vandyke 56
Thorn 50	Ladder 57
Cross 50	Blanket 58
Long-armed Cross 51	Buttonhole 58
Zigzag 51	Closed Buttonhole 58
Herringbone 52	Single Feather 58
Closed Herringbone 52	Up and Down Buttonhole 59
Shadow 52	Open Cretan 59
Basket 53	Feather 60
Wheatear 53	Closed Feather 60
Russian Chain 54	Double Feather 61
Petal 54	Chained Feather 61

Paris

- **Other Name**
  Open square stitch
- **Level**
  Easy
- **Uses**
  Light border; in rows as filling
- **Method**
  Back stitch variation with upright branches
- **Materials**
  Evenweave fabric; any thread

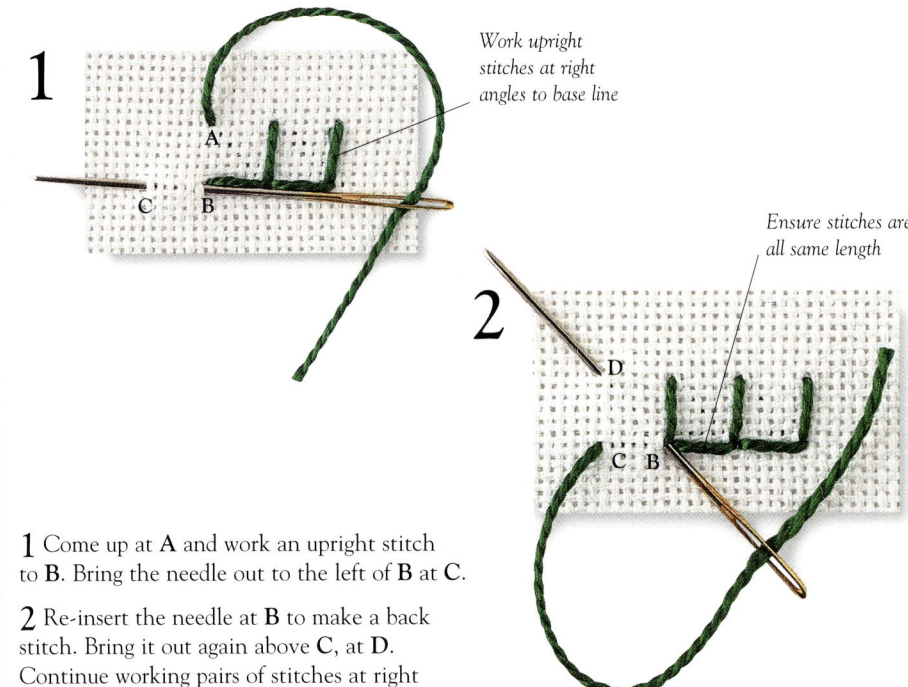

Work upright stitches at right angles to base line

Ensure stitches are all same length

1 Come up at **A** and work an upright stitch to **B**. Bring the needle out to the left of **B** at **C**.

2 Re-insert the needle at **B** to make a back stitch. Bring it out again above **C**, at **D**. Continue working pairs of stitches at right angles in the same way.

Fern

- **Other Name**
  Fern leaf stitch
- **Level**
  Easy
- **Uses**
  Leaf veins and delicate foliage sprays
- **Materials**
  Any fabric; any thread
- **Tip**
  Vary length of stitches when working on a curve

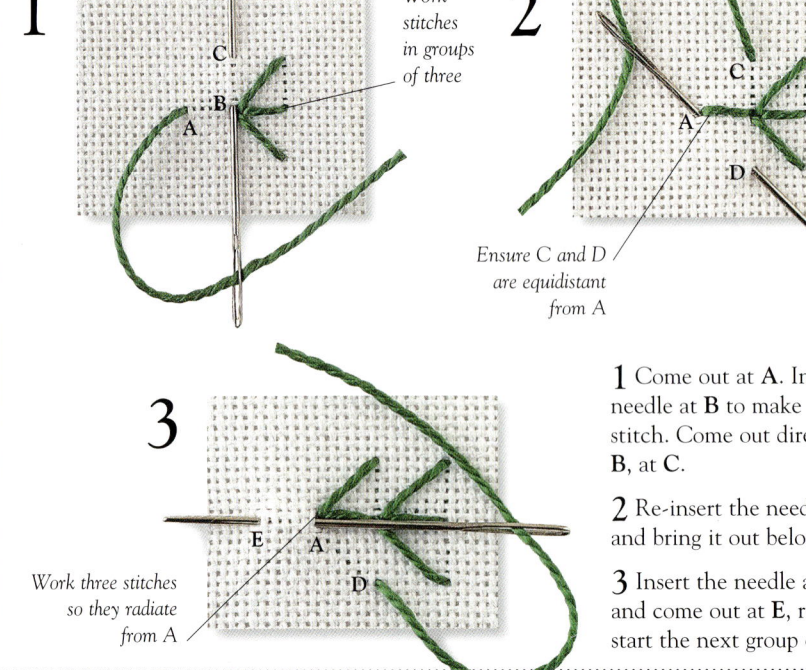

Work stitches in groups of three

Ensure C and D are equidistant from A

Work three stitches so they radiate from A

1 Come out at **A**. Insert the needle at **B** to make a horizontal stitch. Come out directly above **B**, at **C**.

2 Re-insert the needle at **A** and bring it out below **C**, at **D**.

3 Insert the needle again at **A** and come out at **E**, ready to start the next group of stitches.

BORDER STITCHES   49

Bosnian

····· LEVEL ·····
Easy

····· USES ·····
Straight borders or outlines; in rows as filling

····· METHOD ·····
Worked horizontally in two journeys

····· MATERIALS ·····
Any fabric; any thread

1
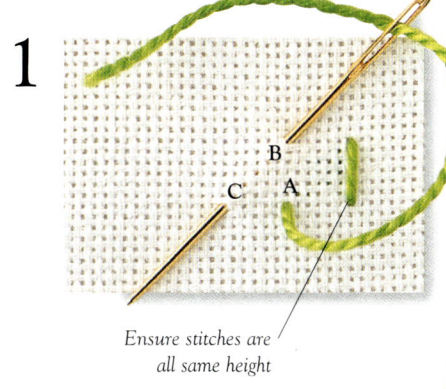
Ensure stitches are all same height

2

Work diagonal stitches to form zigzag line

1 Come up at **A** and make an upright stitch to **B**. Bring the needle out to the left of **A**, at **C**. Continue working a row of evenly spaced straight stitches.

2 Fill the spaces with slanting stitches. Come up at **C**, insert the needle at **B**, then bring it out at **A**. Repeat to the end of the row.

Chevron

····· LEVEL ·····
Easy

····· USES ·····
Straight border; in close rows as light filling; in smocking as surface honeycomb stitch

····· METHOD ·····
Worked horizontally between parallel lines

····· MATERIALS ·····
Any fabric; any thread

1
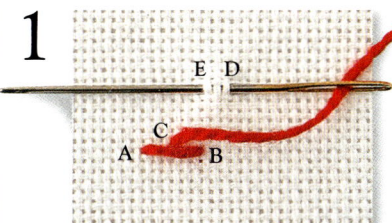

2
Keep thread above needle

Ensure E and F are equidistant from D

Work diagonal stitches at consistent angles   *Make all horizontal stitches same length*

3
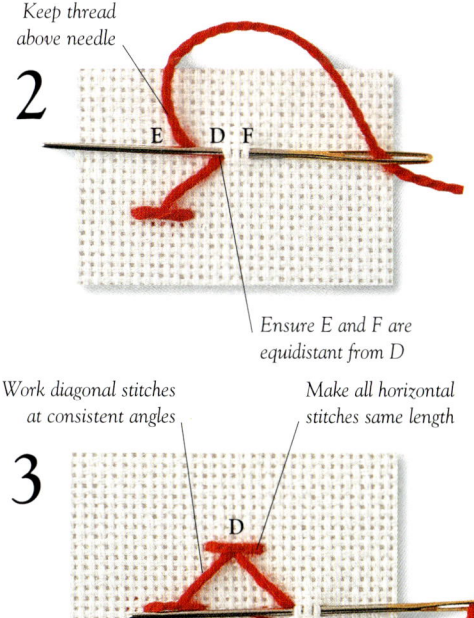

1 Start at **A** and make a horizontal straight stitch to **B**. Bring the needle out at the centre of the stitch, at **C**. Take the needle up to the right and insert it at **D**, then bring it out in line with **D**, at **E**.

2 Take the needle to the right and insert it at **F**. Come out again at **D**.

3 Take the needle down and insert at **G**, then come out at **H**. Insert the needle to the right, at **J**, and bring it out again at **G**. Repeat the sequence to continue.

Thorn

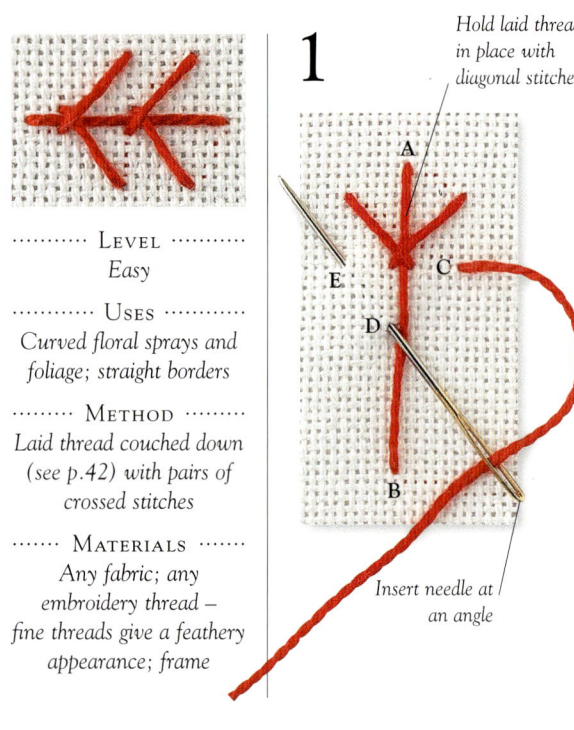

······ LEVEL ······
Easy

······ USES ······
Curved floral sprays and foliage; straight borders

······ METHOD ······
Laid thread couched down (see p.42) with pairs of crossed stitches

······ MATERIALS ······
Any fabric; any embroidery thread – fine threads give a feathery appearance; frame

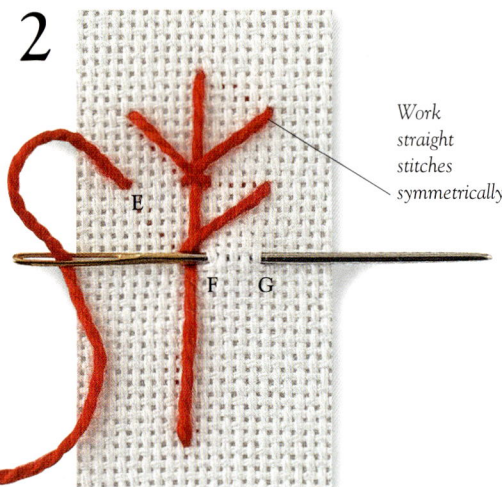

1 Start at **A** and, following the line to be worked, make a long stitch to **B**. Use a second thread to work the couching stitches. Come up at **C** and take the needle across the laid thread to insert at **D**. Bring the needle out at **E**.

2 Insert the needle at **F** and bring it out at **G**, ready to make the next diagonal stitch. Make further pairs of stitches in the same way along the laid thread.

Cross

······ OTHER NAMES ······
Berlin stitch; sampler stitch

······ LEVEL ······
Easy

······ USES ······
Geometric designs; charted patterns; lettering

······ METHOD ······
Worked over equal number of horizontal and vertical threads

······ MATERIALS ······
Evenweave fabric; any embroidery thread

To work in rows:

1 Come up at **A**, insert the needle at **B** and come out at **C**. Repeat to make a series of evenly spaced diagonal stitches.

2 Work the top stitches in the opposite direction. Take the needle across from **C** and insert at **D**. Come out again at **A**. Repeat to complete the row.

To work stitches singly:

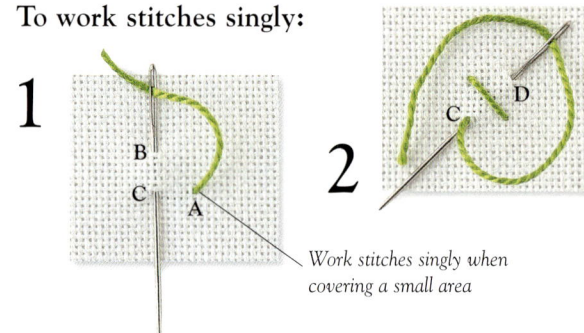

1 Start at **A**. Take the needle diagonally left and insert at **B**, then bring it out at **C**.

2 Insert the needle at **D** to complete the cross. Bring the needle out at **C** to work the next stitch.

BORDER STITCHES 51

Long-armed Cross

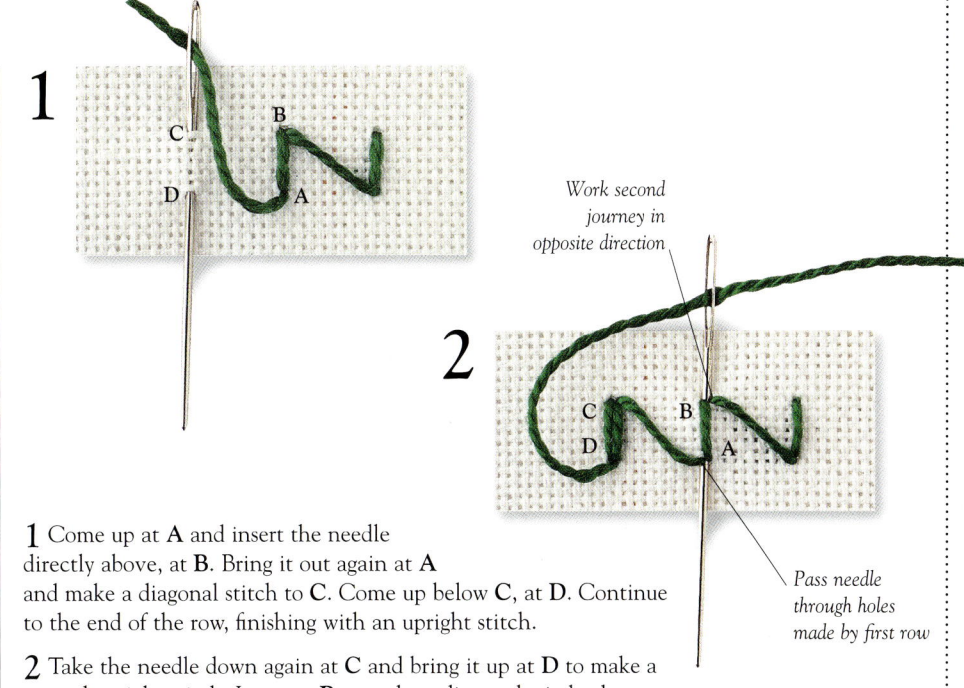

- **Other Names**
  Plaited Slav stitch; long-legged cross stitch
- **Level**
  Intermediate
- **Uses**
  Straight frame or border; in rows as filling
- **Method**
  Cross stitch variation worked horizontally
- **Materials**
  Evenweave fabric; thick embroidery threads – heavier threads give a more raised appearance

Work over twice as many horizontal as vertical threads

Work stitches in pairs

Ensure A and C are equidistant from E

1 Come up at **A** and make a long diagonal stitch to **B**. Come out directly below **B**, at **C**.

2 Take the needle back and insert at **D**, then bring it out directly below, at **E**. Repeat these two steps to the end of the row.

Zigzag

- **Level**
  Easy
- **Uses**
  Open outline; in close rows as open filling
- **Method**
  Alternate upright and diagonal stitches, worked horizontally in two journeys
- **Materials**
  Any fabric; any thread – fine twisted threads give a more open effect

Work second journey in opposite direction

Pass needle through holes made by first row

1 Come up at **A** and insert the needle directly above, at **B**. Bring it out again at **A** and make a diagonal stitch to **C**. Come up below **C**, at **D**. Continue to the end of the row, finishing with an upright stitch.

2 Take the needle down again at **C** and bring it up at **D** to make a second upright stitch. Insert at **B** to make a diagonal stitch, then come up at **A**. Repeat this step until all the crosses are complete.

Herringbone

Other Names
Russian cross stitch; fishnet stitch

Level
Easy

Uses
Decorative straight edging; base for composite stitches; in rows as open filling

Materials
Evenweave fabric; any embroidery thread

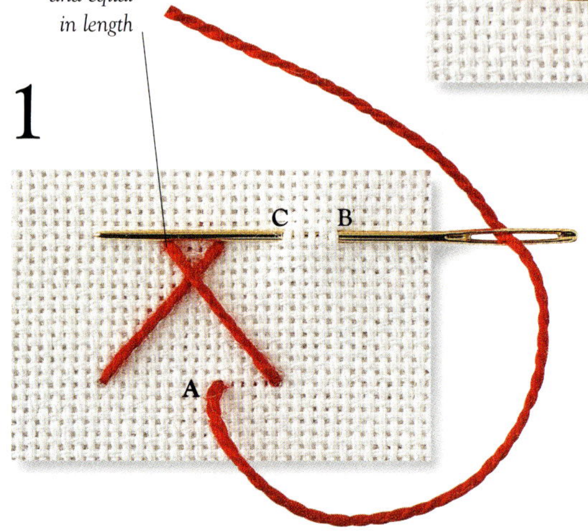

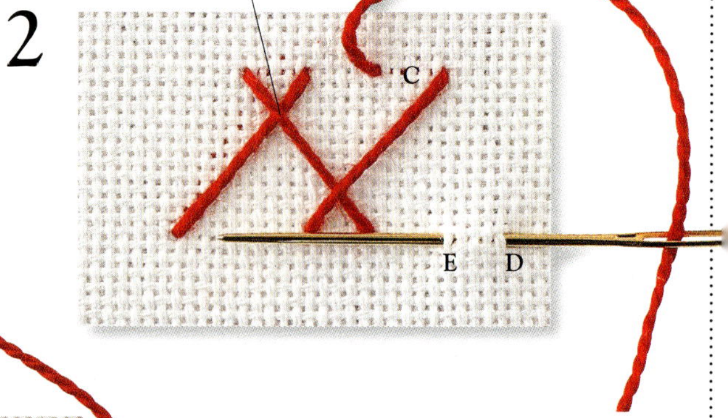

Keep stitches spaced evenly and equal in length

Cross diagonal stitches at top and bottom

1 Come up at **A**, take the needle diagonally up to **B** and insert. Bring it out at **C**, making a small back stitch.

2 Take the needle down and insert at **D**, then bring it through at **E**. Repeat these two steps to the end of the row.

Closed Herringbone

Other Name
Double back stitch

Level
Intermediate

Method
Herringbone variation

Uses
Open border; in rows as lattice filling

Materials
Evenweave fabric; any thread; frame

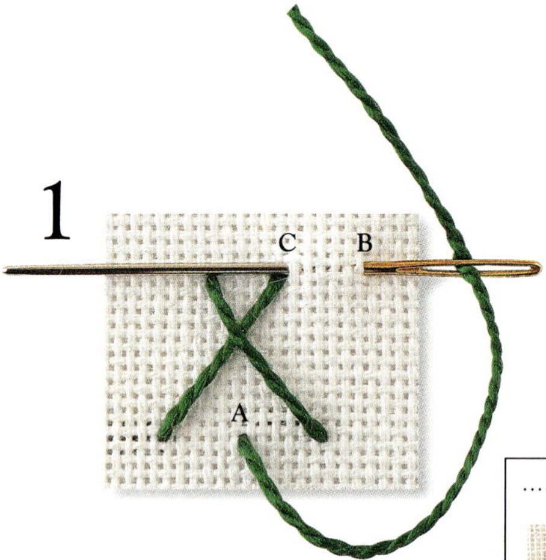

Stitches touch at top and bottom

1 Come up at **A** and make a diagonal stitch across to **B**. Bring the needle out on the same level, at **C**.

2 Take the needle down to **D** and insert, then come through at **E**. Repeat these two steps to continue.

····· **Stitch Variation** ·····

Shadow stitch is formed when closed herringbone stitch is worked on the reverse side of a semi-transparent material. The design is outlined with back stitch and the crossed threads form a dense band of colour, which shows through the fabric. Mount fabric in a frame.

Border Stitches

Basket

- **Level**: Advanced
- **Uses**: Straight bands and borders; in rows as a filling
- **Method**: Alternate forward and backward stitches, worked downwards between two parallel lines
- **Materials**: Any fabric; stranded thread gives a smoother finish

1 Come up at **A** to make the forward stitch. Insert the needle at **B** and bring it up, directly opposite, at **C**.

2 The next stitch is worked backwards. Take the needle across to **D** and insert, then bring it through at **E**. Repeat these two steps to continue.

Keep needle horizontal

Work backward stitches into holes made by previous stitches

Wheatear

- **Level**: Intermediate
- **Uses**: Straight or gently curved outlines; traditionally worked on smocks and childrens' clothes; used singly as filling (see p.81)
- **Method**: Looped stitch, worked from top to bottom
- **Materials**: Any fabric; non-stranded threads give raised effect

1 Start at **A** and make a diagonal stitch down to **B**. Bring the needle up to the right of **A**, at **C** and insert it again at **B**. Come up directly below **B**, at **D**.

2 Slide the needle under both slanted stitches from right to left, and gently draw up the thread.

3 Take the needle down again at **D**. Come out below **A** at **E**, ready to work the next stitch.

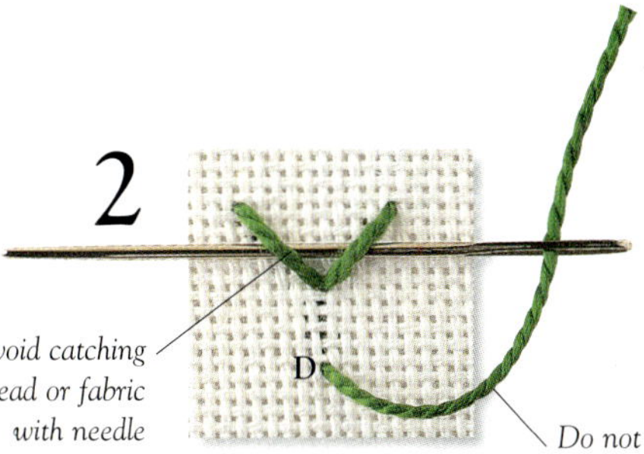

Avoid catching thread or fabric with needle

Do not pull thread too tightly

Work next pair of diagonal stitches into base of loop

Russian Chain

- **Level**
  Easy
- **Uses**
  Straight or curved border; individually as powdered filling
- **Method**
  Worked in detached groups of three chain stitches
- **Materials**
  Any fabric; thick thread

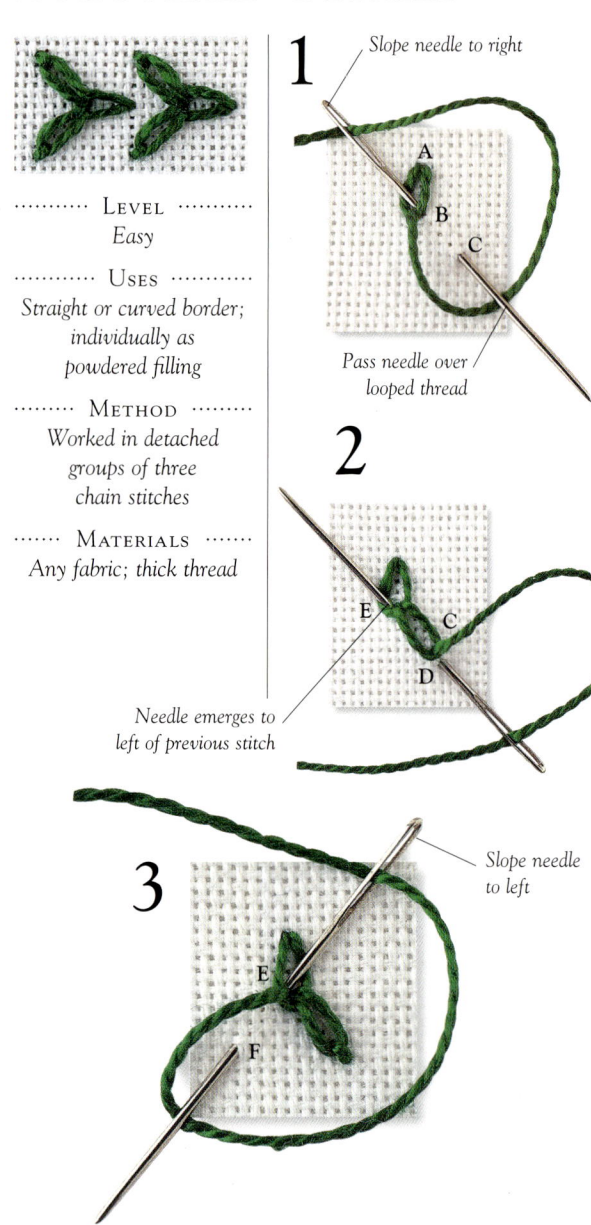

1 Work a chain stitch (see p.44) from **A** to **B**, bringing the needle out to the right of centre. Insert again at **B**, loop the thread from left to right and bring the needle out at **C**.

2 Insert the needle at **D** to make a tie stitch (see p.20), then bring the needle up inside the first loop, at **E**.

3 Make the third chain stitch at an angle from **E** to **F** in the same way. Finish with a tie stitch. Work the next and subsequent groups of stitches directly below the first.

Petal

- **Other Name**
  Pendant chain stitch
- **Level**
  Intermediate
- **Method**
  Angled link stitches combined with a row of stem stitches
- **Uses**
  Curved and straight lines; in rows as filling
- **Materials**
  Any fabric; any thick thread

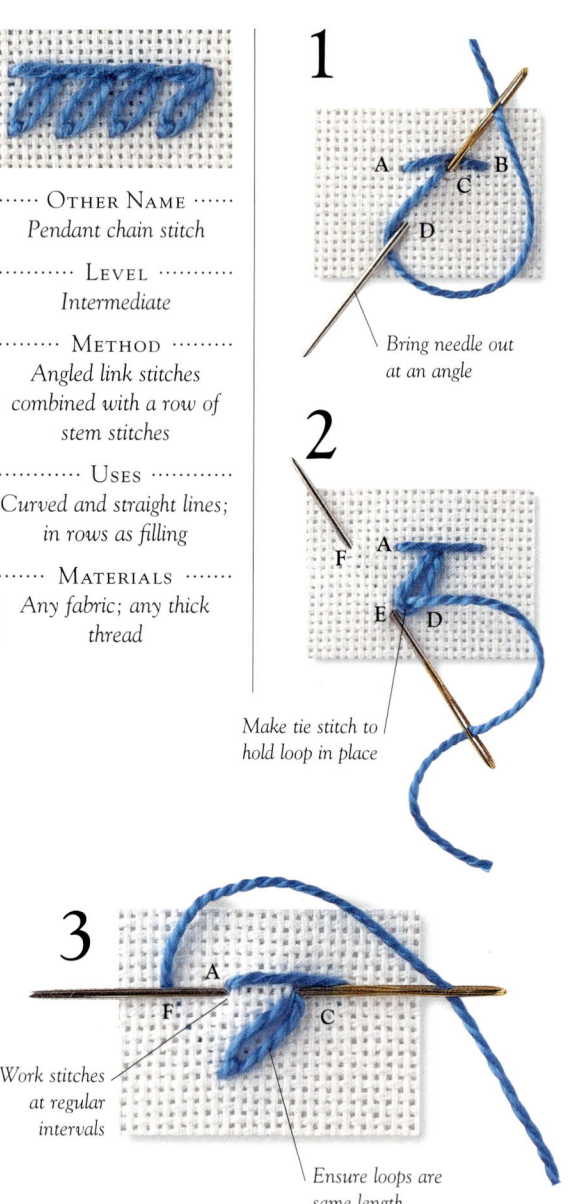

1 Start at **A** and make a straight stitch to **B**. Bring the needle up at the centre of the stitch at **C**. Work a chain stitch (see p.44) from **C** to **D**.

2 Insert the needle at **E** to make a tie stitch (see p.20). Come out to the left of **A** at **F**.

3 Insert the needle again at the top of the loop, at **C**, and come out at **A**, ready to make the next pair of stitches.

BORDER STITCHES 55

Zigzag Chain

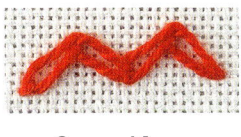

OTHER NAME
Vandyke chain

LEVEL
Intermediate

USES
Straight and gently curved lines and outlines

METHOD
Chain stitches worked at alternate angles

MATERIALS
Any fabric; twisted thread; sharp needle

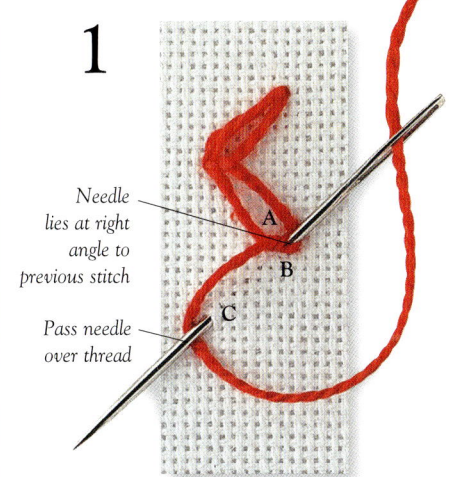

Needle lies at right angle to previous stitch

Pass needle over thread

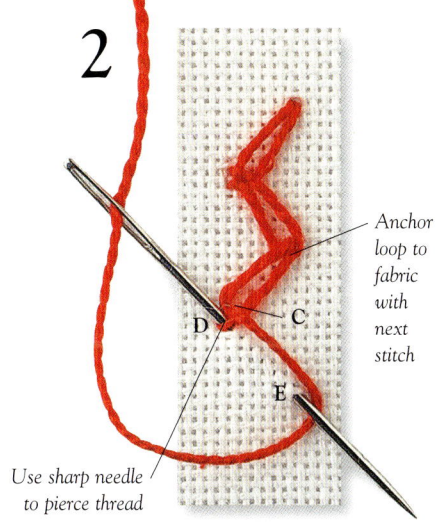

Anchor loop to fabric with next stitch

Use sharp needle to pierce thread

1 Come up inside the previous stitch at **A**. Loop the thread from left to right and insert the needle at **B** so that it pierces the base of the stitch. Bring the needle out at **C**, over the working thread.

2 Loop the thread from right to left and insert the needle at **D**, through the base of the last stitch. Come out at **E** and continue making stitches at right angles. Finish off with a tie stitch (see p.20) over the final loop.

Rosette Chain

OTHER NAME
Bead edging stitch

LEVEL
Advanced

USES
Straight or curved borders

METHOD
Twisted chain variation, worked horizontally

MATERIALS
Any fabric; thick non-stranded thread

Avoid catching threads or fabric with needle

Hold down loop as needle passes over thread

Make stitches small and compact to keep their shape

1 Start at **A**. Loop the thread from left to right and insert the needle at **B**. Come up at **C** and pull the needle through the loop. Slide the needle under the thread to the left of **A** from bottom to top, and pull through gently.

2 Insert the needle at **D** and come up through the loop at **E**, as before. Repeat to continue.

TECHNIQUE VARIATION

Work rosette chain in a circle to create a petalled flower motif. The stitches radiate from a central point and should be evenly spaced.

Loop

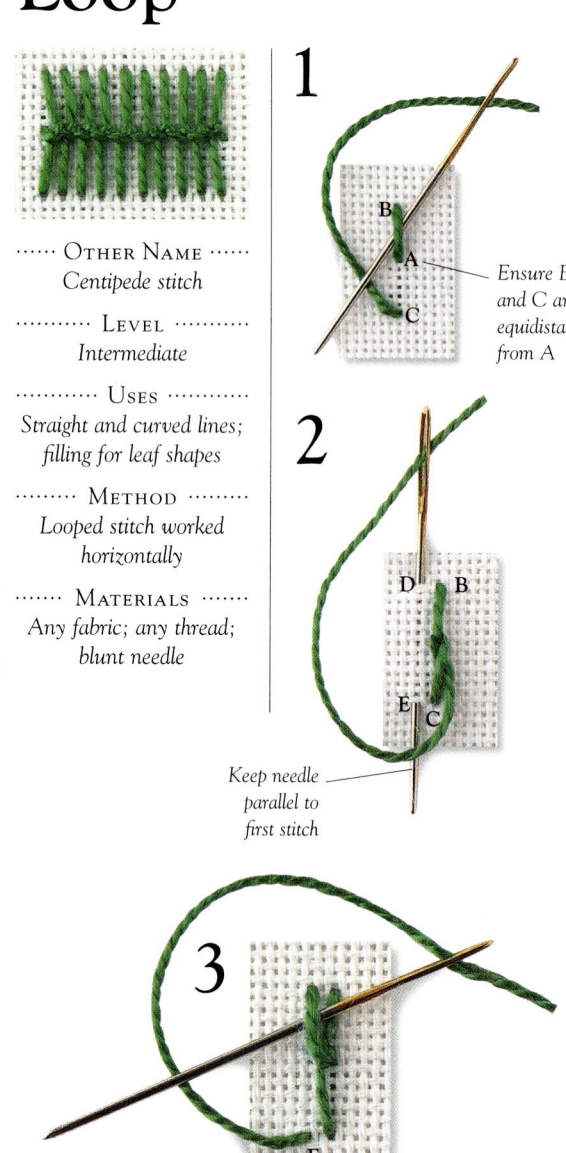

- **Other Name**
  Centipede stitch
- **Level**
  Intermediate
- **Uses**
  Straight and curved lines; filling for leaf shapes
- **Method**
  Looped stitch worked horizontally
- **Materials**
  Any fabric; any thread; blunt needle

Ensure B and C are equidistant from A

Keep needle parallel to first stitch

1 Start at **A**. Make an upright stitch to **B**, then come out directly below **A**, at **C**. Slide the needle under the stitch from right to left, over the working thread.

2 Insert the needle level with **B** at **D**. Come up at **E**, keeping the needle below the working thread.

3 Pass the needle under the previous stitch from right to left, over the working thread. Repeat steps 2 and 3 to continue. Finish off by taking the thread through to the back at the centre of the final stitch.

Flat Vandyke

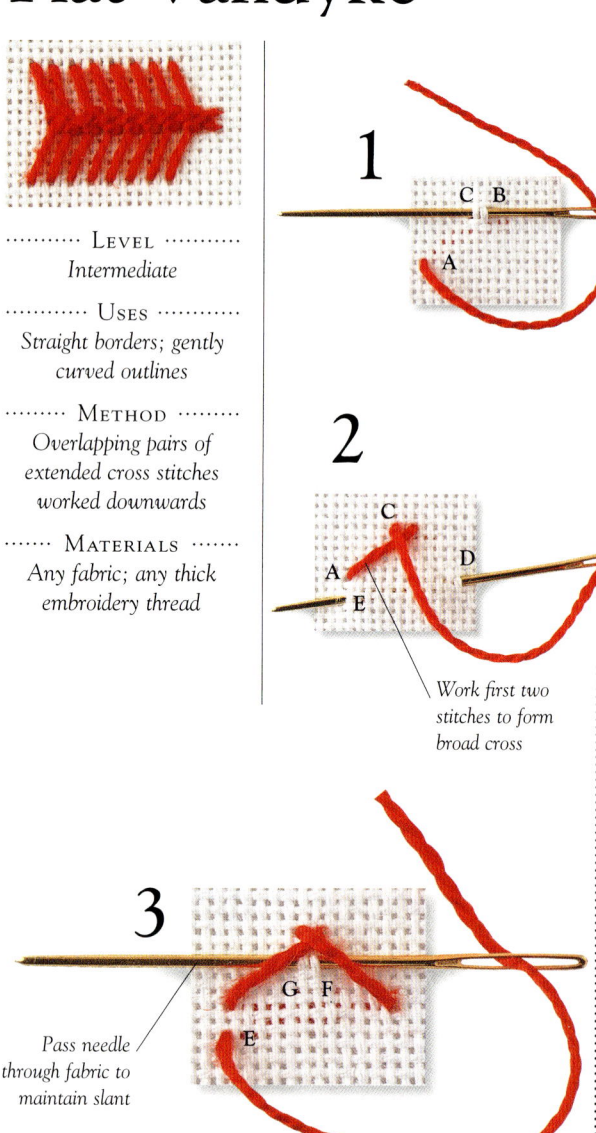

- **Level**
  Intermediate
- **Uses**
  Straight borders; gently curved outlines
- **Method**
  Overlapping pairs of extended cross stitches worked downwards
- **Materials**
  Any fabric; any thick embroidery thread

Work first two stitches to form broad cross

Pass needle through fabric to maintain slant

1 Start at **A**. Make a diagonal stitch up to **B** and bring the needle out to the left of **B**, at **C**.

2 Take the needle down and insert level with **A**, at **D**. Come up below **A**, at **E**.

3 Pass the needle under the crossed stitches from **F** to **G**, picking up two threads of background fabric. Repeat steps 2 and 3 to continue.

Ladder

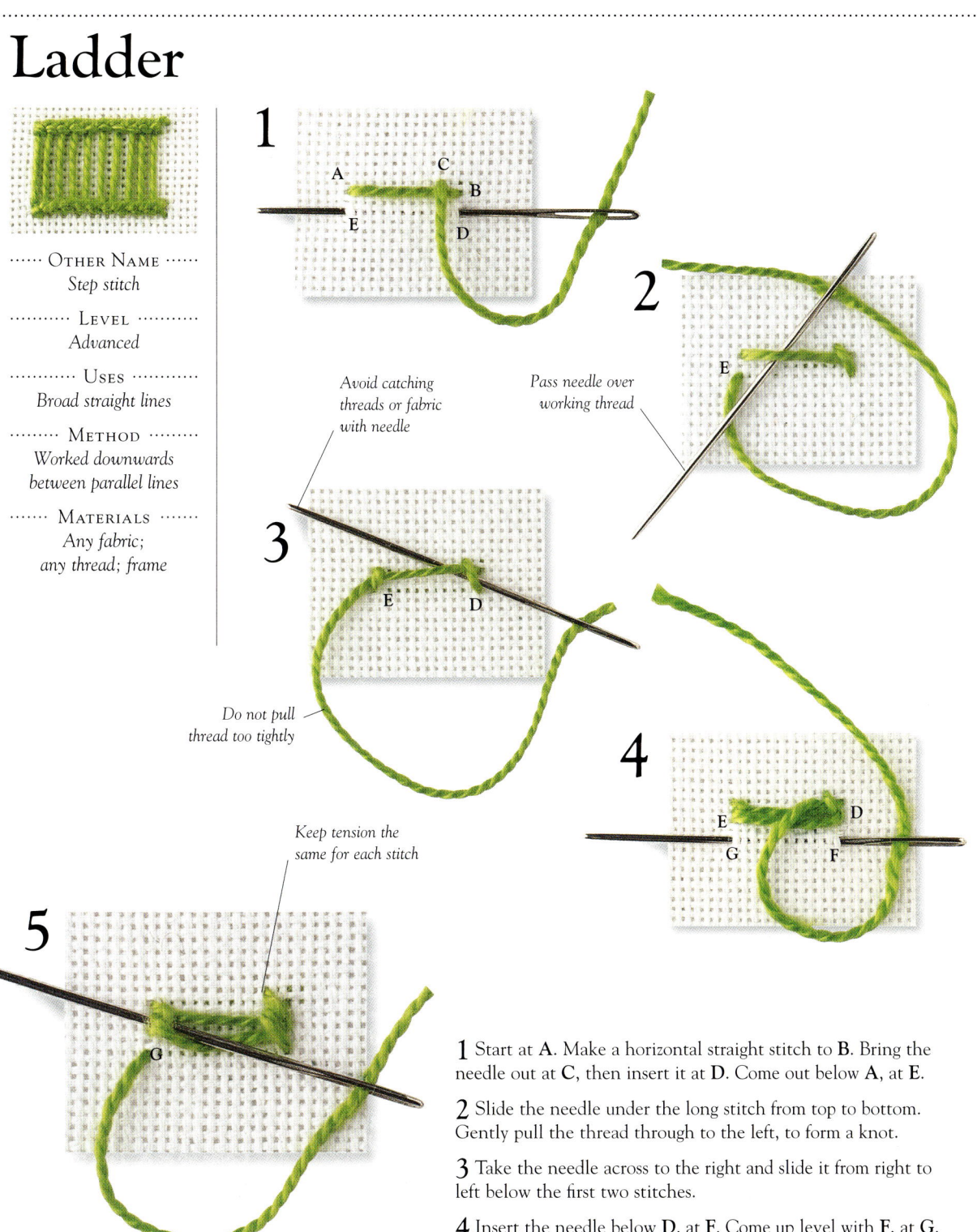

- **Other Name**
  Step stitch
- **Level**
  Advanced
- **Uses**
  Broad straight lines
- **Method**
  Worked downwards between parallel lines
- **Materials**
  Any fabric; any thread; frame

Avoid catching threads or fabric with needle

Pass needle over working thread

Do not pull thread too tightly

Keep tension the same for each stitch

1 Start at **A**. Make a horizontal straight stitch to **B**. Bring the needle out at **C**, then insert it at **D**. Come out below **A**, at **E**.

2 Slide the needle under the long stitch from top to bottom. Gently pull the thread through to the left, to form a knot.

3 Take the needle across to the right and slide it from right to left below the first two stitches.

4 Insert the needle below **D**, at **F**. Come up level with **F**, at **G**.

5 Pass the needle up behind the centre of the left knot from right to left. Repeat from step 3 to continue.

Blanket

Other Name
Open buttonhole stitch

Level
Easy

Method
Looped stitch, worked horizontally

Uses
Straight or curved borders and outlines; finishing edges; securing appliqué shapes; filling (see p.87)

Materials
Woven fabrics or felt; any wool or thread

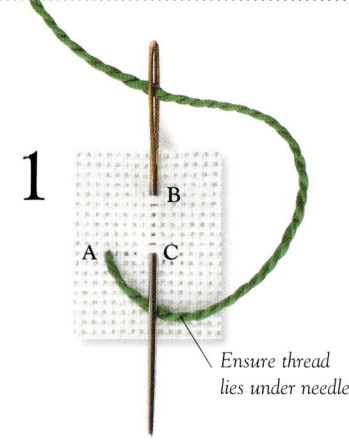

Ensure thread lies under needle

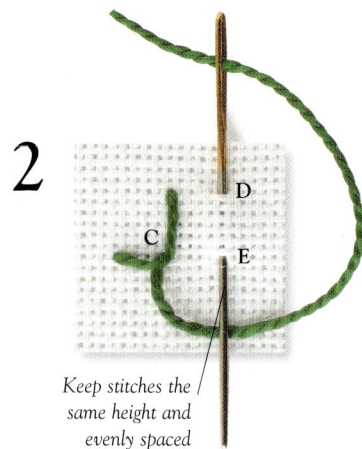

Keep stitches the same height and evenly spaced

1 Start at **A**. Take the needle up and insert at **B**, then bring it out directly below and level with **A**, at **C**.

2 Pull the needle down over the working thread. Insert the needle at **D** then bring it out at **E** to make the next stitch. Repeat this step to continue. Finish off with a tie stitch (see p.20) over the final loop.

Stitch Variation

Buttonhole stitch is worked in the same way but the stitches lie next to each other to create a solid line. The background fabric is completely covered and will not fray, so it is ideal for cutwork (see pp112-113), and neatening hems and hand-worked buttonholes.

Closed Buttonhole

Level
Easy

Method
Triangular blanket stitch variation, worked horizontally

Uses
Decorative edgings and borders; in rows as filling

Materials
Any fabric; any thread

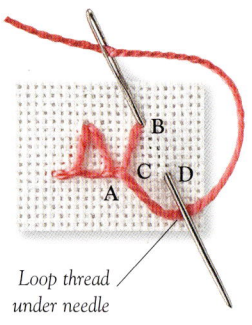

Loop thread under needle

Come up at **A** and insert the needle at **B**. Bring it up close to **A**, at **C**. Pull the needle over the working thread. Re-insert at **B** and come up to the right at **D**. Pull the needle over the loop. Repeat to continue.

Single Feather

Level
Easy

Method
Blanket stitch variation, worked downwards

Uses
Decorative edging; outlines and borders; in smocking; in rows as open filling

Materials
Any fabric; any embroidery thread

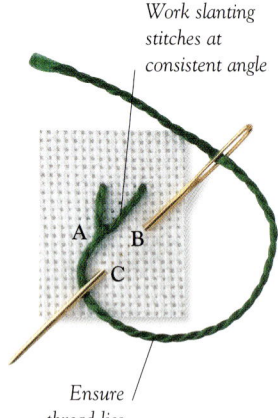

Work slanting stitches at consistent angle

Ensure thread lies under needle

Come up at **A**. Take the needle across to the right and insert it at **B**. Come out below **A**, at **C**. Pull the needle over the working thread. Repeat to continue.

Up and Down Buttonhole

- **Level**
  Intermediate
- **Method**
  Buttonhole stitch variation, worked alternately upwards and downwards
- **Uses**
  Straight or curved lines and edgings; in rows as filling
- **Materials**
  Any fabric; any embroidery thread

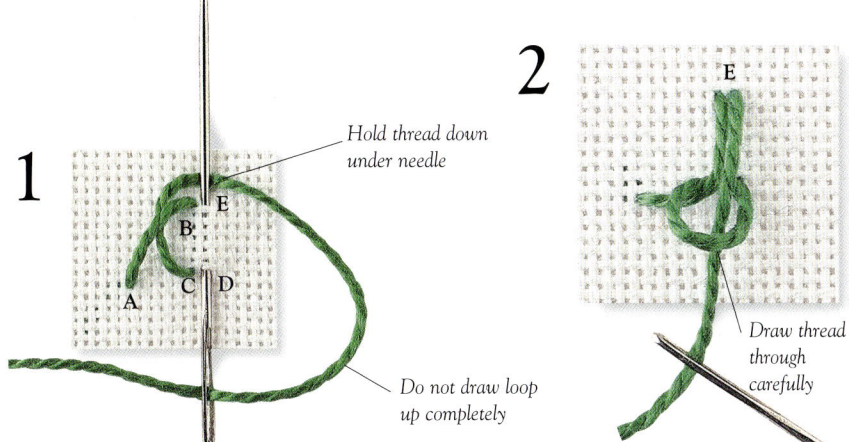

1 Start at **A**. Insert the needle at **B** and bring it out at **C**, as for step 1 of blanket stitch (see left). Insert the needle at **D** and bring it out at **E**, ensuring that the working thread lies under the point. Pull the needle upwards, so that the thread forms a loose loop.

2 Take the needle downwards, pulling gently until the loop tightens around the base of the two upright stitches. Repeat these two steps to continue.

Open Cretan

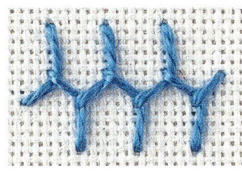

- **Level**
  Easy
- **Method**
  Looped stitch worked from top to bottom
- **Uses**
  Curved or straight lines; open filling
- **Materials**
  Any fabric; any thread – finer threads give a lacy appearance; frame

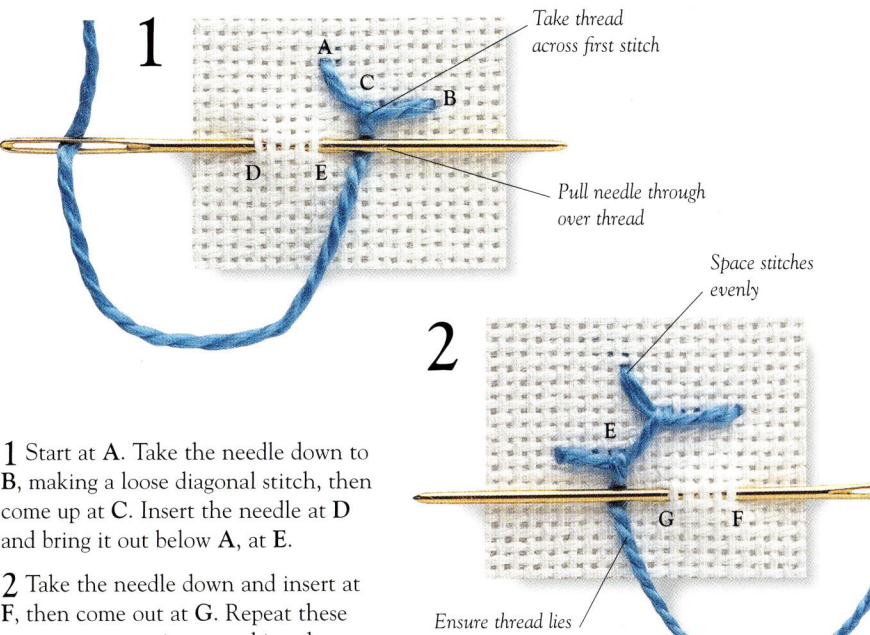

1 Start at **A**. Take the needle down to **B**, making a loose diagonal stitch, then come up at **C**. Insert the needle at **D** and bring it out below **A**, at **E**.

2 Take the needle down and insert at **F**, then come out at **G**. Repeat these two steps to continue, working the stitches alternately from left to right.

Feather

····· OTHER NAMES ·····
*Briar stitch;
single coral stitch*

········· LEVEL ·········
Easy

·········· USES ··········
*Smocking; hems;
crazy patchwork; with
ribbon embroidery*

········ METHOD ········
*Looped stitch, worked
alternately from left to right
in straight or curved lines*

······· MATERIALS ·······
Any fabric; any thread

Ensure thread lies under needle

Do not pull loop too tightly

Make all outside stitches point in same direction

1 Start at **A** and insert the needle to the right, at **B**, leaving a thread loop. Bring the point out over the thread at **C** and pull through.

2 Insert the needle to the left of **C**, at **D**. Come out directly below **A**, at **E**, and pull through over the loop.

3 Insert the needle at **F** and bring it out at **G**, over the loop. Repeat steps 2 and 3 to continue. Finish off with a tie stitch (see p.20) over the final loop.

Closed Feather

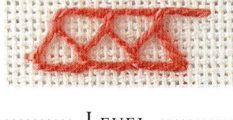

········· LEVEL ·········
Easy

·········· USES ··········
*Straight lines and
borders; in rows
as open filling*

········ METHOD ········
*Feather variation
worked downwards*

······· MATERIALS ·······
*Any fabric;
thick threads will
give a textured effect*

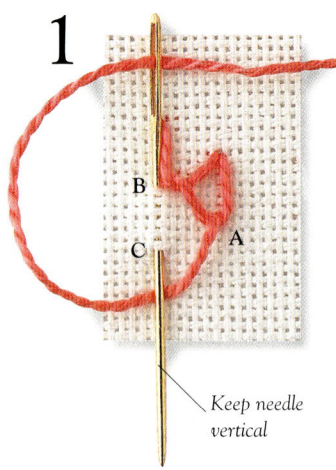

Keep needle vertical

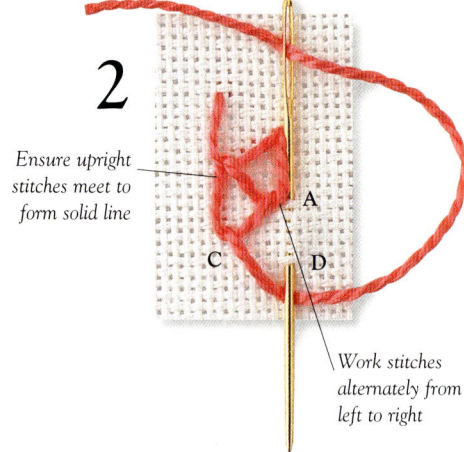

Ensure upright stitches meet to form solid line

Work stitches alternately from left to right

1 Come up at **A**. Take the needle diagonally up to the left and insert at **B**. Bring the point out over the working thread at **C** and pull through.

2 Re-insert the needle at **A**, bring it out at **D** and pull through over the working thread. Repeat these two steps to continue. Finish off with a tie stitch (see p.20) over the last loop.

Double Feather

····· Other Name ·····
Thorn and briar stitch

········· Level ·········
Easy

·········· Uses ··········
Foliage and branches; decorating children's garments

········· Method ·········
Looped stitch, worked alternately from left to right

······· Materials ·······
Any fabric; fine thread will give a lacy effect

1 Work the first two stitches as for feather stitch (see p.60), then make a second stitch to the left. Insert the needle level with **E** at **F**, and come out at **G**. Pull the needle through over the loop.

2 Take the needle across to the right and insert at **H**. Come out at **I** and pull through over the loop.

3 Make a second stitch to the right; take the needle down at **J**, bring it out at **K** and pull through over the loop. Continue working downwards, making two stitches one side, then the other.

Chained Feather

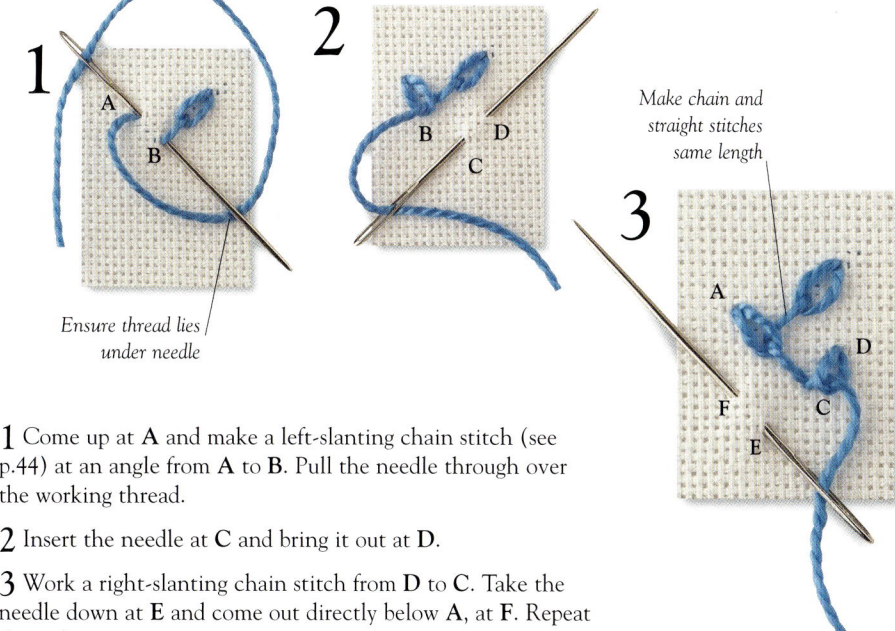

····· Other Names ·····
Feathered chain stitch

········· Level ·········
Intermediate

·········· Uses ··········
Decorative borders; foliage

········· Method ·········
Row of slanting picot stitches set at alternate angles

······· Materials ·······
Any fabric; any thread

1 Come up at **A** and make a left-slanting chain stitch (see p.44) at an angle from **A** to **B**. Pull the needle through over the working thread.

2 Insert the needle at **C** and bring it out at **D**.

3 Work a right-slanting chain stitch from **D** to **C**. Take the needle down at **E** and come out directly below **A**, at **F**. Repeat these three steps to continue.

Composite Border Stitches

This is the most decorative group of stitches which can be worked in single rows, or repeated to create multi-coloured fillings with intricate surface textures. Basic outline and border stitches are embellished with interlacing to create some of them, and others are a combination of two or even three stitches. Magic and Singalese chain are flexible stitches which can be sewn along a curved line, but the rest are all made in straight rows. Use a blunt needle for any interlacing and mount the fabric in an embroidery frame, so that the stitches do not become distorted.

Pekinese 63	Backstitched Herringbone 66
Laced Buttonhole 63	Raised Lattice Band 66
Interlacing Band 63	Double Herringbone 67
Magic Chain 64	Twisted Lattice Band 67
Singalese Chain 64	Butterfly Chain 68
Threaded Chain 65	Raised Chain Band 68
Guilloche 65	Diagonal Woven Band 69
Raised Chevron 66	Striped Woven Band 69
Portuguese Border 69	

COMPOSITE BORDER STITCHES   63

Pekinese

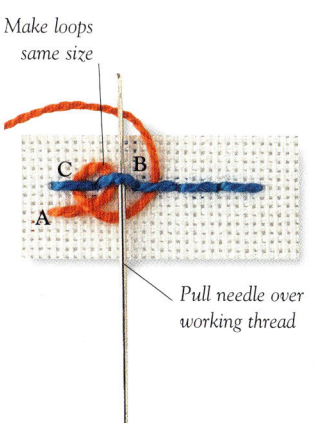
Make loops same size
Pull needle over working thread

····· OTHER NAMES ·····
Chinese stitch; forbidden stitch

········ LEVEL ········
Easy

········ USES ········
Decorative curved and straight outlines; in rows as filling

······· METHOD ·······
Laced back stitch, worked horizontally

······ MATERIALS ······
Any fabric; lacing can be worked in thicker thread; blunt needle

Work a row of back stitch (see p.40). Bring the lacing thread out at **A**. Slide the needle upwards beneath **B**, then pass it downwards under **C**. Draw the thread up gently and continue lacing to the end of the row.

Laced Buttonhole

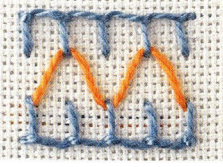

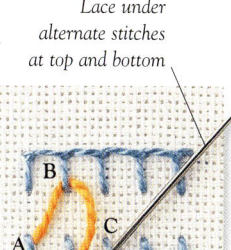
Lace under alternate stitches at top and bottom

····· OTHER NAME ·····
Threaded buttonhole stitch

········ LEVEL ········
Easy

········ USES ········
Decorative straight edgings and borders

······· METHOD ·······
Two rows of blanket stitch with interlacing

······ MATERIALS ······
Any fabric; any thread in two colours; frame; blunt needle

Work two parallel rows of blanket stitch (see p.58) with the upright stitches pointing inwards. Bring the lacing thread out at **A**. Slide the needle under **B**, then beneath **C**. Continue lacing to the end of the row.

Interlacing Band

Use blunt needle for interlacing

Ensure needle crosses thread

····· OTHER NAMES ·····
Double Pekinese stitch; herringbone ladder stitch

········ LEVEL ········
Intermediate

········ USES ········
Braided straight lines

······· METHOD ·······
Two rows of back stitch with looped interlacing

······ MATERIALS ······
Any fabric; any two threads in the same or different thicknesses; frame; blunt needle

1 Work two parallel lines of back stitch (see p.40), starting the bottom row with a half-length stitch. Bring the lacing thread out at **A**. Pass the needle upwards beneath **B**, then slide it downwards under both **C** and **D**.

2 Take the needle to the left and slide it under **E** and **F**, then pull through. Continue lacing up and down to the end of the row.

········ TECHNIQUE VARIATION ········

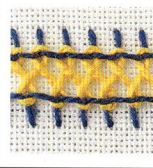

To create a wider, more open border, work the twisted interlacing over two rows of blanket stitch (see p.58), again using two colours.

Magic Chain

····· OTHER NAMES ·····
*Chequered chain stitch;
two-coloured chain stitch*

··········· LEVEL ···········
Intermediate

············ USES ············
Straight or curved outlines

·········· METHOD ··········
*Chain stitch variation
worked with two threads*

········ MATERIALS ········
*Any fabric; two
contrasting threads
in the same weight;
long-eyed needle*

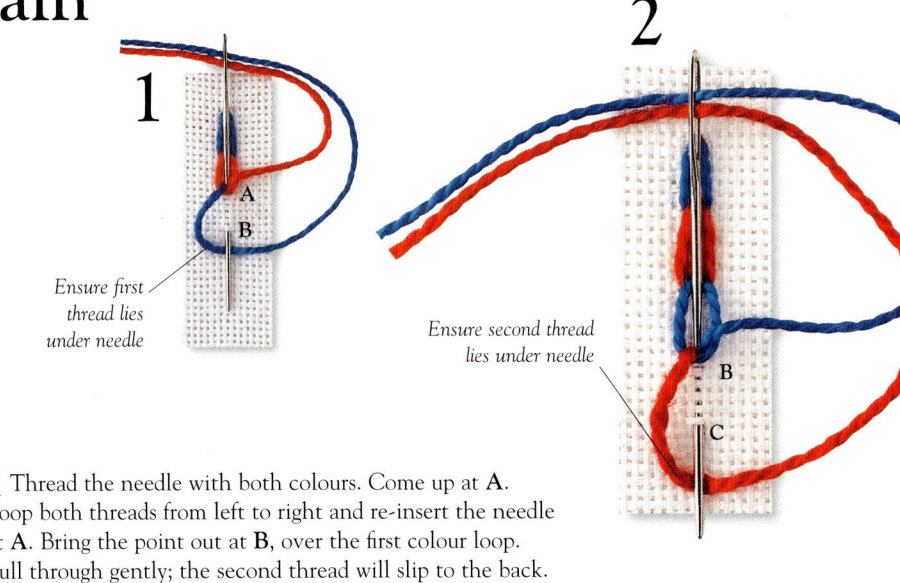

Ensure first thread lies under needle

Ensure second thread lies under needle

1 Thread the needle with both colours. Come up at **A**. Loop both threads from left to right and re-insert the needle at **A**. Bring the point out at **B**, over the first colour loop. Pull through gently; the second thread will slip to the back.

2 Loop the threads from left to right and re-insert the needle at **B**. Bring the point out at **C**, over the second colour loop: pull through. Repeat the steps to the end of the row. Finish with a tie stitch (see p.20) over the last loop.

Singalese Chain

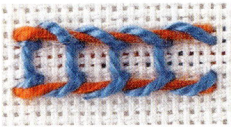

··········· LEVEL ···········
Advanced

············ USES ············
*Decorative borders;
curved or straight
outlines; casing for
narrow ribbon*

·········· METHOD ··········
*Square chain stitch
worked downwards over
contrasting threads*

········ MATERIALS ········
*Any fabric; any two
different coloured threads
of equal weight*

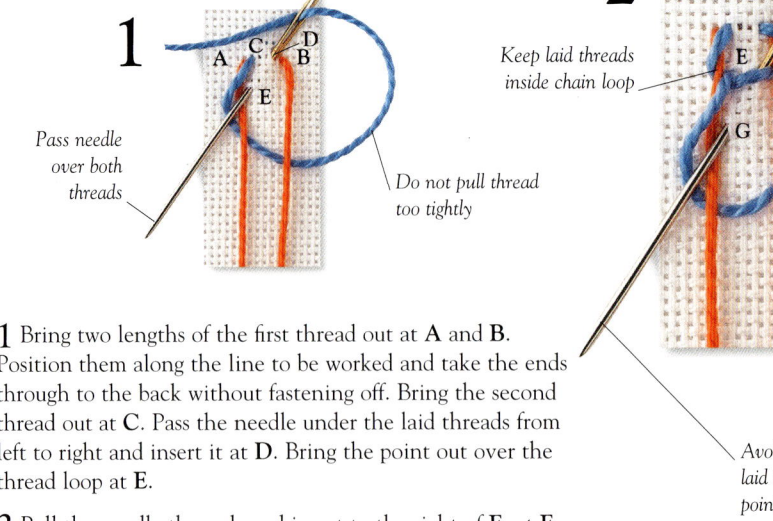

Pass needle over both threads

Do not pull thread too tightly

Keep laid threads inside chain loop

Avoid catching laid thread with point of needle

1 Bring two lengths of the first thread out at **A** and **B**. Position them along the line to be worked and take the ends through to the back without fastening off. Bring the second thread out at **C**. Pass the needle under the laid threads from left to right and insert it at **D**. Bring the point out over the thread loop at **E**.

2 Pull the needle through and insert to the right of **E**, at **F**, then bring it out at **G**, ready to work the next stitch. Repeat this step to continue, easing the laid threads into position. Fasten down the final loop with two tie stitches (see p.20) and finish off the laid threads on the reverse side.

Composite Border Stitches 65

Threaded Chain

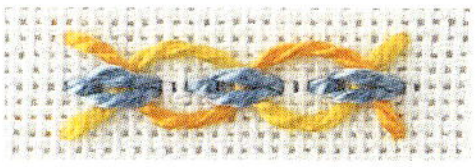

- **Level**
  Intermediate
- **Uses**
  Light borders or outlines
- **Method**
  Row of link stitches with double interlacing
- **Materials**
  Any fabric; any three threads in the same or different colours and weights; blunt needle

Use blunt needle to avoid catching threads

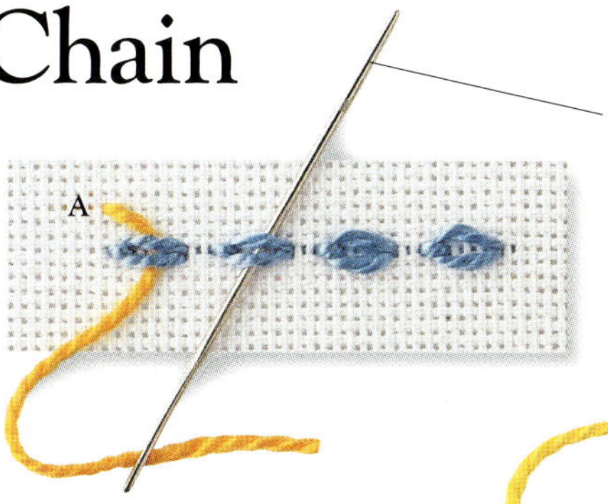

Use thick thread to give raised appearance to interlacing

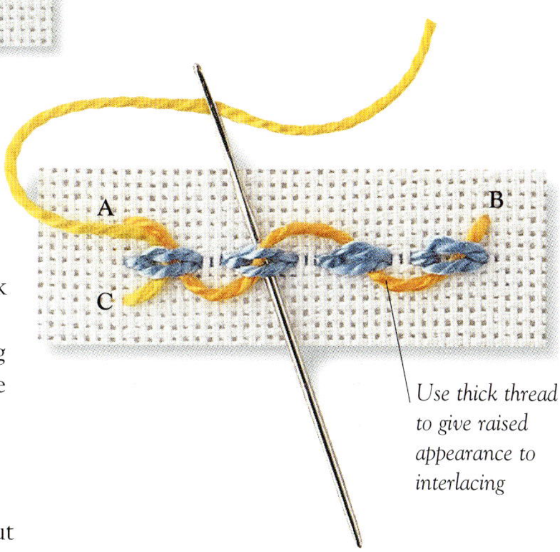

1 Work a foundation of evenly-spaced link stitches (see p.80) in the main colour. Thread the blunt needle with a contrasting colour and come out at **A**. Slide the needle downwards under the first stitch, then upwards beneath the second stitch. Continue to the end of the row.

2 Finish off at **B**. Bring the third colour out at **C** and lace it alternately up and down under the link stitches, filling in the spaces.

Guilloche

- **Level**
  Advanced
- **Uses**
  Multi-coloured straight borders and edgings
- **Method**
  Combination of stem and satin stitches with French knots and interlacing
- **Materials**
  Evenweave fabric; thick thread in three colours; blunt needle

Work out positions of each line and group of stitches before beginning

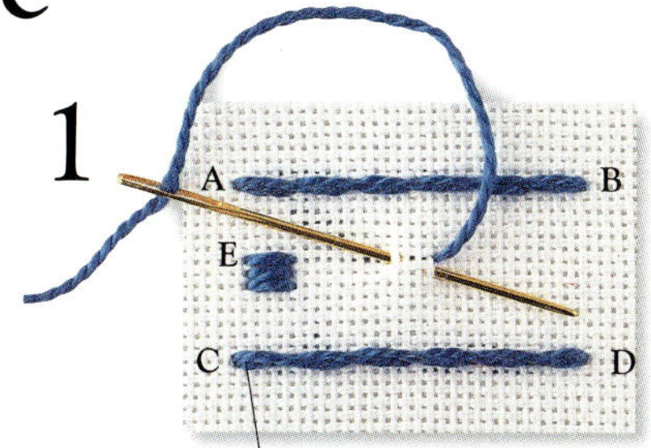

Use blunt needle to avoid catching threads

1 Using the main colour, work two parallel lines of stem stitch (see p.41) from **A** to **B** and from **C** to **D**. Work groups of three short satin stitches (see p.86) at regular intervals between the lines, starting at **E**.

2 Interlace the satin stitches with contrasting threads as for threaded chain stitch (see above).

3 Finish off by working a French knot (see p.76) in the centre of each loop, using the third thread.

Raised Chevron

·········· Level ··········
Intermediate

·········· Uses ··········
Straight outlines and light borders

·········· Method ··········
Chevron stitch worked over two lines of arrowhead stitches

·········· Materials ··········
Any fabric; thicker thread gives more texture – choose two contrasting colours

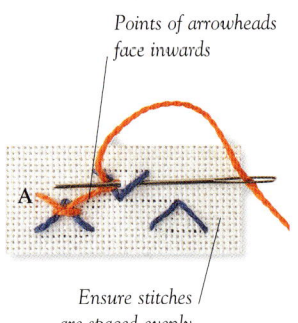

Points of arrowheads face inwards

Ensure stitches are spaced evenly

Stitch two parallel rows of arrowheads (see p.73) in the first colour. Bring the second thread out at **A** and work a band of chevron stitch (see p.49) from left to right, so that the horizontal stitches lie across the points of the arrowhead stitches.

Backstitched Herringbone

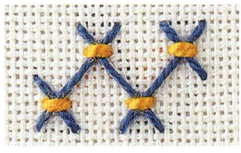

·········· Level ··········
Easy

·········· Uses ··········
Open borders; in rows as a lattice filling

·········· Method ··········
Herringbone stitch with back stitch detail

·········· Materials ··········
Any fabric; two contrasting threads in the same or different weights

Work back stitches over crossed threads

Work a line of herringbone stitch (see p.52). Using the second thread, make a back stitch from **A** to **B**. Bring the needle up at **C**, insert at **D**, and come out at **E**. Continue to the end of the row.

Raised Lattice Band

·········· Level ··········
Advanced

·········· Uses ··········
Decorative borders

·········· Method ··········
Interlaced herringbone stitch worked over padded satin stitch

·········· Materials ··········
Any fabric; lustrous thread in three colours; blunt needle; frame

1

Work upright stitches close together

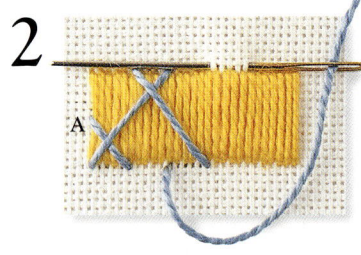

2

3

Ensure lacing is not pulled too tightly

1 Work a foundation of long horizontal surface satin stitch (see p.86). Work a row of upright satin (see p.86) from left to right over the base stitches.

2 Bring the second thread up at **A** and work a row of herringbone stitch (see p.52).

3 Thread the blunt needle with the third colour thread. Come up at **A** and slide the needle upwards, under the centre of the first long diagonal stitch. Take it back down under the second stitch from top to bottom. Continue lacing to the end of the band.

COMPOSITE BORDER STITCHES 67

Double Herringbone

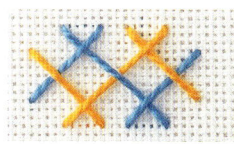

····· OTHER NAME ·····
Indian herringbone stitch

········· LEVEL ·········
Advanced

········· USES ·········
Geometric border; in rows as open filling

········ METHOD ········
Two interlaced rows of herringbone stitch

······· MATERIALS ·······
Any fabric; any thick thread in two colours

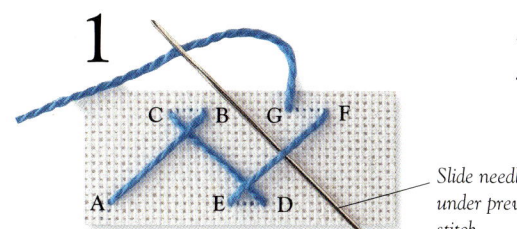

Slide needle under previous stitch

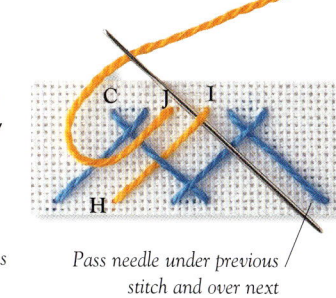

Pass needle under previous stitch and over next

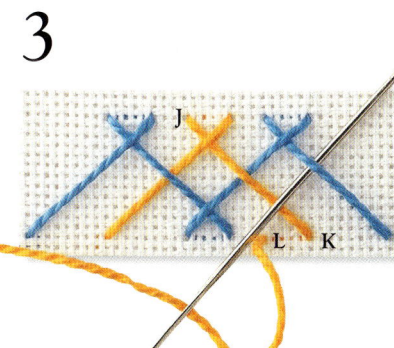

1 Start at **A** and make a diagonal stitch to **B**. Bring the needle out at **C**, pass it under the stitch and take it down at **D**. Come out at **E** and insert at **F**. Bring the needle out at **G** and slide it under the last stitch. Continue to the end of the row.

2 Bring the contrast thread up directly below **C**, at **H**. Slide the needle under the second stitch and insert at **I**. Come out at **J** and pass the needle under the previous stitch.

3 Insert the needle at **K** and come out at **L**. Take it over the first thread and under the second. Repeat steps 2 and 3 to continue.

Twisted Lattice Band

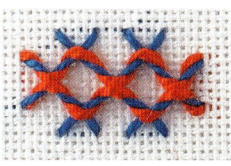

········· LEVEL ·········
Advanced

········· USES ·········
Ornamental border; in rows as filling

········ METHOD ········
Double herringbone stitch with two rows of interlacing

······· MATERIALS ·······
Any fabric; any thick thread in two colours

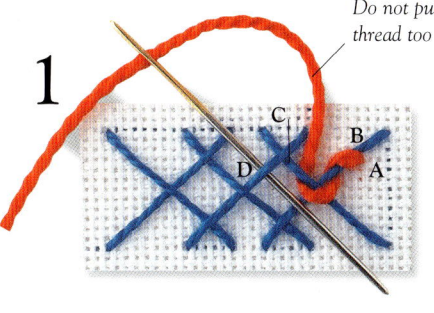

Do not pull lacing thread too tightly

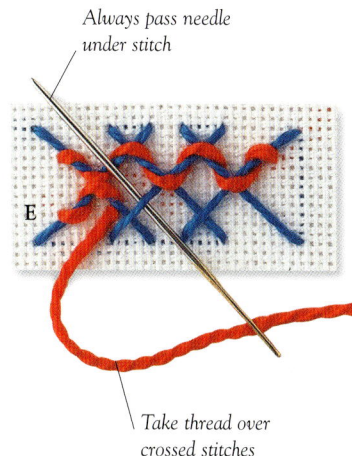

Always pass needle under stitch

Take thread over crossed stitches

1 Work a foundation of double herringbone stitch (see above) in the first colour. Bring the lacing thread out at **A**. Pass the needle downwards under **B**, then upwards under **C**. Slide it beneath the next stitch, at **D**, from top to bottom.

2 Continue weaving the thread under and over the top stitches to the end of the row. Bring the thread out at **E** and interlace the bottom stitches in the same way to complete.

Butterfly Chain

- **Level**
  Intermediate
- **Uses**
  Light frames or borders
- **Method**
  Twisted chain stitch worked over groups of three straight stitches, without piercing fabric
- **Materials**
  Any fabric; thick thread in two colours; blunt needle

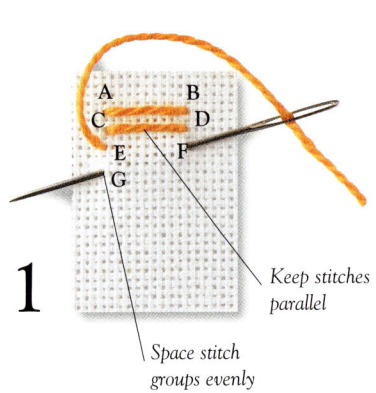

1 *Keep stitches parallel* / *Space stitch groups evenly*

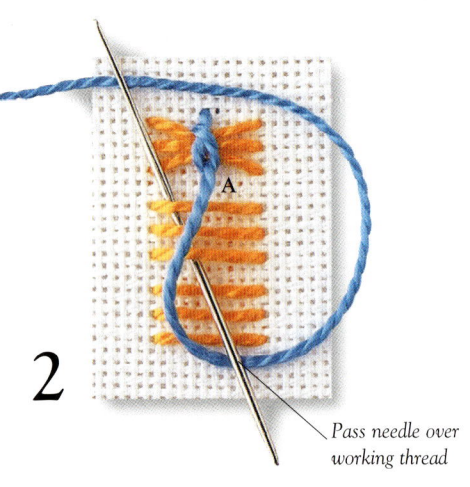

2 *Pass needle over working thread*

1 Start at **A**, and make a horizontal stitch across to **B**. Work two more stitches directly below, from **C** to **D** and **E** to **F**, then bring the needle out at **G** to work the next group of three stitches.

2 Using the contrast thread, work a twisted chain stitch (see p.44) over each group of horizontal stitches. Come through at **A** and loop the thread to the right. Slide the needle under all three stitches and pull it through. Tighten the thread to draw the stitches together.

Raised Chain Band

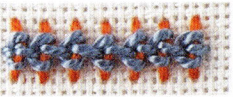

- **Other Name**
  Raised chain stitch
- **Level**
  Intermediate
- **Uses**
  Heavy borders
- **Method**
  Chain stitch worked over straight stitch foundation, without piercing fabric
- **Materials**
  Any fabric; any thick thread in two colours; blunt needle

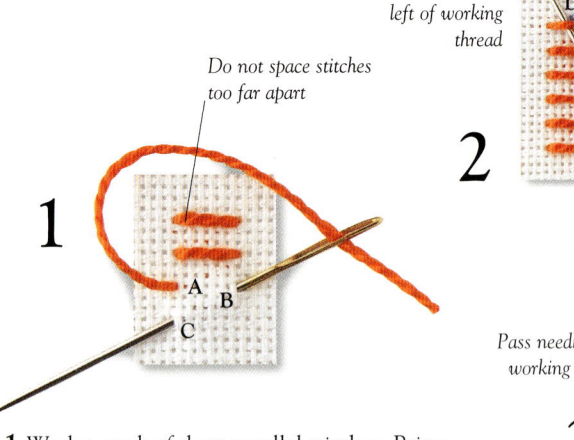

1 *Do not space stitches too far apart*

2 *Keep needle to left of working thread*

3 *Pass needle over working thread* / *Do not pull thread up too tightly*

1 Work a stack of short parallel stitches. Bring the needle out at **A** and take it down at **B**. Come up at **C** and continue working downwards.

2 Bring the second thread out at **D**. Pass the needle under the first stitch from bottom to top.

3 Loop the thread to the right. Slide the needle downwards under the first stitch, to the right of **D**. Repeat steps 2 and 3 to the end of the stack.

COMPOSITE BORDER STITCHES 69

Diagonal Woven Band

····· LEVEL ·····
Advanced

····· USES ·····
Dense striped border or frame

····· METHOD ·····
Two contrasting threads woven through row of straight stitches

····· MATERIALS ·····
Any fabric; any two twisted threads; two blunt needles

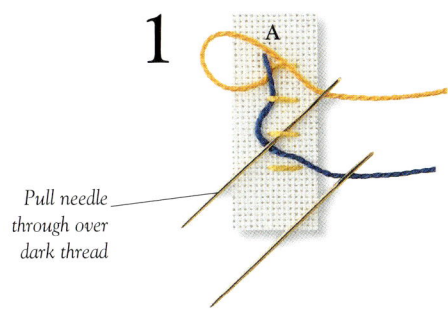

Pull needle through over dark thread

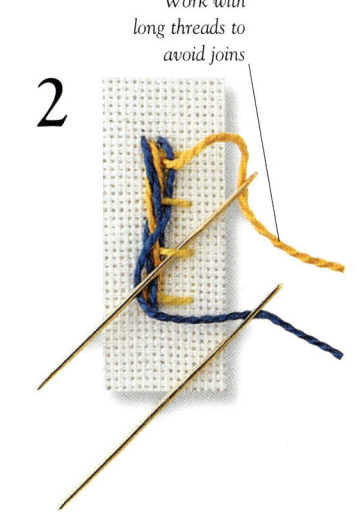

Work with long threads to avoid joins

1 Work a stack of straight stitches (see p.68, raised chain band step 1). Bring the dark thread up at **A**, pass the needle under the second stitch and take it to the right. Bring the light thread up at **A**. Slide the needle to the left below the first stitch and the dark thread, then take it under the third stitch and across the dark thread.

2 Continue weaving downwards, taking the two threads alternately under and over the straight stitches. Work the following rows in the same way, alternating the colour of the first stitch.

····· STITCH VARIATION ·····

To work striped woven band stitch, start every twisted line with the same colour thread, to create solid blocks of alternate colours.

Portuguese Border

····· LEVEL ·····
Advanced

····· USES ·····
Raised borders

····· METHOD ·····
Diagonal stitches woven over straight stitch foundation

····· MATERIALS ·····
Any fabric; twisted thread in two colours; blunt needle

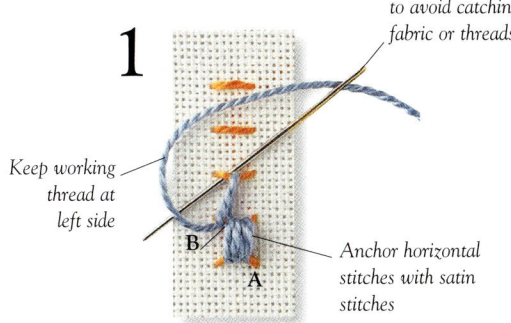

Use blunt needle to avoid catching fabric or threads

Keep working thread at left side

Anchor horizontal stitches with satin stitches

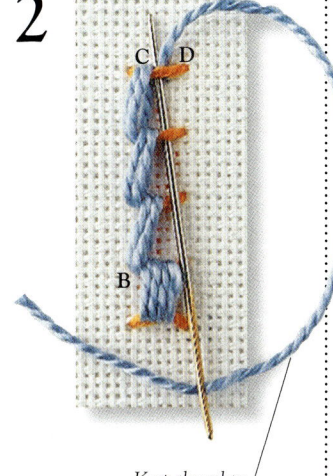

Keep thread to right of stitches

1 Work a stack of horizontal stitches (see p.68, raised chain band step 1). Bring the second thread up at **A** and make three satin stitches (see p.86) over the first two stitches. Come out at **B** and slide the needle downwards under the next two horizontal stitches, making a slanting stitch. Pass the needle under the third horizontal stitch again, to make a second stitch. Continue upwards, working pairs of slanting stitches.

2 At the top of the stack, take the needle down at **C** and out at **D**. Pass it upwards under the top two stitches. Continue as before, slanting the stitches in the opposite direction.

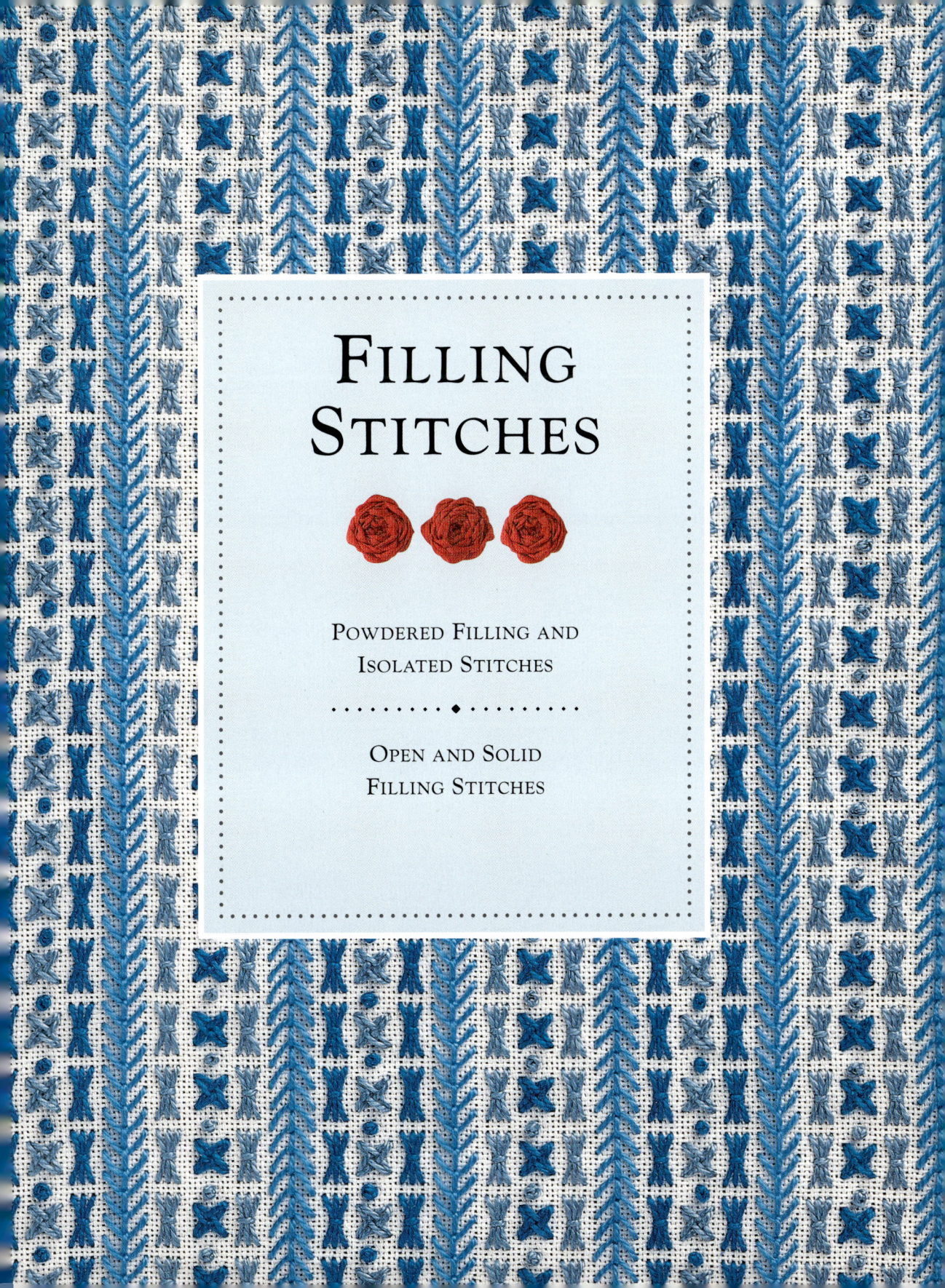

Filling Stitches

Powdered Filling and Isolated Stitches

Open and Solid Filling Stitches

Powdered Filling and Isolated Stitches

These detached stitches are all worked singly and vary considerably in size. The larger versions are often used as accent stitches, while the smaller ones are repeated to form a powdered filling. The stitches can be arranged in several ways: in regular rows to form straight lines and geometric patterns; scattered randomly; spaced apart to allow the background fabric to show through, or sewn close together to form a dense, textured surface. A design usually requires a powdered filling to be contained within an area which has been defined with an outline or border stitch.

Straight 73	Fly 78
Arrowhead 73	Sheaf Filling 78
Dot 73	Crown 78
St George Cross 73	Sorbello 79
Ermine 74	Palestrina Knot 79
Square Boss 74	Link 80
Star 74	Lazy Daisy 80
Woven Star 75	Berry 80
Woven Cross 75	Picot 80
French Knot 76	Detached Wheatear 81
Pistil 76	Tulip 81
Bullion Knot 76	Woven Spider Web 82
Danish Knot 77	Ribbon Rose 82
Four-legged Knot 77	Ribbed Web 82
Sword 77	Buttonhole Wheel 82
Shisha 83	

POWDERED FILLING AND ISOLATED STITCHES | 73

Straight

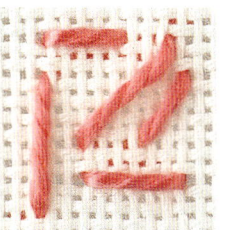

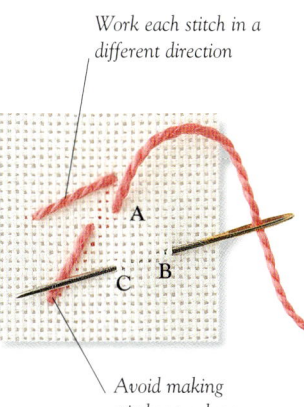

Work each stitch in a different direction

Avoid making stitches too long

····· OTHER NAME ·····
Stroke stitch

····· LEVEL ·····
Easy

····· USES ·····
Foliage; textured filling

····· METHOD ·····
Randomly placed single stitches of varying length

····· MATERIALS ·····
Any fabric; any thread

Come up at **A**. Take the needle down to **B** and insert, then bring it out at **C**. Continue working straight stitches in a random pattern to fill the required area.

Arrowhead

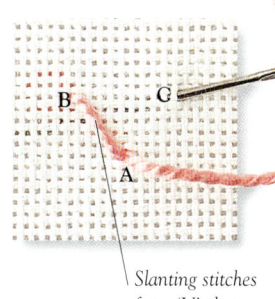

Slanting stitches form 'V' shape

····· LEVEL ·····
Easy

····· USES ·····
Powdered filling; worked in vertical or horizontal rows as border stitch

····· METHOD ·····
Two straight stitches worked at a right angle

····· MATERIALS ·····
Any fabric; thick threads create raised effect

Start at **A**. Make a diagonal straight stitch up to **B**, then come out again at **A**. Insert the needle at **C** to complete.

Dot

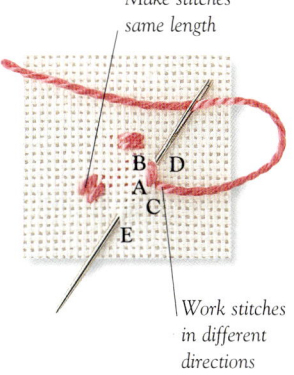

Make stitches same length

Work stitches in different directions

····· OTHER NAME ·····
Backstitched seeding

····· LEVEL ·····
Easy

····· USES ·····
Powdered filling; worked in rows as outline

····· METHOD ·····
Pairs of short, closely spaced back stitches

····· MATERIALS ·····
Any fabric; pearl thread makes stitches stand out

Come up at **A**. Insert the needle at **B** and bring it out at **C**. Insert at **D** to complete the second stitch, then bring the needle up at **E** to work the next pair of stitches.

St George Cross

Ensure second stitch crosses centre of first stitch

····· OTHER NAME ·····
Upright cross stitch

····· LEVEL ·····
Easy

····· USES ·····
Geometric or random fillings; isolated stitch

····· MATERIALS ·····
Any fabric; twisted threads give raised effect

Start at **A** and work a horizontal straight stitch across to **B**. Come out at **C**. Take the needle down over the first stitch and insert at **D** to complete the cross.

Ermine

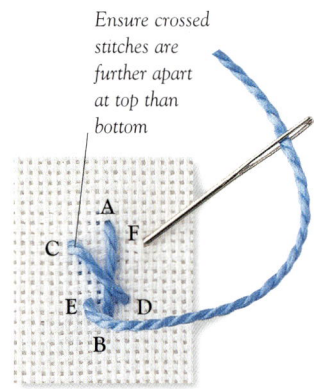

Ensure crossed stitches are further apart at top than bottom

·········· LEVEL ··········
Easy

·········· USES ··········
Scattered or regular filling; in rows as border; isolated stitch; in blackwork

·········· METHOD ··········
Wide cross stitch worked over upright straight stitch

·········· MATERIALS ··········
Evenweave fabric for a regular effect; any thread

Start at **A** and work a vertical straight stitch to **B**. Bring the needle out at **C** and insert at **D**. Come out at **E**. Take the needle across the two stitches and insert at **F** to complete.

Square Boss

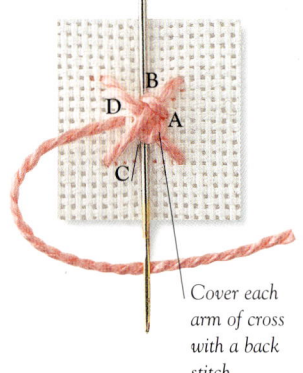

Cover each arm of cross with a back stitch

·········· OTHER NAME ··········
Raised knot

·········· LEVEL ··········
Intermediate

·········· USES ··········
Light fillings; in rows as border; isolated stitch

·········· METHOD ··········
Cross stitch covered by back stitch square

·········· MATERIALS ··········
Any fabric; thick thread gives raised texture

Make a cross stitch (see p.50). Bring the needle out at **A** and take it down at **B**. Come out at **C** and insert at **A**. Bring the needle out at **D** and insert at **C**. Work a back stitch from **B** to **D** to complete.

Star

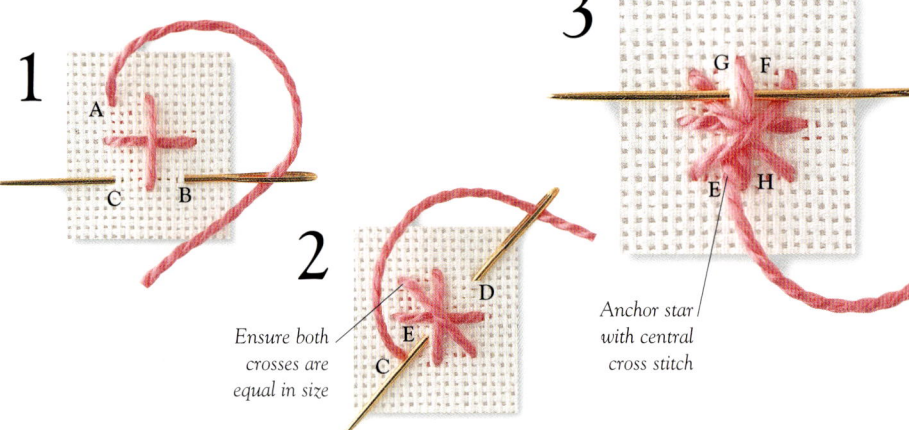

Ensure both crosses are equal in size

Anchor star with central cross stitch

·········· LEVEL ··········
Intermediate

·········· USES ··········
Scattered as light filling; in rows as border; isolated stitch

·········· METHOD ··········
Elongated cross stitch worked over St George cross and cross stitches

·········· MATERIALS ··········
Any fabric; any thread

1 Make a St George cross stitch (see p.73). Bring the needle out at **A**, and work a diagonal stitch down to **B**. Come out to the left of **B**, at **C**.

2 Take the needle diagonally up to **D** and insert. Come out near the centre of the stitch at **E**.

3 Insert the needle at **F,** then bring it out to the left at **G**. Take it down at **H** to complete the cross.

·········· TECHNIQUE VARIATION ··········

For a decorative effect, stitch the small cross in the centre of the star (see step 3) using a different coloured thread.

Powdered Filling and Isolated Stitches 75

Woven Star

- **Level**
  Intermediate
- **Uses**
  Powdered filling; isolated stitch
- **Method**
  Five interwoven straight stitches
- **Materials**
  Any fabric; any thread

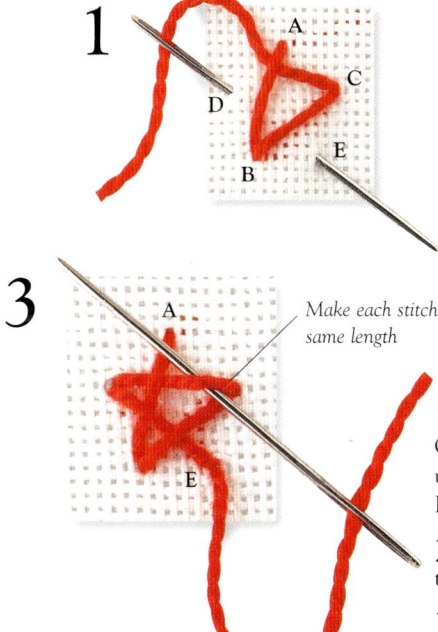

Pass needle over first stitch

Make each stitch same length

1 Start at **A** and work a diagonal stitch down to **B**. Come out at **C** and re-insert at **B**. Bring the needle up again at **C** and slide it under the first stitch. Insert at **D** and come out at **E**.

2 Take the needle over the first thread and under the second, then re-insert at **D**.

3 Come out again at **E**. Slide the needle over the first thread, under the second and insert at **A**.

Woven Cross

- **Level**
  Intermediate
- **Uses**
  Powdered filling; isolated stitch
- **Method**
  Four interwoven straight stitches
- **Materials**
  Any fabric; any thick thread

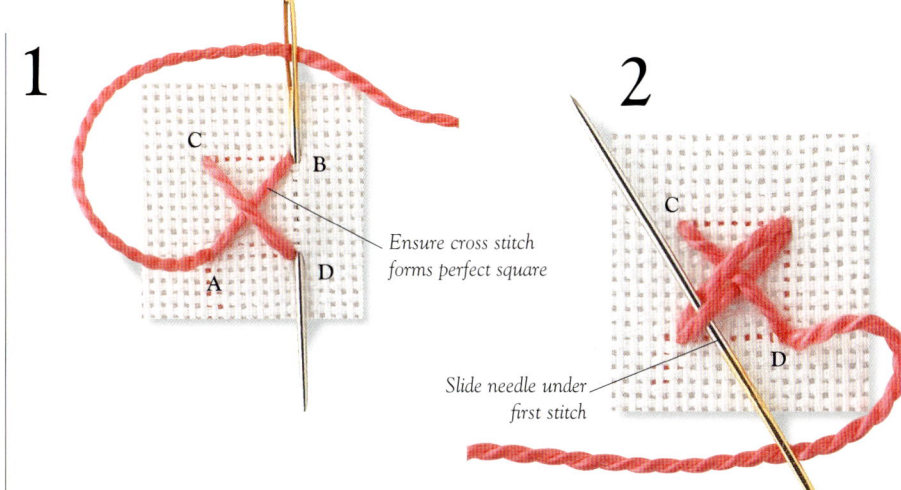

Ensure cross stitch forms perfect square

Slide needle under first stitch

1 Work a cross stitch (see p.50) from **A** to **B** and **C** to **D**. Bring the needle back up at **A**, insert it again at **B** and come out at **D**.

2 Pass the needle under the first thread and over the second, then insert at **C** to complete the cross.

French Knot

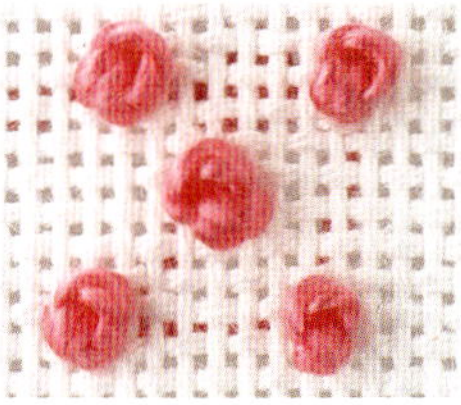

Level
Intermediate

Uses
Light or solid powdered filling; singly as raised highlight

Method
Twisted knotted stitch

Materials
Any fabric; any thread depending on size; small-eyed needle

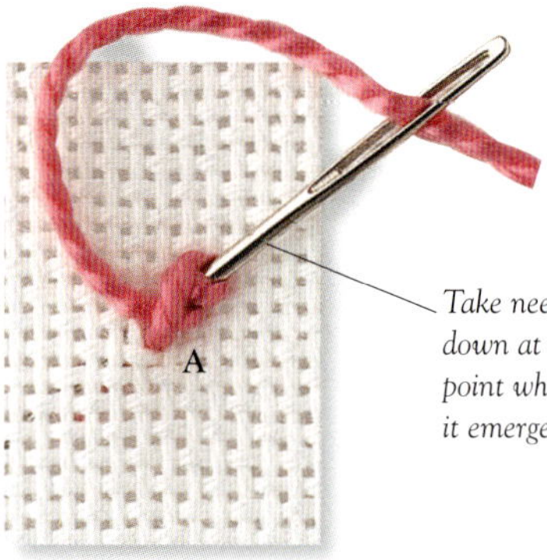

1 Start at **A**. Hold the thread taut and wrap it twice around the needle, then pull it gently to tighten the loops.

2 Maintaining the tension, insert the needle again at **A**, pushing it down through the two loops to form a round knot.

Hold thread to keep it taut

Take needle down at point where it emerged

Stitch Variation
To work pistil stitch, insert the needle a short distance from where it emerged, to form a long tail. Make eight stitches in a circle to create a flower centre or floral shape.

Bullion Knot

Other Names
Caterpillar stitch

Level
Intermediate

Uses
Powdered filling; accent stitch; in rows as border

Method
Long twisted knot

Materials
Any fabric; any twisted embroidery thread

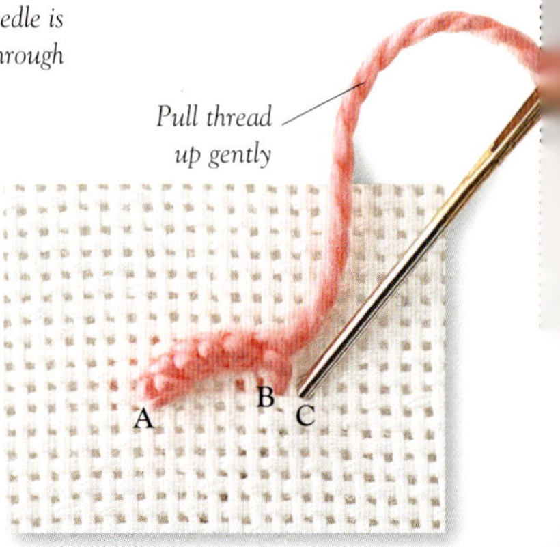

1 Start at **A**. Take the needle down at **B** and bring the point back through at **A**.

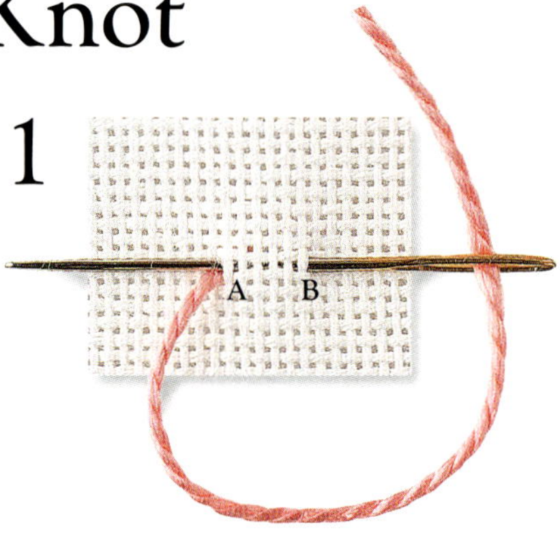

2 Wrap the thread six times around the needle, holding the loops down with a finger. Using the other hand, pull the needle carefully through the fabric and the coiled thread.

3 Take the needle back down at **C** and pull the working thread up so that the loops lie flat.

Hold coiled thread in place as needle is pulled through

Pull thread up gently

POWDERED FILLING AND ISOLATED STITCHES 77

Danish Knot

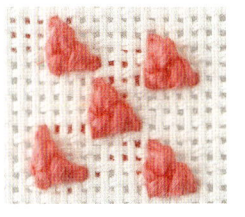

······· Level ·······
Intermediate

······· Uses ·······
*Powdered filling;
triangular accent stitch*

······· Method ·······
*Looped knot worked over
short diagonal stitch*

······· Materials ·······
*Any fabric;
thick twisted thread*

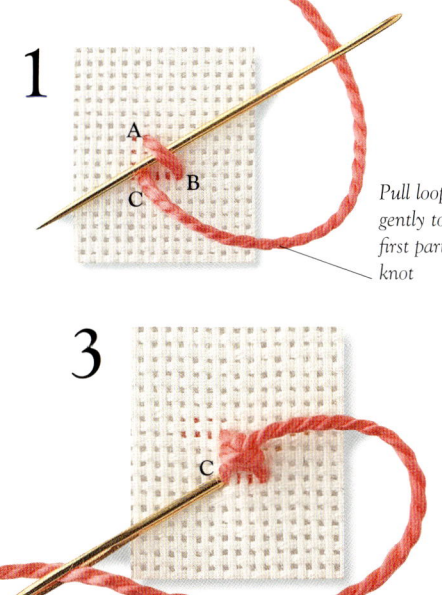

Pull loop up gently to form first part of knot

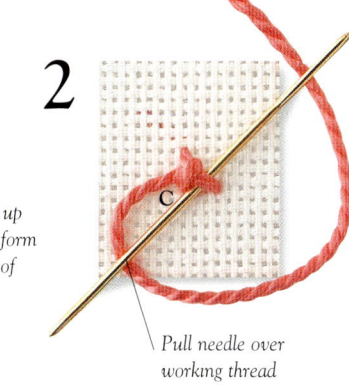

Pull needle over working thread

1 Start at **A** and work a short diagonal stitch down to **B**. Bring the needle out at **C** and slide it under the stitch from right to left.

2 Take the needle across to the right of the knot. Pass it under the diagonal stitch from right to left for a second time.

3 Insert the needle at **C** to complete the knot.

Four-legged Knot

······· Other Name ·······
Knot stitch

······· Level ·······
Intermediate

······· Uses ·······
*Powdered filling;
isolated stitch*

······· Method ·······
*Upright cross with
knotted centre*

······· Materials ·······
Any fabric; any thick thread

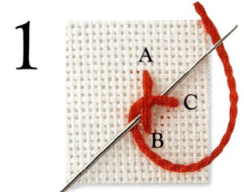

1 Start at **A** and work an upright stitch down to **B**. Come out at **C**. Loop the thread to the left, and slide the needle under the stitch.

2 Pull the thread gently to form a knot. Insert the needle at **D** to complete the stitch.

Sword

······· Level ·······
Easy

······· Uses ·······
*Worked randomly as light
filling; in rows as border*

······· Method ·······
Looped, elongated cross

······· Materials ·······
*Any fabric; any
thick thread*

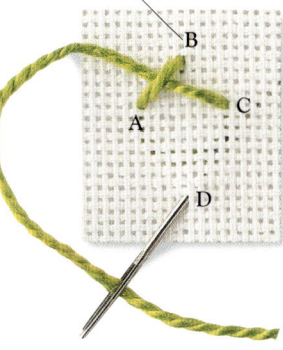

Ensure B is equidistant from A and C

Start at **A** and work a loose diagonal stitch up to **B**. Bring the needle out at **C** and slide it under the stitch from right to left. Take it down at **D**, pulling gently so that the two stitches form a cross.

Fly

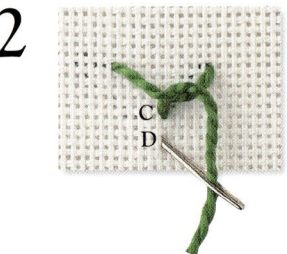

Pull needle over working thread

····· OTHER NAMES ·····
Y-stitch; open loop stitch

········ LEVEL ········
Easy

········ USES ········
Light or heavy filling;
worked in horizontal or
vertical rows as border

········ METHOD ········
Tied loop stitch

········ MATERIALS ········
Any fabric;
any thick thread

1 Start at **A** and work a loose horizontal stitch across to **B**. Bring the needle out at **C**.

2 Take the needle down at **D** to make a tie stitch (see p.20).

Sheaf Filling

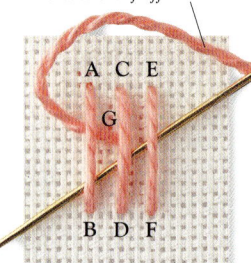

Pull stitches together to create sheaf effect

········ LEVEL ········
Intermediate

········ USES ········
Powdered filling; in rows
as border; isolated stitch

········ METHOD ········
Three upright straight
stitches tied at the centre

········ MATERIALS ········
Any fabric; any thick
thread

Make three parallel straight stitches from **A** to **B**, **C** to **D** and **E** to **F**. Come up at **G** and pass the needle to the left, under the first stitch. Take the needle across to the right and slide it back under the stitches. Take it to the right again and pull the thread up gently. Insert at **G** to complete.

Crown

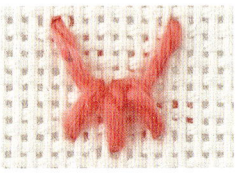

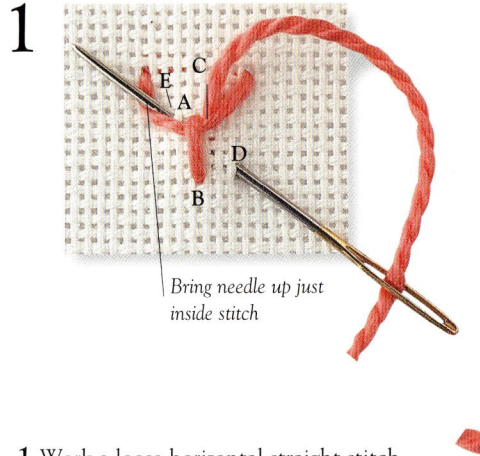

Bring needle up just inside stitch

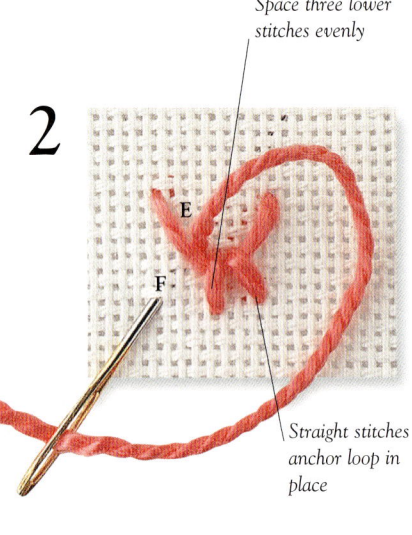

Space three lower stitches evenly

Straight stitches anchor loop in place

········ LEVEL ········
Intermediate

········ USES ········
Powdered filling; in rows
as border; isolated stitch

········ METHOD ········
Looped stitch tied down
with three straight stitches

········ MATERIALS ········
Any fabric; any thick
thread

1 Work a loose horizontal straight stitch. Come out above the thread at **A** and insert the needle at **B**, pulling the loop downwards. Come out at **C**, take the needle over the thread and insert at **D**, then come out at **E**.

2 Take the needle down over the thread and insert at **F** to complete the stitch.

POWDERED FILLING AND ISOLATED STITCHES   79

Sorbello

·········· Level ··········
Intermediate

·········· Uses ··········
In straight rows as filling; in rows as border; isolated stitch

·········· Method ··········
Heavy square knot

·········· Materials ··········
Any fabric; twisted or pearl threads give a raised effect

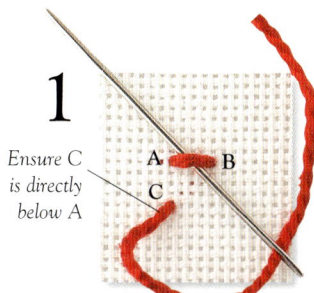

Ensure C is directly below A

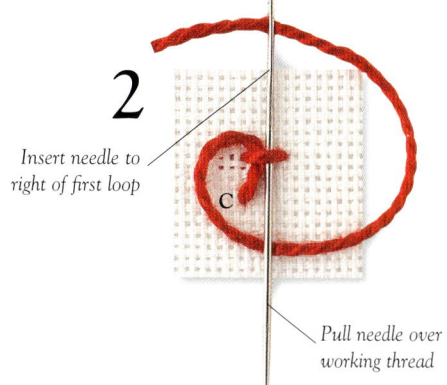

Insert needle to right of first loop

Pull needle over working thread

1 Start at **A** and work a short stitch to **B**. Bring the needle out below **A**, at **C**, and slide it under the stitch from bottom to top.

2 Hold the thread down to the left and pass the needle under the stitch again, this time from top to bottom.

3 Pull the thread gently to make a knot, then insert the needle below **B** at **D** to complete the stitch.

Palestrina Knot

·········· Level ··········
Intermediate

·········· Uses ··········
Geometric filling; worked in rows as border; isolated stitch

·········· Method ··········
Rectangular looped knot

·········· Materials ··········
Any fabric; any thick thread

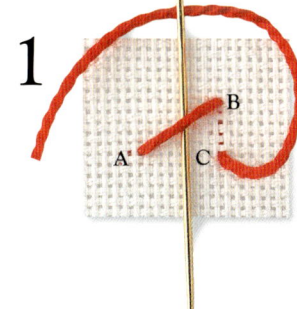

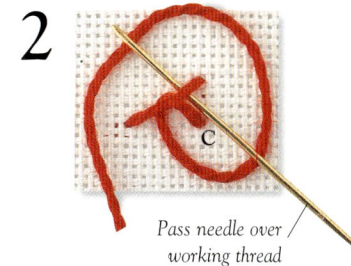

Pass needle over working thread

1 Start at **A** and work a diagonal stitch to **B**. Bring the needle out level with **A**, at **C**, and slide it under the stitch from top to bottom.

2 Pass the needle under the diagonal stitch again, from top to bottom and to the right of the first loop.

3 Pull the thread gently to form a knot, then take the needle down diagonally opposite **C**, at **D**, to complete the stitch.

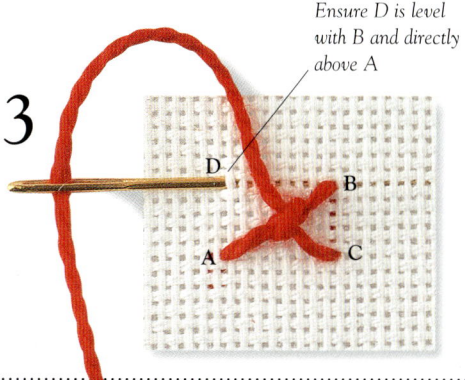

Ensure D is level with B and directly above A

Link

····· OTHER NAME ·····
Detached chain stitch

············· LEVEL ·············
Easy

············· USES ·············
*Scattered as light filling;
leaves and flower petals*

············ METHOD ············
Single looped stitch

··········· MATERIALS ···········
Any fabric; any thread

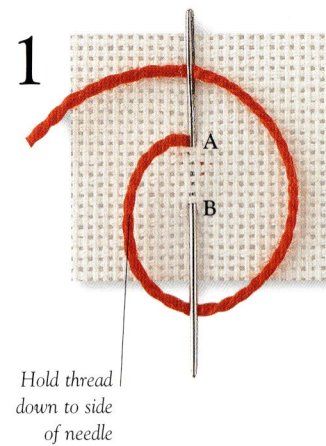

Hold thread down to side of needle

2

Tie stitch secures loop

1 Start at **A**. Make a loop and take the needle down at **A**. Come out at **B** and pull the needle through over the working thread.

2 Insert the needle directly below **B**, at **C**, making a tie stitch (see p.20) to complete.

····················· STITCH VARIATION ·····················

Lazy daisy stitch is formed by making several link stitches in a circle, all starting at the centre. Each stitch represents a petal and the whole looks like a flowerhead.

Berry

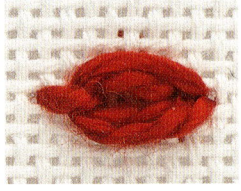

············· LEVEL ·············
Intermediate

············· USES ·············
*Powdered filling;
flowers and leaves*

············ METHOD ············
Double link stitch

··········· MATERIALS ···········
Any fabric; any thread

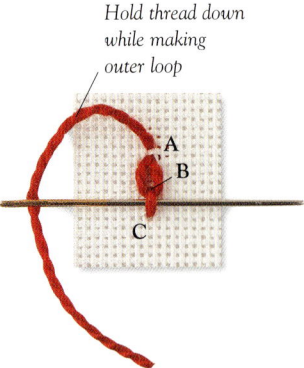

Hold thread down while making outer loop

Make a small link stitch (see above). Bring the needle out at **A** and slide it under the tie stitch between **B** and **C**. Take the needle back up and insert at **A** to complete the stitch.

Picot

····· OTHER NAME ·····
Long-tailed daisy stitch

············· LEVEL ·············
Easy

············· USES ·············
Powdered filling; in circles as floral motif

············ METHOD ············
Link variation with long tie stitch

··········· MATERIALS ···········
Any fabric; any thread

Work elongated tie stitch to form tail

Start at **A** and follow step 1 of link stitch (see above). Take the needle down below **B**, at **C**, to make a long tie stitch.

POWDERED FILLING AND ISOLATED STITCHES   81

Detached Wheatear

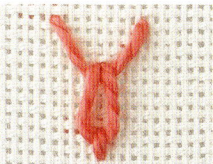

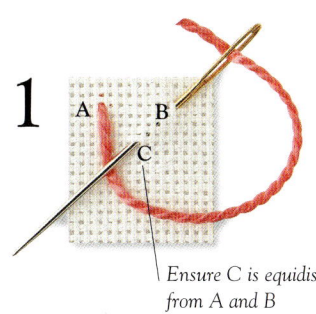

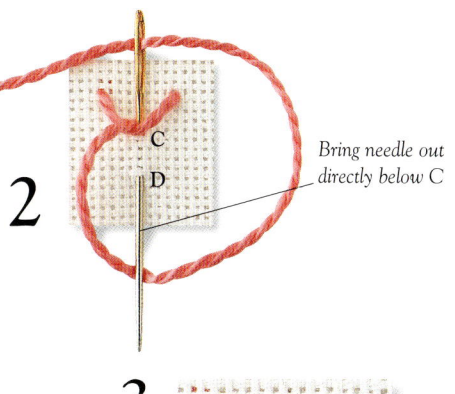

Bring needle out directly below C

Ensure C is equidistant from A and B

····· OTHER NAMES ·····
Tete-de-boeuf stitch; ox-head stitch

········ LEVEL ········
Intermediate

········ USES ········
Powdered filling; isolated stitch

······· METHOD ·······
Link stitch worked over loose straight stitch

······ MATERIALS ······
Any fabric; any thread

1 Start at **A**. Insert the needle at **B** and bring it out at **C**, passing over the working thread.

2 Make a loop and take the needle down at **C**. Come out at **D**, passing the needle over the working thread.

3 Take the needle down at **E** to form a short tie stitch (see p.20) to complete.

Tulip

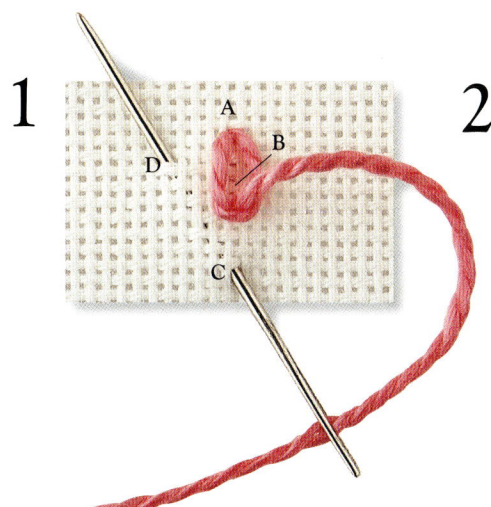

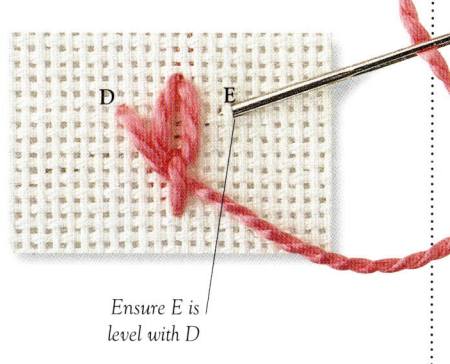

Ensure E is level with D

········ LEVEL ········
Intermediate

········ USES ········
In alternate rows as powdered filling; naturalistic flowers

······· METHOD ·······
Straight stitch worked through link stitch

······ MATERIALS ······
Any fabric; any thread

1 Start at **A** and work a picot stitch (see p.80). Take the needle down at **C** and bring it out to the left, at **D**.

2 Pass the needle under the tie stitch and insert it at **E** to complete the 'leaves'.

········ TECHNIQUE VARIATION ········

Make a slanting straight stitch on either side of the picot stitch, instead of a single one passing beneath the tie stitch (see step 2 above). This creates the effect of two separate leaves at the base of the flower.

Woven Spider Web

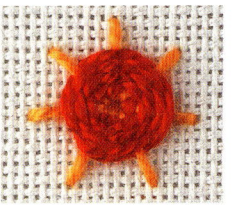

······· LEVEL ·······
Intermediate

······· USES ·······
Isolated stitch; large-scale powdered filling

······· METHOD ·······
Solid circle woven on foundation of seven straight stitches

······· MATERIALS ·······
Any fabric; any thread in two colours; blunt needle

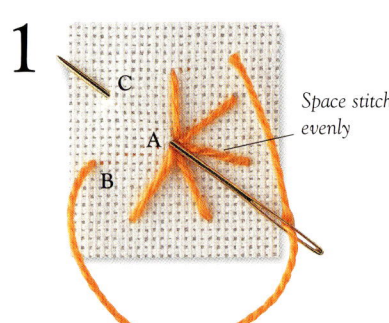

Space stitches evenly

Do not pull thread too tightly

1 Work a foundation of five straight stitches (see p.73), all radiating from **A**. Bring the needle up at **B** and take it back down at **A**. Come out at **C**, ready to work the final stitch.

2 Bring the second thread up at **A**. Working clockwise, weave it alternately over and under the straight stitches until only the tips are left uncovered. Take the needle to the back to finish.

······· STITCH VARIATION ·······

To make a ribbon rose, use a length of narrow silk embroidery ribbon for the weaving in step 2 (see above). Allow it to twist slightly to create the raised petal effect.

Ribbed Web

······· OTHER NAME ·······
Ribbed spider web

······· LEVEL ·······
Intermediate

······· USES ·······
Isolated stitch

······· METHOD ·······
Back stitched spiral over large star stitch

······· MATERIALS ·······
Any fabric; any thick thread in two colours; blunt needle

Work in anti-clockwise direction

Work a star stitch (see p.74) omitting the final cross. Come up at **A**. Slide the needle under the first two stitches to the left, then take it under the second and third stitches, making a back stitch (see p.40). Continue working round the star stitch until only the tips can be seen.

Buttonhole Wheel

······· LEVEL ·······
Intermediate

······· USES ·······
Isolated stitch

······· METHOD ·······
Buttonhole stitch worked within a ring

······· MATERIALS ·······
Any fabric; any thread

Space stitches evenly around outer circle

Mark two concentric circles. Come up at **A**, and insert the needle at **B** on the inner circle. Bring the needle out at **C**, passing it over the working thread. Continue stitching until the ring is complete.

Shisha

·········· LEVEL ··········
Advanced

·········· USES ··········
Indian embroidery; with couched gold threads

·········· METHOD ··········
Mirror disc attached to fabric with ring of twisted stitches

·········· MATERIALS ··········
Any fabric; any thick thread; shisha mirror; frame

1 *Make four straight stitches to anchor mirror*

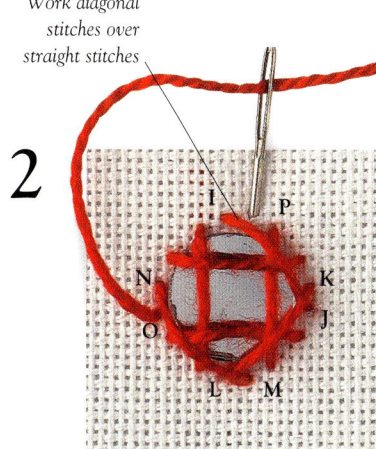

2 *Work diagonal stitches over straight stitches*

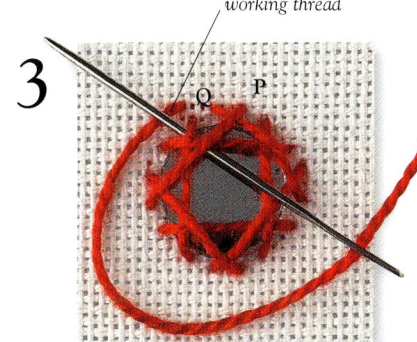

3 *Pass needle over working thread*

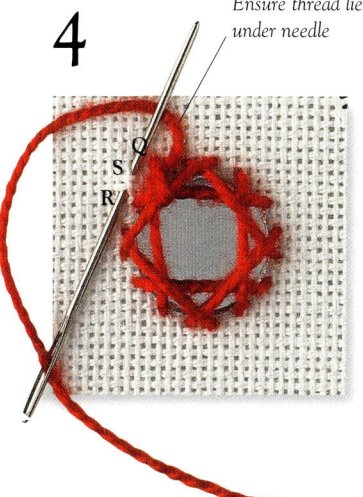

4 *Ensure thread lies under needle*

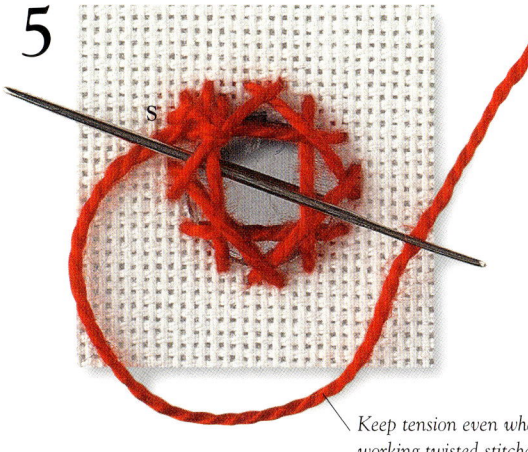

5 *Keep tension even when working twisted stitches*

1 Place the mirror in position. Start at **A** and work a straight stitch down to **B**. Come out at **C** and insert at **D**. Come up at **E** and down at **F**, then come out at **G** and go down at **H**. Bring the needle up at **I**, ready to start the next four stitches.

2 Take the needle down to **J** to make a diagonal stitch. Bring it out at **K** and insert at **L**. Come out at **M**, down at **N**, out at **O**, then take the needle up to **P** and insert.

3 Bring the needle out at **Q**, just outside the straight stitches and pass it beneath the threads from right to left.

4 Insert the needle at **R** and bring it up at **S**, to make a small back stitch. Pull it through over the working thread.

5 Slide the needle back under the straight stitches and pull it through gently over the looped thread. Repeat steps 4 and 5 all the way around the mirror to complete.

Open and Solid Filling Stitches

BOTH TYPES OF filling are stitched within a marked outline, which may be a curved naturalistic shape or a geometric block. Open fillings allow the background to show through, whereas solid fillings produce a densely stitched area and should be worked in a thick thread that covers the fabric completely. Some of these stitches have evolved as shading stitches, using several closely toning threads. With practice, these can produce subtle, three-dimensional effects, especially for flowers and foliage. The fabric should be mounted in a frame for all filling stitches.

Darning 85	Close Fly 89
Double Darning 85	Cretan 89
Brick and Cross 85	Close Cretan 89
Satin 86	Romanian Couching 90
Surface Satin 86	Bokhara Couching 90
Encroaching Satin 86	Spiral Couching 90
Long and Short 87	Couched Filling 91
Buttonhole Filling 87	Laidwork 91
Stem Filling 87	Back Stitch Trellis 92
Leaf 88	Japanese Darning 92
Open Fishbone 88	Cloud Filling 93
Attached Fly 89	Wave Filling 93

Open and Solid Filling Stitches

Darning

····· OTHER NAME ·····
Damask stitch

········ LEVEL ········
Easy

········ USES ········
Solid filling patterns; geometric bands

······· METHOD ·······
Closely spaced rows of running stitch

······ MATERIALS ······
Evenweave fabric; any thread

Work stitches so that spaces between them create a pattern

Come up at **A**, to the right of the start of the stitch above. Insert the needle at **B**, to the right of the end of the stitch above. Bring the needle up one thread to the left, at **C**. Repeat, always following the previous line of stitching.

Double Darning

········ LEVEL ········
Intermediate

········ USES ········
Solid filling stitch that appears the same at front and back

······· METHOD ·······
Double running stitch in closely spaced rows

······ MATERIALS ······
Evenweave fabric; any thread

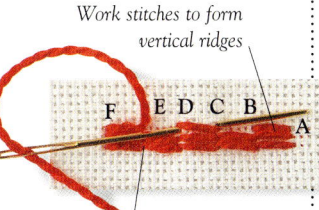

Work stitches to form vertical ridges

Ensure each row of stitches lines up with previous one

Work a row of evenly spaced running stitches (see p.39), from **A** to **B**, **C** to **D** and **E** to **F**. Fill in the spaces on the return journey; bring the needle back out at **E**, insert at **D** and come out at **C**. Work the following rows directly above.

Brick and Cross

········ LEVEL ········
Intermediate

········ USES ········
Open geometric filling

······· METHOD ·······
Alternate cross and groups of straight stitches, worked in vertical rows

······ MATERIALS ······
Evenweave fabric; any thread

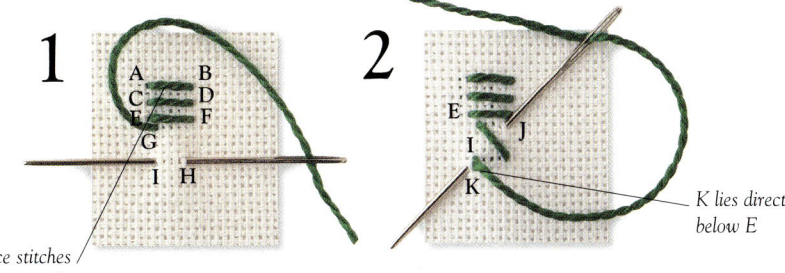

Space stitches equally

K lies directly below E

1 Make three parallel straight stitches from **A** to **B**, **C** to **D** and **E** to **F**. Bring the needle out at **G**. Work a diagonal stitch to **H**, then come out directly below **G**, at **I**.

2 Insert the needle at **J** to complete the cross stitch. Bring the needle out to the left of **I**, at **K**.

3 Insert at **L**, then make two more straight stitches. Come out level with **L**, at **M**, and insert at **N**. Bring the needle out at **O** and insert it at **P** to complete the second cross stitch. Come out at **Q** to begin the next three straight stitches.

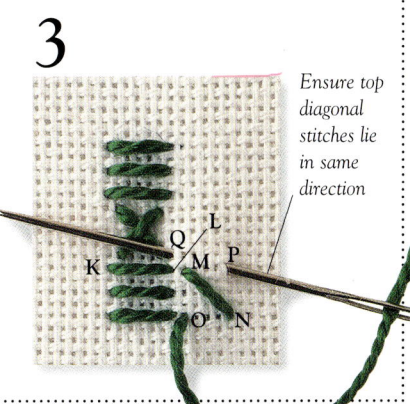

Ensure top diagonal stitches lie in same direction

Satin

····· OTHER NAME ·····
Damask stitch

····· LEVEL ·····
Intermediate

····· USES ·····
Solid filling; bands

····· METHOD ·····
Closely worked straight stitches

····· MATERIALS ·····
Any fabric; any thread – stranded silk or cotton gives lustrous finish

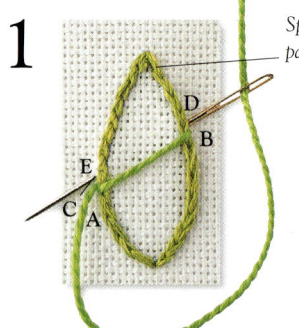

Split stitch creates padded edge

Leave no space between stitches

Work each stitch at same angle

1 Outline the area to be covered with split stitch (see p.40). Start the satin stitch at the widest point of the shape. Work a diagonal stitch from **A** up to **B** and bring the needle out next to **A**, at **C**. Take it down next to **B**, at **D**. Come out at **E** ready for the next stitch.

2 Repeat, varying the stitch length until the top part of the shape is covered. Bring the needle out again just below **A** and work downwards to fill the rest of the shape.

····· TECHNIQUE VARIATION ·····

When working satin stitch over a geometric shape or as a border, work the stitches at a right angle to the outline. Start stitching at one end and work to the other.

Surface Satin

····· LEVEL ·····
Intermediate

····· USES ·····
Solid filling; bands

····· METHOD ·····
Closely worked straight stitches: uses less thread than satin stitch

····· MATERIALS ·····
Any fabric; any thread – stranded silk or cotton for smooth surface; frame

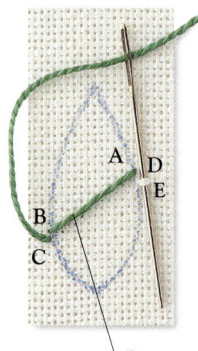

Do not make stitches too long

Mark the required shape. Work a diagonal stitch from **A** down to **B** and come up directly below, at **C**. Take the needle up to **D** and bring it out at **E**. Fill the lower part of the shape in this way. Come back up above **A** to work the remaining area.

Encroaching Satin

····· LEVEL ·····
Intermediate

····· USES ·····
Solid filling for larger areas

····· METHOD ·····
Overlapping narrow rows of satin stitch

····· MATERIALS ·····
Any fabric; any thread, in shades of the same colour; frame

Insert needle just above base of previous stitches

Work a row of satin stitch (see above). On the following rows, bring the needle out at **A** and insert at **B**, between two stitches on the row above. Come up next to **A**, at **C**. Repeat to the row's end.

OPEN AND SOLID FILLING STITCHES   87

Long and Short

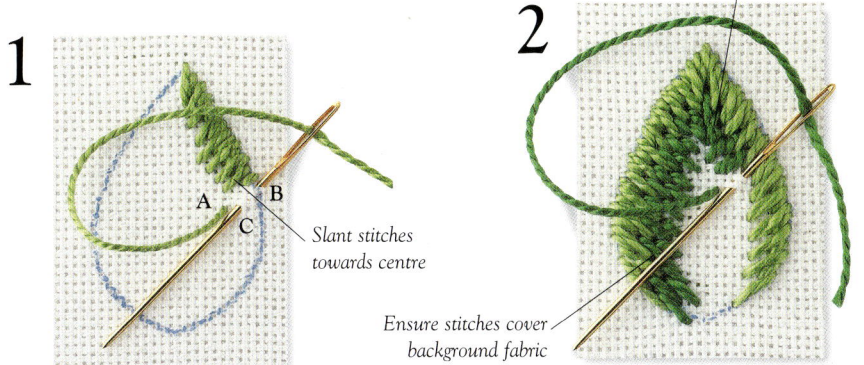

·········· LEVEL ··········
Advanced

·········· USES ··········
Shaded filling, giving three-dimensional effect

·········· METHOD ··········
Interlocking satin stitches

·········· MATERIALS ··········
Any fabric; any thread, in shades of the same colour; frame

1 Mark the outline of the area to be stitched. Work a row of alternate long and short satin stitches (see p.86) around the edge. Come up at **A** and take the needle down at **B** to make a long stitch. Bring it out at **C** to make a short stitch. Continue in this way to complete the first round.

2 Using a darker shade, work a row of long satin stitches which interlock with the first round. Fill in the centre with a third shade.

·········· TECHNIQUE VARIATION ··········

When filling square or rectangular shapes, work the first row in alternate long and short stitches and subsequent rows in long stitches only, so they interlock as before.

Buttonhole Filling

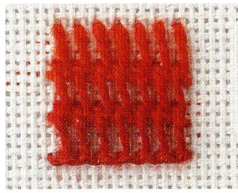
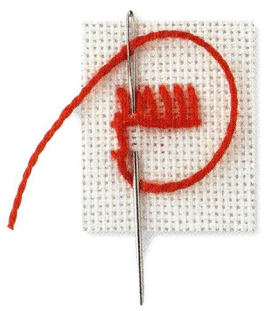

····· OTHER NAME ·····
Buttonhole shading

·········· LEVEL ··········
Intermediate

·········· USES ··········
Shaded filling

·········· METHOD ··········
Overlapping rows of buttonhole stitch

·········· MATERIALS ··········
Any fabric; any thread, in shades of the same colour; frame

Work a row of buttonhole stitch (see p.58) using the lightest thread. With a darker tone, work the second row directly below, so that the upright stitches overlap the base of the previous row. Work subsequent rows in progressively darker tones to create the effect of shading.

Stem Filling

····· OTHER NAME ·····
Stem stitch shading

·········· LEVEL ··········
Intermediate

·········· USES ··········
Shaded filling

·········· METHOD ··········
Closely spaced lines of stem stitch

·········· MATERIALS ··········
Any fabric; any thread, in shades of the same colour

Mark the outline of the area to be stitched. Using the darkest thread, work two rows of stem stitch (see p.41) along one side of the outline. Work the next two rows in a lighter shade. Continue to fill the shape with rows of stem stitch, graduating the colour to create a shaded effect.

Leaf

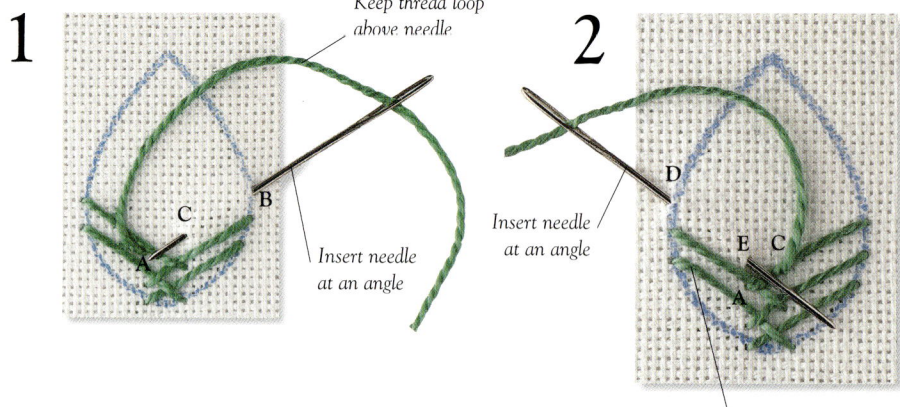

Keep thread loop above needle

Insert needle at an angle

Insert needle at an angle

Work pairs of slanting stitches in alternate directions

Level
Intermediate

Uses
Open filling for leaves, petals and wide borders

Method
Overlapping diagonal stitches worked upwards

Materials
Any fabric; any thread; frame

1 Mark the required shape on the fabric. Come up at **A**, to the left of centre. Insert the needle at **B** and bring it through to the right of centre, at **C**.

2 Take the needle down at **D** and bring it up directly above **A**, at **E**. Repeat these two stitches to fill the space, decreasing the length as the leaf tapers to a point. Work a narrow outline stitch (see pp.38–46) around the outside edge to complete.

Open Fishbone

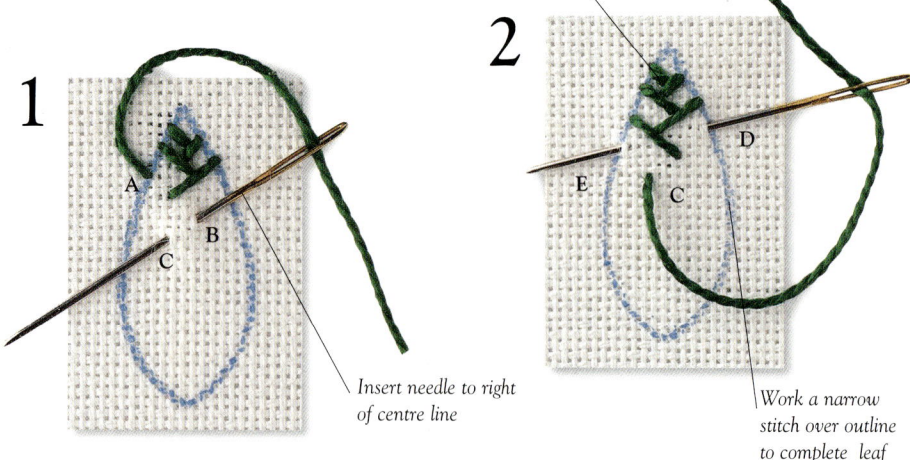

Work stitches alternately up and down

Insert needle to right of centre line

Work a narrow stitch over outline to complete leaf

Level
Easy

Uses
Light filling for small leaf or petal shapes; open borders

Method
Alternate slanting stitches, worked downwards

Materials
Any fabric; any thread; frame

1 Mark the required shape. Come up at **A** and make a downwards slanting stitch to **B**, to the right of centre. Bring the needle out to the left of centre, at **C**.

2 Take the needle up to the right and insert at **D**. Come out at **E**, ready to work the next downwards stitch. Repeat these two stitches to continue, altering the length as the outline widens or narrows.

Open and Solid Filling Stitches 89

Attached Fly

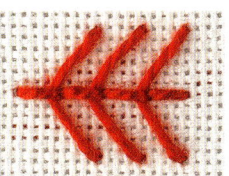

·····Other Name·····
Fishbone

·········Level·········
Easy

·········Uses·········
Open filling for narrow leaf or geometric shapes; light borders

········Method········
Row of linked fly stitches worked downwards

·······Materials·······
Any fabric; any thread; embroidery frame

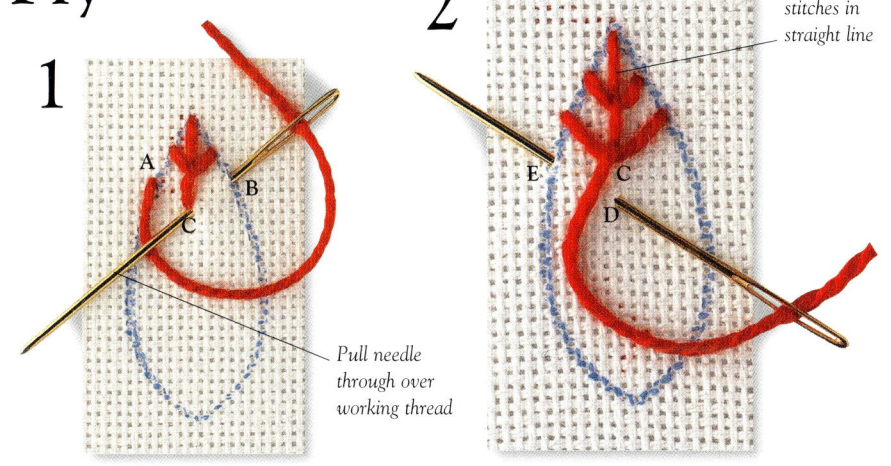

Work upright stitches in straight line

Pull needle through over working thread

1 Mark the outline of the area to be filled. Come out at **A** and insert the needle on the same level, at **B**. Bring it up in the centre at **C**.

2 Insert the needle directly below **C**, at **D**, to make a straight stitch, and bring it out at **E**. Repeat steps 1 and 2 to continue, varying the stitch length as required.

·······Stitch Variation·······

Close fly stitch is made by reducing the length of the straight stitches (see step 2).

Cretan

·····Other Name·····
Cretan filling

·········Level·········
Easy

·········Uses·········
Open filling for leaf or geometric motif; borders

········Method········
Looped vertical stitch, worked downwards

·······Materials·······
Any fabric; any thread; frame

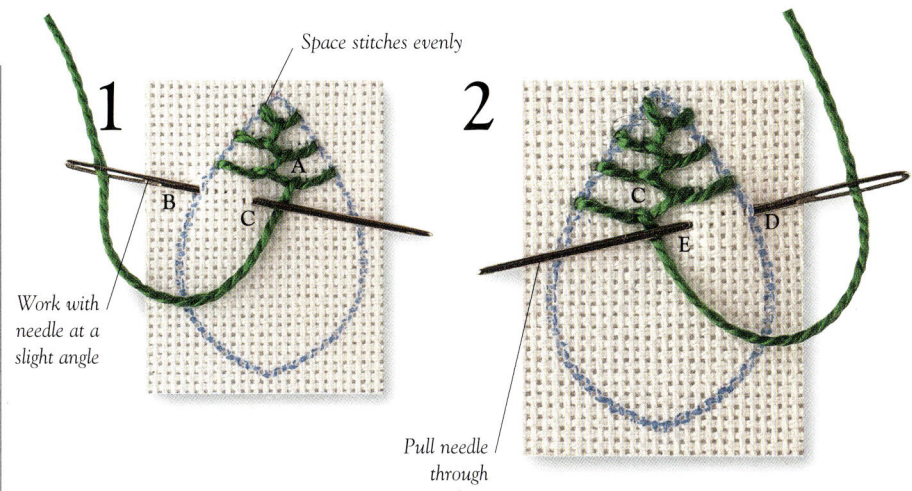

Space stitches evenly

Work with needle at a slight angle

Pull needle through over loop

1 Mark the shape to be filled. Come up to the right of centre at **A**, then take the needle across to **B** and insert. Come out to the left of centre at **C**. Pull the needle through over the working thread.

2 Take the needle down at **D** and come out at **E**. Repeat these two steps to fill the required area.

·······Stitch Variation·······

Close Cretan stitch is formed by working each new stitch immediately below the last, so no space is left between them.

Romanian Couching

·········· LEVEL ··········
Intermediate

·········· USES ··········
Solid filling for large areas

·········· METHOD ··········
Closely spaced long couched stitches

·········· MATERIALS ··········
Any fabric; any thread – stranded cotton gives smooth surface; frame

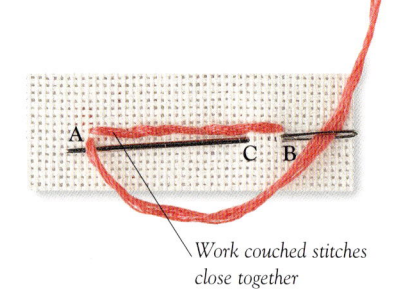

Work couched stitches close together

Do not work couching stitches too tightly

Ensure E and F are level

1 Come up at **A** and work a long horizontal stitch across to **B**. Bring the needle out level with **A**, at **C**.

2 Make a couching stitch: take the needle over the long stitch and insert at **D**. Draw the thread up gently to tighten. Come out at **E**, ready to make the next couching stitch.

·········· STITCH VARIATION ··········

Bokhara couching is worked in the same way, but the couching stitches are much shorter and made at a steep angle.

Spiral Couching

·········· LEVEL ··········
Intermediate

·········· USES ··········
Solid filling for circles; metal thread embroidery

·········· METHOD ··········
Laid threads worked within a circle

·········· MATERIALS ··········
Any fabric; thick or fragile threads; finer couching thread; frame

Work first round of couching stitches at right angles

Ensure laid threads cover fabric completely

Lay threads in a clockwise spiral

1 Mark a circle and bring the couching thread up just above the centre, at **A**. Fold the laid thread in half, pass the needle through the loop and insert at **B** to make a couching stitch. Curve the threads to the right. Work three more stitches, to complete the round. Make another round of four couching stitches.

2 Continue couching the laid threads in a spiral, spacing the stitches further apart as it increases in diameter. Take the ends through to the back to finish.

OPEN AND SOLID FILLING STITCHES 91

Couched Filling

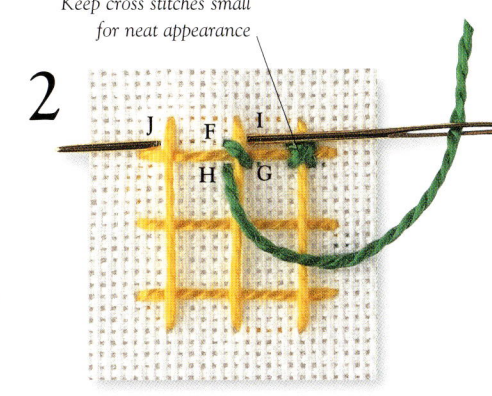

Work upright stitches at right angles to horizontal stitches

Keep cross stitches small for neat appearance

Ensure stitches are parallel and spaced evenly

LEVEL
Intermediate

USES
Decorative open filling

METHOD
Straight stitch grid with cross stitch couching

MATERIALS
Any fabric; thread in two colours of the same or different thicknesses; frame

1 Using the first colour, make a foundation of horizontal straight stitches (see p.73). Come up at **A** to start working the vertical stitches. Take the needle down at **B**, then bring it out at **C**. Insert at **D** and come out at **E**, ready for the final stitch.

2 Work a cross stitch over each intersection of the straight stitches. Bring the second colour up at **F**. Take the needle down over the crossed threads and insert at **G**. Come up at **H** and insert at **I**, then come out at **J**, ready to make the next cross.

Laidwork

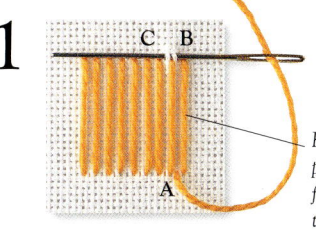

Keep stitches parallel so no fabric shows through

Ensure diagonal stitches are spaced evenly

LEVEL
Advanced

USES
Decorative solid filling

METHOD
Surface satin stitch with trellis of couched straight stitches

MATERIALS
Any fabric; thread in three colours; frame

Work tie stitches over crossed threads

1 Work a row of upright surface satin stitches (see p.86), leaving one stitch width between each. Bring the needle out at **A**, insert at **B** and come up at **C**. Repeat along the row to fill in the spaces.

2 Using the second thread, work a series of diagonal stitches across the foundation. Come up at **D** to start the second layer of stitches. Take the needle down at **E**, then bring it out at **F** and insert at **G**. Come out at **H**, ready to complete the trellis.

3 Work the short tie stitches (see p.20) in the third colour. Come up at **I**, take the needle down at **J** and bring it out again at **K**. Repeat at each intersection.

Back Stitch Trellis

·········· Level ··········
Intermediate

·········· Uses ··········
Open geometric filling

·········· Method ··········
Intersecting diagonal rows of back stitch

·········· Materials ··········
Any fabric – evenweave for a regular effect; any embroidery thread

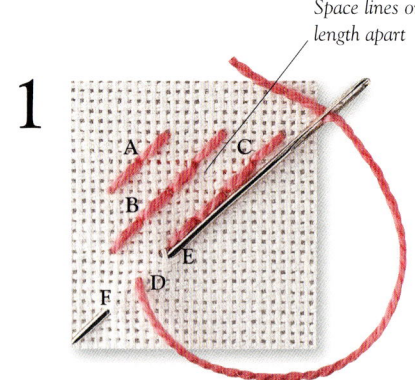

1

Space lines one stitch length apart

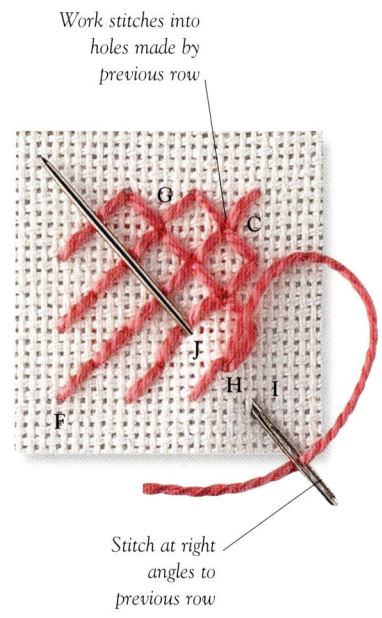

2

Work stitches into holes made by previous row

Stitch at right angles to previous row

1 Work a series of diagonal, parallel rows of back stitch (see p.40). Start the first row at **A**, the second at **B** and the third at **C**. Come out at **D**, insert the needle at **E** and bring it out at **F**. Continue until the required area is filled.

2 Work the next row in the opposite direction, starting at **C**, then **G**. Come out at **H**, insert at **I** and come up at **J**. Repeat to complete the trellis.

Japanese Darning

·········· Level ··········
Intermediate

·········· Uses ··········
Open geometric filling for larger areas

·········· Method ··········
Combination of running and straight stitches

·········· Materials ··········
Any fabric – evenweave is easier to use; any embroidery thread

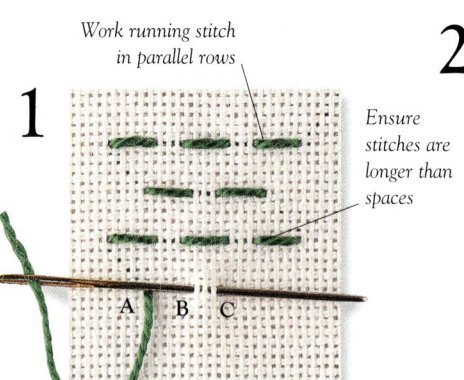

1

Work running stitch in parallel rows

Ensure stitches are longer than spaces

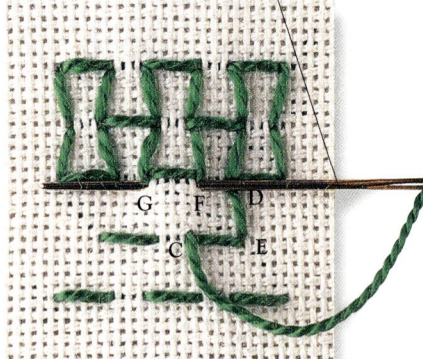

2

Work slanting stitches into holes made by running stitches

1 Work several horizontal rows of running stitch (see p.39), positioned so that the stitches in each row lie beneath the spaces in the row above. Come up at **A**, insert the needle at **B** and bring it out at **C**. Repeat to fill the required area.

2 Link the rows of running stitch with slanting stitches. Bring the needle out at **D** and take it down at **E**. Come up at **C**, go down at **F**, then up at **G**, ready to make the next stitch. Continue to the end of the row, before proceeding to the one below.

OPEN AND SOLID FILLING STITCHES 93

Cloud Filling

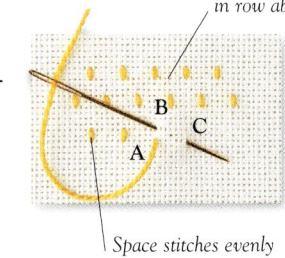

Position each stitch between two in row above

1

Space stitches evenly

2

Use blunt needle for lacing

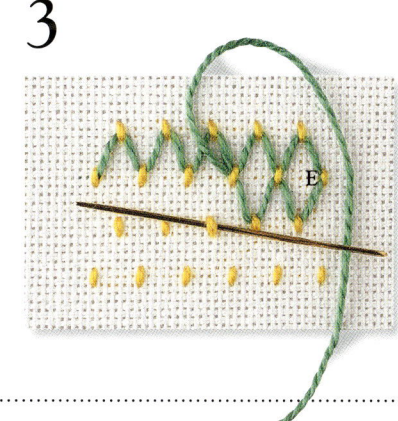

3

····· OTHER NAME ·····
Mexican stitch

········· LEVEL ·········
Intermediate

·········· USES ··········
Open filling; crewel work

········ METHOD ········
Interlaced rows of short upright stitches

······· MATERIALS ·······
Any fabric – evenweave for regular effect; any thread in two colours; blunt needle

1 Work a foundation of short upright stitches, arranged in staggered rows. Come up at **A** and make a straight stitch to **B**, then bring the needle out at **C**. Repeat to fill the required area.

2 Bring the second thread up at **D**. Slide the needle under the first stitch in the top row from left to right. Pass it beneath the second stitch on the row below and continue lacing to the end.

3 Come up at **E**. Slide the needle under the first stitch on the third row, from right to left. Take it under the next stitch on the second row. Repeat to the end, then thread further rows in the same way.

Wave Filling

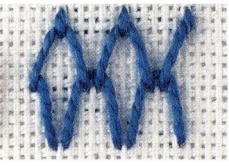

1

Pick up a small amount of fabric with needle

2

Needle passes under two threads

········· LEVEL ·········
Intermediate

·········· USES ··········
Shaded or single colour open filling; crewel work

········ METHOD ········
Interlinked horizontal rows of looped stitches

······· MATERIALS ·······
Any fabric; any thread in one or more colours; frame

1 Work a base row of short, evenly spaced upright stitches. Come up at **A** and slide the needle under the first stitch. Take it back down to **B** and insert. Come out just to the left, at **C** and repeat to the end of the row.

2 Start the next row at **D**. Pass the needle under the next two stitches of the row above. Take it down and insert at **E**, then come out at **F**. Continue to the end of the row.

········ TECHNIQUE VARIATION ········

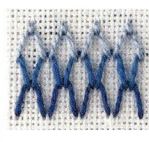

Create a subtly shaded effect by stitching each successive row in a darker shade of the same colour.

Openwork

Pulled Fabric Stitches

Drawn Thread and Insertion Stitches

Cutwork and Edging Stitches

Pulled Fabric Stitches

Many of these stitches were originally worked as white-on-white stitches to decorate household linen, but their diversity and intricate patterns only really become apparent when coloured threads are used. They form all-over designs which vary in density; some are open and lacy, but others have a more solid pattern of stitches. Work on evenweave fabric which has been mounted in a frame. Avoid stretching the fabric too taut; it has to be fairly loose to allow the stitches to be worked evenly. Use strong thread in a weight to match the background fabric, and pull each stitch tightly to draw the fabric threads together.

Window Filling 97	Step 100
Three-sided 97	Mosaic Filling 101
Honeycomb Filling 98	Diagonal Satin Filling 101
Russian Filling 98	Back Stitch Rings 102
Diagonal Raised Band 99	Algerian Eye 102
Punch 99	Outlined Diamond Eyelet 103
Cobbler Filling 100	

PULLED FABRIC STITCHES 97

Window Filling

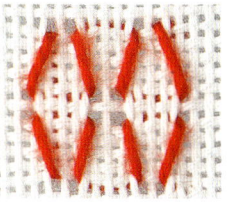

·········· LEVEL ··········
Easy

·········· USES ··········
Dense filling

·········· METHOD ··········
Diamond trellis with
four small holes

·········· MATERIALS ··········
Evenweave fabric;
any thread; blunt
needle; frame

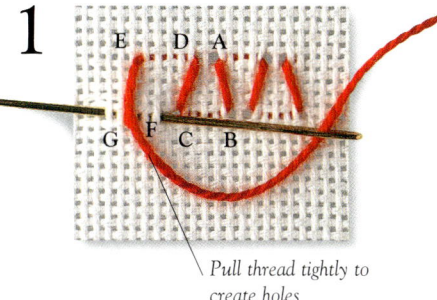

Pull thread tightly to create holes

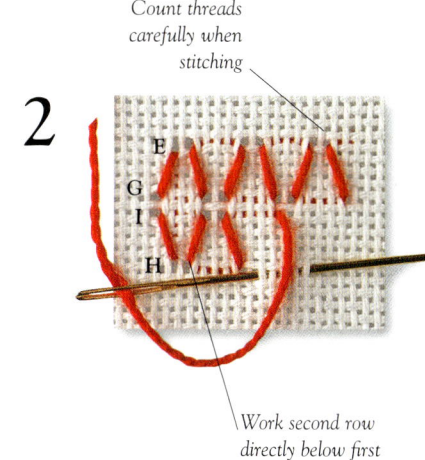

Count threads carefully when stitching

Work second row directly below first

1 Come up at **A**. Work a diagonal stitch over five horizontal and two vertical threads, down to **B**. Come out five threads to the left, at **C**, then insert one thread to the left of **A**, at **D**. Bring the needle out five threads to the left, at **E** and go down one thread to the left of **C**, at **F**. Come out at **G** and continue to the end of the row.

2 Stitch the next row as a mirror image of the first. Come up at **H**, eleven threads below **E**, and insert one thread below **G**, at **I**. Repeat these two rows to continue.

·········· STITCH VARIATION ··········

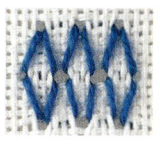

Pulled wave filling, which has open holes, is worked in the same way, but no space is left between the stitches.

Three-sided

·········· OTHER NAME ··········
Straight line stitch

·········· LEVEL ··········
Easy

·········· USES ··········
Narrow borders

·········· METHOD ··········
Double back stitch
worked in triangles

·········· MATERIALS ··········
Evenweave fabric;
any thread; blunt
needle; frame

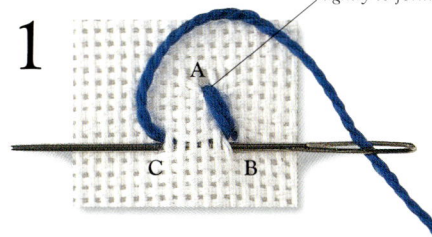

Draw thread up tightly to form holes

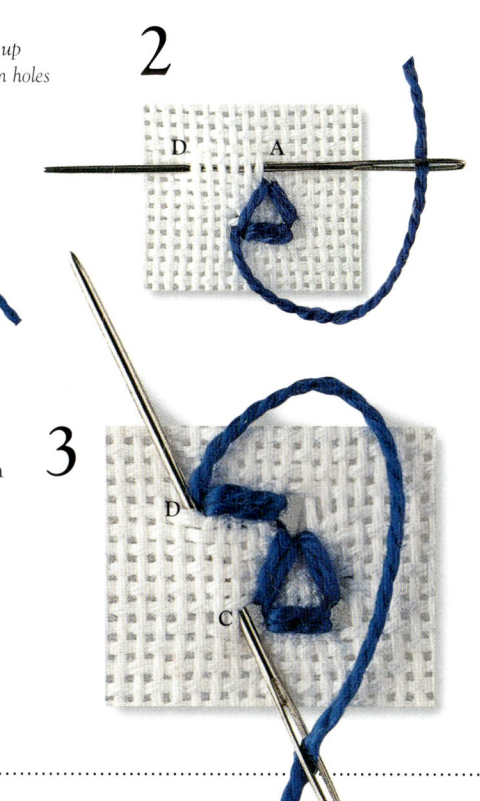

1 Start at **A** and work a diagonal stitch over six horizontal and three vertical threads down to **B**. Come out again at **A** and re-insert at **B** to make a double back stitch. Come up six threads to the left of **B** at **C** and work another double back stitch.

2 Work another double back stitch up to **A** and come out six threads to the left, at **D**.

3 Take the needle down to **C** and make a double stitch. Repeat to the end of the row.

Honeycomb Filling

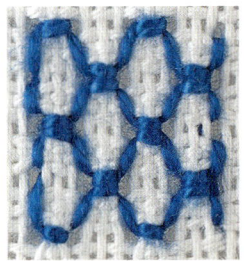

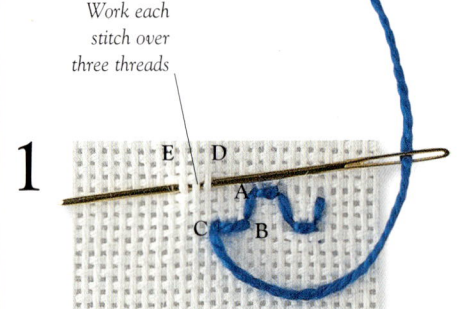

Work each stitch over three threads

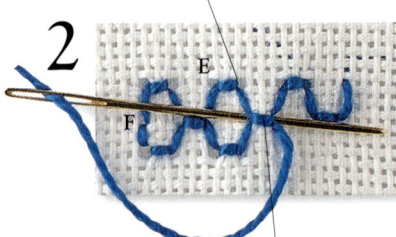

Ensure stitches are all worked at right angles to each other

Make a double horizontal stitch at point where rows meet

.... **Level** ....
Intermediate

.... **Uses** ....
Light filling with semi-open appearance

.... **Method** ....
Worked to form hexagonal lattice

.... **Materials** ....
Evenweave fabric; any thread; blunt needle

1 Start at top right. Come up at **A**, go down at **B** and bring the needle out at **C**. Re-insert at **B** and come up again at **C**, then go down at **D**. Come up at **E**, re-insert the needle at **D**, and bring it out again at **E**. Repeat these four stitches to the end of the row.

2 Work the second row as a mirror image of the first. Start at **F**, and turn the work upside-down if desired. Repeat these two rows to fill the required area.

Russian Filling

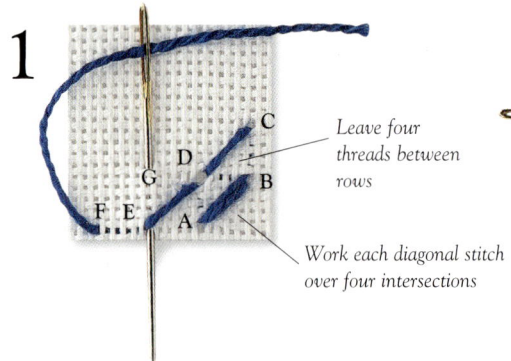

Leave four threads between rows

Work each diagonal stitch over four intersections

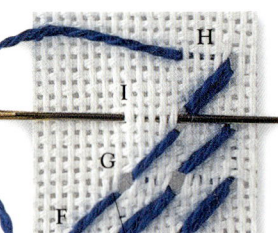

Pull stitches tightly to create large holes

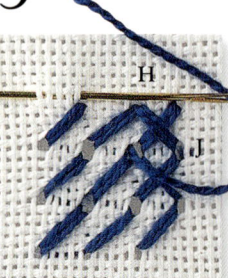

.... **Level** ....
Advanced

.... **Uses** ....
Dense filling with open holes

.... **Method** ....
Crossed diagonal stitches worked in two journeys

.... **Materials** ....
Evenweave fabric; any thread; blunt needle

1 Start at bottom right. Work a diagonal stitch from **A** to **B**. Come up at **C** and insert the needle at **D**. Bring it back up at **B**, down at **A**, then up again at **D** and down at **E**. Start the next row with a stitch from **F** to **G** and come up at **E**. Repeat these two rows until the top right corner of the area being filled is reached.

2 Work a stitch from **H** to **I** to square off the top edge, then continue working diagonal rows to fill the space.

3 The second journey, which completes the crosses, starts from **J** to **H**. Turn the work through 45 degrees to the left and stitch as before.

Diagonal Raised Band

Level
Easy

Uses
Ridged diagonal borders

Method
Diagonal row of tightly worked cross stitches

Materials
Evenweave fabric; any thread; blunt needle; frame

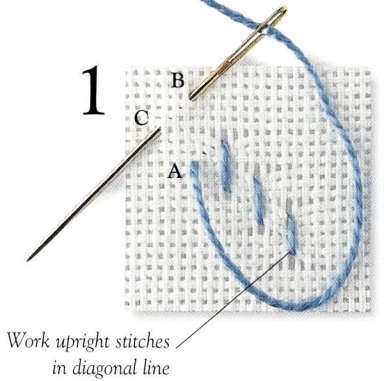

Work upright stitches in diagonal line

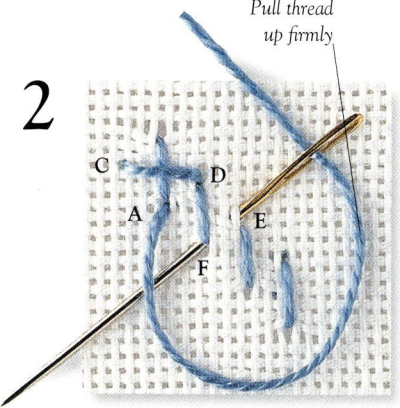

Pull thread up firmly

1 Work a row of upright stitches. Come out at **A**, take the needle up over six threads and insert it at **B**. Bring the needle out three intersections to the left, at **C**.

2 Insert the needle at **D** and bring it out again at **A**. Insert at **E** and come out at **F**, and continue to the end of the row.

·······Stitch Variation·······

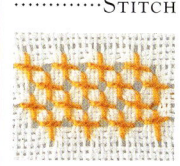

Ridged filling is made by working diagonal raised band stitch in adjacent rows to make a solid pattern.

Punch

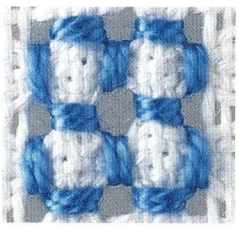

Level
Easy

Uses
Open filling with large holes

Method
Double back stitch worked in square grid

Materials
Evenweave fabric; any thread; blunt needle; frame

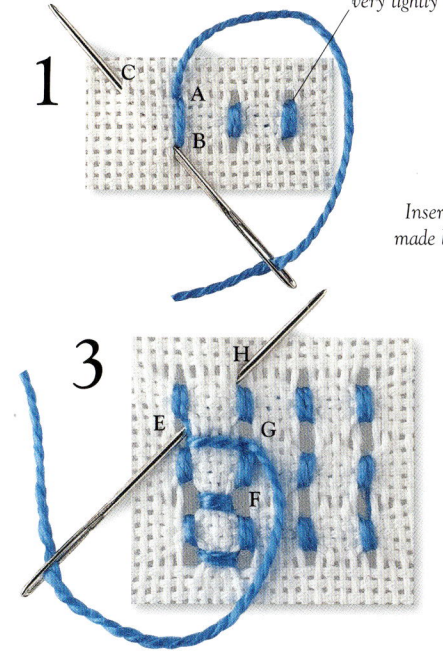

Work double stitches very tightly

Insert needle into hole made by previous stitch

1 Come up at **A** and work an upright stitch over four threads to **B**. Make a second stitch in the same holes, then come out five intersections to the left, at **C**. Repeat to the end of the row.

2 Bring the needle out five threads below the final stitch, at **D**. Work a double back stitch between **D** and **E**, then come up five threads to the right, at **F**. Continue to the end of the row then repeat to fill the required area.

3 Work horizontal stitches between the upright rows. Come up at **G** and make a double back stitch to **E**. Bring the needle out at **H**, then continue working up and down the rows.

Cobbler Filling

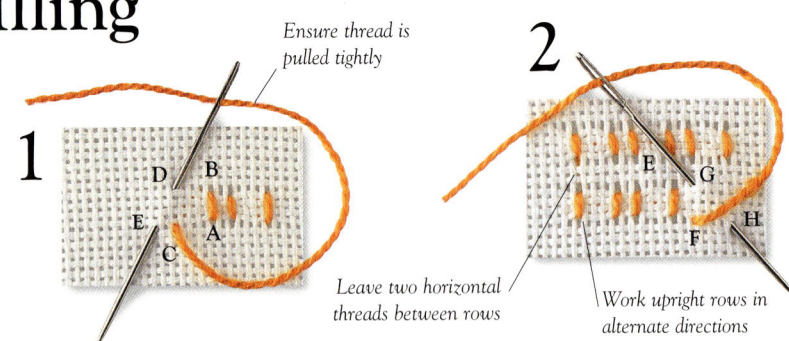

·········· LEVEL ··········
Intermediate

·········· USES ··········
Light, open filling

·········· METHOD ··········
Straight stitches worked in vertical and horizontal rows to form pattern of detached squares

·········· MATERIALS ··········
Evenweave fabric; any thread; blunt needle; frame

Ensure thread is pulled tightly

Leave two horizontal threads between rows

Work upright rows in alternate directions

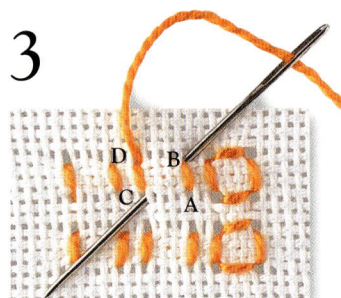

1 Come up at **A** and take the needle up over four threads to **B**. Bring it out four threads to the left of **A** at **C**. Insert at **D** and come up two threads to the left of **C** at **E**. Repeat to the end of the row.

2 Work the following rows of upright stitches in line with the first. Bring the needle up six threads below the previous stitch, at **F**. Insert at **G** and come up at **H**.

3 Join the pairs of stitches to form squares. Bring the needle up at **D**, take it down at **B** and up at **C**. Insert at **A**, then continue working down and up the rows.

Step

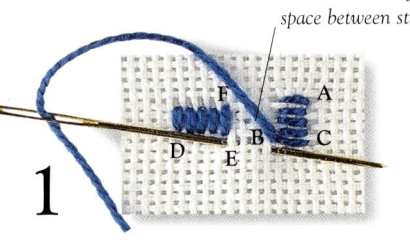

·········· LEVEL ··········
Intermediate

·········· USES ··········
Dense filling

·········· METHOD ··········
Diagonal rows made up of blocks of satin stitch set at alternate angles

·········· MATERIALS ··········
Evenweave fabric; any thread; blunt needle; frame

Do not leave any space between stitches

Ensure blocks meet at each corner

Work each satin stitch over four threads

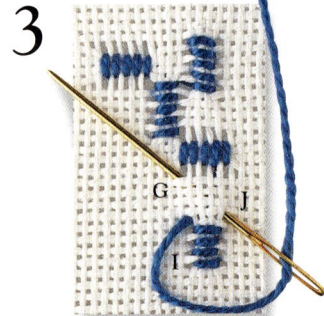

1 Start at **A**. Work a block of five horizontal stitches over four threads, ending with **B** to **C**. Come up eight threads to the left of **B**, at **D**. Work five upright stitches over four threads, ending with **E** to **F**. Come out at **B**, insert at **E** and work four more horizontal stitches.

2 Come up eight threads below **B**, at **G**. Insert at **H**, work four more upright satin stitches.

3 Bring the needle out eight threads below **G**, at **I**. Work five stitches over four threads, ending at **J**. Come up at **G** to make a block of upright stitches. Continue making alternate blocks to fill the required area.

Pulled Fabric Stitches 101

Mosaic Filling

..... Level .....
Advanced

..... Uses .....
Dense chequered filling

..... Method .....
Block of satin stitch set in a square with back stitch centre

..... Materials .....
Evenweave fabric; any thread; blunt needle; frame

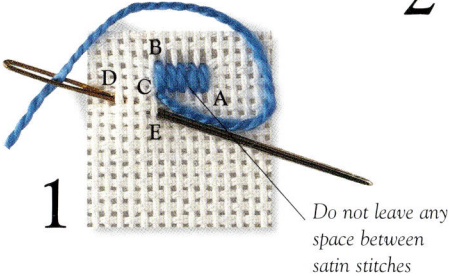

Do not leave any space between satin stitches

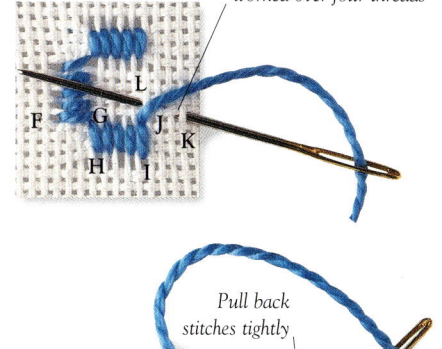

Ensure all satin stitches are worked over four threads

Pull back stitches tightly

1 Start at **A**. Work five satin stitches (see p.86) over four threads, finishing at **B**. Come out at **C**. Insert four threads to the left, at **D**, and come out at **E**.

2 Work four more horizontal stitches, finishing at **F**. Come up at **G** and insert the needle four threads below, at **H**. Work four more upright stitches, ending at **I**. Come up at **J**, insert at **K** and come out at **L**.

3 Work four more stitches, ending at **M**. Come back up at **A** and insert at **J**. Work three more back stitches from **C** to **A**, **G** to **C** and **J** to **G** to complete. Start the next stitch to the left (see Gallery p.31).

Diagonal Satin Filling

..... Level .....
Intermediate

..... Uses .....
Dense geometric filling

..... Method .....
Diagonal rows of satin stitch diamonds, worked in alternate directions

..... Materials .....
Evenweave fabric; any thread; blunt needle; frame

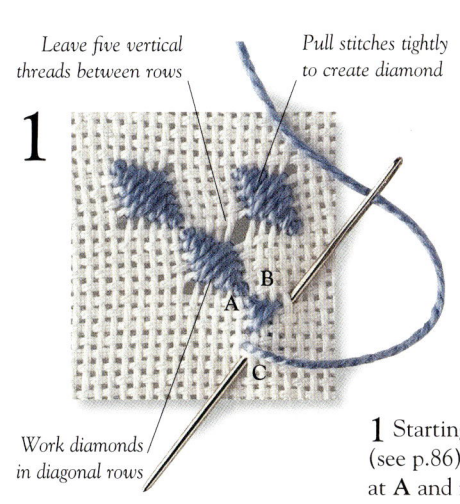

Leave five vertical threads between rows

Pull stitches tightly to create diamond

Work diamonds in diagonal rows

Stitch into holes made by previous blocks

1 Starting at top right, work a series of satin stitch (see p.86) diamonds to fill the required area. Come up at **A** and make a diagonal stitch over one intersection to **B**. Work four more stitches, increasing the length of each by one thread. Come up at **C** to work the longest stitch, then complete the diamond with four stitches which decrease in size.

2 Fill in the spaces with further rows of diamonds worked in the same way but in the opposite direction.

Back Stitch Rings

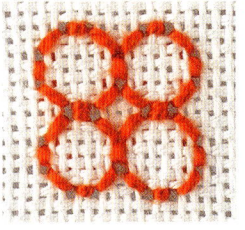
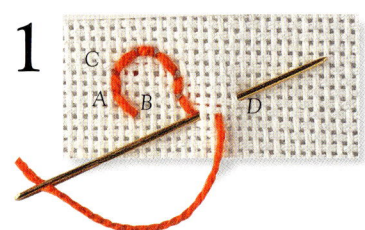

1

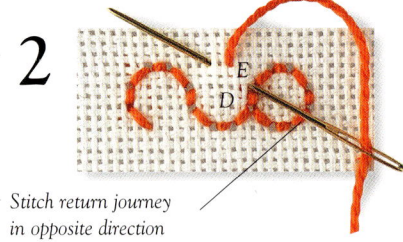

2

Stitch return journey in opposite direction

·········· **Level** ··········
Intermediate

·········· **Uses** ··········
Filling for large areas

·········· **Method** ··········
Intersecting rows of back stitch forming pattern of small circles

·········· **Materials** ··········
Evenweave fabric; any thread; blunt needle; frame

3

Work each back stitch over two vertical threads

1 Start at **A** and take the needle down over two intersections, at **B**. Come up two threads above **A**, at **C**, then continue working alternate straight and diagonal back stitches to form a row of semi-circles.

2 Work a full circle at the end of the row. The lines cross at the upright stitches; work a second back stitch between **E** and **D**, then continue stitching from right to left.

3 Come up at **F** to start the next row. Work from left to right, making a second horizontal stitch between **G** and **H**, and at each point where two rows meet.

Algerian Eye

1

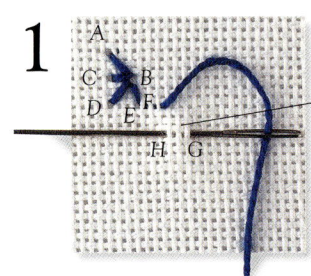

Work stitches over three vertical threads

2

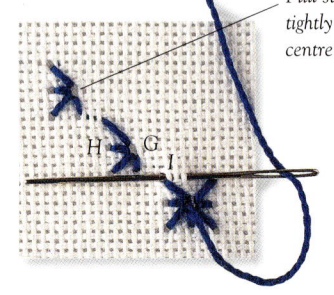

Pull stitches tightly to create centre holes

·········· **Level** ··········
Intermediate

·········· **Uses** ··········
Chequerboard filling for large areas

·········· **Method** ··········
Straight stitch stars worked in two journeys

·········· **Materials** ··········
Evenweave fabric; any thread; blunt needle; frame

3

1 Start at **A** and take the needle down over three intersections, at **B**. Come up three threads to the left, at **C** and insert at **B**. Bring the needle up at **D**, down at **B**, up at **E** and down at **B**. Come out three threads to the right of **E**, at **F**. For the next half star, go down over three intersections, at **G**, and up at **H**.

2 Continue stitching downwards, working half stars to fill the required area. Complete the final star with four more straight stitches, finishing at **I**. Insert at **G** to continue the second journey.

3 Come up at **J**, six threads to the right of the top star, ready to work the next diagonal row of stars.

Outlined Diamond Eyelet

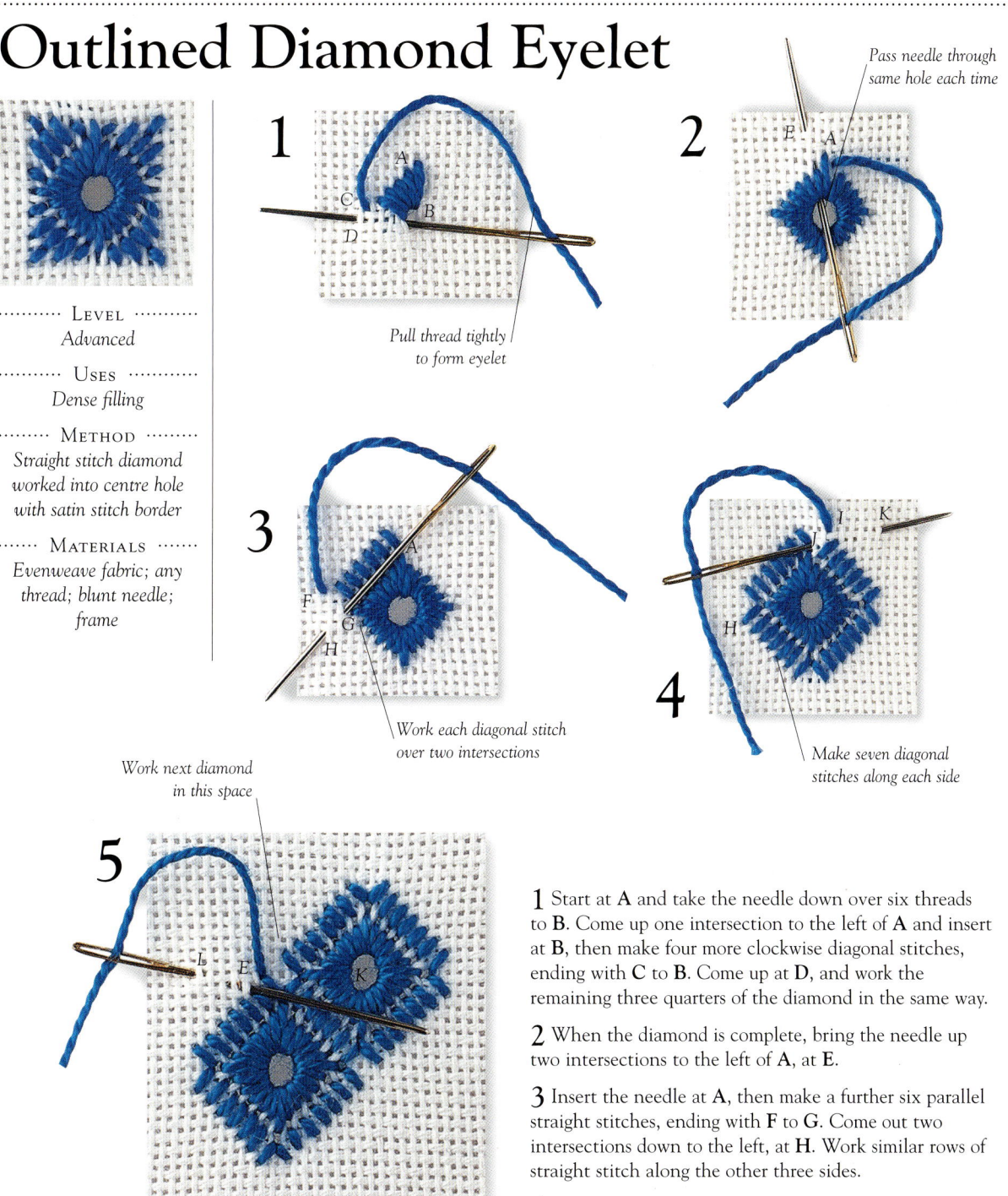

Level — Advanced

Uses — Dense filling

Method — Straight stitch diamond worked into centre hole with satin stitch border

Materials — Evenweave fabric; any thread; blunt needle; frame

1 Start at **A** and take the needle down over six threads to **B**. Come up one intersection to the left of **A** and insert at **B**, then make four more clockwise diagonal stitches, ending with **C** to **B**. Come up at **D**, and work the remaining three quarters of the diamond in the same way.

2 When the diamond is complete, bring the needle up two intersections to the left of **A**, at **E**.

3 Insert the needle at **A**, then make a further six parallel straight stitches, ending with **F** to **G**. Come out two intersections down to the left, at **H**. Work similar rows of straight stitch along the other three sides.

4 Make the final stitch from **I** to **J**. Come up six threads to the right, at **K**, and repeat steps 1 to 3 to work the next diamond.

5 To work the next diamond to the left, come back up at **E** and take the needle down six threads to the left, at **L**.

Drawn Thread and Insertion Stitches

Drawn thread hem and border stitches developed as a method of producing a decorative neatened edge on a piece of fabric. They should be worked on evenweave fabric from which a band of threads has been withdrawn. The remaining threads are then bunched together with tightly pulled stitches to form a regular pattern. Insertion stitches, also known as faggoting, have developed from old seaming techniques into a group of intricate stitches, which can be worked on plain or evenweave fabric. The two edges being joined must be mounted on paper so that the stitches can be spaced evenly.

Single Hem 105	Laced Insertion 108
Ladder Hem 105	Cretan Insertion 108
Serpentine Hem 105	Faggot Bundles 108
Antique Hem 105	Knotted Insertion 109
Italian Border 106	Buttonhole Insertion 109
Four-sided 106	Needleweaving Bars 110
Chevron Border 107	Zigzag Clusters 110
Diamond Border 107	Corded Clusters 110

DRAWN THREAD AND INSERTION STITCHES 105

Single Hem

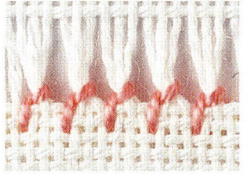

········ Level ········
Easy

········ Uses ········
Simple open border for hemmed edge

········ Method ········
Small groups of threads pulled into clusters along hem; worked on wrong side of fabric

········ Materials ········
Evenweave fabric; any thread; blunt needle

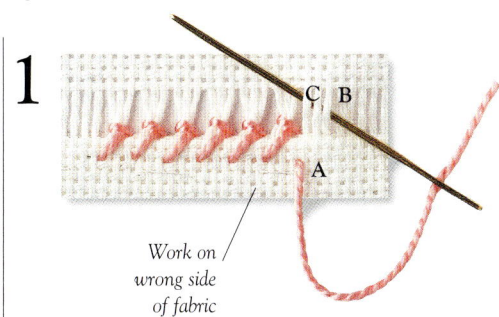

Work on wrong side of fabric

Pull thread tightly to bunch threads

Work each stitch over same number of threads

1 Draw out a few threads along the edge of the fabric (see p.21). Fold a double hem to the base of the threads and tack down. Come up at **A** and slide the needle under three threads to the right, from **B** to **C**.

2 Take the needle down at **B** and bring it out at **D**. Repeat these two steps to continue.

········ Stitch Variation ········

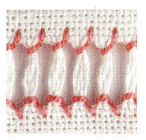

Ladder hem stitch is worked over a wider band of drawn threads. Work as for single hem stitch, then turn the fabric upside down and work a second row over the same groups of threads, making a series of bars.

Serpentine Hem

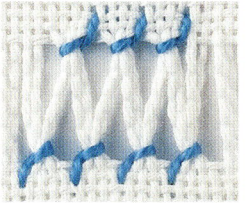

········ Other Name ········
Trellis hem stitch

········ Level ········
Easy

········ Uses ········
Decorative edging

········ Method ········
Two staggered rows of hem stitch worked to create slanting bars

········ Materials ········
Evenweave fabric; any thread; blunt needle

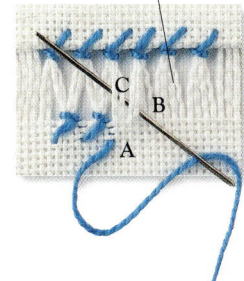

Withdraw several threads to create wide band

Work a row of hem stitch over groups of four threads (see above), then turn the fabric upside down. Come up at **A**. Pass the needle under two threads from each group, from **B** to **C**, and work a second row of hem stitch.

Antique Hem

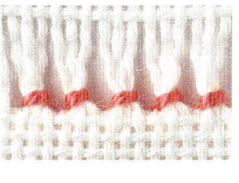

········ Level ········
Easy

········ Uses ········
Plain border for hem

········ Method ········
Hem stitch variation in which horizontal stitches only show on right side

········ Materials ········
Evenweave fabric; any thread; blunt needle

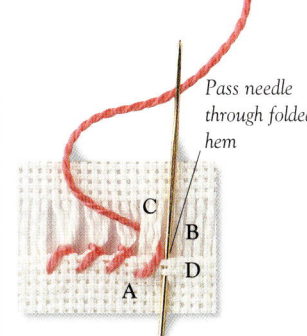

Pass needle through folded hem

Prepare the fabric as for single hem stitch (see above). With the wrong side facing, come up at **A**. Slide the needle under three threads to the right, from **B** to **C**. Insert the needle through the edge of the fold at **B** and come out at **D**. Pull up the thread; repeat this step to continue.

Italian Border

···· Other Name ····
Italian hem stitch

········ Level ········
Easy

·········· Uses ··········
Open band; with hem stitch as decorative border

········ Method ········
Open border stitch, worked in two journeys

······· Materials ·······
Evenweave fabric; any thread; blunt needle

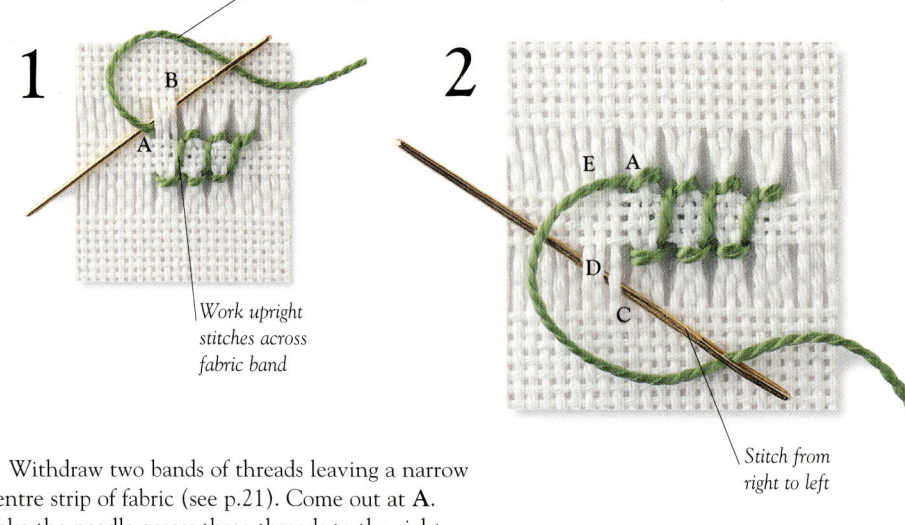

Draw up loop to pull threads together

Work upright stitches across fabric band

Stitch from right to left

1 Withdraw two bands of threads leaving a narrow centre strip of fabric (see p.21). Come out at **A**. Take the needle across three threads to the right and then slide it behind the fabric from **B** to **A**.

2 Take the needle down to **C**. Slide it behind three threads and come out at **D**. Go back down at **C** and come up at **E**, three threads to the left of **A**. Repeat steps 1 and 2 to continue.

Four-sided

········ Level ········
Intermediate

·········· Uses ··········
Open bands; can also be worked as pulled fabric stitch

········ Method ········
Pulled straight stitches, worked horizontally to form square pattern

······· Materials ·······
Evenweave fabric; any thread; blunt needle

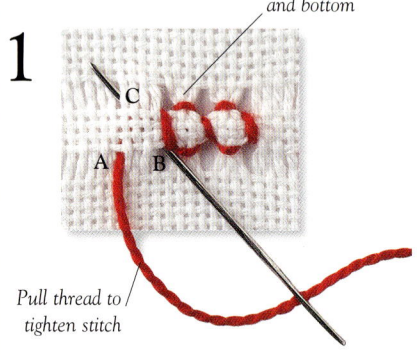

Work over same threads at top and bottom

Pull thread to tighten stitch

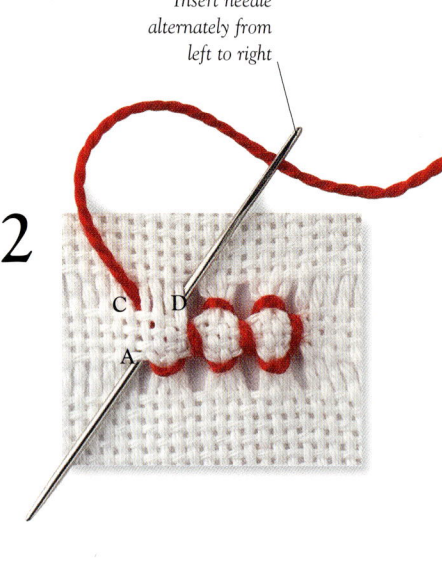

Insert needle alternately from left to right

1 Withdraw two bands of threads leaving a narrow strip of fabric between them (see p.21). Come up at **A**. Take the needle down four threads to the right, at **B**. Bring it out directly above **A**, at **C**.

2 Take the needle down four threads to the right, at **D** and come up at **A**. Go down at **C** to make a vertical stitch and come up four threads to the left of **A**, ready to start the next stitch. Repeat these two steps to continue.

Chevron Border

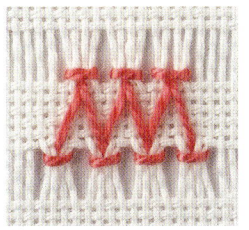

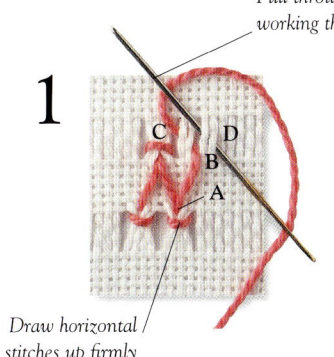

Pull through over working thread

Draw horizontal stitches up firmly

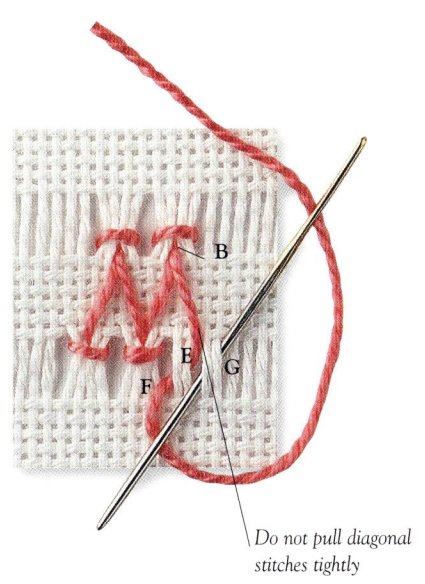

Do not pull diagonal stitches tightly

·········· **Level** ··········
Intermediate

·········· **Uses** ··········
Decorative open bands; with hem stitch as edging

·········· **Method** ··········
Chevron stitch variation; worked horizontally

·········· **Materials** ··········
Evenweave fabric; any thread; blunt needle

1 Prepare the fabric as for step 1 below. Come up at **A**. Take the needle diagonally up and slide it behind two threads from **B** to **C**. Take the needle across four threads to the right, and insert at **D**. Come up again at **B**.

2 Insert the needle at **E**. Slide it behind two threads to the left and come up at **F**. Take the needle across four threads and insert at **G**. Bring it out at **E** and pull through over the working thread. Repeat these two steps to the end of the row.

Diamond Border

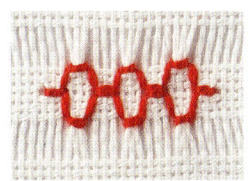

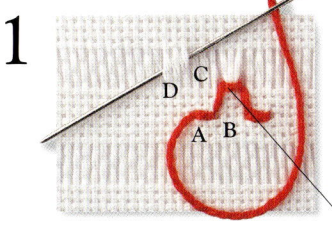

Work each horizontal stitch over same number of threads

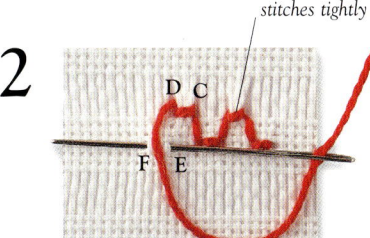

Pull horizontal stitches tightly

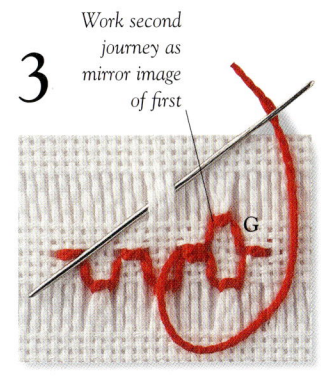

Work second journey as mirror image of first

·········· **Level** ··········
Intermediate

·········· **Uses** ··········
Open border with hexagonal pattern

·········· **Method** ··········
Pulled straight stitches, worked in two journeys

·········· **Materials** ··········
Evenweave fabric; any thread; blunt needle

1 Withdraw two bands of thread leaving a narrow strip of fabric between them (see p.21). Come up in the centre, at **A**. Take the needle down three threads to the right, at **B**, then bring it out at **A** again. Insert directly above, at **C** and slide the needle under three threads to the left, coming up at **D**.

2 Take the needle down at **C** and come back up at **D**. Insert it directly below, at **E** and come out on the same level, at **F**. Repeat steps 1 and 2 to the end of the row.

3 Turn the fabric the other way up to work the second journey. Come up at **G** and stitch as before.

Laced Insertion

····· OTHER NAME ·····
Laced faggot stitch

········ LEVEL ········
Easy

········ USES ········
Decorative joining stitch

······· METHOD ········
Two hems worked with Antwerp edging stitch, linked with interlacing

······ MATERIALS ······
Evenweave fabric; thick thread; blunt needle

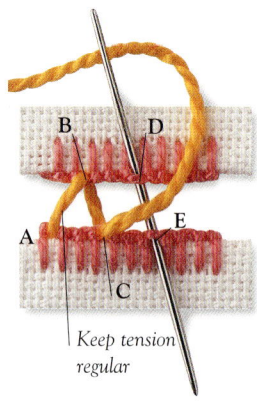

Keep tension regular

Mount the fabric (see p.21). Work a row of Antwerp edging stitch (see p.112) along each hem. Come up at **A**. Pass the needle down over **B**. Slide it under **C**, from back to front. Take it over **D**, from front to back; repeat to the end of the seam.

Cretan Insertion

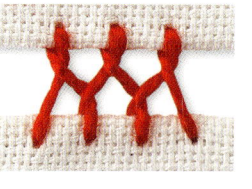

········ LEVEL ········
Easy

········ USES ········
Simple join for two straight edges

······· METHOD ········
Open Cretan stitch adapted as insertion

······ MATERIALS ······
Evenweave fabric; thick thread; blunt needle

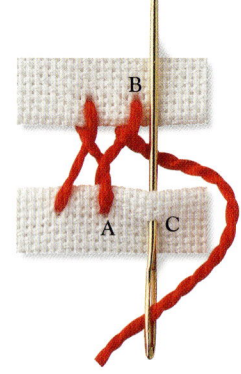

Mount the fabric on paper (see p.21). Take the needle through to the back at **A**, then insert it from the front at **B**. Bring it through behind the diagonal thread and take it down at **C**. Pull through over the working thread. Repeat to the end of the seam.

Faggot Bundles

········ LEVEL ········
Intermediate

········ USES ········
Decorative method of joining two edges

······· METHOD ········
Groups of two stitches bound by a third, worked from top to bottom

······ MATERIALS ······
Evenweave fabric; any thread; blunt needle

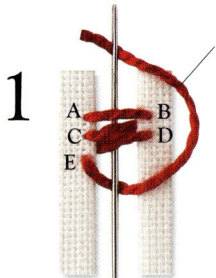

Loop thread from left to right

Pull thread tightly to bunch stitches

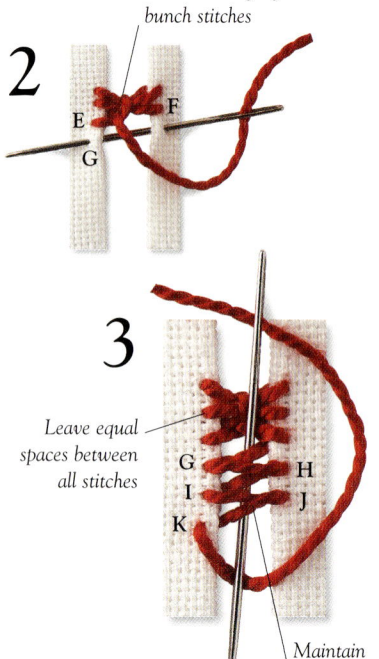

Leave equal spaces between all stitches

Maintain even tension

1 Mount the fabric (see p.21). Start on the left, at **A** and work a straight stitch across to **B**, on the right. Make another stitch from **C** to **D**, then come out at **E**. Pass the needle behind all the threads, then pull through over the loop.

2 Insert the needle at **F**, then bring it out below **E** at **G**, ready to start the next group of stitches.

3 Insert at **H**, then make another stitch from **I** to **J**. Come out at **K**, take the needle behind the three diagonal and two horizontal threads, and pull through over the working thread. Repeat steps 1 to 3 to continue.

Knotted Insertion

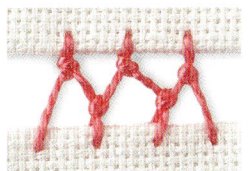
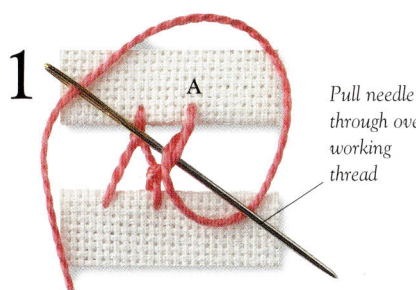
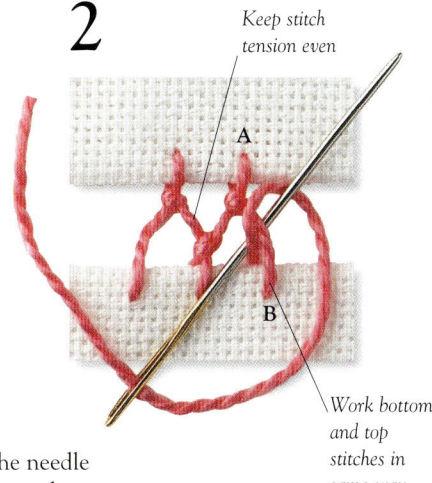

····· Other Name ·····
Knotted faggot stitch

········· Level ·········
Advanced

·········· Uses ··········
Decorative method of joining two edges

········ Method ········
Knotted joining stitch worked horizontally

······· Materials ·······
Evenweave fabric; thick thread; blunt needle

1 Mount the fabric on paper (see p.21). Take the needle down through the top hem at **A** and bring it out to the left of the diagonal stitch. Loop the working thread to the right and pass the needle under both threads. Pull the thread up tightly to form a knot.

2 Take the needle down to the bottom hem and insert at **B**. Bring it through to the left of the diagonal stitch and loop the thread to the right. Slide the needle under both threads and pull through tightly. Continue stitching alternately up and down to the end of the seam.

Buttonhole Insertion

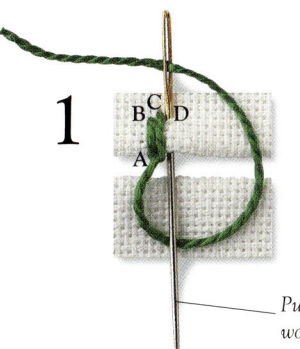
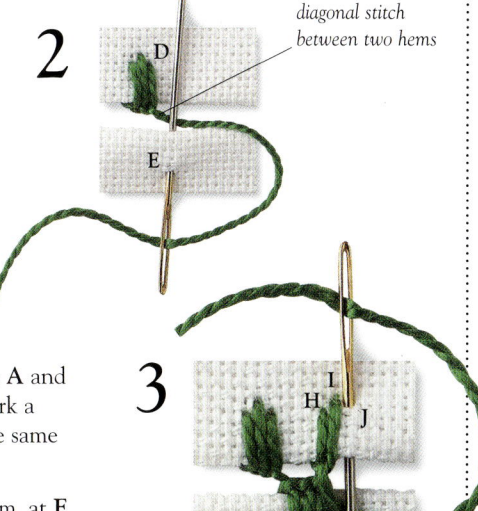

····· Other Name ·····
Buttonhole faggot stitch

········· Level ·········
Advanced

·········· Uses ··········
Decorative joining method

········ Method ········
Groups of three buttonhole stitches worked alternately from top to bottom

······· Materials ·······
Evenweave fabric; thick thread; blunt needle

1 Mount the fabric on paper (see p.21). Start at **A** and work a buttonhole stitch (see p.58) up to **B**. Work a second, longer stitch to **C**, then come out on the same level as **B**, at **D**, to work the third stitch.

2 Take the needle down through the bottom hem, at **E** and pull it through over the working thread.

3 Work two more buttonhole stitches at **F** and **G**, varying the length as before, then take the needle back up to the top hem at **H**. Make two more stitches at **I** and **J**, then continue to the end of the seam.

Needleweaving Bars

Work each bar over even number of threads

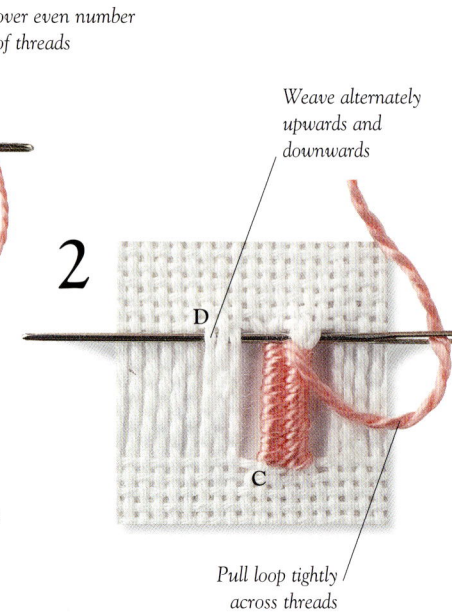

Weave alternately upwards and downwards

Pull loop tightly across threads

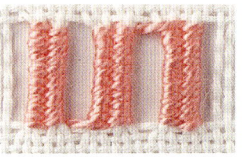

······ Other Name ······
Woven bars

······ Level ······
Advanced

······ Uses ······
Flat, heavy borders

······ Method ······
Weaving stitch, worked horizontally

······ Materials ······
Evenweave fabric; any thread; blunt needle

1 Withdraw a band of threads from the fabric. (see p.21). Come up at **A** and take the needle across three threads to the right. Insert it at **B** and bring it back through at **A**. Insert over three threads to the left at **C**, then come back out in the centre, at **A**. Continue weaving upwards.

2 When the bar is complete, bring the needle out three threads to the left, at **D**. Work downwards as before, then continue weaving bars to the end of the row.

Zigzag Clusters

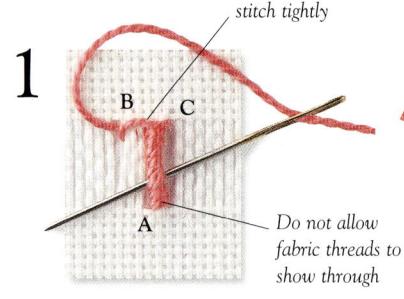

Pull double stitch tightly

Do not allow fabric threads to show through

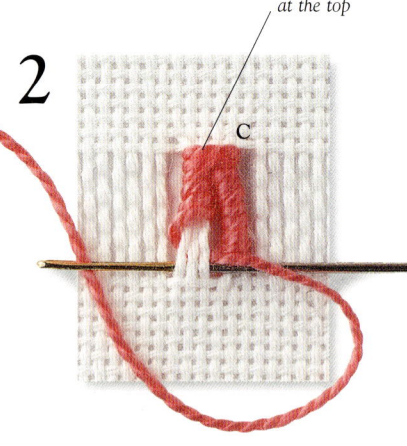

Join clusters at the top

······ Level ······
Advanced

······ Uses ······
Heavy open borders

······ Method ······
Round, wrapped bars worked over foundation of drawn threads

······ Materials ······
Evenweave fabric; any thread; blunt needle

1 Withdraw a band of threads (see p.21). Start at **A** and take the needle over three threads to the right. Come back up at **A**, then pass the needle in front of and behind the threads. Continue wrapping to the top, then come out three threads to the left, at **B**. Take the needle across six threads and insert at **C**, then come back up at **B**. Insert again at **C** and come up between the two groups of threads.

2 Take the needle back over three threads and continue wrapping to the bottom. Start the next and subsequent clusters three threads to the left.

····· **Stitch Variation** ·····

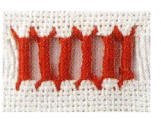

Corded clusters are worked in the same way, but without the double linking stitches.

Cutwork and Edging Stitches

Edging stitches give an ornamental finish to a hem, and look particularly effective when worked in a thick, twisted thread. The stitches should be spaced regularly, but they can be worked on evenweave or plainweave fabric. Cutwork stitches, like the other types of openwork, were grouped under the name of 'white work'. Eyelets in various shapes can be used to decorate collars, mats and garments or combined with satin stitch to create *Broderie Anglaise* designs on lawn. Work these stitches on fine plainweave cotton or linen, in white or coloured threads, with or without a frame.

Antwerp Edging 112

Scalloped Edge 114

Sailor Edging 112

Ring Picot Edge 114

Looped Edge 113

Buttonhole Eyelet 115

Half Chevron 113

Overcast Eyelet 115

Square Eyelet 115

Antwerp Edging

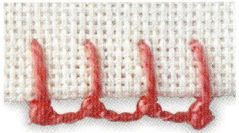

····· Other Name ·····
Knotted blanket stitch

········· Level ·········
Intermediate

········· Uses ·········
Decorative hems

········ Method ········
Blanket stitch variation, worked horizontally over edge of fabric

······· Materials ·······
Any fabric; thick twisted threads give best stitch definition

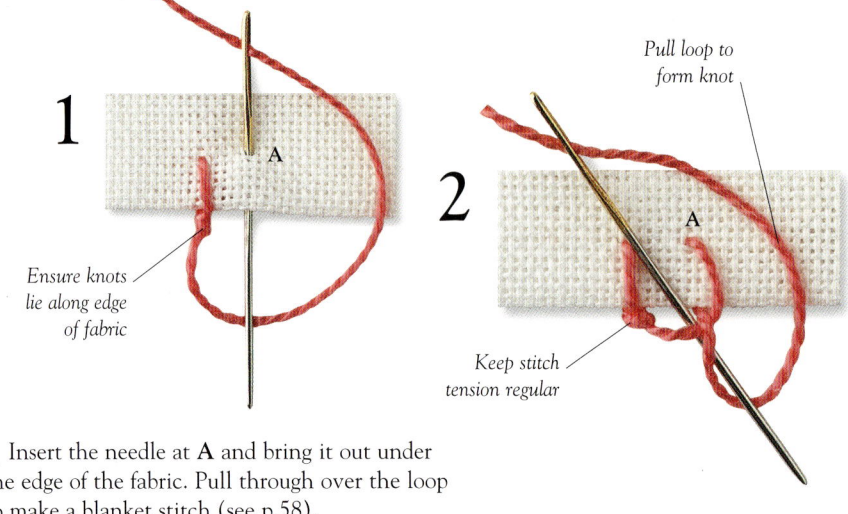

1 Insert the needle at **A** and bring it out under the edge of the fabric. Pull through over the loop to make a blanket stitch (see p.58).

2 Take the needle back to the left and pass it behind the two threads. Draw up the working thread to form a knot. Repeat these two steps to continue along the edge.

Sailor Edging

········· Level ·········
Intermediate

········· Uses ·········
Decorative hems

········ Method ········
Blanket stitch variation, worked downwards over edge of fabric

······· Materials ·······
Any fabric; any twisted thread

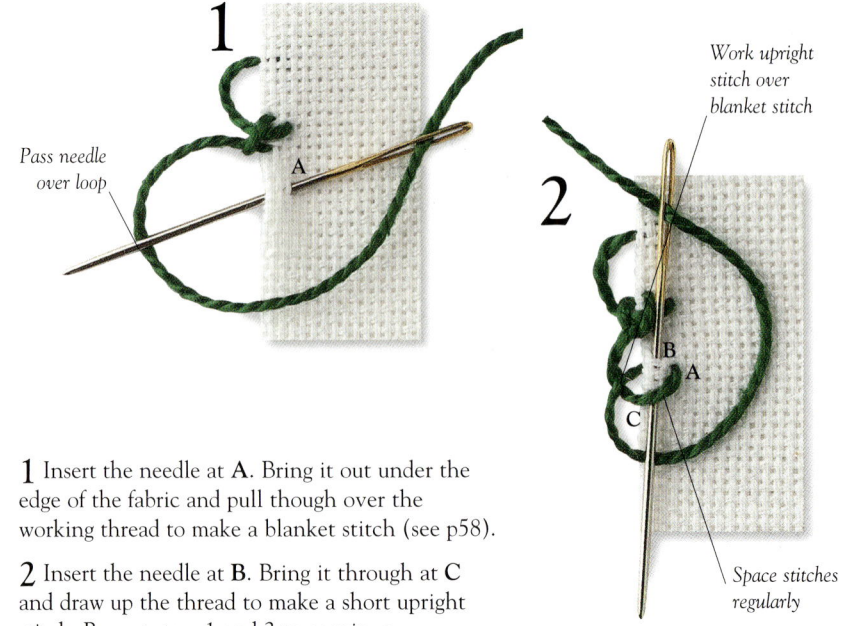

1 Insert the needle at **A**. Bring it out under the edge of the fabric and pull though over the working thread to make a blanket stitch (see p58).

2 Insert the needle at **B**. Bring it through at **C** and draw up the thread to make a short upright stitch. Repeat steps 1 and 2 to continue.

Looped Edge

········ Level ········
Intermediate

········ Uses ········
Solid stitch for hems and neatening raw edges; foundation for laced insertion stitch

········ Method ········
Looped edging stitch, worked horizontally

········ Materials ········
Any fabric; any thread depending on fabric

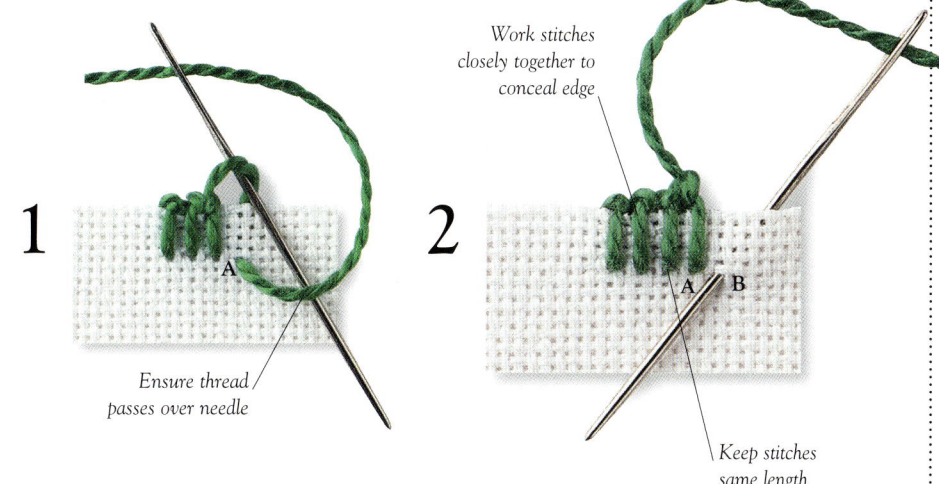

1 Come up at **A**. Take the needle to the left and pass it downwards through the loop. Pull up the thread gently.

2 Bring the needle out at **B**, ready to make the next stitch. Repeat these two steps to continue.

Half Chevron

········ Level ········
Intermediate

········ Uses ········
To neaten folded edges and hems

········ Method ········
Chevron stitch variation, worked over edge of fabric

········ Materials ········
Any fabric; any thread

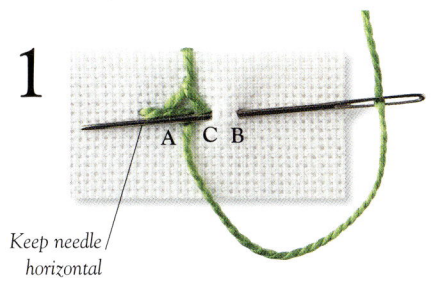

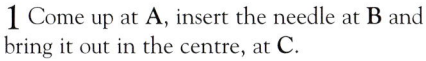

1 Come up at **A**, insert the needle at **B** and bring it out in the centre, at **C**.

2 Loop the thread from left to right. Take the needle behind the fabric and bring it through over the working thread, at **D**.

3 Insert the needle to the right of **B**, at **E**, then bring it through again at **B**. Repeat steps 1 to 3 to continue along the edge.

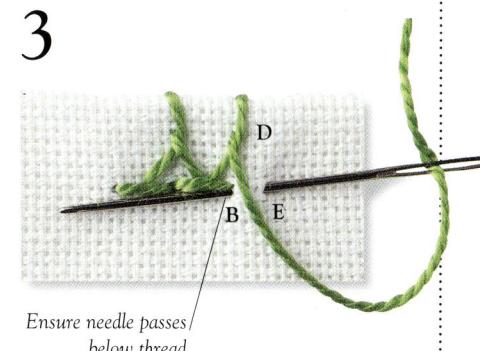

Scalloped Edge

·········· Level ··········
Intermediate

·········· Uses ··········
Neatening curved and scalloped raw edges

·········· Method ··········
Buttonhole stitch worked over running stitch foundation

·········· Materials ··········
Closely woven fabric; any fine thread; embroidery scissors

1

Do not leave any space between rows

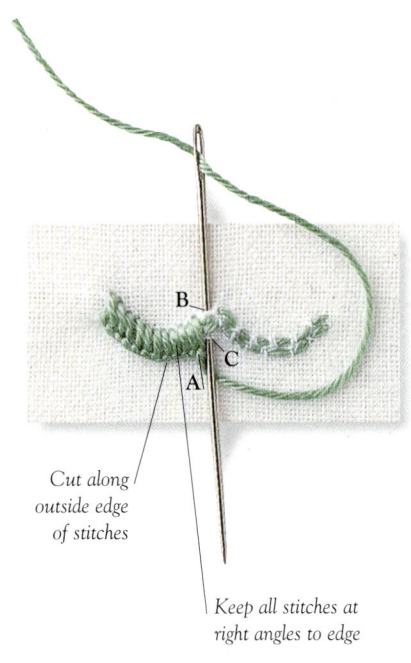

2

Cut along outside edge of stitches

Keep all stitches at right angles to edge

1 Sew two foundation rows of closely spaced running stitch (see p.39) along the outline of the edge to be worked.

2 Work a row of buttonhole stitch (see p.58) over the foundation, following the curve of the outline. Come up at **A**, insert at **B** and pull the needle through at **C**. Repeat to the end of the line. When the stitching is complete, trim away the surplus fabric using sharp embroidery scissors.

Ring Picot Edge

·········· Level ··········
Advanced

·········· Uses ··········
Decorative trim on buttonholed edges

·········· Method ··········
Buttonhole stitch worked over thread loop

·········· Materials ··········
Closely woven fabric, any fine thread; embroidery scissors

1

Pull needle through to make buttonhole stitch

2

Do not pull stitches too tightly

3

1 Sew a line of closely spaced running stitch (see p.39) along the edge to be worked. Make a row of buttonhole stitch (see p.58) over it, finishing at the right edge of the picot, at **A**. Take the needle back to **B** and pass it under the horizontal thread to form the foundation loop. Slide the needle under the loop from right to left, over the working thread and gently pull through.

2 Work a series of buttonhole stitches to cover the foundation loop.

3 Continue working buttonhole stitch along the marked line. When complete, carefully trim away the surplus fabric using sharp embroidery scissors.

CUTWORK AND EDGING STITCHES   115

Buttonhole Eyelet

Level
Advanced

Uses
Circular holes; laced eyelets

Method
Buttonhole stitch worked in a ring around central opening

Materials
Closely woven fabric; any fine thread; sharp scissors

Reinforce opening with running stitch

Turn surplus fabric to wrong side

Space stitches evenly in a ring

1 Mark two concentric circles on the fabric. Outline the inner circle with a round of closely spaced running stitch (see p.39).

2 Clip the knot and make two cuts at right angles across the inner circle. Using the point of the needle, ease the fabric to the wrong side and finger press in place.

3 Come up at **A** on the outer circle and work a circle of buttonhole stitch (see p.58) into the centre. Trim any surplus fabric on the wrong side.

Overcast Eyelet

Level
Advanced

Uses
Broderie Anglaise; openwork

Method
Small open circle with bound edge

Materials
Fine cotton or linen; any fine thread

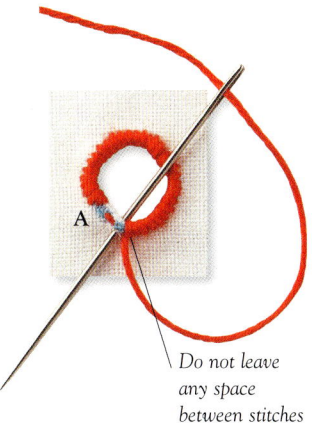

Do not leave any space between stitches

Draw a circle onto the fabric and prepare as for steps 1 and 2 above. Bring the needle up a short distance away from the folded edge, at **A** and work a ring of short stitches into the space.

Square Eyelet

Level
Advanced

Uses
Broderie Anglaise; openwork

Method
Cut square with bound edge

Materials
Any fine fabric; fine thread

Work longer stitches at corners

Mark the outline and work a round of running stitch over it. Make two diagonal cuts across the square and finger press the surplus fabric to the wrong side. Come up at **A** and work a round of straight stitches into the opening, angling them at each corner.

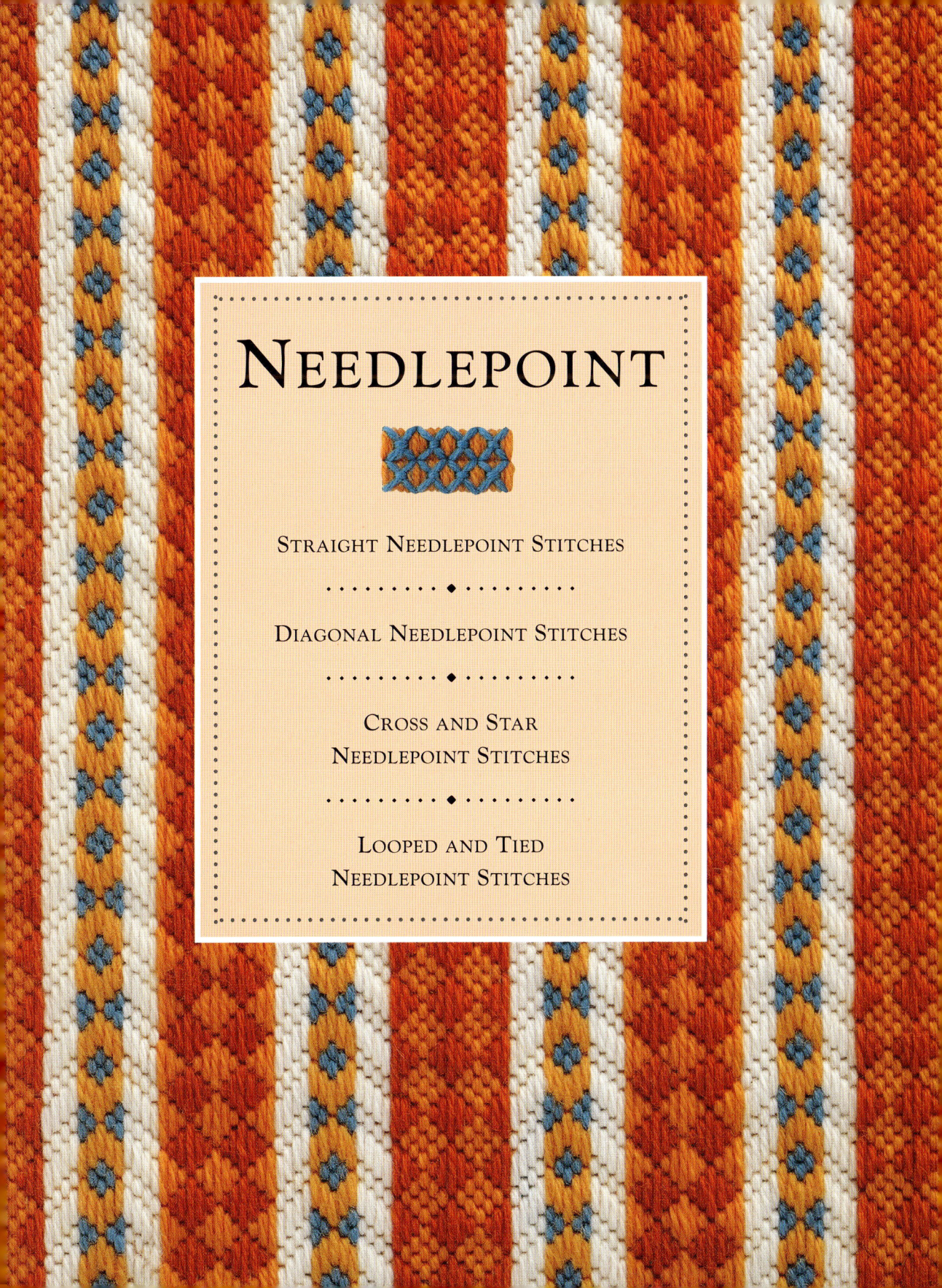

Needlepoint

- Straight Needlepoint Stitches
- Diagonal Needlepoint Stitches
- Cross and Star Needlepoint Stitches
- Looped and Tied Needlepoint Stitches

Straight Needlepoint Stitches

T<small>HIS VERSATILE GROUP</small> of stitches includes stripes, zigzags, diamonds and other geometric patterns which can be used for fillings and backgrounds on various scales, using one or more colours. They are all stitched either horizontally or vertically, so that the thread lies parallel to the grain of the canvas. This means that they do not distort the square weave in the same way as diagonal stitches and, with care, they can be worked without a frame. The stitches are all sewn on single canvas, and the thread, yarn or wool used must be thick enough to conceal the background completely.

Upright Gobelin **119**	Straight Cushion **123**
Gobelin Filling **119**	Scottish Diamond **123**
Parisian **119**	Diamond **124**
Hungarian **120**	Long Stitch Triangles **124**
Hungarian Diamond **120**	Lozenge **125**
Single Twill **121**	Straight Milanese **125**
Double Twill **121**	Double Brick **126**
Bargello **121**	Brick Filling **126**
Chevron **122**	Long and Short Brick **127**
Hungarian Ground **122**	Basket Filling **127**

Straight Needlepoint Stitches 119

Upright Gobelin

····· Other Name ·····
Straight Gobelin stitch

····· Level ·····
Easy

····· Uses ·····
Ridged fillings and backgrounds

····· Method ·····
Horizontal rows of vertical straight stitches, worked alternately from right to left

····· Materials ·····
Single canvas; any thread

Work each stitch over four threads

Starting at top left, make an upright stitch from **5A** to **1A** and repeat to the end of the line. Begin the next row at **9F** to **5F** and stitch towards the left. Repeat these two rows to fill the required area.

Gobelin Filling

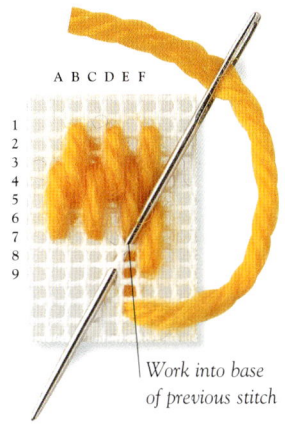

····· Level ·····
Easy

····· Uses ·····
Twill effect backgrounds and shaded fillings

····· Method ·····
Interlocking horizontal rows of upright stitches

····· Materials ·····
Single canvas; any thread

Work into base of previous stitch

Start at top left. Work the first stitch from **7A** to **3A**, the second from **5B** to **1B** and repeat to the end of the line. Begin the next row at **9F** to **5F** and **11E** to **7E** and work towards the left; repeat these two rows to continue.

Parisian

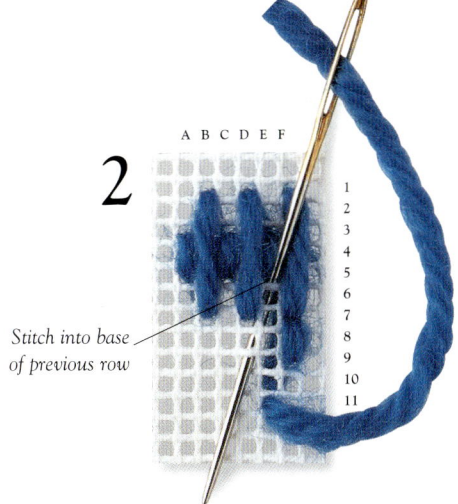

····· Level ·····
Easy

····· Uses ·····
Textured fillings and large background areas

····· Method ·····
Interlocking horizontal rows of alternate long and short upright stitches

····· Materials ·····
Single canvas; any thread

Work each row in pairs of long and short stitches

Stitch into base of previous row

1 Start at the top left corner. Work a short stitch over two threads from **5A** to **3A** and a long stitch over six threads from **7B** to **1B**. Repeat these two stitches to the end of the line.

2 Begin the next row with a short stitch from **9F** to **7F** and a long stitch from **11E** to **5E**, then work alternate long and short stitches to the end of the row. Repeat these two steps to fill the required area.

····· Technique Variation ·····

To create a secondary pattern within Parisian stitch, work all the long stitches in a dark yarn, then fill the spaces with short stitches in a contrasting colour.

Hungarian

·········· Level ··········
Easy

·········· Uses ··········
Textured fillings

·········· Method ··········
Horizontal rows of small interlocking diamonds

·········· Materials ··········
Single canvas; any thread in one or two colours

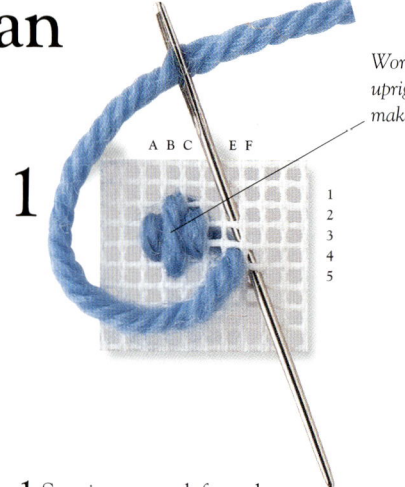

Work three upright stitches to make diamond

1 Starting at top left, make a short stitch over two threads from **4A** to **2A**. Work a long stitch from **5B** to **1B**, then another short stitch from **4C** to **2C**. Miss one space, then come up at **4E** to start the next diamond. Continue to the end of the line.

2 Using a contrasting colour, come up at **6E** to start the next row. Repeat the sequence of three stitches and one space, working from right to left.

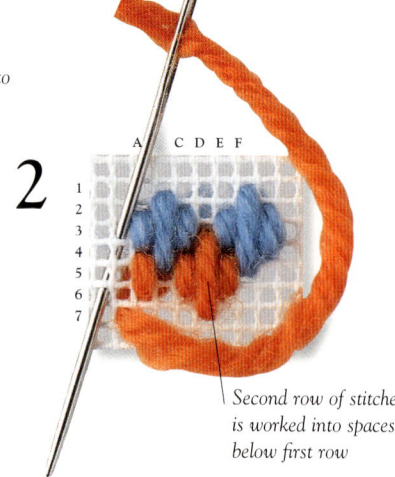

Second row of stitches is worked into spaces below first row

·········· Technique Variation ··········

When Hungarian stitch is worked in just a single colour it produces a smooth, brocade-like texture which provides a good background for detailed tent stitch designs.

Hungarian Diamond

·········· Level ··········
Easy

·········· Uses ··········
Striped backgrounds and fillings

·········· Method ··········
Hungarian stitch variation on larger scale

·········· Materials ··········
Single canvas; any thread

Work progressively longer and shorter stitches

Stitch second row in opposite direction, working into spaces left below first

1 Start at top left. Work three progressively longer stitches from **5A** to **3A**, **6B** to **2B** and **7C** to **1C**, then a shorter stitch from **6D** to **2D**. Repeat these four stitches to the end of the row and work two shorter stitches to complete the final diamond.

2 Use a second colour for the next row. Start with a short stitch from **9K** to **7K** and continue as above, working from right to left. Repeat these two rows to fill the required area.

STRAIGHT NEEDLEPOINT STITCHES   121

Single Twill

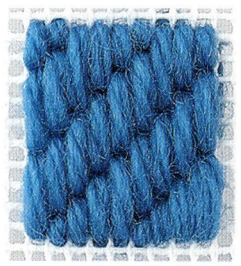

Work each stitch a single thread higher than preceding stitch

·········· LEVEL ··········
Easy

·········· USES ··········
Ridged fillings and woven effect backgrounds

·········· METHOD ··········
Diagonal rows of vertical straight stitches

·········· MATERIALS ··········
Single canvas; any thread

Start at the top left with a straight stitch from **9A** to **5A**. Work the next from **8B** to **4B** and continue stitching upwards. Start the next row at **9E** to **5E**, and continue working downwards. Repeat these two rows to continue.

Bargello

·········· OTHER NAMES ··········
Florentine stitch; flame stitch

·········· LEVEL ··········
Easy

·········· USES ··········
Large patterned areas

·········· METHOD ··········
Straight stitch worked in wide zigzag bands

·········· MATERIALS ··········
Single canvas; any yarn in a selection of toning and contrasting colours

Insert needle into base of previous stitch

1 Start at the left with a straight stitch from **11A** to **7A**. Make three stitches upwards from **9B** to **5B**, **7C** to **3C** and **5D** to **1D**. Work the next three stitches downwards, leaving two threads between each, ending at **7G**. Come up at **9H** and repeat this sequence to the end of the row.

2 Stitch the next row in the same way, starting at **15A** and using a lighter shade of the same colour. The third row is worked in a paler yarn, starting at **19A**. Repeat these three rows to continue.

Double Twill

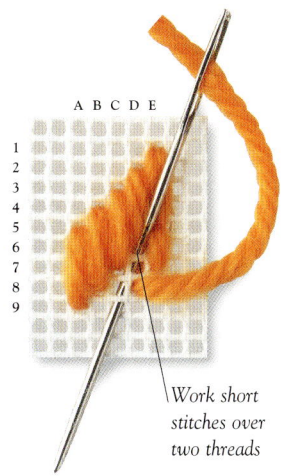

Work short stitches over two threads

·········· LEVEL ··········
Easy

·········· USES ··········
Textured fillings and backgrounds

·········· METHOD ··········
Alternate rows of long and short upright stitches, worked diagonally

·········· MATERIALS ··········
Single canvas; any thread

Work the first row as for single twill stitch (see above). Start the second row with **7E** to **5E** and continue working short stitches downwards. Repeat these two rows to fill the required area.

·········· TECHNIQUE VARIATION ··········

To create a wider zigzag with a stepped effect, work blocks of two and three stitches in the centre of the diagonals. Add in a contrasting colour yarn to give more visual interest.

Chevron

······· Level ·······
Easy

······· Uses ·······
Backgrounds and fillings

······· Method ·······
Alternate zigzag bands of long and short stitches

······· Materials ·······
Single canvas; any thread in one or two colours

Work long stitches over four threads

Work short stitches over two threads

1 Start at the top left corner with a stitch from **8A** to **4A**. Work three more stitches upwards from **7B** to **3B**, **6C** to **2C** and **5D** to **1D**, then two downwards stitches from **6E** to **2E** and **7F** to **3F**. Repeat this sequence to the end of the row.

2 Begin the next row with a short stitch from **7J** to **5J**. Continue stitching from right to left, working into the base of the previous row. Repeat these two rows to continue.

······· Technique Variation ·······

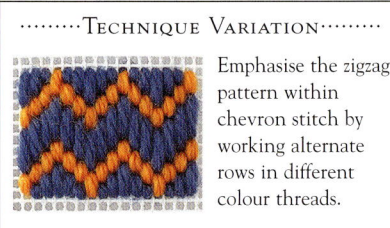

Emphasise the zigzag pattern within chevron stitch by working alternate rows in different colour threads.

Hungarian Ground

······· Level ·······
Intermediate

······· Uses ·······
Geometric fillings

······· Method ·······
Alternate straight stitch zigzags and diamonds

······· Materials ·······
Single canvas; any thread

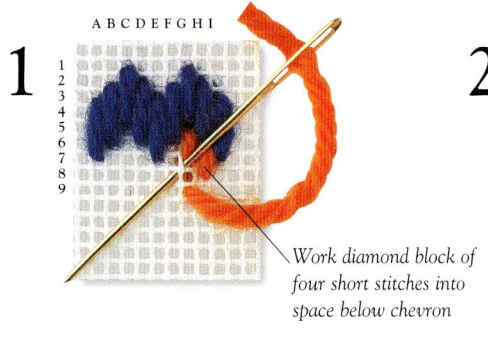

Work diamond block of four short stitches into space below chevron

Work third row as mirror image of first

1 Start at the top left corner. Work three long stitches upwards from **7A** to **3A**, **6B** to **2B** and **5C** to **1C** and one stitch downwards from **6D** to **2D**, then repeat this block to the end of the line. Using the second colour, make four short stitches from **8H** to **6H**, **7G** to **5G**, **9G** to **7G** and **8F** to **6F**. Start the next diamond at **8D**.

2 With the first colour, work three stitches downwards from **11I** to **7I**, **12H** to **8H** and **13G** to **9G**, then two stitches upwards from **12F** to **8F** and **11E** to **7E**. Repeat to the end of the row, then fill in the spaces with diamonds.

STRAIGHT NEEDLEPOINT STITCHES   123

Straight Cushion

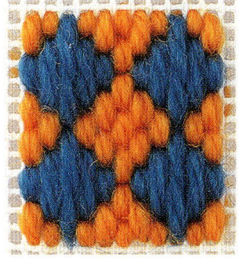

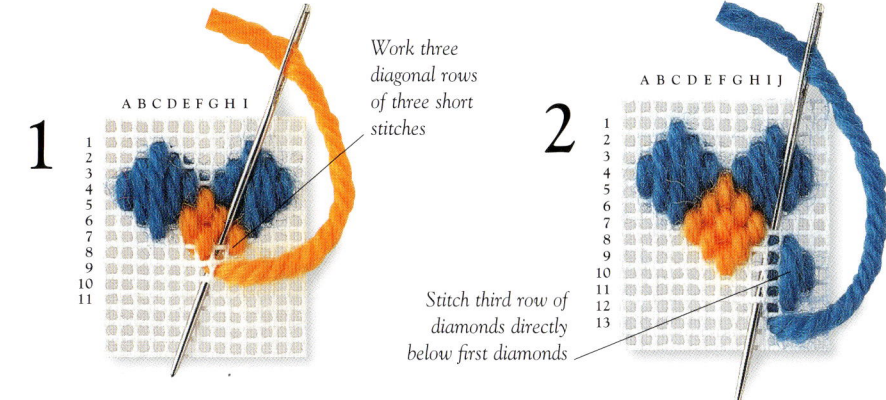

1 Work three diagonal rows of three short stitches

2 Stitch third row of diamonds directly below first diamonds

·········· LEVEL ··········
Intermediate

·········· USES ··········
Chequerboard fillings

·········· METHOD ··········
Alternate rows of diamonds worked in long and short straight stitches

·········· MATERIALS ··········
Single canvas; any thread or yarn in two colours

1 Work the first row as step 1 of Scottish diamond stitch (see below) starting at **5A**. Using a second colour, work three rows of stitches, from **8H** to **6H**, **7G** to **5G**, **6F** to **4F**; **7E** to **5E**, **8F** to **6F**, **9G** to **7G** and **10F** to **8F**, **9E** to **7E** and **8D** to **6D**.

2 Work the third row as the first, starting at **11K** and stitching from right to left. Continue working alternate rows of dark and light diamonds.

·········· TECHNIQUE VARIATION ··········

Work straight cushion stitch in two shades of the same colour, instead of two contrasting yarns, to give a subtle brocade effect for fillings or large-scale backgrounds.

Scottish Diamond

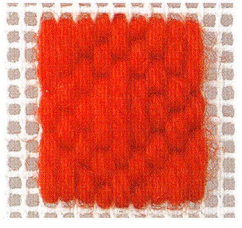

·········· LEVEL ··········
Intermediate

·········· USES ··········
Textured fillings and backgrounds

·········· METHOD ··········
Straight stitch chevrons and diamonds worked in alternate rows

·········· MATERIALS ··········
Single canvas; any thread

Make five stitches for each diamond

Work short stitches over two threads

1 Start at top left. Work five upright stitches in a diamond shape from **7B** to **5B**, **8C** to **4C**, **9D** to **3D**, **8E** to **4E** and **7F** to **5F**. Repeat to the end of the line, leaving one space between each diamond.

2 Work a zigzag line above and below the diamonds. Start at **4A** to **6A**, then work three stitches upwards from **3B** to **5B**, **2C** to **4C** and **1D** to **3D**, and two downwards from **2E** to **4E** and **3F** to **5F**. Repeat to the end of the row, then work a mirror image below, starting at **8M** to **6M**. Continue working alternate rows of diamonds and chevrons to fill the required area.

Diamond

.... LEVEL ....
Easy

.... USES ....
Fillings and backgrounds

.... METHOD ....
Large-scale variation of Hungarian stitch

.... MATERIALS ....
Single canvas; any thread in one or two colours

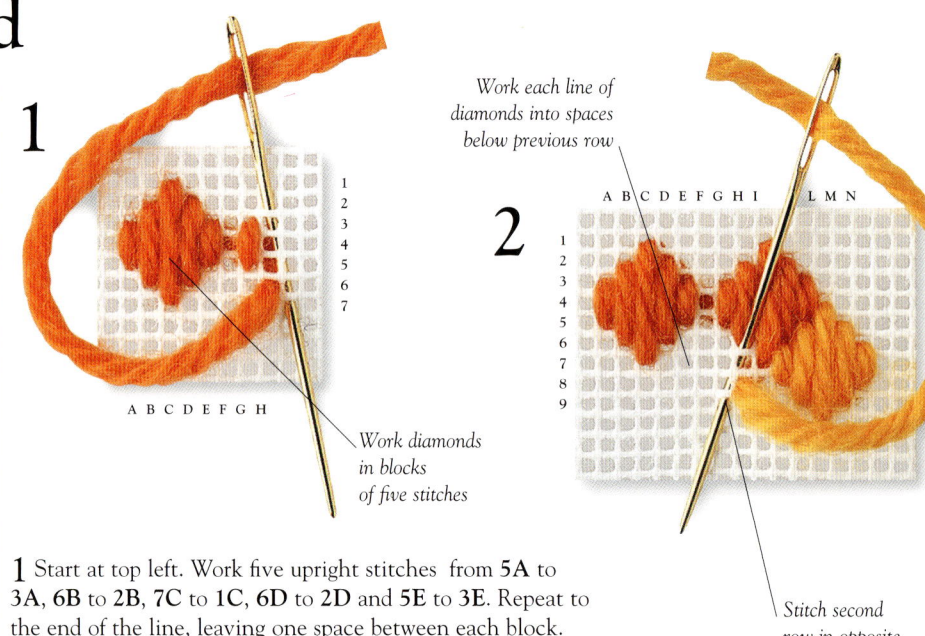

1 *Work diamonds in blocks of five stitches*

2 *Work each line of diamonds into spaces below previous row*

Stitch second row in opposite direction

1 Start at top left. Work five upright stitches from **5A** to **3A**, **6B** to **2B**, **7C** to **1C**, **6D** to **2D** and **5E** to **3E**. Repeat to the end of the line, leaving one space between each block.

2 The second row is worked from right to left, using the same or a different colour. Start the first block at **8N** to **6N**, then repeat these two rows to continue.

Long Stitch Triangles

.... LEVEL ....
Easy

.... USES ....
Textured single-colour background or filling

.... METHOD ....
Two rows of interlocking straight stitch triangles, repeated horizontally

.... MATERIALS ....
Single canvas; any thread

1 *Work eight upright stitches to form first triangle*

2 *Make longest stitches below shortest stitches of previous row*

Stitch second row from right to left

1 Start in the top left corner with five progressively longer stitches, worked from **2A** to **1A**, **3B** to **1B**, **4C** to **1C**, **5D** to **1D** and **6E** to **1E**. Work three shorter stitches from **5F** to **1F**, **4G** to **1G** and **3H** to **1H**. Repeat this block to the end of the line.

2 Make a long stitch from **7Q** to **2Q**, then work four shorter stitches from **7P** to **3P**, **7O** to **4O**, **7N** to **5N** and **7M** to **6M**, and three longer stitches from **7L** to **5L**, **7K** to **4K** and **7J** to **3J**. Repeat these two rows to fill the required area.

Lozenge

······· Level ·······
Intermediate

······· Uses ·······
Harlequin filling or background for large areas

······· Method ·······
Elongated diamonds, worked in interlocking diagonal rows

······· Materials ·······
Single canvas; two colours of any thread

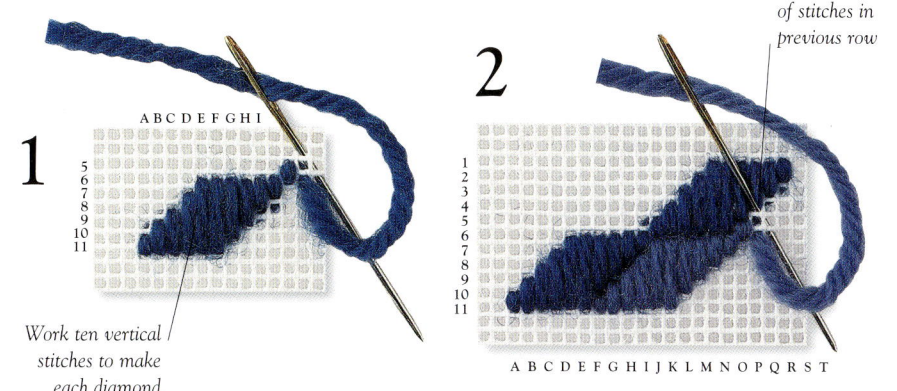

Work ten vertical stitches to make each diamond

Stitch into base of stitches in previous row

1 Start at bottom left with five stitches from **11A** to **10A**, **11B** to **9B**, **11C** to **8C**, **11D** to **7D** and **11E** to **6E**. Complete the diamond with five more stitches from **11F** to **6F**, **10G** to **6G**, **9H** to **6H**, **8I** to **6I** and **7J** to **6J**. Begin the next diamond at **6K** to **5K** and contine working upwards.

2 Using a different colour, begin the second row at **11G** to **10G**. Work the third row in the first colour, starting at **11M** to **10M**. Fill in the required space above the stitches with further rows in alternate colours.

Straight Milanese

······· Level ·······
Intermediate

······· Uses ·······
Background or filling

······· Method ·······
Interlocking rows of triangles worked vertically to create a wave pattern

······· Materials ·······
Single canvas; any thread in one or two colours

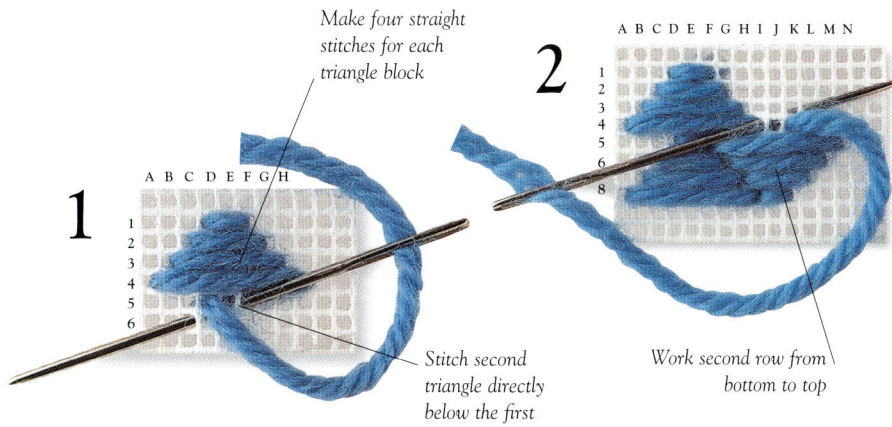

Make four straight stitches for each triangle block

Stitch second triangle directly below the first

Work second row from bottom to top

1 Start at top left. Work four horizontal stitches from **1D** to **1F**, **2C** to **2G**, **3B** to **3H** and **4A** to **4I**. Begin the next triangle at **5D** to **5F** and continue downwards to the end of the row.

2 Begin the next row with four stitches from **8K** to **8I**, **7L** to **7H**, **6M** to **6G** and **5N** to **5F**. Continue working upwards, then repeat these two rows to fill the required area.

······· Technique Variation ·······

For a more geometric effect, work alternate rows in contrasting or toning colours, to emphasize the triangular formation of straight milanese stitch.

Double Brick

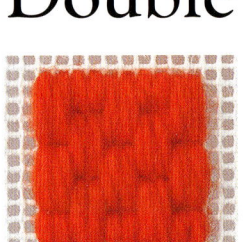

····· Other Name ·····
Double Gobelin filling

········ Level ········
Easy

········· Uses ·········
Single colour filling

······· Method ·······
Interlocking rows of double straight stitches

······ Materials ······
Single canvas; any thread

1

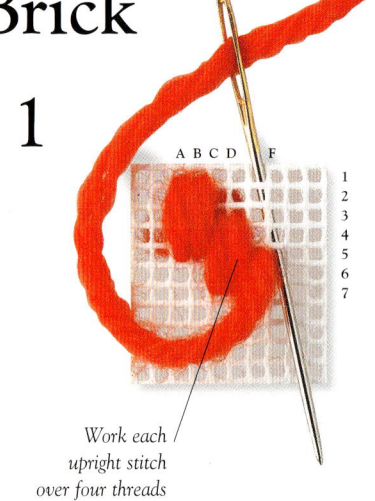

Work each upright stitch over four threads

2

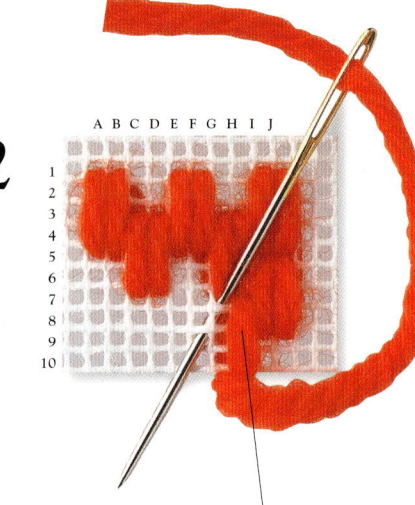

Stitch second row from right to left

1 Start at top left. Work two parallel stitches from **5A** to **1A** and **5B** to **1B**, then two more from **7C** to **3C** and **7D** to **3D**. Come up at **5E** and continue working pairs of staggered straight stitches to the end of the row.

2 Work the second and subsequent rows in the same way, starting with a pair of stitches from **9J** to **5J** and **9I** to **5I**.

Brick Filling

········ Level ········
Intermediate

········· Uses ·········
Small-scale fillings

······· Method ·······
Pairs of horizontal straight stitches divided by vertical stitches

······ Materials ······
Single canvas; any thread in two colours

1

Work each horizontal stitch over four threads

2

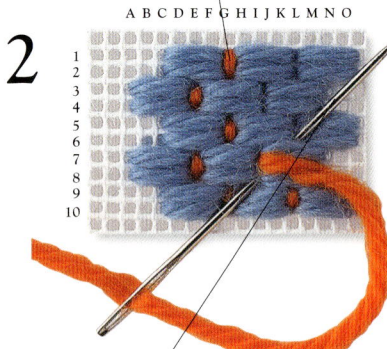

Work each upright stitch over one thread

Avoid catching long stitches with needle

1 Starting at bottom left, work two horizontal stitches from **10G** to **10C** and **9G** to **9C**, then a second staggered pair from **8E** to **8A** and **7E** to **7A**. Continue upwards, then work the second row downwards in the same way, starting at **1K** to **1G**. Repeat these two rows to fill the required area.

2 Using a contrasting thread, work short upright stitches at the points where pairs of stitches meet, starting with **1G** to **2G**.

····· Technique Variation ·····

Working the vertical stitches (see step 2, above) in the same thread as the horizontal stitches produces a more textured surface with a quilted appearance.

STRAIGHT NEEDLEPOINT STITCHES 127

Long and Short Brick

····· OTHER NAME ·····
Brick stitch

········· LEVEL ·········
Intermediate

·········· USES ··········
Fillings and backgrounds

········ METHOD ········
Alternate pairs of long
and short stitches

······· MATERIALS ·······
Single canvas; one or two
colours of any thread

Leave two spaces between each pair of straight stitches

Work each long stitch over six horizontal threads

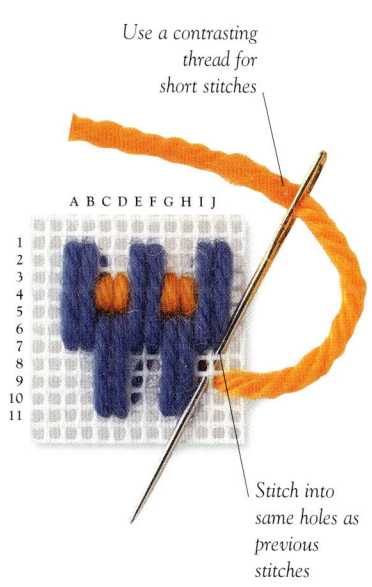

Use a contrasting thread for short stitches

Stitch into same holes as previous stitches

1 Start at top left and work two stitches from **7A** to **1A** and **7B** to **1B**. Make two more from **7E** to **1E** and **7F** to **1F**. Repeat to the end of the row, leaving two spaces between each pair of stitches. Start the next row with **11H** to **5H** and **11G** to **5G** and continue working from right to left.

2 Fill in the spaces with pairs of short stitches, starting with **5C** to **3C** and **5D** to **3D**. Repeat these two steps to continue.

Basket Filling

········· LEVEL ·········
Intermediate

·········· USES ··········
Large-scale woven-look
filling or background

········ METHOD ········
Straight stitch worked in
alternate vertical and
horizontal blocks

······· MATERIALS ·······
Single canvas; any thread

Slip needle under vertical stitch before inserting

Work each stitch over six threads

1 Start at top left. Work a block of five upright stitches from **7B** to **1B**, **7C** to **1C**, **7D** to **1D**, **7E** to **1E** and **7F** to **1F**, then work a block of five horizontal stitches from **2L** to **2F**, **3L** to **3F**, **4L** to **4F**, **5L** to **5F** and **6L** to **6F**. Repeat to the end of the line.

2 Work five upright stitches below the horizontal block, starting with **12K** to **6K** and ending with **12G** to **6G**. Work a horizontal block under the upright block, starting at **7A** to **7F** and ending with **12A** to **12F**. Repeat to the end of the line, then repeat these two rows to continue.

Diagonal Needlepoint Stitches

THIS SECTION STARTS with tent stitch and its variations, which are the most frequently used needlepoint stitches. Like all the other diagonal stitches, they are worked at a slant across the thread intersections. This can have the effect of distorting the square weave of the canvas, even when it is mounted in a frame. The finished piece should be stretched and blocked back into shape. Some diagonal stitches are worked on single canvas, others on double. Always match the thickness of the thread or yarn to the weight of the canvas being used, so that no background threads are visible.

Half Cross 129	Cashmere 132
Basketweave Tent 129	Diagonal 133
Tent 129	Byzantine 133
Trammed Tent 129	Jacquard 134
Gobelin 130	Moorish 135
Encroaching Gobelin 130	Milanese 135
Reversed Sloping Gobelin 131	Mosaic 136
	Cushion 136
Canvas Stem 131	Scottish 137
Florence 132	Chequer 137

Half Cross

.... Level ....
Easy

.... Uses ....
Charts; printed canvases

.... Method ....
Small slanting stitches

.... Materials ....
Double canvas; thick yarn

.... Tip ....
Turn work upside-down for return journey to stitch rows in same direction

Start at top left. Stitch over one intersection, from **2A** to **1B** and **2B** to **1C**, then repeat to the end of the line. Begin the next row with **2F** to **3E** and **2E** to **3D**. Repeat these two rows to continue.

Basketweave Tent

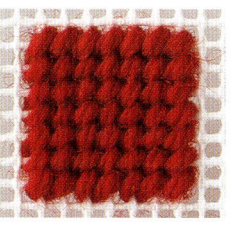

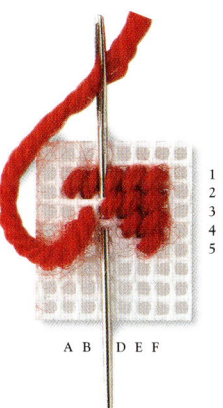

.... Other Names ....
Continental stitch; diagonal tent stitch

.... Level ....
Intermediate

.... Uses ....
Backgrounds and fillings

.... Method ....
Tent stitch worked in diagonal rows

.... Materials ....
Single canvas; any thread

Starting at top right, make a stitch from **2E** to **1F**. Work the next row upwards from **3E** to **2F** and **2D** to **1E** and the third downwards from **2C** to **1D**, **3D** to **2E** and **4E** to **3F**. Begin the following row with **5E** to **4F**: continue working up, then down.

Tent

.... Other Name ....
Petit point

.... Level ....
Easy

.... Uses ....
Backgrounds; detailed charted or printed patterns

.... Method ....
Worked horizontally

.... Materials ....
Single canvas; any thread

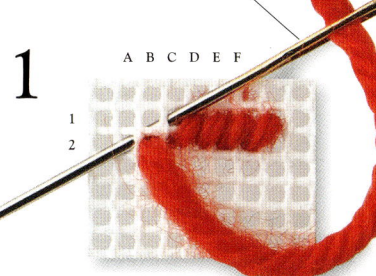

Take needle behind two threads to make long stitch on reverse side

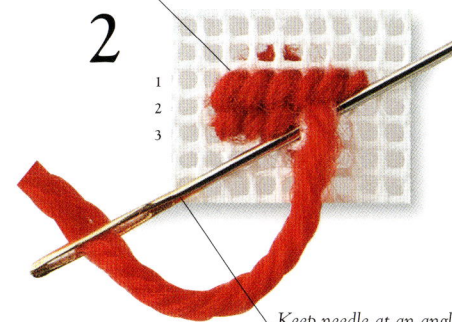

Work each stitch in same direction

Keep needle at an angle

1 Start at top right and sew a diagonal stitch from **2F** to **1G**. Work the second stitch from **2E** to **1F** and repeat to the end of the row.

2 Turn the canvas the other way up and repeat step 1 or work the second row from left to right, starting with **2B** to **3A**. Repeat these two rows.

.... Stitch Variation ....

Trammed tent stitch is sewn over long straight stitches worked through the small holes on a double canvas. This gives a ridged effect and because it is hardwearing, this stitch is often used for seat covers.

Gobelin

····· Other Names ·····
Oblique Gobelin;
gros point

········ Level ········
Easy

········ Uses ········
Backgrounds and fillings

······· Method ·······
Long diagonal stitches
worked in horizontal rows

······ Materials ······
Single canvas, any thread

Work each stitch over one vertical and two horizontal threads

Work into base of previous stitch

1 Start at top right. Make the first diagonal stitch from **3G** to **1H** and the next from **3F** to **1G**. Repeat to the end of the line.

2 Begin the return journey with two stitches from **5A** to **3B** and **5B** to **3C**, and continue to the end of the row. Repeat these two rows to fill the required area.

Encroaching Gobelin

········ Level ········
Easy

········ Uses ········
Backgrounds; filling for
plain or shaded areas

······· Method ·······
Overlapping rows of
diagonal stitches, worked
horizontally

······ Materials ······
Single canvas; any yarn

Stitch over one vertical and three horizontal threads

Work over five horizontal threads to fill larger areas

Work second row so stitches overlap first row by one thread

1 Starting at top right, work a row of diagonal stitches, beginning with **4F** to **1G** and **4E** to **1F**.

2 Work the first stitch of the next row from **6A** to **3B** and the second from **6B** to **3C**. Continue to the end of the line and repeat these two steps to continue.

DIAGONAL NEEDLEPOINT STITCHES 131

Reversed Sloping Gobelin

LEVEL
Easy

USES
Plain or shaded fillings and backgrounds

METHOD
Vertical rows of diagonal straight stitches worked alternately down and up

MATERIALS
Any canvas; any thread

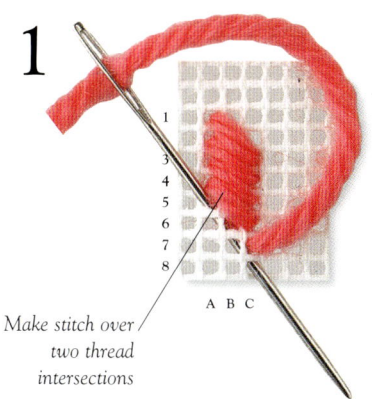

Make stitch over two thread intersections

Work second row at right angles to first

1 Start at top left and work a diagonal stitch from **3C** to **1A**. Work the next stitch from **4C** to **2A** and repeat downwards to the end of the line.

2 Begin the next line with a stitch in the opposite direction from **6E** to **8C**, then continue working upwards. Repeat these two rows.

·········· TECHNIQUE VARIATION ··········

To produce a shaded effect, work the stitches in the lower part of the stitched area with a selection of progressively darker tones of the main colour.

Canvas Stem

LEVEL
Intermediate

USES
Textured background, filling or chevron border

METHOD
Two upright rows of diagonal stitches, set in a V-shape, and divided by lines of back stitch

MATERIALS
Double canvas; two colours of any yarn

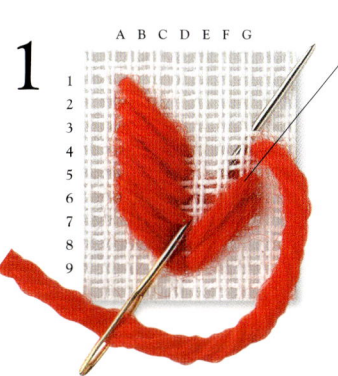

Work each stitch over three thread intersections

Ensure back stitches conceal horizontal threads

Use contrasting thread for back stitch

1 Starting at top left, make a diagonal stitch from **4D** to **1A**. Work the second stitch directly below, from **5D** to **2A**, and continue stitching downwards. Begin the next row at **6G** to **9D**. Make another stitch from **5G** to **8D** and continue working upwards. Repeat these two rows to cover the required area.

2 Make two back stitches from **4D** to **3D** and **5D** to **4D** and continue downwards. Work further rows of back stitch into the holes between the lines of diagonal stitches.

Florence

···· OTHER NAME ····
Diagonal mosaic stitch

········ LEVEL ········
Easy

········· USES ·········
Plain or striped fillings

········ METHOD ········
Alternate long and short slanting stitches, worked diagonally

······ MATERIALS ······
Any canvas; any thread

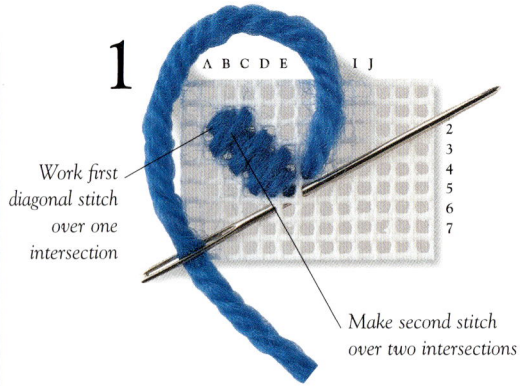

Work first diagonal stitch over one intersection

Make second stitch over two intersections

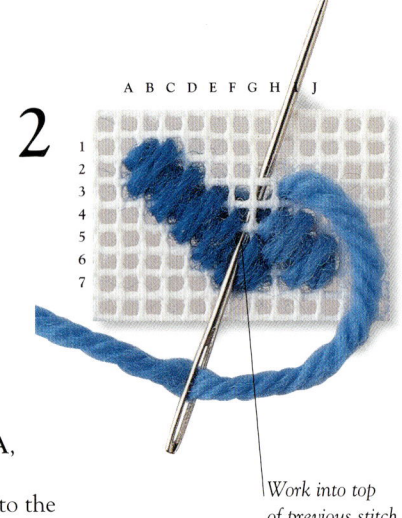

Work into top of previous stitch

1 Start at top left. Make a short stitch from **1B** to **2A**, followed by a longer stitch from **1C** to **3A**. Continue working alternate long and short stitches downwards to the bottom edge of the area being filled.

2 The next row is worked upwards using the same or a different colour yarn. Begin with a short stitch from **6J** to **7I** and a long one from **5J** to **7H** and repeat to the end of the row. Repeat these two steps to continue.

Cashmere

········ LEVEL ········
Easy

········· USES ·········
Textured plain or striped backgrounds and fillings

········ METHOD ········
Groups of three diagonal stitches worked vertically

······ MATERIALS ······
Any canvas; any thread

Work in blocks of one short and two long stitches

Stitch second row in opposite direction

1 Starting at top left, make a short diagonal stitch from **1B** to **2A**. Work two longer stitches from **1C** to **3A** and **2C** to **4A**. Repeat these three stitches, working downwards to the end of the row.

2 The next row is worked upwards. Make a short stitch from **8H** to **9G** and the next two long stitches from **7H** to **9F** and **6H** to **8F**. Repeat steps 1 and 2 to fill the required area.

······ TECHNIQUE VARIATION ······

Work alternate rows in a second colour to create a pattern of ridged diagonal stripes.

Diagonal

Work in blocks of four stitches

- **Level**
  Easy
- **Uses**
  Plain or striped filling or background for large areas
- **Method**
  Graduated straight stitches worked in diagonal rows
- **Materials**
  Any canvas; one or two colours of any thread

Work the second row in the same or a contrasting colour

1 Start at the top left corner. Each row is made up of blocks of four stitches, beginning with **1C** to **3A**, **1D** to **4A**, **1E** to **5A** and **2E** to **5B**. Work the first stitch of the next block from **3E** to **5C** and continue working downwards.

2 The next row is worked upwards in the same way. Make the first block from **13I** to **15G**, **12I** to **15F**, **11I** to **15E** and **11H** to **14E**. Repeat these two rows to continue and fill in the spaces with additional diagonal stitches (see p.19).

Technique Variation

For a more unusual effect, use one colour to sew the diagonal stitch, then work rows of contrasting back stitch (see p.40) between the lines. This will conceal any canvas that may show through and creates the illusion of a set of diagonal laid threads couched by zigzag lines of back stitch.

Byzantine

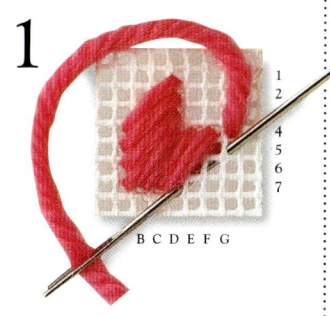

- **Other Name**
  Step stitch
- **Level**
  Easy
- **Uses**
  Large scale fillings and backgrounds
- **Method**
  Diagonal straight stitches, worked in zigzag lines
- **Materials**
  Any canvas; any thread

1 Start at top left. Each zigzag is made up of repeated blocks of six diagonal stitches. Work the first four stitches downwards from **1D** to **4A**, **2D** to **5A**, **3D** to **6A** and **4D** to **7A**. The next two stitches are worked to the right, from **4E** to **7B** and **4F** to **7C**. Start the next block at **4G**.

2 Work the second row level with and to the right of the first, starting at **1J** to **4G**. Make further rows to the right to fill the area required.

3 Complete any space at the bottom left corner with extra zigzags, starting at **10A** to **7D**, then work short stitches to fill the gaps (see p.19).

Jacquard

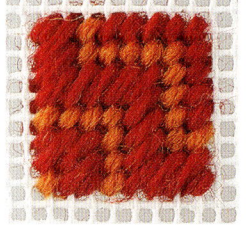

- **Level**
  Intermediate
- **Uses**
  Zigzag filling for large areas
- **Method**
  Stepped rows of alternate diagonal and tent stitch
- **Materials**
  Single canvas; one or two colours of any thread

1

Make eight stitches for each block

2

Work each diagonal stitch over two intersections

3
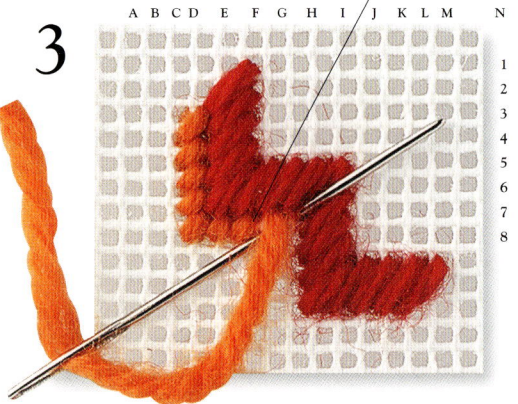

Work tent stitch over one intersection

4

Fill in unworked canvas with part stitches

1 Start at top left. Work a block of five diagonal stitches downwards from **3D** to **1F**, **4D** to **2F**, **5D** to **3F**, **6D** to **4F** and **7D** to **5F**, and three to the right from **7E** to **5G**, **7F** to **5H** and **7G** to **5I**.

2 Repeat this block to the bottom right corner of the area to be filled.

3 Using the second colour, work a block of five tent stitches downwards from **4C** to **3D**, **5C** to **4D**, and **6C** to **5D**, **7C** to **6D** and **8C** to **7D** and three to the right from **8D** to **7E**, **8E** to **7F**, **8F** to **7G**. Repeat this block to the end of the row.

4 Repeat step 1, starting with **6A** to **4C**, then continue working these two rows in alternate colours to fill the space.

Technique Variation

Work this stitch in one single colour to create a brocade-like background. Lustrous threads give a smooth, shiny surface that will add to the woven effect.

Moorish

·········· LEVEL ··········
Intermediate

·········· USES ··········
Large-scale filling with zigzag pattern

·········· METHOD ··········
Alternate rows of graduated diagonal stitches and tent stitch

·········· MATERIALS ··········
Any canvas; any thread in one or two colours

Work diagonal stitches to form row of square blocks

Make tent stitch over one intersection

1 Start at top left. Work three diagonal stitches which increase in length from **2B** to **1C**, **3B** to **1D** and **4A** to **1E**, then a shorter stitch from **4C** to **2E**. Repeat these four stitches to continue the row.

2 Using the second thread, work a stepped line of tent stitch to the left of the first row. Start with **2B** to **3A**, **3B** to **4A**, **4B** to **5A** and **4C** to **5B**, then repeat these four stitches. Repeat steps 1 and 2 to continue, working each successive row into the spaces left by the row before.

Milanese

·········· LEVEL ··········
Intermediate

·········· USES ··········
Brocade-like background or filling for larger areas

·········· METHOD ··········
Diagonal rows of alternate long and short back stitch forming triangular pattern

·········· MATERIALS ··········
Any canvas; any thread

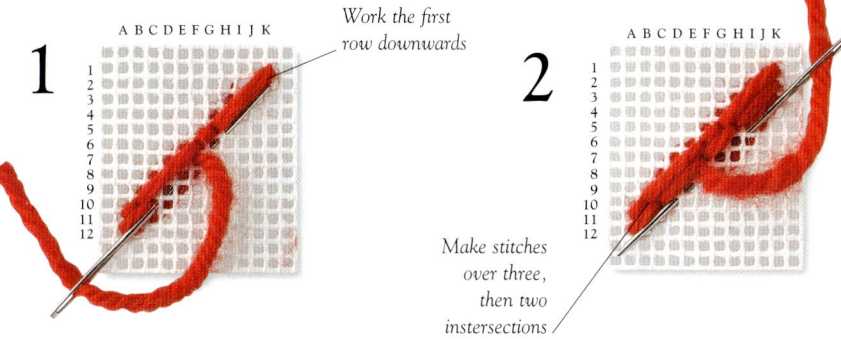

Work the first row downwards

Make stitches over three, then two instersections

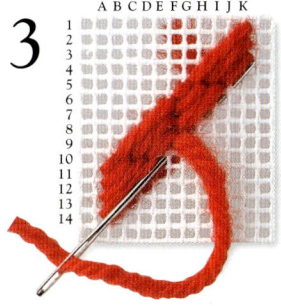

1 Start at top right. Work a long stitch from **5G** to **1K** and a short stitch from **6F** to **5G**, then repeat these two stitches to the end of the line. Start the next row with a short stitch from **10C** to **12A** and a long stitch from **7F** to **10C**, and repeat these two stitches, working upwards.

2 Start the third row with **5I** to **3K** and **8F** to **5I**, and repeat these two stitches, working downwards.

3 Work the fourth row upwards, starting with **10E** to **14A** and **9F** to **10E**. Repeat these four rows to continue.

Mosaic

·········· Level ··········
Easy

·········· Uses ··········
Fine textured backgrounds

·········· Method ··········
Long and short diagonal stitches worked in horizontal rows to form square pattern

·········· Materials ··········
Any canvas, any thread

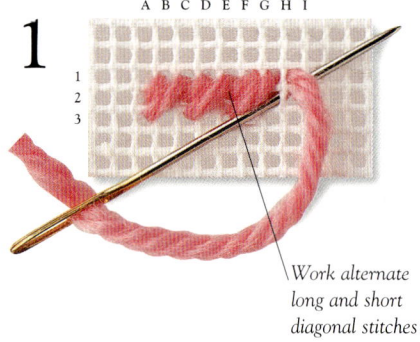

Work alternate long and short diagonal stitches

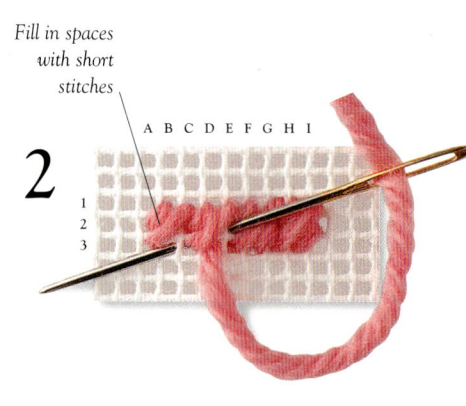

Fill in spaces with short stitches

1 Start at top left with two diagonal stitches from **1B** to **2A** and **1C** to **3A**. Repeat these two stitches to the end of the line.

2 Work the second row in the opposite direction. Make a short stitch from **3H** to **2I** to complete the first square, then continue working towards the left. Repeat these two rows to fill the required area.

·········· Technique Variation ··········

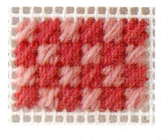

Change the visual effect by working the squares in two or more toning or contrasting colours to make a chequerboard pattern, ideal for filling smaller areas.

Cushion

·········· Level ··········
Easy

·········· Uses ··········
Filling or background with regular pattern of squares

·········· Method ··········
Graduated diagonal stitches worked in squares

·········· Materials ··········
Any canvas; any thread

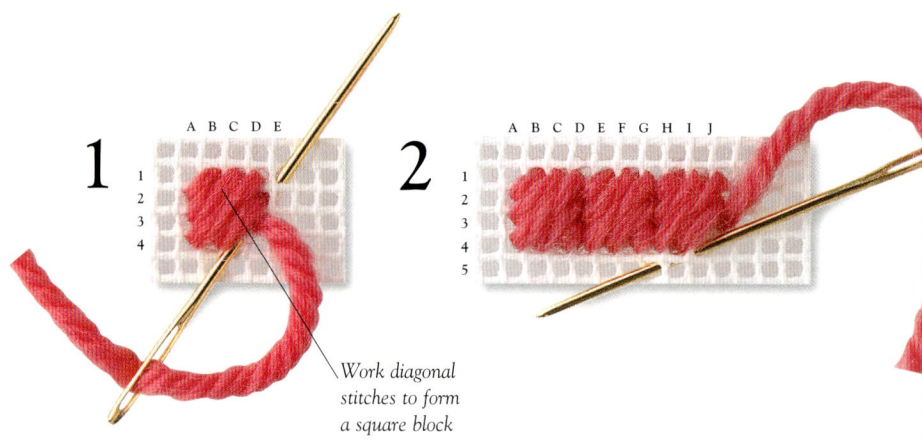

Work diagonal stitches to form a square block

1 Starting at the top left corner, work five stitches from **1B** to **2A**, **1C** to **3A**, **1D** to **4A**, **2D** to **4B** and **3D** to **4C**. Start the next block at **1E** to **2D** and continue to the end of the row.

2 Work the second row in the opposite direction, starting at **5G** to **4H**. Repeat steps 1 and 2 until the required space is filled.

·········· Technique Variation ··········

To prevent the canvas distorting, the square blocks can be worked in alternate directions using one or two colours.

DIAGONAL NEEDLEPOINT STITCHES 137

Scottish

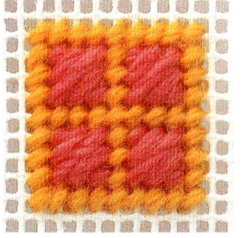

·········· LEVEL ··········
Intermediate
·········· USES ··········
Filling for large areas
·········· METHOD ··········
Cushion stitches framed with a line of tent stitch
·········· MATERIALS ··········
Any canvas; any thread

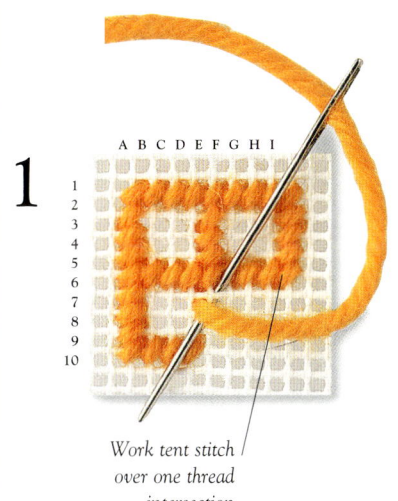

Work tent stitch over one thread intersection

Make five diagonal stitches to fill square

1 Starting at top left, work the tent stitch frame (see p.129). Make a grid of horizontal and vertical rows, leaving a square of three canvas threads between the lines.

2 Fill the squares with cushion stitch (see p.136), using a second colour. Work the first block from **2C** to **3B**, **2D** to **4B**, **2E** to **5B**, **3E** to **5C** and **4E** to **5D**, then come up at **2G** to start the next square.

Chequer

·········· LEVEL ··········
Intermediate
·········· USES ··········
Textured fillings
·········· METHOD ··········
Alternate large cushion stitches and square tent stitch blocks
·········· MATERIALS ··········
Any canvas; any thread in one or two colours

Leave four threads between each cushion stitch

Fill in spaces with squares of tent stitch

1 Start at top left with the first cushion stitch. Make seven diagonal stitches from **1B** to **2A**, **1C** to **3A**, **1D** to **4A**, **1E** to **5A**, **2E** to **5B**, **3E** to **5C** and **4E** to **5D**. Begin the next block with **1J** to **2I** and start the next row at **6E** to **5F**.

2 Using a second colour, work squares of tent stitch (see p.139) in the spaces between the cushion stitches. Starting with **2H** to **1I**, work four stitches, then work another three rows directly below. Repeat to fill all the unworked squares.

Cross and Star Needlepoint Stitches

THIS SECTION INCLUDES all the stitches that are worked with a combination of horizontal, vertical and diagonal stitches. The various cross stitches feature two or more straight stitches that cross over each other, while the individual stitches that make up the star stitches radiate from a central point. The heavier cross variations are all worked on double canvas to give better coverage; the other stitches use single canvas. Whichever background is being used, the chosen thread should be thick enough to cover the canvas completely. This group of stitches should all be worked in a frame.

Cross 139	Plaited Gobelin 144
Diagonal Cross 139	Greek 144
Double Cross 139	Plait 145
Upright Cross 140	Fishbone 145
Diamond Cross 140	Fern 146
Smyrna Cross 140	Fir 146
Double Leviathan 141	Rhodes 147
Diagonal Tweed 141	Half Rhodes 147
Broad Cross 142	Star 148
Cross-corner Cushion 142	Eye 148
Brighton 143	Diamond Eye 149
Rice 143	Fan 149

CROSS AND STAR NEEDLEPOINT STITCHES 139

Cross

····· Other Name ·····
Berlin stitch

····· Level ·····
Easy

····· Uses ·····
Charted and printed designs; backgrounds

····· Method ·····
Individual cross stitches, worked horizontally

····· Materials ·····
Double canvas; any thread or yarn

Work each diagonal stitch over one intersection

Start at top right with two stitches from **1E** to **2D** and **1D** to **2E**. Begin the next cross at **1D** to **2C** and continue to the left. Work the first cross of the next row at **3A** to **2B** and **3B** to **2A**, then continue to the right. Repeat these two rows.

Diagonal Cross

····· Level ·····
Easy

····· Uses ·····
Backgrounds and fillings

····· Method ·····
Single cross stitches, worked in diagonal rows

····· Materials ·····
Single canvas; any thread

Stitch over two intersections

Start at bottom left. Work three crosses from **5A** to **7C** and **5C** to **7A**; **7E** to **5C** and **7C** to **5E**; **5C** to **3A** and **5A** to **3C**. Begin the next row at **1A** to **3C** and **1C** to **3A**, and start the second cross at **3C** to **5E**. Repeat these two rows.

Double Cross

····· Level ·····
Intermediate

····· Uses ·····
Two-coloured backgrounds

····· Method ·····
Spaced cross stitches with overlapping rows of elongated crosses

····· Materials ·····
Double canvas; thin and thick thread in two colours

Work each cross over one thread intersection

Make crosses below spaces in previous row

Work second stitch of each cross in same direction

1 Start at top right, using the fine thread. Make two crosses from **2H** to **3G** and **2G** to **3H**, then **2F** to **3E** and **2E** to **3F** and continue towards the left. Begin the next row with **4C** to **5B** and **4B** to **5C** and **4E** to **5D** and **4D** to **5E**. Repeat these two rows.

2 Fill in the spaces with rows of long crosses in the thick thread, worked in alternate directions. Start with **4F** to **1G** and **4G** to **1F** and work towards the left. Begin the next row with a cross from **6A** to **3B** and **6B** to **3A** and continue towards the right.

Upright Cross

······ OTHER NAME ······
Straight cross

······ LEVEL ······
Easy

······ USES ······
Fine textured backgrounds

······ METHOD ······
Crosses worked singly in interlocking diagonal rows

······ MATERIALS ······
Any canvas; any thread

Start at top left with two crosses from **3B** to **1B** and **2A** to **2C**, and **4C** to **2C** and **3B** to **3D**; continue downwards. Start the next row with **7D** to **5D** and **6C** to **6E**, **6C** to **4C** and **5B** to **5D** and continue upwards. Repeat these two rows to fill the required area.

Diamond Cross

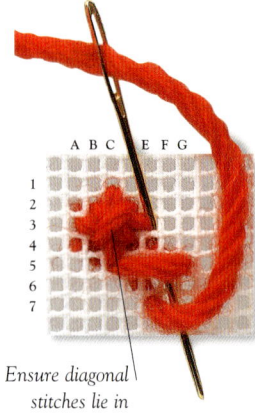

······ LEVEL ······
Intermediate

······ USES ······
Raised backgrounds and textured fillings

······ METHOD ······
Cross stitches worked over larger upright cross stitches

······ MATERIALS ······
Single canvas; any thread

Ensure diagonal stitches lie in same direction

Start at top left. Work an upright cross from **3E** to **3A** and **5C** to **1C** covered by a cross from **4D** to **2B** and **4B** to **2D**. Begin the next stitch at **5G** to **5C**, then continue working in diagonal rows.

Smyrna Cross

······ OTHER NAME ······
Leviathan stitch

······ LEVEL ······
Easy

······ USES ······
Raised backgrounds

······ METHOD ······
Upright cross worked over cross stitch

······ MATERIALS ······
Single canvas; any thread

Work stitch over five thread intersections

Always work stitches in same order

1 Start at top left with a diagonal stitch from **1A** to **5E** crossed by a second stitch from **5A** to **1E**. Bring the needle out at **5C**.

2 Make an upright stitch to **1C** and a horizontal stitch from **3A** to **3E**. Bring the needle out at **1E** to begin the next stitch, then continue working in horizontal rows.

······ TECHNIQUE VARIATION ······

Work alternate crosses in toning or contrasting colours to create an all-over chequer pattern, for a colourful background.

Double Leviathan

········· LEVEL ·········
Intermediate

········· USES ·········
Highly textured filling

········· METHOD ·········
Smyrna cross variation

········· MATERIALS ·········
Single canvas; any yarn or thread – lustrous pearl cotton gives good result

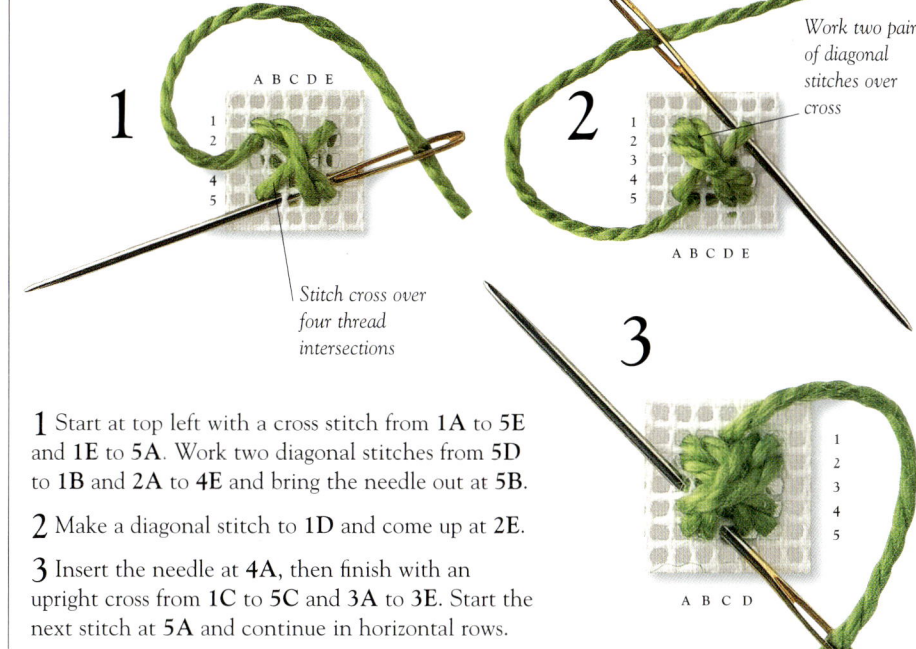

Stitch cross over four thread intersections

Work two pairs of diagonal stitches over cross

1 Start at top left with a cross stitch from **1A** to **5E** and **1E** to **5A**. Work two diagonal stitches from **5D** to **1B** and **2A** to **4E** and bring the needle out at **5B**.

2 Make a diagonal stitch to **1D** and come up at **2E**.

3 Insert the needle at **4A**, then finish with an upright cross from **1C** to **5C** and **3A** to **3E**. Start the next stitch at **5A** and continue in horizontal rows.

Diagonal Tweed

········· LEVEL ·········
Intermediate

········· USES ·········
Two-colour filling with raised surface

········· METHOD ·········
Smyrna crosses alternated with large crosses covered by small upright crosses

········· MATERIALS ·········
Single canvas; two colours of any thread

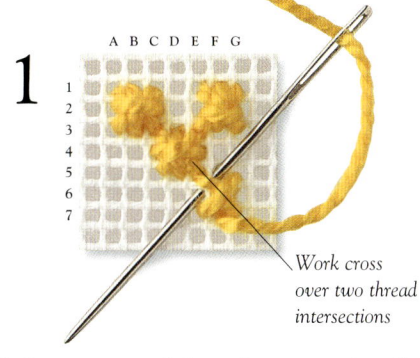

Work cross over two thread intersections

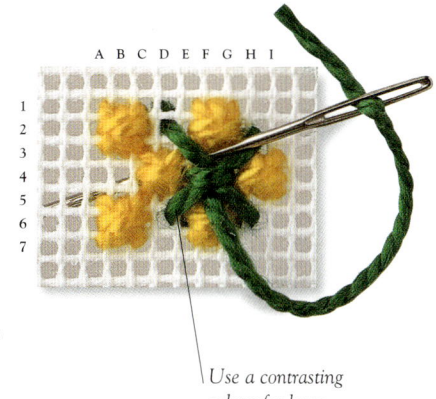

Use a contrasting colour for large double crosses

1 Starting at top left, work a series of small Smyrna cross stitches (see left). Leave two threads between each stitch and work the crosses in subsequent rows beneath these gaps.

2 Using the second thread, work a cross stitch from **6H** to **2D** and **6D** to **2H**. Make a horizontal stitch from **4E** to **4G**, then an upright stitch from **6F** to **3F**. Start the next large cross at **6D** and repeat along the row.

Broad Cross

·········· LEVEL ··········
Intermediate

·········· USES ··········
Basketweave filling for large areas

·········· METHOD ··········
Large square crosses worked in horizontal rows

·········· MATERIALS ··········
Single canvas; any thread

Work straight stitches over six thread intersections

Insert needle into base of previous row

1 Start at top left. Work a block of three upright stitches from **7C** to **1C**, **7D** to **1D** and **7E** to **1E**, crossed by three horizontal stitches from **5A** to **5G**, **4A** to **4G** and **3A** to **3G**. Begin the next block at **7I** to **1I** and continue to the end of the row.

2 The second row fits into the spaces between the crosses; begin the first block at **11F** and work subsequent rows in the same way, alternately from right to left.

Cross-corner Cushion

·········· LEVEL ··········
Intermediate

·········· USES ··········
Filling for large areas

·········· METHOD ··········
Cushion stitch variation with two layers of stitches, forming a diagonal pattern

·········· MATERIALS ··········
Single canvas; any thread – twisted embroidery cotton gives good results

Work square over five thread intersections

Work second layer of stitches at right angles to first

1 Start at top left with a square of nine graduated diagonal stitches starting at **2F** to **1E** and ending with **6B** to **5A**.

2 Work five more stitches in the opposite direction, from **1F** to **6A**, **2F** to **6B**, **3F** to **6C**, **4F** to **6D** and **5F** to **6E**.

3 Repeat steps 1 and 2 along the row, reversing every other square. Work the next and subsequent rows as a mirror image of the one above.

Brighton

· · · · · · Level · · · · · ·
Intermediate

· · · · · · Uses · · · · · ·
Dense fillings and backgrounds

· · · · · · Method · · · · · ·
Straight stitch hexagons, interspersed with contrasting upright crosses

· · · · · · Materials · · · · · ·
Single canvas; two colours of any thread

Alternate direction of diagonal stitches for each block

Work upright cross in space between diagonal stitches

1 Starting at top left, make a hexagonal block of five diagonal stitches from **1C** to **3A**, **1D** to **4A**, **1E** to **5A**, **2E** to **5B** and **3E** to **5C**.

2 Reverse the direction for the second hexagon, starting at **3I** to **1G**. Repeat these two blocks to the end of the line. Work each subsequent row as a mirror image of the one above.

3 Using a contrasting thread, work an upright cross from **4E** to **6E** and **5D** to **5F**. Repeat to fill each space.

Rice

· · · · · · Other Name · · · · · ·
William and Mary stitch

· · · · · · Level · · · · · ·
Intermediate

· · · · · · Uses · · · · · ·
Solid lattice filling

· · · · · · Method · · · · · ·
Back stitch square worked over large cross stitch

· · · · · · Materials · · · · · ·
Single canvas; one thick and one fine thread

Make each cross over five intersections

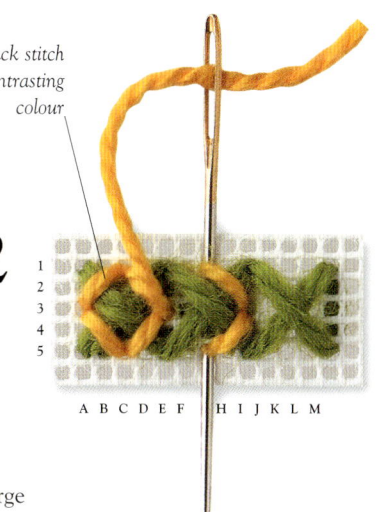

Work back stitch in contrasting colour

1 Start at top left. Using the thick thread, make a large cross stitch from **5A** to **1E** and **5E** to **1A**. Begin the next cross at **5E** to **1I** and continue along the row.

2 With the fine thread, work four back stitches over the first cross from **3E** to **5C**, **1C** to **3E**, **3A** to **1C** and **5C** to **3A**. Repeat for each cross, starting the next back stitch square at **3I** to **5G**. Work the following rows in the same way, directly below the first.

Plaited Gobelin

·········· LEVEL ··········
Easy

·········· USES ··········
Woven effect backgrounds; filling for large areas

·········· METHOD ··········
Gobelin variation, worked in overlapping rows

·········· MATERIALS ··········
Double canvas; tapestry yarn or other thick thread

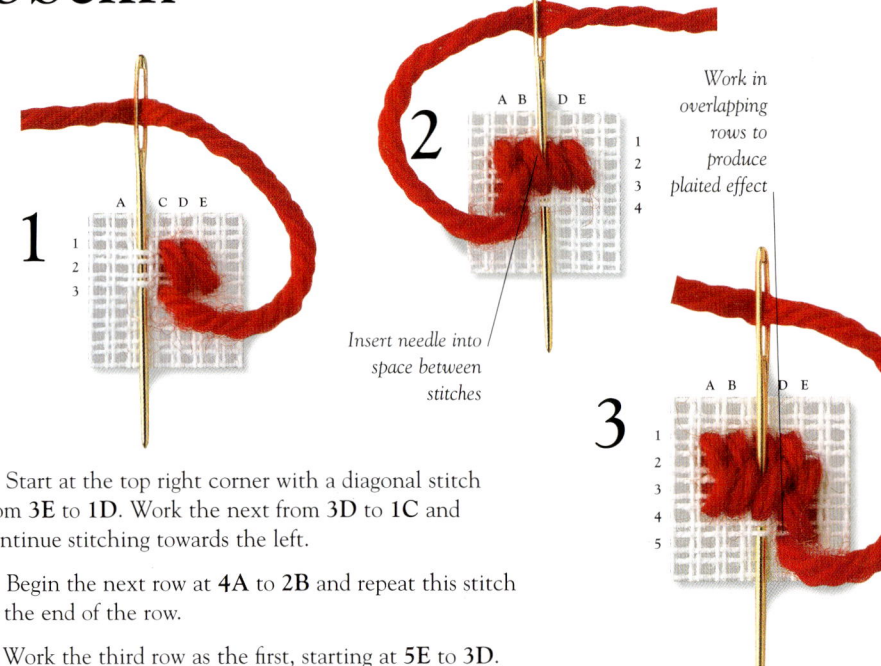

Insert needle into space between stitches

Work in overlapping rows to produce plaited effect

1 Start at the top right corner with a diagonal stitch from **3E** to **1D**. Work the next from **3D** to **1C** and continue stitching towards the left.

2 Begin the next row at **4A** to **2B** and repeat this stitch to the end of the row.

3 Work the third row as the first, starting at **5E** to **3D**. Continue working alternately to the left, then right.

Greek

·········· LEVEL ··········
Easy

·········· USES ··········
In single rows as outline; textured filling

·········· METHOD ··········
Herringbone variation, worked in horizontal rows

·········· MATERIALS ··········
Double canvas; any thick thread

Work alternate long and short diagonal stitches

1 Start at top left. Make a short stitch from **1C** to **3A**, then a long stitch from **1A** to **3E**. Come up at **3C**.

2 Make a short stitch to **1E**, then continue working alternate long and short stitches to the end of the line.

3 Work the second row in the opposite direction starting with **5G** to **3E** and **3G** to **5C**. Repeat these two rows to continue.

CROSS AND STAR NEEDLEPOINT STITCHES   145

Plait

- **Level** — Easy
- **Uses** — Solid ridged backgrounds, in single row as outline
- **Method** — Rows of overlapping straight stitches
- **Materials** — Double canvas; any thick thread

Work stitches in pairs

Work long stitch across short stitch

Come up at base of first stitch

1 Start at top left with a diagonal stitch from **3B** to **1A**, crossed by a longer stitch from **3A** to **1C**. Come out at **3C** to start the next pair of stitches.

2 Work a short stitch up to **1B** and come out at **3B**. Continue working pairs of stitches to the end of the line, then stitch the second and subsequent rows directly below the first.

TECHNIQUE VARIATION

Plait stitch can also be worked in vertical rows, depending on the effect required and the shape of the area to be filled.

Fishbone

- **Level** — Intermediate
- **Uses** — Textured chevron filling for large areas
- **Method** — Diagonal stitches worked in alternate directions in vertical rows
- **Materials** — Double canvas; tapestry yarn or other thick thread

Work first row upwards

Work short stitch across top of long stitch

Make long stitch over three intersections

1 Start at bottom left. Make a long diagonal stitch from **7A** to **4D** and a short stitch from **4C** to **5D**. Come up at **6A** and repeat these two stitches to the end of the row.

2 Work the second row downwards. Make the first two stitches from **1D** to **4G** and **4F** to **3G**, then come up at **2D**. Repeat steps 1 and 2 to fill the required area.

TECHNIQUE VARIATION

Repeat step 1 only to vary the surface of the stitch and work the rows in alternate light and dark colours to make a pattern of bold ridged vertical stripes.

Fern

········ LEVEL ········
Easy

········ USES ········
Ridged fillings and backgrounds

········ METHOD ········
Pairs of overlapping diagonal stitches worked in vertical rows

········ MATERIALS ········
Double canvas; any thick thread or yarn

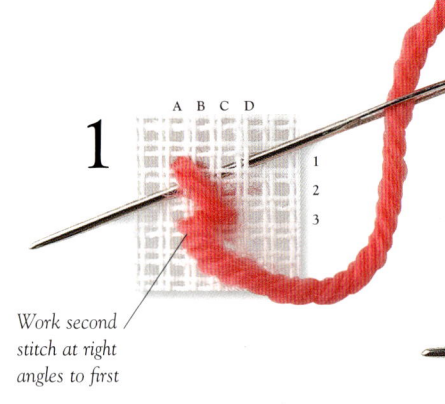

Work second stitch at right angles to first

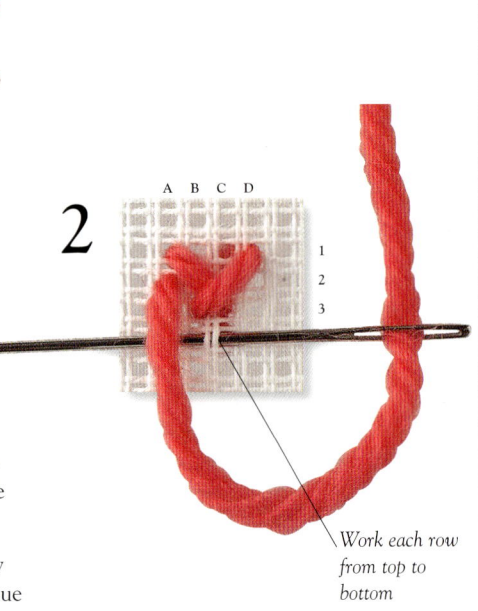

Work each row from top to bottom

1 Start at top left. Make two diagonal stitches from **1A** to **3C** and **3B** to **1D**. Bring the needle out at **2A** ready to start the next stitches.

2 Work the next pair of stitches directly below the first, from **2A** to **4C** and **4B** to **2D**. Continue working downwards to the end of the row. Start the next row at **1D**.

Fir

········ OTHER NAME ········
Leaf stitch

········ LEVEL ········
Intermediate

········ USES ········
Filling for large areas

········ METHOD ········
Interlocking rows of hexagonal blocks

········ MATERIALS ········
Any canvas; any thread

Work second side as mirror image of first

Make eleven straight stitches for each block

1 Start at top left with an upright stitch from **1D** to **5D**. Work three slanting stitches from **2C** to **5D**, **3B** to **6D** and **4A** to **7D**. Make two more stitches directly below, from **5A** to **8D** and **7A** to **9D**. Come up at **2E**.

2 Make six stitches to mirror step 1 from **2E** to **5D**, to **7G** to **9D**. Start the second block with **1J** to **5J** and continue working to the right. Stitch the next row into the spaces below the first.

········ TECHNIQUE VARIATION ········

Work an upright stitch from **5D** to **9D** to vary the leaf shape and stitch the rows in two contrasting colours to create a striped filling.

Cross and Star Needlepoint Stitches 147

Rhodes

·········· Level ··········
Intermediate

·········· Uses ··········
3-dimensional fillings or background

·········· Method ··········
Raised square stitch worked in straight rows

·········· Materials ··········
Single canvas; any thread

Work stitches anti-clockwise

Make ten slanting stitches to form square

Ensure each block is worked in same order

1 Start at top left and work four diagonal stitches from **6A** to **1F**, **6B** to **1E**, **6C** to **1D** and **6D** to **1C**. Come up at **6E**.

2 Work another two stitches from **6E** to **1B**, and **6F** to **1A**. Insert the needle at **1B**, then come up at **4F**.

3 Make three more stitches to complete the square from **4F** to **3A**, **3F** to **4A** and **2F** to **5A**. Come up at **6F**, ready to make the next block. Work the following rows directly below.

Half Rhodes

·········· Level ··········
Intermediate

·········· Uses ··········
Striped raised filling for large areas or backgrounds

·········· Method ··········
Rhodes stitch variation worked in diagonal rows

·········· Materials ··········
Single canvas; any thread in one or two colours

Stitch each block in same direction

Work the second row into the spaces below the first

1 Start at top left. Make five overlapping straight stitches from **5A** to **1E**, **5B** to **1D**, **5C** to **1C**, **5D** to **1B** and **5E** to **1A**. Come up at **7D** to make the next block, then continue working downwards to the right.

2 Stitch the second row in a different colour, starting at **9A** to **5E**. Work the next and subsequent rows directly below the first.

Star

····· Other Name ·····
Algerian eye stitch

········· Level ·········
Intermediate

········· Uses ·········
Fine textured filling

········ Method ········
Straight stitch stars worked in horizontal rows

······· Materials ·······
Single canvas; thick thread

Always insert needle into same hole

Work second star to right of first

1 Start at top left with four straight stitches from **1E** to **3C**, **1C** to **3C**, **1A** to **3C** and **3A** to **3C**.

2 Work four more stitches to complete the star, from **5A** to **3C**, **5C** to **3C**, **5E** to **3C** and **3E** to **3C**. Begin the next star at **1E** and repeat steps 1 and 2 to continue. Work the next row directly below.

Eye

········· Level ·········
Intermediate

········· Uses ·········
Large scale filling

········ Method ········
Square blocks of straight stitch with open centres, outlined with back stitch

······· Materials ·······
Single canvas; thick thread; embroidery scissors

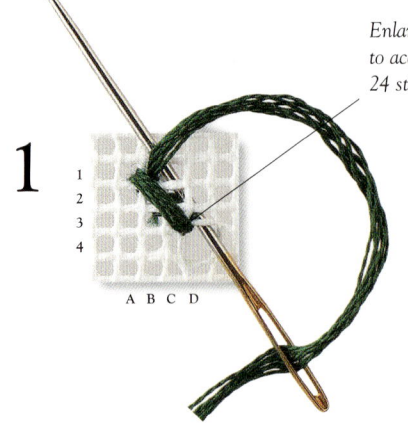

Enlarge centre hole to accommodate 24 stitches

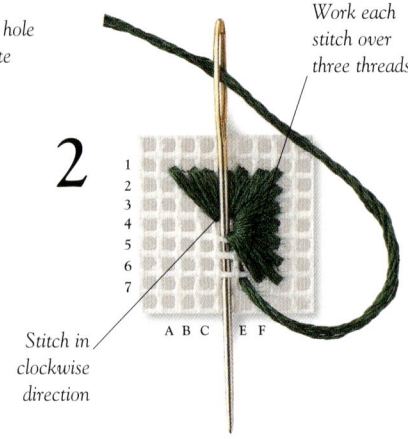

Work each stitch over three threads

Stitch in clockwise direction

1 Start at top left. Enlarge the hole at **4D** by carefully twisting the scissor point between the canvas threads. Work two straight stitches from **1A** to **4D** and **1B** to **4D**.

2 Make eleven more stitches into **4D**, starting from **1C**, **1D**, **1E**, **1F**, **1G**, **2G**, **3G**, **4G**, **5G**, **6G** and **7G**. Work the second half as a mirror image of the first, then start the next block at **1G**. Finish off by outlining each square with back stitch (see p.40), worked over one thread.

······· Technique Variation ·······

The back stitch outline stitch can be worked in a contrasting colour to create a square grid pattern across the canvas.

Cross and Star Needlepoint Stitches

Diamond Eye

······· LEVEL ·······
Advanced

······· USES ·······
Geometric background or filling for large areas

······· METHOD ·······
Straight stitch diamonds with open centres, outlined in back stitch

······· MATERIALS ·······
Single canvas; thick thread

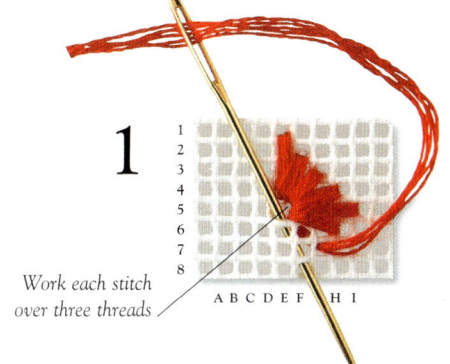

Work each stitch over three threads

Always insert needle into same hole

1 Start at top left with an upright stitch from **1E** to **5E**. Make seven more stitches into the same hole from **2F**, **3G**, **4H**, **5I**, **6H**, **7G**, **8F** and **9E**, then work the second half of the diamond as a mirror image of the first.

2 Work the next block in the same way, starting with **5I** to **9I**, and stitch the next row directly below the first. When the area is complete, outline each diamond with back stitch (see p.40) worked over one thread, to conceal any canvas that may show through.

Fan

······· OTHER NAME ·······
Ray stitch

······· LEVEL ·······
Easy

······· USES ·······
Fine textured filling

······· METHOD ·······
Blocks of radiating stitches, worked in horizontal rows

······· MATERIALS ·······
Single canvas; thick thread

Insert the needle at same point for every stitch

Work stitches in opposite direction to first row

1 Starting at bottom left, make an upright stitch from **4A** to **7A**. Work six more stitches into the same hole, from **4B**, **4C**, **4D**, **5D**, **6D** and **7D**, to form a square. Start the next block at **4D** to **7D** and continue working towards the right.

2 Work the next row directly above the first and stitch in the opposite direction, starting at **1G** to **4G**. Repeat steps 1 and 2 to continue.

Looped and Tied Needlepoint Stitches

THIS GROUP INCLUDES some of the most advanced and interesting stitches, which can be used when unusual textures and multi-coloured patterns are required. The looped Rya and Turkey stitches, traditionally used for rugs, are ideal for stitching raised areas within a design and can be trimmed to give a plush finish. The tied and twisted stitches consist of long, straight stitch held down with shorter stitches to give a dense, ridged surface. All the stitches in this section should be worked in a frame on single canvas. Ensure that the thread or yarn used covers all of the background threads.

Rya **151**	Old Wheatsheaf **153**
Turkey **151**	Tied Gobelin **154**
Houndstooth **152**	French **154**
Knitting **153**	Pineapple **155**
Arrow **155**	

Rya

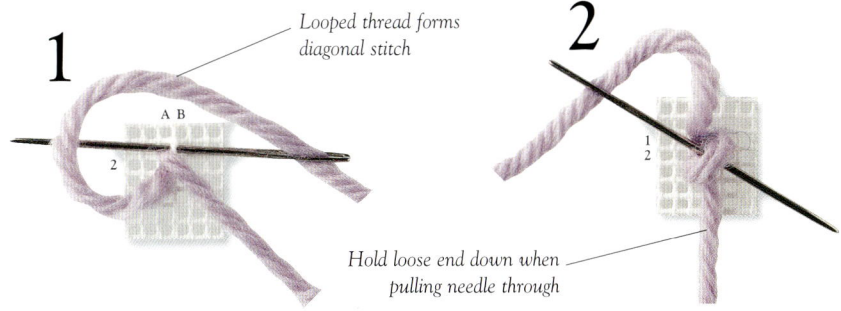

Looped thread forms diagonal stitch

Hold loose end down when pulling needle through

.... Level ....
Advanced

.... Uses ....
Looped or cut pile stitch
for carpet-like texture

.... Method ....
Looped stitch worked
over knitting needle in
horizontal rows

.... Materials ....
Single canvas; thick thread

1 Start at bottom left. Take the needle down at **1A** and bring it through at **2A**, leaving a short tail. Insert at **1B** and come back out at **1A**.

2 Pass the needle back under the diagonal loop and pull both ends tightly. Hold the knitting needle below the stitches and take the thread over and under it to form a loop.

3 Repeat steps 1 and 2 to continue, starting the second stitch at **1B**. Work the next and subsequent rows directly above the first. Trim the pile if a tufted effect is required.

Turkey

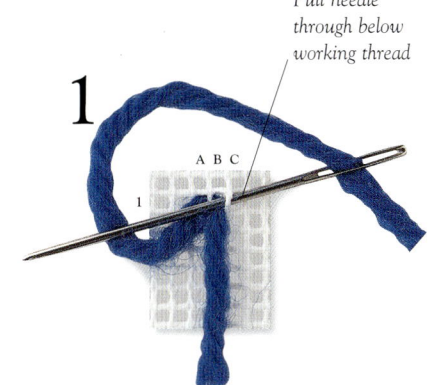

Pull needle through below working thread

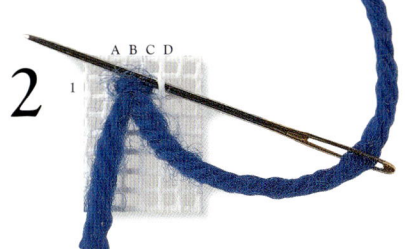

Keep loops same length

Hold loop down while making next stitch

.... Other Name ....
Ghiordes knot stitch

.... Level ....
Advanced

.... Uses ....
Tufted filling; background

.... Method ....
Looped stitch, with cut pile

.... Materials ....
Single or rug canvas; thick
thread or yarn

1 Start at bottom left. Insert the needle at **1B** and bring it out at **1A**. Take it down at **1C** and come out again at **1B**.

2 Repeat step 1, starting at **1D**. Leave a loop of thread between the stitches.

3 Continue working towards the right, ensuring the loops are the same length. Work each following row one space above. When the stitching is complete, cut and trim the loops to create a pile.

Houndstooth

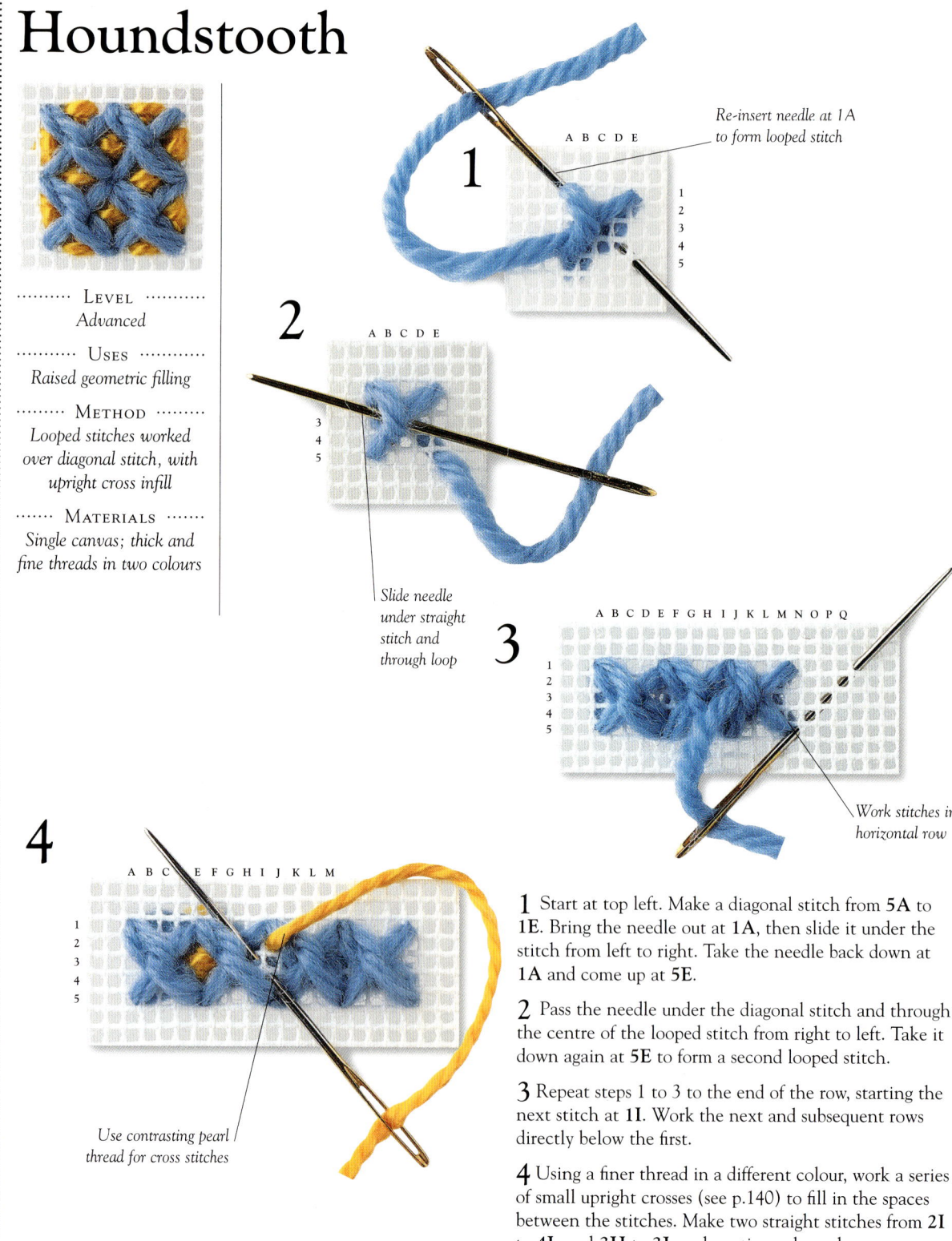

Level
Advanced

Uses
Raised geometric filling

Method
Looped stitches worked over diagonal stitch, with upright cross infill

Materials
Single canvas; thick and fine threads in two colours

Re-insert needle at 1A to form looped stitch

Slide needle under straight stitch and through loop

Work stitches in horizontal row

Use contrasting pearl thread for cross stitches

1 Start at top left. Make a diagonal stitch from **5A** to **1E**. Bring the needle out at **1A**, then slide it under the stitch from left to right. Take the needle back down at **1A** and come up at **5E**.

2 Pass the needle under the diagonal stitch and through the centre of the looped stitch from right to left. Take it down again at **5E** to form a second looped stitch.

3 Repeat steps 1 to 3 to the end of the row, starting the next stitch at **1I**. Work the next and subsequent rows directly below the first.

4 Using a finer thread in a different colour, work a series of small upright crosses (see p.140) to fill in the spaces between the stitches. Make two straight stitches from **2I** to **4I** and **3H** to **3J**, and continue along the row.

Knitting

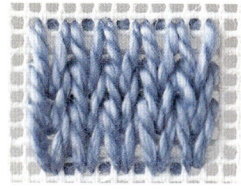

- **Level** — Easy
- **Uses** — Filling resembling knitted stocking stitch
- **Method** — Overlapping diagonal stitches worked vertically in alternate directions
- **Materials** — Single canvas; any thread

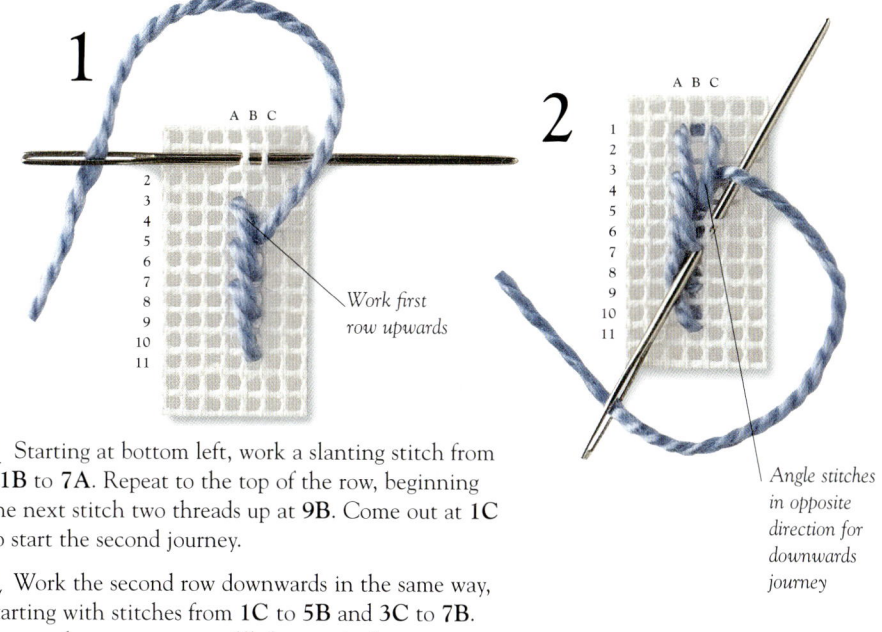

1 Starting at bottom left, work a slanting stitch from **11B** to **7A**. Repeat to the top of the row, beginning the next stitch two threads up at **9B**. Come out at **1C** to start the second journey.

2 Work the second row downwards in the same way, starting with stitches from **1C** to **5B** and **3C** to **7B**. Repeat these two steps to fill the required area.

Old Wheatsheaf

- **Level** — Advanced
- **Uses** — In single row as border; filling for large areas
- **Method** — Sheaf filling variation with contrast interlacing
- **Materials** — Single canvas; any thread in two contrasting colours

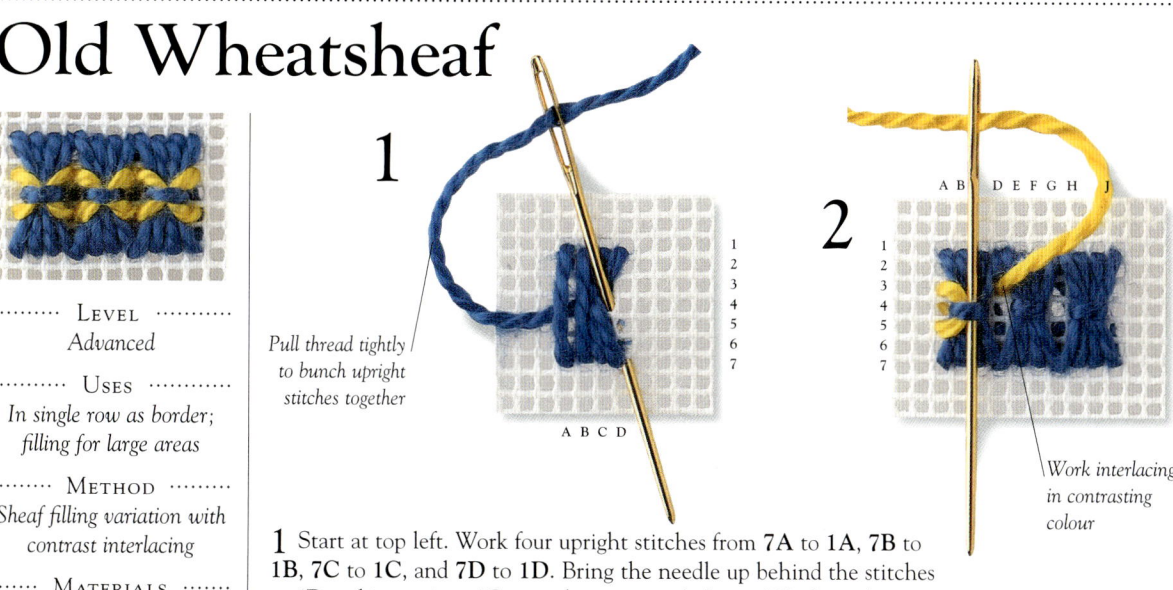

1 Start at top left. Work four upright stitches from **7A** to **1A**, **7B** to **1B**, **7C** to **1C**, and **7D** to **1D**. Bring the needle up behind the stitches at **4B** and insert it at **4C** to make a tie stitch (see p.20). Start the next sheaf at **7D** to **1D**. Work the following rows directly below the first.

2 Using the second thread, bring the needle up at **3A**. Slide it downwards under the tie stitch, and insert at **5A**. Come up at **3D**, pass the needle under the tie stitch again, and take it down at **5D**. Lace each sheaf in the same way.

Tied Gobelin

····· Other Names ·····
Knotted stitch

········ Level ········
Intermediate

········· Uses ·········
Filling with ridged texture

········ Method ········
Horizontal rows of interlocking tied diagonal stitches

······· Materials ······
Single canvas; any thread

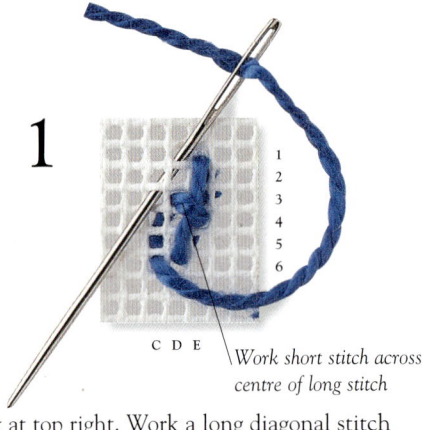

Work short stitch across centre of long stitch

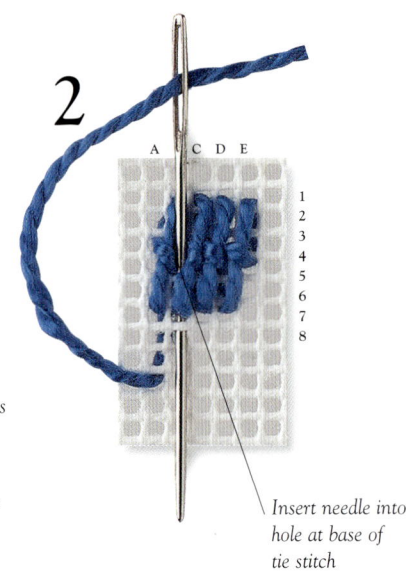

Insert needle into hole at base of tie stitch

1 Start at top right. Work a long diagonal stitch from **6D** to **1E**, crossed by a short stitch from **4E** to **3D**. Make the next pair of stitches from **6C** to **1D** and **3C** to **4D**, and continue working to the left.

2 The next row is stitched in the opposite direction. Work the first two stitches from **9A** to **4B** and **7B** to **6A** and repeat to the end of the row. Repeat these two rows to fill the required area.

French

········ Level ········
Intermediate

········· Uses ·········
Textured, ridged filling or background

········ Method ········
Pairs of tied upright stitches worked in horizontal rows

······· Materials ······
Single canvas; any thread

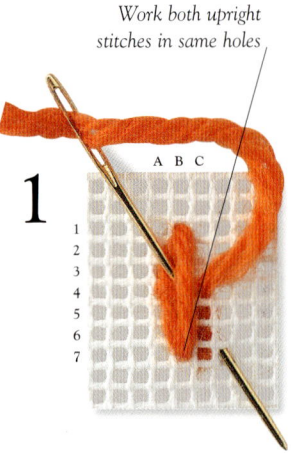

Work both upright stitches in same holes

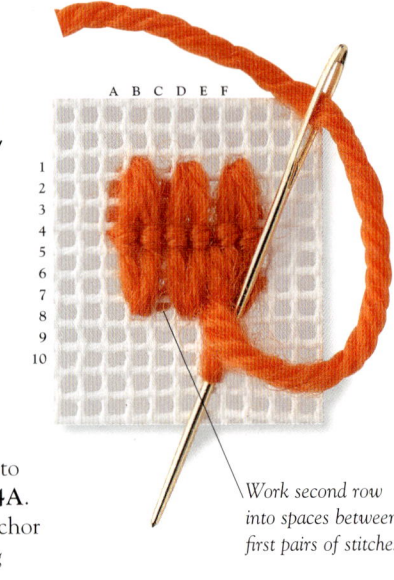

Work second row into spaces between first pairs of stitches

1 Start at top left. Make an upright stitch from **7B** to **1B** held down by a tie stitch (see p.20) from **4B** to **4A**. Work a second upright stitch from **7B** to **1B** and anchor it with a tie stitch from **4C** to **4B**. Continue making pairs of tied stitches to the end of the row.

2 Work the next row in the opposite direction, starting with an upright stitch from **10E** to **4E** and a tie stitch from **7E** to **7F**. Repeat these two rows to continue.

LOOPED AND TIED NEEDLEPOINT STITCHES 155

Pineapple

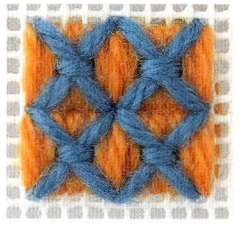

.... LEVEL ....
Advanced

.... USES ....
Two-coloured geometric filling for large areas

.... METHOD ....
Tied cross stitches worked over upright Gobelin stitch

.... MATERIALS ....
Single canvas; any thread in two colours

Work upright stitches in a multiple of five

Work tie stitch over cross

Insert needle between upright stitches

1 Start at top left and work a row of upright Gobelin stitch (see p.119) starting at **5A** to **1A**. Using the second thread, make a diagonal stitch from **5A** to **1E** and come out at **5E**.

2 Insert the needle at **1A** to complete the cross, then make a horizontal tie stitch (see p.20) from **3B** to **3D**. Continue working crosses along the row, then work subsequent rows directly below.

Arrow

.... LEVEL ....
Intermediate

.... USES ....
Textured filling; in single rows as a border

.... METHOD ....
Angled variation of sheaf filling, worked in rows

.... MATERIALS ....
Single canvas; any thread

Work upright stitches over four threads

Pull thread up tightly to draw stitches to right

1 Starting in the top left corner, work three upright stitches from **5A** to **1A**, **5B** to **1B**, and **5C** to **1C**. Bring the needle out at **3D** and slide it under the three stitches from right to left.

2 Take the needle back down at **3D** and bring it out at **5C**, ready to make the next upright stitch. Repeat steps 1 and 2 to continue, and work the following rows directly below the first.

Index

A

Aida cloth, 13
Algerian eye stitch, 31, 102
  see also star stitch
alternating stem stitch, *see* cable stitch
antique hem stitch, 31, 105
Antwerp edging stitch (knotted blanket stitch), 32, 112
  with interlacing, 108
appliqué, 56
arrow stitch, 35, 155
arrowhead stitch, 27, 73
Assisi stitch, *see* double running stitch
Assisi work, 39
attached fly stitch (fishbone stitch), 29, 89

B

back stitch, 8, 24, 40
  double back stitch, *see* closed herringbone stitch
  with needlepoint, 133
  outlining shadow stitch, 52
  threaded back stitch, 24, 40
backstitched herringbone stitch, 27, 66
back stitch rings, 31, 102
back stitched seeding, *see* dot stitch
back stitch trellis, 8, 30, 92
bands, 6, 39, 86
  drawn thread work, 106–107
  woven, 13
bargello stitch (Florentine stitch; flame stitch), 33, 121
bars, needleweaving (woven), 32, 110
basket filling stitch, 33, 127
basket stitch, 25, 53
basketweave pattern, 142
basketweave tent stitch (Continental stitch; diagonal tent stitch), 33, 129
bead edging stitch, *see* rosette chain stitch
beaded stitch, *see* coral stitch
beginning to stitch, 18
Berlin stitch, *see* cross stitch
Berlin wools, 6
berry stitch, 28, 80
Binca, 13
blackwork, 39, 74
blanket stitch (open buttenhole stitch), 26, 58
with braided interlacing, 63
knotted blanket stitch, *see* Antwerp edging stitch
blocking needlepoint, 21, 128
Bokhara couching, 90
border stitches, 48–61
  chevron, 31, 107
  composite, 6269
  diamond, 31, 107
  Italian, 31, 106
Bosnian stitch, 25, 49
braided interlacing, 63
briar stitch, *see* feather stitch
brick and cross stitch, 29, 85
brick filling, 33, 126
brick stitch (long and short brick stitch), 33, 127
  double (double gobelin filling), 33, 126
Brighton stitch, 34, 143
broad chain stitch (reversed chain stitch), 24, 45
broad cross stitch, 34, 142
Broderie Anglaise, 111, 115
bullion knot (caterpillar stitch), 28, 76
butterfly chain stitch, 27, 68
buttonhole eyelet, 32, 115
buttonhole filling stitch (buttonhole shading stitch), 29, 87
buttonhole insertion stitch (buttonhole faggot stitch), 32, 109
buttonhole stitch, 26, 58
  closed, 26, 58
  laced (threaded), 26, 63
  open, *see* blanket stitch
  ring picot edge, 114
  scalloped edge, 114
  up and down, 26, 59
  wheel, 28, 82
Byzantine stitch (step stitch), 34, 133

C

cable chain stitch, 24, 45
cable stitch (alternating stem stitch; side-to-side stem stitch), 24, 41
canvas, 13
  binding edges, 17
  mounting, 17
  printed, 129, 139
  working stitches, 19
canvas stem stitch, 33, 131
cashmere stitch, 34, 132
caterpillar stitch, *see* bullion knot
centipede stitch, *see* loop stitch
chain stitch (*point de chainette;* tambour stitch), 8, 24, 44
  broad (reversed), 24, 45
  butterfly, 27, 68
  cable, 24, 45
  detached, *see* link stitch
  feathered, *see* chained feather stitch
  magic (chequered; two-coloured), 26, 64
  pendant, *see* petal stitch
  raised (raised chain band), 27, 68
  rosette (bead edging stitch), 25, 55
  Russian, 25, 54
  Singalese, 26, 64
  square (open; Roman; ladder stitch), 24, 44
  threaded, 26, 65
  tie stitches, working, 20
  twisted, 24, 44
  zigzag (Vandyke) 25, 55
chained feather stitch (feathered chain stitch), 26, 61
chalk pencil, 12
charted patterns, 39, 50
  needlepoint, 129, 139
chequer stitch, 137
chequered chain stitch, *see* magic chain stitch
chequers, 123, 136, 140
chevron border stitch, 31, 107
chevron stitch:
  as border stitch, 25, 49
  half, 32, 113
  needlepoint stitch, 33, 122
  raised, 26, 66
Chinese stitch, *see* Pekinese stitch
close Cretan stitch, 89
close fly stitch, 89
closed buttonhole stitch, 26, 58
closed feather stitch, 26, 60
closed herringbone stitch (double back stitch), 25, 52
cloud filling stitch (Mexican stitch) 30, 93
cobbler filling stitch, 30, 100
composite stitches:
  base stitches, 39, 40, 52
  border stitches, 62–69
  outline stitches, 38
Continental stitch, *see* basketweave tent stitch
coral stitch (beaded stitch; knotted stitch; snail trail), 24, 43
  single, *see* feather stitch
corded clusters, 32, 110
cordonnet stitch, *see* whipped running stitch
cotton fabrics, 13, 17, 111
cotton threads, 14
couched filling stitch, 29, 91
couching, 7, 24, 42
  Bokhara couching, 90
  Romanian couching, 29, 90
  satin couching (trailing stitch), 42
  spiral couching, 29, 90
  stitches, 44, 50
  tie stitches, working, 20
counted thread work, 13, 47
  working stitches, 20
Cretan insertion stitch, 31, 108
Cretan stitch (Cretan filling stitch), 29, 89
  close, 89
  open 26, 59
crewel stitch, *see* stem stitch
crewel wool, 14
crewel work, 93
cross-corner cushion, 34, 142
cross stitch (Berlin stitch; sampler stitch), 7, 8
  border stitch, 25, 50
  broad, 34, 142
  diagonal, 34, 139
  diamond, 34, 140
  double, 34, 139
  half, 33, 129
  long-armed (long-legged; plaited Slav stitch), 25, 51
  needlepoint stitch, 34, 139
  Russian, *see* herringbone stitch
  St George (upright), 27, 73
  Smyrna (Leviathan stitch), 34, 140
  upright (straight), 34, 140
  working, 50
  woven, 27, 75
crown stitch, 28, 78
cushion stitch, 8, 34, 136
  cross-corner, 43, 142
  straight, 33, 123
cut pile stitches, 7, 150, 151
cutwork:
  reinforcing, 29
  stitches, 58, 111–115

D

damask stitch, *see* darning stitch; satin stitch

INDEX

Danish knot, 28, 77
darning in, 18
darning stitch (damask stitch), 29, 85
  double, 29, 85
  Japanese, 30, 92
detached chain stitch, *see* link stitch
detached wheatear stitch (ox-head stitch; *tete-de-boeuf* stitch), 28, 81
diagonal cross stitch, 34, 139
diagonal mosaic stitch, *see* Florence stitch
diagonal needlepoint stitches, 20, 21, 128–137
diagonal raised band, 30, 99
diagonal satin filling stitch, 31, 101
diagonal stitch, 34, 133
diagonal tent stitch, *see* basketweave tent stitch
diagonal tweed stitch, 34, 141
diagonal woven band, 27, 69
diamond border stitch, 31, 107
diamond cross stitch, 34, 140
diamond eye stitch, 35, 149
diamond eyelet, outlined, 31, 103
diamond stitch, 33, 124
  Scottish, 33, 123
dot stitch (backstitched seeding), 27, 73
double back stitch, *see* closed herringbone stitch
double brick stitch (double gobelin filling), 33, 126
double cross stitch, 34, 139
double darning stitch, 29, 85
double feather stitch (thorn and briar stitch), 26, 61
double gobelin filling, *see* double brick stitch
double herringbone stitch (Indian herringbone stitch), 27, 67
double knot stitch (Old English knot stitch; Palestrina stitch; Smyrna stitch), 24, 43
double Pekinese stitch, *see* interlacing band
double running stitch (Assisi stitch; Holbein stitch), 39
double twill stitch, 32, 121
drawn thread work, 13
  fabrics for, 21
  needles for, 15
  pulling out threads, 21
  stitches, 104–107, 110
dressmaker's pencils and pens, 12

E

edge stitch, looped, 32, 113
edges:
  finishing stitches, 58, 113–114
  neatening, 17
  ring picot, 32, 114
  scalloped, 32, 114
edging stitch:
  Antwerp (knotted blanket stitch), 32, 112
  sailor, 32, 112
edging stitches, 111–115
embroidery hoop, 16
  mounting fabric, 17
  preparing inner ring, 16
embroidery threads, 14
encroaching gobelin stitch, 33, 130
encroaching satin stitch, 29, 86
ending thread, 18
equipment, 12
ermine stitch, 27, 74
evenweave fabric, 13
  for drawn thread work, 21, 104
  needles for, 15
eye stitch, 35, 148
  diamond, 35, 149
eyelets, 111
  buttonhole, 32, 115
  outlined diamond, 31, 103
  overcast, 32, 115
  square, 32, 115

F

fabric, 13
  preparing, 17
faggot bundles, 31, 108
faggoting, *see* insertion stitches
fan stitch (ray stitch), 35, 149
feather stitch (briar stitch; single coral stitch), 26, 60
  chained (feathered chain stitch), 26, 61
  closed, 26, 60
  double (thorn and briar stitch), 26, 61
  single, 36, 58
felt, 13
fern stitch (fern leaf stitch), 8
  border stitch, 25, 48
  needlepoint stitch, 35, 146
filling stitch, gobelin, 32, 119
filling stitches, 71–93
  open/solid, 84–93
  powdered/isolated, 72–83
  working, 20
finishing off, 21
fir stitch (leaf stitch), 35, 146
fishbone stitch, 35, 145
  open, 29, 88
  see also attached fly stitch
fishnet stitch, *see* herringbone stitch
flame stitch, *see* bargello stitch
flat stitches, 7, 47
flat Vandyke stitch, 25, 56
Florence stitch (diagonal mosaic stitch), 33, 132
Florentine stitch, *see* bargello stitch
flower thread, 14
fly stitch (open loop stitch; Y-stitch), 28, 78
  attached (fishbone stitch), 29, 89
  close, 89
forbidden stitch, *see* Pekinese stitch
four-legged knot, 28, 77
four-sided stitch, 31, 106
frames, 16
  free-standing, 16, 19
  mounting techniques, 17
freestyle embroidery, 13, 20
French knot, 15, 27, 76
French stitch, 35, 154

G

geometric designs, 50
  bands, 39, 84
  borders, 67
  filling stitches, 85, 86, 92
  needlepoint, 118, 123, 125
Ghiordes knot stitch, *see* Turkey stitch
gingham, 13
gobelin filling, 32, 119
  double, *see* double brick stitch
gobelin stitch (oblique gobelin; *gros point*), 33, 130
  encroaching, 33, 130
  plaited, 35, 144
  reversed sloping, 33, 131
  tied (knotted stitch), 35, 154
  upright (straight), 32, 119
gold thread, 7, 83
Greek stitch, 35, 144
gros point, *see* gobelin stitch
guilloche stitch, 26, 65

H

half chevron stitch, 32, 113
half cross stitch, 33, 129
half Rhodes stitch, 35, 147
hand-held fabric, 19
hand sewing, 15, 39
Hardanger fabric, 13
hem stitch:
  antique, 31, 105
  Italian, *see* Italian border stitch
  ladder, 31, 105
  serpentine (trellis), 31, 105
  single, 31, 105
hems, decorative, 111–113
herringbone ladder stitch, *see* interlacing band
herringbone stitch (fishnet stitch; Russian cross stitch), 25, 47, 52
  backstitched, 27, 66
  closed (double back stitch), 25, 52
  double (Indian), 27, 67
  mounting fabrics, 17
Holbein stitch, *see* double running stitch
honeycomb filling stitch, 30, 98
hoop frame, *see* embroidery hoop
houndstooth stitch, 35, 153
Hungarian diamond stitch, 32, 120
Hungarian ground stitch, 33, 122
Hungarian stitch, 32, 120

I

Indian embroidery, 8, 44, 83
Indian herringbone stitch, *see* double herringbone stitch
insertion stitch, 7, 104, 108–109
  buttonhole (buttonhole faggot stitch), 32, 109
  Cretan, 31, 108
  knotted (knotted faggot stitch), 32, 109
  laced (laced faggot stitch), 31, 108
  mounting fabric, 21
interlacing, 15
  braided, 63
  composite border stitches, 62, 63, 65–67
  filling stitches, 93
  needlepoint, 153
  outline stitches, 38, 39, 40
interlacing band (double Pekinese stitch; herringbone ladder stitch), 26, 63
Italian border stitch (Italian hem stitch), 31, 106
Italian hem stitch, *see* Italian border stitch

J

Jacquard stitch, 34, 134
Japanese darning stitch, 30, 92

K

knitting stitch, 35, 153
knot stitch, *see* four-legged knot
  double (Old English knot stitch; Palestrina stitch; Smyrna stitch), 24, 43
knots, 7, 47
  bullion, (caterpillar stitch), 28, 76
  Danish, 28, 77
  four-legged (knot stitch), 28, 77
  French, 27, 76
  Palestrina, 28, 79
  raised (square boss stitch), 27, 74
knotted blanket stitch, *see* Antwerp edging stitch
knotted insertion stitch (knotted faggot stitch), 32, 109
knotted stitch, *see* coral stitch; tied gobelin

L

laced buttonhole stitch (threaded buttonhole stitch), 26, 63
laced insertion stitch (laced faggot stitch), 31, 108
  foundation stitch, 113
lacing:
  mounting on board, 21
  mounting on frame, 17
  see also interlacing
ladder hem stitch, 31, 105
ladder stitch (step stitch) 8, 26, 57
  see also interlacing band; square chain stitch
laidwork stitch, 30, 91
lattice bands, 27, 66
lattice filling, 52, 143
lazy daisy stitch, 28, 80
leaf stitch, 29, 88
  see also fir stitch
left-handed workers, 18
lettering, 38, 40, 44, 50
leviathan stitch, *see* Smyrna cross stitch
  double, 34, 141
linen, 13, 16, 111
  for drawn thread work, 21
  neatening edges, 17
link stitch (detached chain stitch), 28, 80
long and short brick stitch (brick stitch), 33, 127
long and short stitch, 29, 87
long-armed cross stitch (long-legged; plaited Slav stitch), 25, 51
long stitch triangles, 33, 124
long-tailed daisy stitch, *see* picot stitch
loop stitch (centipede stitch), 25, 56
  open, *see* fly stitch
looped edge stitch, 32, 113
looped stitches, 7, 47
  needlepoint, 151
  working, 19, 20
lost knot method, 18
lozenge stitch, 33, 125

M

magic chain stitch (chequered chain stitch; two-coloured chain stitch), 26, 62, 64
metal thread work, 42, 90
  threads, 14
Mexican stitch, *see* cloud filling stitch
Milanese stitch, 34, 135
  straight, 33, 125
mirrorwork, 83
monograms, 38, 42
Moorish stitch, 34, 135
mosaic filling stitch, 31, 101
mosaic stitch, 34, 136
  diagonal, *see* Florence stitch
mounting:
  finished work, 21, 62
  in frame, 17
  insertion stitching, 21

N

needle threader, 12, 15
needlepoint, 16
  beginning to stitch, 18
  blocking, 21, 128
  cross stitches, 138–147
  diagonal stitches, 21, 128, 137
  distortion, 21, 118, 128
  looped stitches, 150–152
  star stitches, 138, 148–149
  straight stitches, 118–127
  tied and twisted stitches, 150, 153–155
  working stitches, 18–20
needles, 15
  threading, 15
needleweaving bars (woven bars), 32, 110

O

oblique gobelin stitch, *see* gobelin stitch
old English knot stitch, *see* double knot
old wheatsheaf stitch, 35, 153
open buttonhole stitch, *see* blanket stitch
open chain stitch, *see* square chain stitch
open Cretan stitch, 26, 59
open embroidery stitches, 18
open filling stitches, 84–85, 88–89, 91–93
  working, 20
open fishbone stitch, 29, 88
open loop stitch, *see* fly stitch
open square stitch, *see* Paris stitch
openwork, 7, 95–115
  working stitches, 21
outline stitch, *see* stem stitch
outline stitches, 38–47
outlined diamond eyelet, 31, 103
overcast eyelet, 32, 115
ox-head stitch, *see* detached wheatear stitch

P

Palestrina knot, 28, 79
Palestrina stitch, *see* double knot stitch
Paris stitch (open square stitch), 25, 48
Parisian stitch, 32, 119
  with secondary pattern, 119
part stitches, 20
patchwork, 8, 60
pearl cotton threads, 14
pearl stitch, 24, 42
Pekinese stitch (Chinese stitch; forbidden stitch), 26, 63
  double, *see* interlacing band
pens and pencils, 12
perle cotton, 54, 73
Persian wool, 14
petal stitch (pendant chain stitch) 25, 54
petit point, *see* tent stitch
picot edge, ring, 32, 114
picot stitch (long-tailed daisy stitch), 28, 80
pictures, embroidered, 6, 7
pineapple stitch, 35, 155
pins, 12
pistil stitch, 27, 76
plainweave fabric, 13, 15
plait stitch (Spanish stitch), 35, 145
plaited gobelin stitch, 35, 144
plaited Slav stitch, *see* long-armed cross stitch
plush finish, 150
point de chainette, *see* chain stitch
Portuguese border stitch, 69
powdered filling stitches, 54, 72–83
  working, 20
pressing fabrics, 17, 21
pulled fabric work, 13, 15
  stitches, 96–103
pulled wave filling stitch, 30, 97
punch stitch, 30, 99

Q

quilted effect, needlepoint, 126
quilting, 38

R

raised band, diagonal, 30, 99
raised chain band (raised chain stitch), 27, 68
raised chevron stitch, 26, 66
raised knot, *see* square boss stitch
raised lattice band, 27, 66
ray stitch, *see* fan stitch
reversed chain stitch, *see* broad chain stitch
reversed sloping gobelin stitch, 33, 131
Rhodes stitch, 35, 147
  half, 35, 147
ribbed web (ribbed spider web), 28, 82
ribbon, 14
ribbon embroidery, 60
  casing stitch, 64
  foundation stitch for, 44
  ribbon rose, 28, 82
rice stitch (William and Mary stitch), 35, 143
ridged filling stitch, 30, 99
ring picot edge, 32, 114
rings, backstitched, 31, 102
Roman chain, *see* square chain stitch
Romanian couching, 29, 90
rope stitch, 8, 24, 46
rose, ribbon, 28, 82
rosette chain stitch (bead edging stitch), 25, 55
ruler, 12
running stitch, 24, 39
  beginning stitching with, 18
  double (Assisi stitch; Holbein stitch), 24, 39

INDEX

whipped (cordonnet stitch), 24, 39
Russian chain stitch, 25, 54
Russian cross stitch *see* herringbone stitch
Russian filling stitch, 30, 98
Rya stitch, 35, 150, 151

S

sailor edging stitch, 32, 112
St George cross stitch (upright cross stitch), 27, 73
sampler stitch, *see* cross stitch
samplers, 7
satin couching (trailing stitch), 24, 42
satin filling stitch, diagonal, 31, 101
satin stitch (damask stitch), 29, 86
  encroaching, 29, 86
  surface, 29, 86
  scalloped edge, 32, 114
scissors, 12
Scottish diamond stitch, 33, 123
Scottish stitch, 34, 137
scroll frame, 16, 17
scroll stitch (single knotted line stitch), 24, 46
seat covers, 129
serpentine hem stitch (trellis hem stitch), 31, 105
shaded effects, 14,
  filling stitches, 84, 87, 93
  needlepoint, 119, 131
shadow stitch, 25, 52
sheaf filling stitch, 28, 78
sheaf stitch variations, 153, 155
shears, 12
shisha stitch, 8, 28, 83
side-to-side stem stitch, *see* cable stitch
silk taffeta, 13
silk threads, 14
Singalese chain stitch, 26, 62, 64
single coral stitch, *see* feather stitch
single feather stitch, 26, 58
single hem stitch, 31, 105
single knotted line stitch, *see* scroll stitch
single twill stitch, 32, 121
skeins, 15
slipper, embroidered, 7
smocking stitches, 49, 60
Smyrna cross stitch (leviathan stitch), 34, 140
Smyrna stitch, *see* double knot stitch
snail trail, *see* coral stitch
soft cotton thread, 14
solid filling stitches, 84-87, 90-91
  padded edge, 40
  working, 20
Sorbello stitch, 28, 79
Spanish stitch, *see* plait stitch
spider webs, 28, 82
spiral couching, 29, 90
split stitch, 24, 40
square boss stitch (raised knot), 27, 74
square chain stitch (ladder stitch; open chain stitch; Roman chain), 24, 44
square eyelet, 32, 115
stabbing technique, 19
star stitch:
  as filling stitch, 27, 74
  in needlepoint (Algerian eye stitch), 35, 148
  with central cross, 74
  woven, 27, 75
stem filling stitch (stem stitch shading), 29, 87
stem stitch (crewel stitch; outline stitch), 24, 41
  alternating stem stitch, *see* cable stitch
  canvas stem stitch, 33, 131
  rope-like effect, 41
  side-to-side stem stitch, *see* cable stitch
stem stitch shading, *see* stem filling stitch
step stitch, 31, 100
  see also Byzantine stitch; ladder stitch
stitch length, 18
stitch ripper, 12
stitching techniques, 18–21
straight cross, *see* upright cross stitch
straight cushion stitch, 33, 123
straight gobelin stitch, *see* upright gobelin stitch
straight line stitch, *see* three-sided stitch
straight Milanese stitch, 33, 125
straight stitch (stroke stitch), 6, 7, 27, 73
stranded cotton, 14
stretcher frame, 16, 17
striped pattern, needlepoint, 145
striped woven band, 27, 69
stroke stitch, *see* straight stitch
surface satin stitch, 29, 86
sword stitch, 28, 77

T

tambour stitch, *see* chain stitch
tape measure, 12
tapestry needles, 15
tapestry wool, 14
tension, 18, 19
tent stitch (*petit point*) 6, 7, 33, 129
  basketweave (diagonal; Continental stitch), 33, 129
  trammed, 33, 129
tete-de-boeuf stitch, *see* detached wheatear stitch
thimble, 12
thorn and briar stitch, *see* double feather stitch
thorn stitch, 25, 50
threaded back stitch, 24, 40
threaded buttonhole stitch, *see* laced buttonhole stitch
threaded chain stitch, 26, 65
  preparing, 15
  threads, 14
  working length, 15
three-dimensional effects, 84, 87, 147
three-sided stitch (straight line stitch) 30, 97
ticking, 13
tie stitches, working, 20
tied gobelin stitch (knotted stitch), 35, 154
tied stitches, needlepoint, 150, 153–155
trailing stitch, *see* satin couching
trammed tent stitch, 33, 129
trellis, back stitched, 8, 30, 92
trellis hem stitch, *see* serpentine hem stitch
triangles, long stitch, 33, 124
tulip stitch, 28, 81
Turkey stitch (Ghiordes knot stitch), 7, 35, 150, 151
twill effect, needlepoint, 119
twill stitch, double/single, 32, 121
twisted chain stitch, 24, 44
twisted lattice band, 27, 67
twisted skeins, 14, 15
two-coloured chain stitch *see* magic chain stitch

U

up and down buttonhole stitch, 26, 59
upright cross stitch (straight cross), 34, 140
  see also St George cross stitch

upright gobelin stitch (straight gobelin stitch), 32, 119

V

Vandyke chain stitch, *see* zigzag chain stitch
Vandyke stitch, flat, 25, 57

W

wave filling stitch, 30, 93
  pulled, 30, 97
weave, marking, 17
web, ribbed, 28, 82
wheatear stitch, 25, 53
  detached (ox-head stitch; *tete-de-boeuf* stitch), 28, 81
wheel, buttonhole 28, 82
whipped running stitch (cordonnet stitch), 39
white work, 96, 111
William and Mary stitch, *see* rice stitch
window filling stitch, 8, 30, 97
wools, 14
woven band, diagonal, 27, 69
woven bands, linen, 13
woven bars, *see* needleweaving bars
woven cross stitch, 27, 75
woven spider web, 28, 82
woven star stitch, 27, 75

Y

Y-stitch, *see* fly stitch

Z

zigzag chain stitch (Vandyke chain), 25, 55
zigzag clusters, 32, 110
zigzag stitch, 25, 51

Acknowledgments

Author's acknowledgments

No writer can work in isolation, and this book would not have been possible without the joint skills of the art and editorial teams at both Dorling Kindersley and C&B Packaging. I would like to extend my thanks to all the many colleagues and friends who have contributed their experience and commitment over the past year.

I am indebted to Samantha Gray, who first suggested my name to the publishers. Nigel Duffield, Mary Lindsay, Sarah Hall, and Cathy Shilling at DK have given me every encouragement, along with their invaluable guidance and enthusiasm, from the outset.

Managing editor Kate Yeates has been my mainstay: her dedication and constant good humour have helped me through to the end of the project. Special thanks also to Roger Bristow and Helen Collins at C&B Packaging for their invaluable creative input, to Sam Lloyd for patiently photographing all the many stitch samples and to Heather Dewhurst for editing my text so meticulously.

Lis Gunner embroidered my designs for the chapter openers and gave me useful advice about stitching.

Debbie Kilby of Anything Left-Handed (Tel: 0208 770 3727) advised me on techniques for left-handed workers.

Finally, I must thank my husband Jonathan Hayden-Williams for always being there for me, and my sister Emma Ganderton and father Colin Ganderton for their unfailing support, for which I am ever grateful.

Dorling Kindersley would like to thank the following:

DMC Creative World Ltd for supplying the needles, pearl cottons, tapestry yarns, evenweave linen and canvas used to create the step-by-step examples and finished stitch samples. Thanks in particular to Cara Ackerman for all her help. For further information about DMC products contact them at: Pullman Road, Wigston, Leicestershire, LE18 2DY. Tel: 0116 281 1040.

Additional assistance

Editorial: Nicola Munro
Design: Cathy Shilling
Administration: Christopher Gordon
Additional Photography: (p.12)
Andy Crawford, Steve Gorton

Jet and Rocket Aircraft of World War 2

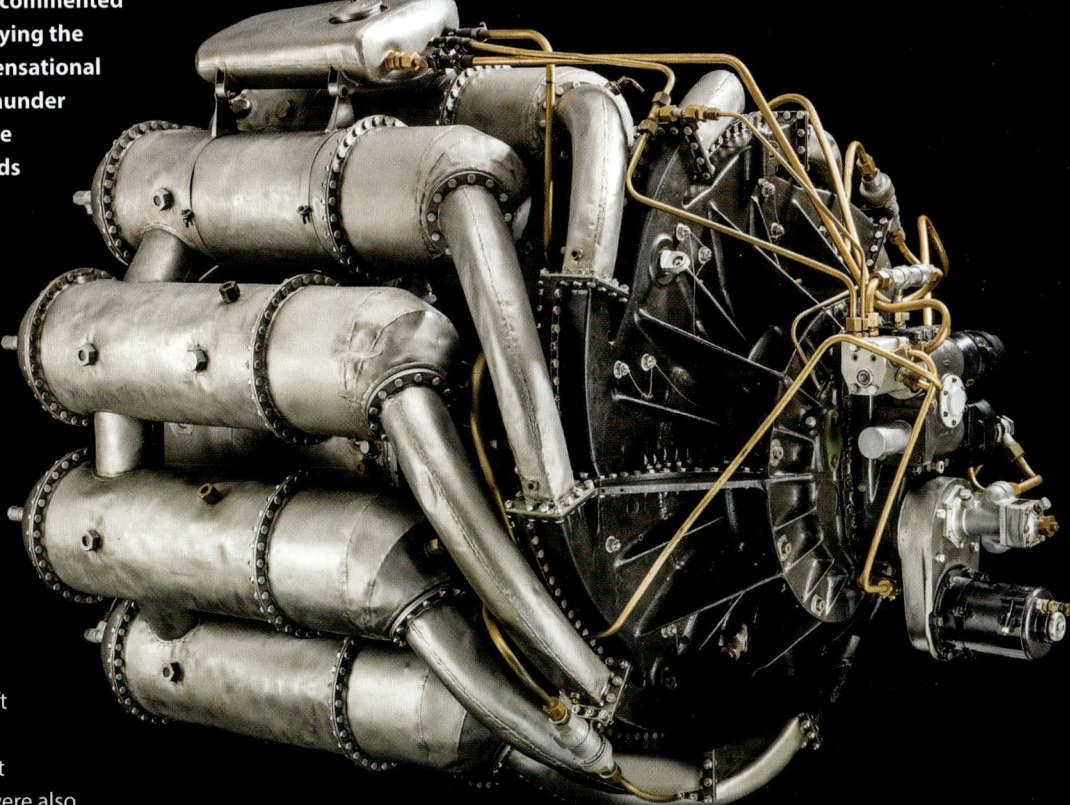

'It felt as though angels were pushing'. So commented famous Luftwaffe ace Adolf Galland on flying the world's first operational jet fighter, the sensational Messerschmitt Me 262. Indeed, when the thunder of jet engines first began to echo around the skies during World War 2, it was as if the gods themselves had entered the battle.

Forged from the technology of war, the jet engine heralded a new age in aviation, one that promised to propel man and machine to hitherto unimagined speeds. The potential was exciting, yet terrifying. Although pioneered by British inventor Frank Whittle, it was Germany that embraced the power of the jet engine, recognising that its development would be vital in winning the arms race. Initially the British were more reticent about diverting valuable resources to such an unproven concept, but soon the risk was too great to ignore. It then became a battle to get the first jet aircraft into service. It was perhaps inevitable that the resulting machines were some of the most fascinating and innovative of the war… and were also some of the most dangerous. From the fertile minds of the German designers came the likes of the rocket-powered Messerschmitt Me 163 Komet, the unique Arado Ar 234 bomber and the menacing shark-like Messerschmitt Me 262, the most numerous jet fighter of World War 2. Meanwhile, the honour of being the first operational Allied jet fell to the British Gloster Meteor, rushed into service in 1944 to counter the German threat. Meanwhile, Japan had been busy replicating German technology and applied rocket power to a more sinister means, that of Kamikaze missions. Spurred into action, the might of the American war machine also entered the 'battle of the jets', though its designs were just too late to see operational service… in this war at least.

In the event, the first generation of jet and rocket aircraft were too underpowered and too late on the scene to significantly alter the course of World War 2, but the foundations for the future had been set, and the jet engine was soon to take over the world. **Allan Burney**

AVIATION ARCHIVE SERIES

'Jet and rocket aircraft of World War 2' is No 34 in the successful Aviation Archive series. Featured are some of the most innovative and technologically challenging aircraft that were developed, flown or built during World War 2. Aircraft are listed in chronological sequence of first flight under country of manufacture. Because of space restrictions, we have excluded hybrid machines that combined propeller and jet technology. The coverage includes many exclusive and rare shots that have never been published before. The words and photographs are complemented by 'period' cutaways from the talented pens of the 'Flight' and 'Aeroplane' artists of the era, together with specially selected aircraft profiles.

Cover: **Messerschmitt Me 262 'Yellow 5', WNr501232, of 9./KG(J)6 in May 1945.**
Antonis Karidis

Aviation Archive Series
Jet and Rocket Aircraft of World War 2

- **Editor:** Allan Burney • **Design:** Philip Hempell
- **Publisher and Managing Director:** Adrian Cox • **Executive Chairman:** Richard Cox • **Commercial Director:** Ann Saundry • **Group Editor:** Nigel Price
- **Distribution:** Seymour Distribution Ltd +44 (0)20 7429 4000 • **Printing:** Warners (Midlands) PLC, The Maltings, Manor Lane, Bourne, Lincs PE10 9PH.

All rights reserved. The entire content of Aviation Archive is © Key Publishing 2017. Reproduction in whole or in part and in any form whatsoever is strictly prohibited without the prior permission of the Publisher. We are unable to guarantee the bona fides of any of our advertisers. Readers are strongly recommended to take their own precautions before parting with any information or item of value, including, but not limited to, money, manuscripts, photographs or personal information in response to any advertisements within this publication. Published by Key Publishing Ltd, PO Box 100, Stamford, Lincs PE19 1XQ. Tel: +44 (0) 1780 755131. Fax: +44 (0) 1780 757261. Website: www.keypublishing.com **ISBN:** 9781912205110

Jet and Rocket Aircraft of W

🇩🇪 GERMANY
- 6 HEINKEL He 178
- 10 HEINKEL He 280
- 12 MESSERSCHMITT Me 163
- 18 MESSERSCHMITT Me 262
- 28 ARADO Ar 234
- 34 MESSERSCHMITT Me 328
- 35 JUNKERS Ju 287
- 36 HORTEN Ho 229
- 37 FIESELER Fi 103R
- 38 HEINKEL He 162
- 44 BACHEM Ba 349 NATTER
- 46 HENSCHEL He 132
- 47 MESSERSCHMITT Me P1101

🇮🇹 ITALY
- 48 CAPRONI CAMPINI N.1

🇯🇵 JAPAN
- 50 YOKOSUKA MXY-7 OHKA
- 52 MITSUBISHI J8M SHŪSU
- 53 NAKAJIMA J1N KIKKA

🇬🇧 UNITED KINGDOM
- 54 GLOSTER E.28/39
- 58 GLOSTER METEOR
- 66 DE HAVILLAND VAMPIRE

⭐ UNITED STATES
- 72 BELL P-59 AIRACOMET
- 78 LOCKHEED P-80 SHOOTING STAR
- 84 MCDONNELL FD PHANTOM
- 86 BELL XP-83
- 88 NORTHROP XP-79B
- 92 DOUGLAS XB-43 JETMASTER

USSR
- 96 BEREZNYAK-ISAYEV BI-1

CONTENTS | 5

ld War 2

Heinkel He 178

For such a small unassuming aircraft, the historical significance of the Heinkel He 178 is immense. As the world's first aircraft to fly under the power of a jet engine, it pioneered one of the greatest technological revolutions known to mankind… and yet to this day it remains largely unheralded.

Famed German aircraft designer Professor Ernst Heinkel was passionate about high-speed flight and was keen on exploring alternative forms of aircraft propulsion. It was in 1936, that a young engineer named Hans von Ohain took out a patent on using the exhaust from a gas turbine as a means of propulsion. Hans von Ohain had started development of the turbojet engine in the early 1930s and by 1935 he had developed a test engine to demonstrate his ideas. He asked Ernst Heinkel, for support rather than approach the German engine industry. Heinkel saw the promise in von Ohain's invention and by the end of February 1937, the He S-1 turbojet engine with hydrogen fuel was tested and produced a thrust of 250lb at 10,000rpm. Although the German air ministry (Reichsluftfahrtministerium – RLM) respected Heinkel for his aircraft visions, it was not particularly interested in developing unproven technology at a time when the German nation was gearing up for total war in Europe. Therefore, Heinkel continued his jet engine initiative as a company private venture. Heinkel was so impressed with the engine tests, that he pressed for an accelerated flight engine programme. Von Ohain's team developed the He S-3 and this became the engine that would power the He 178, a single-seat, single-engine aircraft designed specifically for testing the turbojet flight concept.

Despite its ground-breaking nature, the He 178 airframe was pretty much of conventional design. The fuselage was tubular and contoured for maximum airflow. The wooden wings were high-mounted and fitted aft of the cockpit, which lay at the extreme front end of the fuselage. The tail was of traditional configuration, featuring a single vertical tail fin and a pair of horizontal tailplanes. All wing surfaces were straight in

their design and curved at their tips – save for the second prototype which, though never flown under power, showcased clipped wing tips. The undercarriage was a typical 'tail dragger' arrangement. The main landing gear was intended to be retractable into wells in the fuselage, but in the event remained fixed in the 'down' position throughout the flight trials. The engine itself was buried deep in the fuselage, being fed by a nose-mounted intake to which ductwork managed airflow to the engine. The engine exhausted through a circular nozzle at the extreme aft of the fuselage.

The first tests took place at the beginning of August 1939 and consisted of a series of taxiing trials at Rostock. During one of these tests on 24 August, the aircraft became briefly airborne. However, history records that the first proper flight took place on 27 August 1939 when test pilot Erich Warsitz took He 178 into the air, thus heralding the age of jet-powered flight. Although the take-off was textbook, it was an eventful first flight. Firstly, the undercarriage refused to retract and during the second circuit of the airfield a bird was sucked into the intake causing the engine to cut out. Fortunately, Warsitz made a safe power-off landing, thereby saving the machine.

Now that Heinkel had proven the concept of jet aircraft, he approached the RLM for support. Reluctantly the RLM agreed to a demonstration flight on 1 November 1939, watched by Ernst Udet, Erhard Milch and engineer Helmut Schelp. Although the aircraft was projected to have a top speed of 435mph, during the demonstration it did not break 200mph, owing to the basic design and limited power of its engine. The watching crowd were unimpressed and decided against diverting valuable resources to the project. However, what Heinkel did not realise was that the RLM was developing its own jet engines. In 1939, BMW was building its 003 and Junkers was working on its Jumo 004 turbojet engines. These were axial-flow turbojets and not centrifugal-flow turbojets. Axial-flow turbojets promised much higher flight speeds unlike centrifugal-flow turbojets being developed at Heinkel and by Frank Whittle in England.

In the event, the He 178 proved its worth as a technology demonstrator intended to test the viability of the new propulsion method and lay the foundation for a new breed of aircraft designs still to come. Only two of its kind were produced and both were lost to separate Allied bombing raids – the first in 1943 while under the care of the Berlin Air Museum and the second, while in storage at Rostock, in 1945.

Below: *A simple design, the technological advances of the Heinkel He 178 all lay under the skin. Despite its revolutionary powerplant, the German Air Ministry was not impressed by the aircraft's performance.*

GERMANY

*Right: **The He 178 was designed around von Ohain's third engine design, the HeS 3, which burned diesel fuel. The result was a small aircraft with a metal fuselage of conventional configuration and construction. The jet intake was in the nose, and the aircraft was fitted with a tailwheel undercarriage.***

Professor Ernst Heinkel

In 1922 Ernst Heinkel established the Heinkel-Flugzeugwerke company at Warnemunde. After Adolf Hitler came to power, Heinkel's designs formed a vital part of the Luftwaffe's growing strength in the years leading up to World War 2. This included the Heinkel He 59, the Heinkel He 115 and the iconic Heinkel He 111. Heinkel was a critic of Hitler's regime and in 1942 the government took control of his factories. At the end of the war Heinkel was arrested by the Allies but evidence of anti-Hitler activities led to his acquittal and he was allowed to re-establish his aviation company in Germany. Ernst Heinkel died in 1958.

Heinkel He 178 V5

Engine:	1 x Heinkel HeS 3 turbojet
Power:	990lb thrust
Crew:	1
Wingspan:	23ft 3in (7.2m)
Length:	24ft 6in (7.48m)
Height:	6ft 10in (2.1m)
Loaded weight:	3,572lb (1,620kg)
Max Speed:	380mph (598km/h)
Range:	125 miles (200km)
Armament:	None

HEINKEL He 178

Hans von Ohain

Born in 1911, Hans Joachim Pabst von Ohain was a German physicist who designed the first operational jet engine. His initial design ran in March 1937, and it was one of his engines that powered the world's first flyable all-jet aircraft, the Heinkel He 178 (He 178 V1) in late August 1939. In spite of these early successes, other German designs quickly eclipsed Ohain's, and none of his engine designs entered widespread production or operational use.

Left: **The He S-3 engine that powered the world's first jet aircraft.**

Below left: **Hans von Ohain leads a toast after the successful flight of the Heinkel He 178. On the left side of the image Ernst Heinkel raises his glass in celebration.**

Bottom left: **Rear fuselage details of the He 178 displaying the conventional layout of the world's most unconventional aircraft of the time.**

Below: **The He 178 V2 (note the squared-off wingtips). This particular aircraft only flew as an unpowered glider.**

Heinkel He 280

Heinkel He 280 V5

Engine:	2 x Heinkel HeS 8A turbojets
Power:	1,650lb thrust each
Crew:	1
Wingspan:	40ft (12.2m)
Length:	34ft 1in (10.4m)
Height:	10ft 0in (3.04m)
Loaded weight:	9,482lb (4,301kg)
Max Speed:	559mph (900km/h) for 30 seconds, 510mph (821km/h) maintained speed
Service Ceiling:	37,720ft (11,497m) estimated
Range:	404 miles (650km)
Armament:	3 x MG 151 20mm cannon

The story of the futuristic Heinkel He 280 could so easily have been different. Had its potential been realised from the start, it may well have become one of the most significant weapons of World War 2. Although circumstances meant that it never entered operational service, it has the distinction of being the first turbojet-powered fighter aircraft in the world.

Despite failing to impress the German air ministry (Reichsluftfahrtministerium, RLM) with his first jet aircraft, Heinkel's faith in the concept never wavered. Eventually this vision was matched by the RLM following the appointment of a young forward-looking engineer Helmut Schelp. Motivated by the threat of war and possibility of conflict with Britain, he pushed Heinkel into continuing development of the ambitious Heinkel He 280, the first jet–powered aircraft to be developed as a fighter.

The He 280 was a single-seat, twin-engine, all-metal, turbojet-powered aircraft, credited with speeds in excess of 550mph. Its twin HeS 8 turbojets were mounted beneath each wing, the latter being attached mid-fuselage and featuring straight leading edges but curved trailing edges. The armament was housed in the nose and was designed to comprise an array of six MG 151 20mm cannons, though only three were ever installed in the prototypes. The pilot sat just ahead of the main wing roots with good visibility forward, above and to the sides. A powered-tricycle landing gear was one of its notable design features, as was the tail unit which comprised of two fins and rudders mounted either side of a single elevator. The He 280 offered a compressed-air powered ejection seat, the world's first aircraft to be so equipped.

The first flight of the Heinkel He 280 V1 (DL+AS) was on 2 September 1940 as a glider, but owing to engine delays it was not fitted with its HeS 8 powerplants, which produced around 1,000lb of thrust each, until March 1941.

Top: The Heinkel He 280 on its maiden flight, with test pilot Fritz Schäfer at the controls. Note the absence of engine cowlings, that were not fitted owing to excessive fuel leak.

Above: The third Heinkel 208 prototype, V3 GJ+CB, was destroyed in a crash landing. A total of nine prototypes were produced, each with varying powerplant configurations as needed. He 280 V1 became the first aircraft to feature a live ejection when the pilot had to abandon the aircraft after the controls froze up. He 280 V4 saw the system fitted with six pulsejets whilst He 280 V5 and He 280 V6 became the first aircraft in the series fitted with three 20mm cannon armament. The He 280 V7 prototype would later become a glider for high-speed aerodynamic research and He 280 V8 was designed with a 'V' type tail unit instead of the twin fin set up.

Left: A case of what might have been. An artist's impression of the Heinkel He 280 streaking through the clouds, cannons blazing. Had the aircraft not suffered such problems with its powerplant, it could well have become the scourge of Allied bombers.

Then, on 2 April it became the world's first purpose-built jet fighter when it took to the air for the first time, in the hands of test pilot Fritz Schäfer. It was a private event carried out at under 1,000ft and with the engine cowlings removed as the powerplants had a tendency to leak fuel. Schäfer reportedly told Heinkel that the He 280 was a little difficult to control in turns, but that an experienced pilot should be able to fly it easily. He also reported the He 280 to be a little sluggish on landing but said that otherwise it handled well. Three days later, the first official flight took place in front of a distinguished crowd of RLM officials and Luftwaffe officers, including Ernst Udet. Once again interest was not overwhelming, but officials did agree that work on the jet engine should be intensified

Over the next year, progress was slow due to tail flutter and ongoing engine problems, the latter resulting in the crash landing of the third prototype which destroyed the airframe. Eventually the RLM ordered Heinkel to abandon the HeS 8 and HeS 30 to focus all development on a follow-on engine, the HeS 011, a more advanced but problematic design. Meanwhile, the first He 280 prototype was re-equipped with pulsejets and towed aloft to test them. Bad weather caused the aircraft to ice up, and before the jets could be tested, pilot Helmut Schenk became the first person to put an ejection seat to use. The seat worked perfectly, but the aircraft was lost and never found. With the HeS 011 not expected for some time, by the end of 1943 Heinkel opted for the rival BMW 003 to power prototypes 5 and 6. On 22 December, a mock dogfight was staged for RLM officials in which the He 280 was matched against an Fw 190. Here, the jet demonstrated its vastly superior speed, completing four laps of an oval course before the Fw 190 could complete three. At last, the RLM became interested and placed an order for 20 pre-production test aircraft, to be followed by 300 production machines.

However, by this time, the aircraft was competing with the Messerschmitt Me 262, an aircraft that had longer range, was more heavily equipped and was a sturdier design, though reportedly was not as agile as the Heinkel. Nevertheless, on 27 March 1943, Erhard Milch cancelled the project and Heinkel was ordered to abandon the He 280 to focus attention on bomber development and construction.

Messerschmitt Me 163

The skies over Nazi Germany, summer 1944. The Luftwaffe has detected an incoming formation of US Army Air Force 'heavies'. Some 30,000ft below the gleaming bare-metal B-17s, a diminutive swept-wing, tailless fighter ignites its volatile rocket engine and with a terrifying roar streaks down the runway. Once airborne it points its nose to the heavens and zoom-climbs high above the bomber stream. With the rocket motor now nearing the end of its fuel, the pilot scans ahead to ascertain the position of his target, and then launches into a steep dive. Tearing down through the enemy formation, the pilot unleashes a volley of 30mm cannon fire, breaking through the ranks of lumbering bombers… The futuristic interceptor in this scenario was the Messerschmitt Me163 and was arguably the most radical fighter to be put into service during World War 2.

The chief designer of the Messerschmitt Me 163, Dr Alexander Lippisch, had accumulated many years of experience in the design of tailless sailplanes, and it was from this peaceful background that he drew the inspiration for something altogether different… a rocket-propelled fighter. In 1937 the research section of the German air ministry (Reichsluftfahrtministerium, RLM) commissioned Lippisch to draft a design for an aircraft that would serve as a testbed for a new type of rocket engine, the Walter R I-203 with a rating of 400kg thrust. This engine worked on the principle of a steam generator into which the two different fuel types (T-Stoff, which consisted mainly of concentrated hydrogen peroxide, and Z-Stoff, based on a solution of calcium permanganate in water), were sprayed using compressed air. This in turn drove a turbine, which powered a pump to deliver T-Stoff to the combustion chamber. Such was the volatile nature of the rocket fuels that the pilot was outfitted in a special flying suit made of asbestos-Mipolamfibre.

Lippisch and his design team were brought within the fold of Messerschmitt in January 1939 and began work on an existing tailless research glider, to receive the rocket propulsion. In this configuration, the aircraft was flown in summer 1940. After completing a successful test campaign an order was received for six prototypes of an aircraft to be designated Me 163A. By this time a new motor was available, the improved Walter II-203b. The

Messerschmitt Me 163B-1a

Engine:	1 x Walter HWK 509A-2
Power:	3,800lb thrust
Length:	19ft 1in (5.84m)
Height:	9ft 1in (2.77m)
Wingspan:	30ft 7in (9.32m)
Max T/O weight:	9,061lb (4,110kg)
Max speed:	596mph (960km/h)
Service ceiling:	39,700ft (12,100m)
Endurance:	7min 30sec
Armament:	2 x MK 108 cannon

*Below: **The diminutive size of the Messerschmitt Me 163 is apparent in this view of BV45, C1+05 with Eprobungskommando 16, at Bad Zwischenahn, July 1944.***

Right: ***The fuselage of the Me 163 was constructed of light alloy, with the surface of the aircraft covered by numerous detachable panels in order to provide access to the various internal subsystems. The largest single internal item was the tank for the T-Stoff rocket fuel, which had a capacity of 1,040 litres. The tank was located in the space between the cockpit and the powerplant. Additional T-Stoff reserves were carried in a series of smaller tanks, which were found either side of the cockpit. Meanwhile, the C-Stoff reserve was located in a pair of 173-litre tanks between the wing spars as well as in two 73-litre tanks in the leading edges of the wing.***

company also had a yet more powerful rocket engine in the works, and Lippisch was tasked to scheme the production of the Me 163 on the basis of this. In the meantime, the six Me 163A prototypes would be powered by a modified version of the II-203b.

The first of the prototypes reverted to powerless configuration to conduct gliding tests after launch from a Bf 110. By summer 1941 however, prototypes were available with the Walter rocket engine, and these entered testing at Peenemünde. The initial Me 163A V1 proved itself capable of attaining speeds of 310mph (500km/h) on its maiden flight.

Left: ***Trailblazer – an Me 163A gaining speed soon after taking off at Peenemünde and before making its usual spectacular almost vertical climb skywards.***

Below: ***The prototype V1(A), KE + SW, taking off on a test flight from Kallshagen, Peenemünde, with the record breaking test pilot, Heini Dittmar at the controls, in September 1941. Propelled by a rocket engine fuelled by a volatile combination of chemicals, the Me 163 offered only around six minutes' of powered flight, but was capable of climbing to a height of over 30,000ft in just 2.5min.***

GERMANY

Messerschmitt Me 163, BV45, C1+05 with Eprobungskommando 16, at Bad Zwischenahn, July 1944.

Above: Rudolf Opitz being assisted into his Komet at Bad Zwischenahn. His one-piece flying suit and overboots were made from a special acid resistant material, which was supposed to protect the occupant from the corrosive T-Stoff in the far from likely event of a rough landing - assuming his aircraft did not explode.

Below: Although a relatively tight fit for a well-proportioned pilot, the cockpit was nevertheless reasonably comfortable. A hinged window was provided on the port side of the cockpit canopy, with an additional air inlet on the underside of the nose. However, there was no provision for pressurisation. The canopy itself was a less-than-robust Plexiglas moulding. Although he was not provided with an ejection seat, the pilot was afforded some protection in combat by front and back armour.

After the experience gained with the six Me 163A prototypes, Messerschmitt was authorised to complete an initial pre-production run of 10 Me 163A-0 fighters, with manufacture being undertaken under subcontract by Wolf Hirth Segelflugzeugbau. These did not yet represent the definitive operational configuration, and were instead intended for use as pilot trainers, to allow the Luftwaffe to gain experience on what was an entirely new type of interceptor.

After a significant redesign, six pre-production prototypes were ordered for the Me 163B production fighter, to be followed by the first batch of 70 series-built aircraft of the same variant. The first 70 B-models were completed at Regensburg and were used to iron out the last remaining technical and operational problems. The production aircraft were differentiated from the half-dozen prototypes by their Me 163B-1a designation. Among the modifications was a revised wing, designed to combat the threat of an uncontrolled spin, although the threat of stall remained ever-present. The definitive rocket motor was the II-211, which was fully controllable and which now used C-Stoff in place of the previous Z-Stoff. The new chemical was based on hydrazine hydrate solution in methyl alcohol. That the new fuel was no less hazardous than its predecessor was made clear when two engines exploded during testing, destroying the entire building in which they were contained.

Dubbed Komet (comet), the first of the pre-production Me 163Bs was flown in summer 1942 and by early 1943 flight testing had progressed to a stage whereby it was decided that a test squadron could be established within the Luftwaffe. The unit was to be based at Peenemünde, the nascent home of German rocket developments.

The Luftwaffe harboured ambitious plans of developing a network of interconnected fighter stations equipped with Komets, that could tackle enemy bomber streams approaching from any direction. The concept involved airfields located around 100km apart, forming a protective ring, and allowing recovering Me 163s to glide back to different bases if required. In the event, only a single unit would be equipped with Me 163s in any meaningful numbers.

It was the summer of 1944 before the Me 163 finally entered combat. Based at Brandis, near Leipzig, I./Jagdgeschwader 400 was created in May 1944, and began to receive aircraft from late July. On the 28th of that month the Komet saw action for the first time, in the first-ever operational use of a rocket-powered manned fighter. On that occasion five Me 163s were launched against a formation of B-17s. It was an inauspicious debut. The Komet pilots

Left: A direct comparison between the Me163 A and B. The photograph was taken soon after the first of the Klemm-built aircraft were delivered to Bad Zwischenahn in January 1944.

GERMANY

Messerschmitt retained a few Me 163B prototypes for test purposes at Lechfeld up to the end of September 1944. Me 163 BV6 was designated to be fitted with a pressurised cockpit, but there is no firm evidence that this was in fact carried out. BV6 was fitted with the Walter 109-509 B-1 rocket motor.

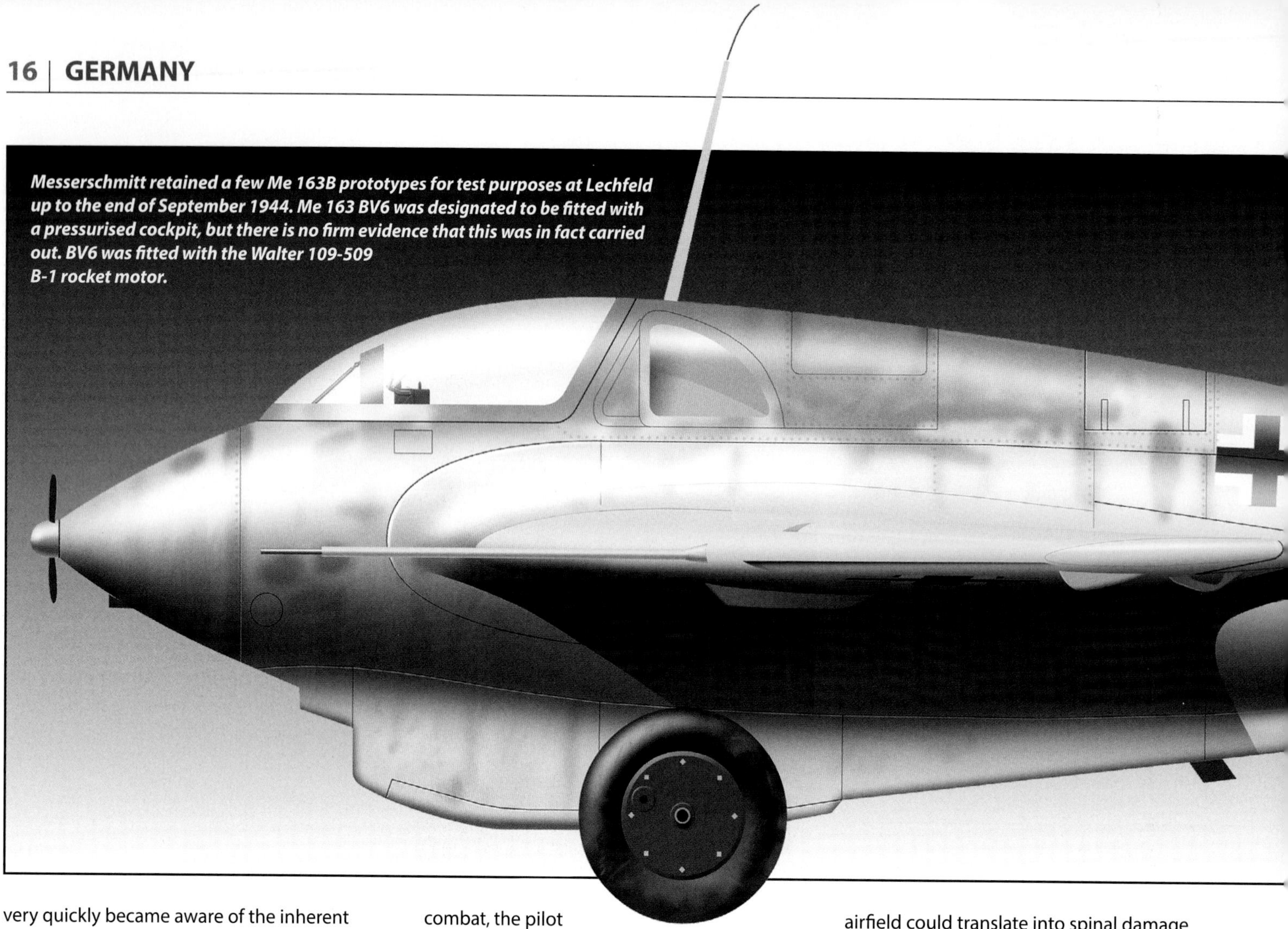

very quickly became aware of the inherent difficulties in engaging the enemy in such a fast-flying fighter. While the American 'heavies' were far from fast, combined with the speed of the Me 163 in its attacking dive the pilots had to get the target in the crosshairs at a closing velocity of some 800mph (1,300km/h)! The window of opportunity in which to press home an attack with any chance of success was just three seconds. After having broken from

*Below: **A member of the groundcrew of Me 163 BV47, PK+QR, C1+06, is seen here refuelling the tank with C-Stoff propellant.***

combat, the pilot of the Komet now faced the challenging task of getting his mount back on terra firma. The undercarriage of the Me 163 was a hangover from its sailplane origins, and was poorly suited to a rocket-propelled fighter. After take-off the pilot jettisoned the wheeled dolly, which meant that landing had to be achieved using a sprung skid. For a successful recovery, the Komet had to be dead into wind. If not, the aircraft would slew violently, and the pilot ran the risk of overturning, since the rudder provided no control at slow speeds. The bumps of an uneven airfield could translate into spinal damage transmitted via the skid, and also ran the risk of shaking up the propellants and creating a devastating explosion.

In the event, the Me 163 accounted for just a handful of the daylight raiders, while sustaining heavy attrition among its own ranks. Ultimately, the two operational squadrons of Me 163s claimed just nine bomber kills, while 14 of their own number fell to enemy fighters and bombers. However, these combat losses represented a relatively moderate toll of just 5 per cent, and a staggering 80 per cent of attrition was as a result of take-off or landing accidents, often in association with the unstable rocket fuels.

While its ensuing combat record was less than stellar, the Me 163 was nonetheless a milestone in aviation history. A small aircraft with a big impact. Ultimately, the Me 163 represented a daring gamble on behalf of Germany's wartime aviation industry. Never before had attempts been made to conceive a fighter that offered such levels of straight-line speed and high-altitude performance. Had the gamble paid off, the rocket fighter could have presented the Allies with an insoluble problem. By the time production of the Komet was wound up in February 1945, almost 400 examples of all versions had been completed, perhaps 300 of which made it as far as front-line service.

MESSERSCHMITT Me 163 | 17

Above: **Produced by the Hellmuth Walter Werke, the HWK 509A was originally known by the designation II-211. It was a notably compact engine, with a weight of just over 220lb (100kg) and a length of 7ft (2.13m).**

Left: **With its engine ignited, Me 163B White 4 begins its take-off run.**

Below left: **A rare shot of an Me 163 in flight. Original armament of the Komet was a pair of Mauser 20mm cannon of the MG 151 type. However, from the 47th aircraft onwards, a pair of 30mm MK 108 cannon, provided by Rheinmetall-Borsig, replaced these weapons. Each 30mm cannon was provided with 60 rounds of ammunition.**

Below: **This Messerschmitt Me 163B, was brought to the UK after the war and given the number VF241 at the Royal Aircraft Establishment, Farnborough, and put on public display.**

Messerschmitt Me 262

From nowhere they came, falling upon the masses of US bombers. Sleek, fast and powerful, the world's first operational jet fighters easily evaded the defending fighters and pulverised the lumbering bombers with lethal cannon fire. The revolutionary Messerschmitt Me 262 had been unleashed. Nicknamed 'Schwalbe' (Swallow), with its swept wings and shark-like appearance the Me 262, represented an aviation marvel. However, the Allies' continuous bombardment of Germany's factories ensured that the world's first operational jet fighter could never meet its potential. But in its brief yet brilliant career, the Me 262 changed air warfare and dictated fighter design to this day.

The iconic Messerschmitt Me 262 was born from German turbojet engine development in the mid-1930s, conceived by engineer Hans-Joachim Pabst von Ohain. By 1938, a Messerschmitt design team had drawn up concepts for an interceptor fighter with two jet engines as 'Project 1065'. Conceived in 1938, the Me 262 was designed by a team led by Dr Waldemar Voigt. It went through a long gestation period, not making its first flight until 18 April 1941, and then only under the power of a Junkers Jumo 210G piston engine of about 700hp. Jet engine development, although more advanced in Germany than elsewhere, was still in a primitive state, and the turbine engines intended for the sleek fighter were not ready. As the aircraft's future looked promising, the German Air Ministry (Reichsluftfahrtministerium – RLM) ordered more prototypes. Finally, Me 262 V1 was fitted with two BMW 003 turbojets as well as the standard prop in the nose as the engines were still unreliable, a wise move as both jets failed on its maiden flight. The Jumo 004 was a more promising turbojet, and on 18 July 1942 the Me 262 became a true jet when it took to the air in the hands of test pilot Fritz Wendel.

The new fighter had turbojets in nacelles under the middle of the wings. The characteristic swept-back design was the result of a need to place the centre of gravity aft to compensate for heavier-than-expected engines. It was only later that the benefits of swept wings were appreciated. Also, to improve low-speed handling, slats were incorporated to the front of the outer wings that extended automatically.

The pilot sat high in a canopy offering all-round visibility that tilted open to the right. The front window glass was bullet-proofed and the seat (non ejection) was armoured. Also referred to as the 'weapons pod', the nose section housed the armament and non-steerable nosewheel assembly, which, when retracted, protruded into a raised channel within the weapons bay. Armament included: four 30mm MK108 cannon (A-2a variant had two cannon); 24 2.2in (55mm) R4M air-to-air rockets; two 551lb (250kg) bombs or two 1,102lb (500kg) bombs (A-2a only).

The Me 262 became a ray of hope in the increasingly dark skies of the German Luftwaffe. However, its future was threatened by a number of influential figures who favoured the advancement of proven piston aircraft. But by 1943 an order was placed for 100 jet fighters. Even then, the Me 262 was plagued by bureaucratic obstacles when Hitler demanded that the fighter be converted into a 'Jabo' (bomber). For Erhard Milch, the German Field Marshal who oversaw the development of the Luftwaffe, the idea of robbing the Me 262 of its superior speed was unacceptable. So, with the Führer believing that the Me 262 was in production as a bomber, work continued on its development in the fighter role. On learning that his order has been ignored, Hitler was furious and Messerschmitt engineers feverishly converted the fighters to carry two 550lb (250kg) bombs.

*Below: **The menacing shark-like shape of the Me 262 terrorised Allied bomber crews in the latter stages of World War 2. This airframe was the first Me 262 to come into Allied hands when its German test pilot defected on 31 March 1945. The aircraft was then shipped to the US for testing.***

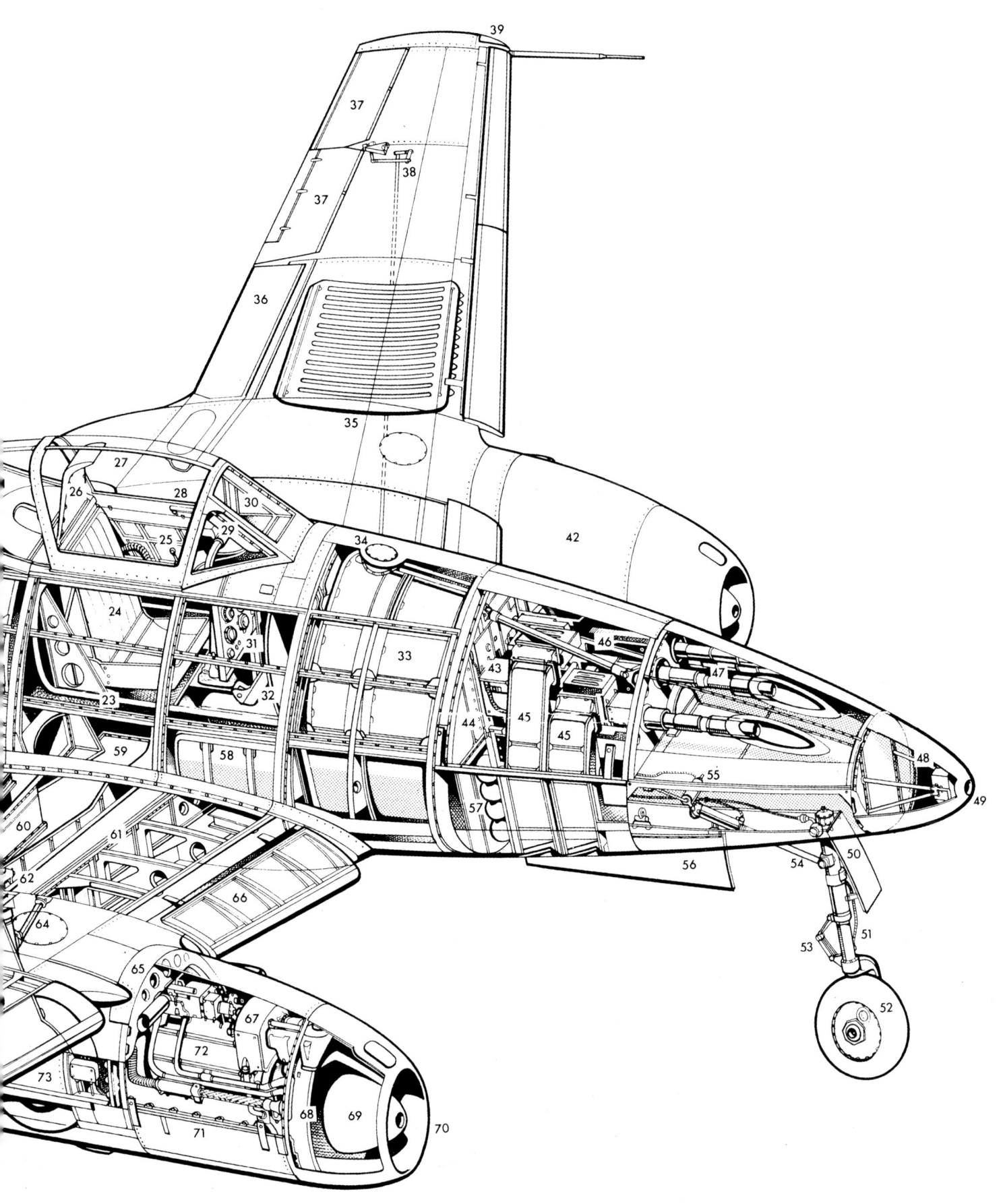

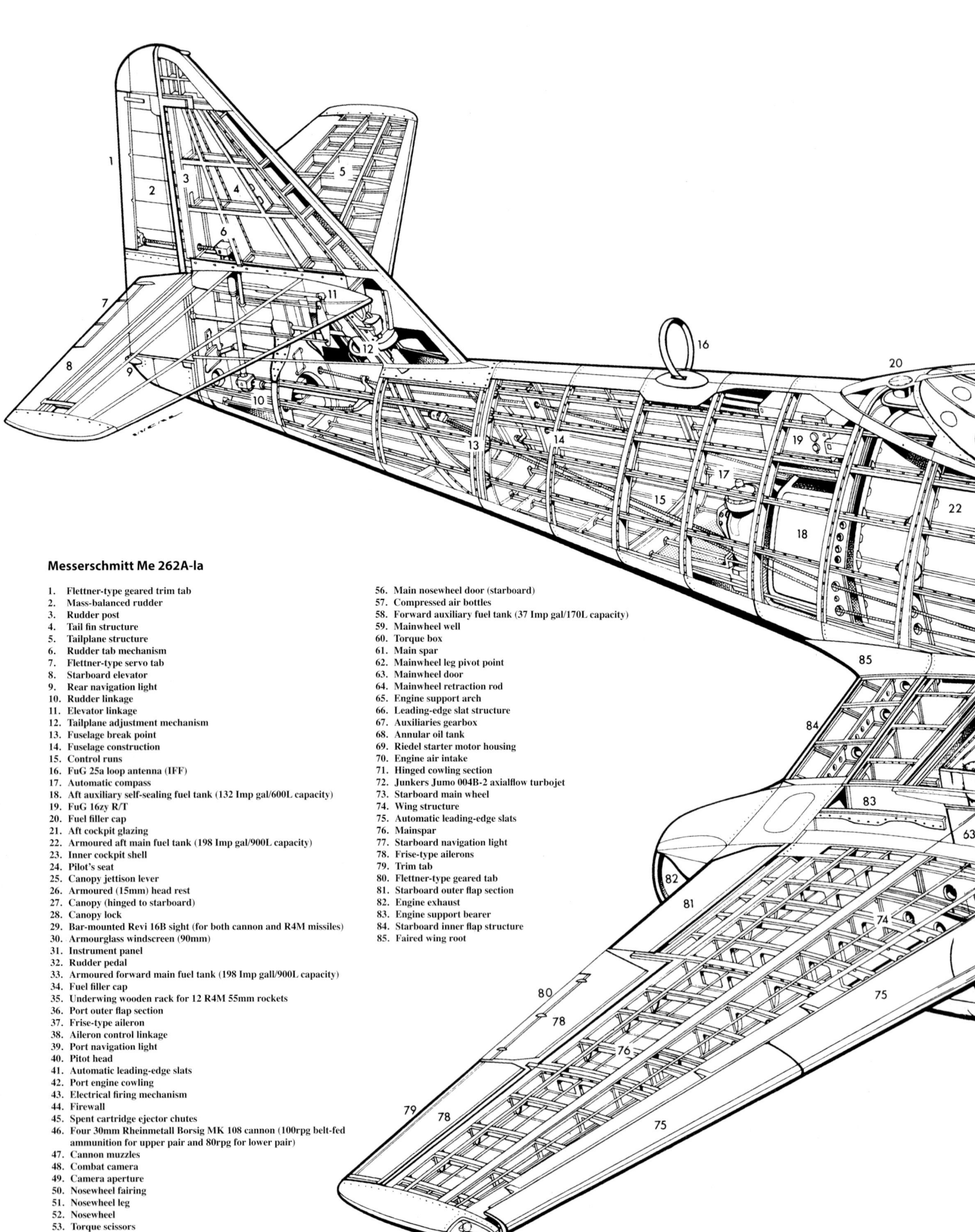

Messerschmitt Me 262A-la

1. Flettner-type geared trim tab
2. Mass-balanced rudder
3. Rudder post
4. Tail fin structure
5. Tailplane structure
6. Rudder tab mechanism
7. Flettner-type servo tab
8. Starboard elevator
9. Rear navigation light
10. Rudder linkage
11. Elevator linkage
12. Tailplane adjustment mechanism
13. Fuselage break point
14. Fuselage construction
15. Control runs
16. FuG 25a loop antenna (IFF)
17. Automatic compass
18. Aft auxiliary self-sealing fuel tank (132 Imp gal/600L capacity)
19. FuG 16zy R/T
20. Fuel filler cap
21. Aft cockpit glazing
22. Armoured aft main fuel tank (198 Imp gal/900L capacity)
23. Inner cockpit shell
24. Pilot's seat
25. Canopy jettison lever
26. Armoured (15mm) head rest
27. Canopy (hinged to starboard)
28. Canopy lock
29. Bar-mounted Revi 16B sight (for both cannon and R4M missiles)
30. Armourglass windscreen (90mm)
31. Instrument panel
32. Rudder pedal
33. Armoured forward main fuel tank (198 Imp gall/900L capacity)
34. Fuel filler cap
35. Underwing wooden rack for 12 R4M 55mm rockets
36. Port outer flap section
37. Frise-type aileron
38. Aileron control linkage
39. Port navigation light
40. Pitot head
41. Automatic leading-edge slats
42. Port engine cowling
43. Electrical firing mechanism
44. Firewall
45. Spent cartridge ejector chutes
46. Four 30mm Rheinmetall Borsig MK 108 cannon (100rpg belt-fed ammunition for upper pair and 80rpg for lower pair)
47. Cannon muzzles
48. Combat camera
49. Camera aperture
50. Nosewheel fairing
51. Nosewheel leg
52. Nosewheel
53. Torque scissors
54. Retraction jack
55. Hydraulic lines
56. Main nosewheel door (starboard)
57. Compressed air bottles
58. Forward auxiliary fuel tank (37 Imp gal/170L capacity)
59. Mainwheel well
60. Torque box
61. Main spar
62. Mainwheel leg pivot point
63. Mainwheel door
64. Mainwheel retraction rod
65. Engine support arch
66. Leading-edge slat structure
67. Auxiliaries gearbox
68. Annular oil tank
69. Riedel starter motor housing
70. Engine air intake
71. Hinged cowling section
72. Junkers Jumo 004B-2 axialflow turbojet
73. Starboard main wheel
74. Wing structure
75. Automatic leading-edge slats
76. Mainspar
77. Starboard navigation light
78. Frise-type ailerons
79. Trim tab
80. Flettner-type geared tab
81. Starboard outer flap section
82. Engine exhaust
83. Engine support bearer
84. Starboard inner flap structure
85. Faired wing root

MESSERSCHMITT Me 262 | 23

Right: **The futuristic shape of Willy Messerschmitt's revolutionary masterpiece was far in advance of any other aircraft of its time.**

Left: **Me 262A-1a 'White 10', WNr 170041, of Erprobungskommando 262 at Lechfeld in July 1944.**

Below left: **Me 262A-1a 'White 3' as flown by Hans-Guido Mutke of 7./JG 7, based at Fürstenfeldbruck, Germany. On 25 April 1945, Mutke landed this aircraft at Dübendorf, Switzerland. He claimed that he got lost during a combat mission and landed there by mistake, although there were suspicions that he'd defected. The Swiss authorities never attempted to fly the fighter, keeping it in storage and returning it to Germany on 30 August 1957. Mutke was also famous for making the controversial claim that he broke the sound barrier in 1945 in an Me 262.**

Below: **The prototype Me 262 being refuelled between test flights. Note the protective cages over the jet intakes.**

The 'Jabo' version achieved little in France and Hitler reluctantly reversed his order to return production to the fighter variant.

The first experimental fighter unit to receive the Me 262 was Erprobungskommando 262, and the jet was bloodied on 26 July 1944 when a Mosquito was shot down. The first active unit to fly the Me 262 in anger was Kommando Nowotny, formed by Maj Walter Nowotny in September 1944, and its first confirmed kill was a B-24. However, the unit suffered a mortal blow when Nowotny was shot down and killed when marauding P-51s braved the airfield defences and swooped down on his Me 262 during landing. Disbanded shortly afterwards, Kommando Nowotny claimed 22 kills for the loss of 26 Me 262s.

The legendary JG 7 was formed in August 1944 from the remnants of Kommando Nowotny, KG 1 and JG 3. Much training followed, but the unit suffered from an inadequate supply of replacement parts and fuel, 10 Me 262s being lost due to mechanical failure. However, the unit had improved by February 1945, delivering concentrated attacks on heavy bomber streams and being instrumental in establishing how the jet was to be implemented in the anti-bomber role.

As the Me 262 was so advanced and untested in war, there was much debate from senior JG 7 pilots on how to employ tactics against the heavies. Piston fighters enjoyed head-on attacks, but the high speed of the Me 262 made this impossible. Therefore, a traditional rear attack was employed, the jets using their incredible speed and cannons to devastating effect. This, of course, meant that the Me 262 had to withstand concentrated gunfire from the bombers.

Whatever the tactics used, the sheer number of Allied aircraft made the jet attacks almost irrelevant. On 18 March 1945, 37 Me 262s engaged 1,221 American bombers and 636 escorting fighters. It was also on this day that the new R4M 4kg air-to-air rocket was introduced. Nicknamed the 'Hurricane' due to its distinctive smoke trail when fired, the R4M, armed with a potent Hexogen warhead, was greatly feared and a single hit could rip a bomber apart. In the frantic engagement, 12 bombers and a fighter were shot down for the loss of three jets. Even on their biggest day, when JG 7 flew 38 sorties and knocked down 14 bombers and two fighters for the loss of four Me 262s, the Luftwaffe 'Wolf Packs' could only shoot down enough aircraft to represent a one per cent loss for the Allies.

Perhaps the most famous of Me 262 units, JV 44, 'the squadron of experts', was established on 5 February 1945 and was commanded by Adolf Galland under the direct order of Hitler. Despite its late entry into the war and facing radically superior numbers, JV 44 went on to claim 56 kills before Germany surrendered.

The vastly superior performance of the Me 262 gave confidence to the fortunate pilots who flew it, but the Allied dominance of the air was so complete that the Schwalbe never reached its full potential. The airfields from which it flew were under constant attack, and in the last days of the war, the remaining Me 262 units were forced to operate from makeshift bases constructed along Germany's famous autobahns. Although 1,443 Me 262s were completed, it is estimated that only about 300 saw combat.

Right: **The Me 262 was a deadly enemy of the US bomber streams raiding Germany, but there were too few in number and they arrived too late in the conflict to affect the outcome. This B-24 (44-50838 of the 714th Bombardment Squadron, 448th Bombardment Group based at RAF Seething) was shot down east of Hamburg by an R4M rocket fired by an Me 262. No parachutes were seen. Germany surrendered a month after this image was taken.**

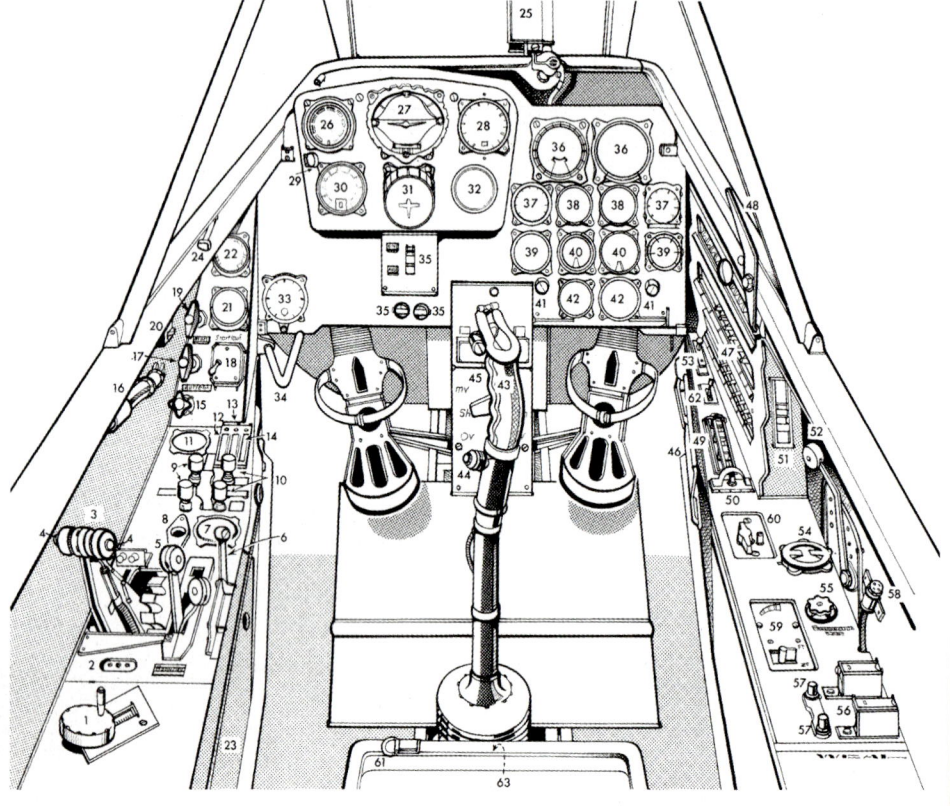

Messerschmitt Me 262 cockpit

1. Handwheel for rudder trimming
2. Contact for pilot's gloves (electric heating)
3. Power lever
4. Pressbuttons for starting device
5. Switch lever for fuel cock battery
6. Lever for tailplane adjustment
7. Tailplane position indicator
8. Master battery cut-off switch
9. Contactor switch for landing flaps
10. Contactor switch for undercarriage
11. Pressure gauge for compressed air
12. Indicator signal for port undercarriage
13. Indicator signal for nosewheel
14. Indicator signal for starboard undercarriage
15. Oxygen valve
16. Breathing tube
17. Emergency lever for landing flaps
18. Switch box for RATOG
19. Emergency handle for undercarriage
20. Knife switch (contactor) for jet pipe adjustment
21. Oxygen flow meter
22. Oxygen pressure gauge
23. Cable line for jettisoning RATOG
24. Ventilation (air vent) lever
25. Reflex (or reflector) sight and base
26. Airspeed indicator
27. Turn-and-bank indicator combined with artificial horizon
28. Rate-of-climb indicator
29. Indicator signal for Pitot head heating
30. Sensitive/coarse altimeter
31. Pilot's repeater compass
32. AFN indicator
33. Board clock
34. Nosewheel brake handle
35. Fire safety cut-out switches
36. RPM indicator
37. Gas pressure indicator
38. Injection pressure indicator
39. Gas temperature indicator
40. Oil pressure indicator
41. Residual level indicator
42. Fuel supply gauge
43. Control column
44. Pneumatic (gun) loading button
45. Fuse switchbox
46. Board (document) case holder
47. Main switchboard
48. Canopy jettison lever
49. Signal flare firing gear
50. Contactor for FuG 25a detonator charge
51. Deviation table
52. Bomb load emergency release
53. Switch for window-shield heating
54. Frequency switch
55. Frequency control for air-to-air communications set
56. Starting switch
57. Changing-over (or reversing) button for RPM indicator
58. Contact for pilot's helmet leads
59. Junction box (wall socket)
60. Control unit for R/T
61. Loop for seat-type parachute
62. Selector (or throw-over) switch for signal flare ammo
63. Pilot's seat adjusting gear

MESSERSCHMITT Me 262 | 25

Me 262 A-1a

Engine:	2 x Junkers Jumo 004 B-1 turbojets
Power:	1,980lb each
Length:	34ft 9in (10.60m)
Wingspan:	41ft 6in (12.60m)
Height:	11ft 6in (3.50m)
Empty weight:	8,366lb (3,795kg)
Loaded weight:	14,272lb (6,473kg)
Max T/O weight:	15,720lb (7,130kg)
Maximum speed:	559mph (900km/h)
Range:	652nm (1,050km)
Service ceiling:	37,565ft (11,450m)

Junkers Jumo 004

The Junkers Jumo 004 was the world's first turbojet engine to see operational use. Some 8,000 of these powerplants were produced and they powered the experimental Horten Ho 229, the Arado Ar 234 recce-bomber and the Me 262. The first prototype engines, which showed great promise, had been built without restrictions on scarce materials such as nickel, cobalt and molybdenum. However, wartime necessities would only allow low-grade metals. As a consequence, its lifetime expectancy was poor.

GERMANY

Left: *On 8 November 1944, Lt James W. Kenny of the US 357th Fighter Group flying a Mustang, managed to score hits on a Me 262 piloted by Lt Franz Schall of Kommando Nowotny. Because of the damage sustained, Schall bailed out.*

Right: *Following trials with radar fitted to a single-seater, it was decided to equip two-seaters still on the production line with FuG 218 Neptun V radars, with prominent 'Stag's Antlers' aerials on the nose. Seven of these night fighter variants, designated Me 262B-1a/U1, were used by 10/NJG.II in April 1945 in the defence of Berlin, the only unit to be so equipped. At the end of hostilities these were handed over to the Allied forces and 'Red 6' was sent to the US where it wore the identifier 'FE-610'.*

Below: *The Me262 was to mutate into the world's fastest and deadliest killing machine. The Me 262A-1a/U4 'Pulkzerstörer' packed a 50mm cannon and was the ultimate bomber killer. In the event only two (some sources quote three) prototypes of this version were completed. V083 is pictured in its post USAAF capture guise as* Wilma Jeanne, *named after the wife of Col Harold Watson, who was dispatched to oversee the retrieval of advanced technology and its transport back to the states. Later renamed* Happy Hunter II, *V083 was lost during a ferry flight to Cherbourg when a turbine blade failed.*

Bottom right: *A line of wrecked Me 262s discovered by advancing Allied troops in a field in Germany.*

Arado Ar 234

Not only did Germany field the first operational jet fighter, but it also flew the first operational jet bomber, the appropriately-named Arado Ar 234B Blitz (Lightning). Propelled by two Junkers Jumo 004 B turbojets, this graceful aircraft had a top speed of 456mph (735km/h), making it virtually immune to attacks from piston-engined Allied fighters. The relatively few Ar 234s that reached Luftwaffe units before the end of the German surrender provided excellent (if futile) service, particularly as reconnaissance aircraft.

Development of the Ar 234 began in 1940 when the German air ministry (Reichsluftfahrtministerium – RLM) issued an order to Dr Walter Blume, technical director of the state-owned Arado concern, to design and build a high-speed, high-flying reconnaissance aircraft propelled by the turbojet engines then under development by BMW and Junkers. Rüdiger Kosin led the design team that produced one of the most recognisable of all of the wartime jet designs. The fuselage was pencil-like in its approach with a rounded nose cone and well-tapered rear. The entire nose was made up of the single-seat cockpit which provided excellent visibility of the oncoming action with only light framing being involved. The rounded fuselage incorporated slab sides for a deep approach required of the internal fuel stores, avionics and cockpit. Engines were held in streamlined nacelles, hung under the straight high-mounted wing. To reduce weight and free space for larger fuselage fuel tanks, the initial prototype series dispensed with a conventional landing gear in favour of retractable skids mounted beneath the fuselage and nacelles. The aircraft would taxi and take off atop a wheeled trolley that the pilot jettisoned as the jet left the runway.

Engine problems repeatedly delayed the flight testing of the first Ar 234. BMW and Junkers both experienced trouble building jet engines in quantities sufficient for both the Me 262 and Ar 234 programmes. Although Arado completed the Ar 234 V1 airframe in late 1942, the Messerschmitt aircraft took priority and claimed the trickle of flight-ready engines that Junkers managed to turn out. Thus, the first Ar 234 turbojet-powered prototype finally achieved its first flight on 30 July 1943 from Rheine Airfield and the five other prototype aircraft soon followed the initial V1. The second prototype, Arado Ar 234 V2, crashed on 2 October 1943 at Rheine near Münster after suffering a fire in its port wing, failure of both engines and various instrumentation failures. The aircraft

Below: The sleek lines of the world's first operational jet bomber, the Arado Ar 234. In the definitive B-models, the undercarriage was wholly-retractable and arranged in a tricycle format with two main landing gear legs and a nose leg. All three positions held a large 'donut-style' landing wheel of low pressure, intended to counter the rather narrow undercarriage track.

dived into the ground killing its pilot. Prototype V3 was given an ejector seat and pressurised cockpit while being outfitted with rockets for assisted take-off. Prototypes V6 and V8 were reserved as static test beds for a four-engined development still to come.

Luftwaffe pilot Erich Sommer carried out the first Ar 234 combat mission on 2 August 1944, in the V5 prototype on a reconnaissance sortie over the Allied beachhead in Normandy. He encountered no opposition during his two-hour flight, and gathered more useful intelligence than the Luftwaffe obtained during the previous two months.

Meanwhile, the Air Ministry directed Arado to redesign the landing gear and give the jet a bombing capability. Kosin and his team enlarged the fuselage slightly to accommodate a conventional tricycle landing gear and added a semi-recessed bomb bay under the fuselage. To allow the pilot to act as a bombardier, Kosin mounted a Lotfe 7K bombsight in the fuselage floor ahead of the control column, which the pilot swung out of his way to use the sight. A Patin PDS autopilot guided the aircraft during the bombing run. The pilot-bombardier used another periscope sight during shallow-angle, glide bombing.

*Above: **Prototypes of the Arado Ar 234 featured a skid and trolley system to save weight.***

The bomber version, designated Ar 234B-0, became the first subtype built in quantity. The Air Ministry ordered 200 Ar 234Bs and Arado built them at a new Luftwaffe airfield factory at Alt Lönnewitz in Saxony. The factory finished and delivered all 200 by the end of December 1944 but managed to roll out another 20 by war's end. The initial order had called for two versions of the Ar 234B: the B-1 reconnaissance aircraft and the B-2 bomber, but in the end Arado built only the B-2 version and converted these into reconnaissance models when required. The Ar 234B included an ejection seat, Patin PDS autopilot system and, due to the thirsty nature of early turbojet engines, were given optional external auxiliary fuel tanks for improved range. As a bomber, the Ar 234B-2

Arado Ar 234B-2

Engine:	2 × Junkers Jumo 004B-1 axial flow turbojet engines
Power:	1,990lb thrust each
Crew:	1
Wingspan:	47ft 3in (14.4m)
Length:	41ft 6in (12.64m)
Height:	14ft 1in (4.29m)
Loaded weight:	21,605lb (9,800kg)
Max Speed:	461mph (742km/h)
Service ceiling:	33,000ft (10,000m)
Range:	967 miles (1,556km)
Payload:	Up to 3,309lb (1,500kg) of bombs on external racks

GERMANY

was capable of 3,300lb (1,497kg) of stores and entered operation in late 1944, remaining active into 1945. The design proved aerodynamically efficient and relatively stable with little in the way of engineering corrections required.

Plans called for more advanced versions of the Arado jet, including the Ar 234C powered by four BMW 003 A-1 engines. However, only 14 Ar 234Cs left the Arado factory before Soviet forces overran the area. The four-engine Ar 234 was, however, the fastest jet aircraft of World War 2.

Only one Luftwaffe unit, KG 76 (Kampfgeschwader or Bomber Wing 76), was equipped with Ar 234 bombers before Germany's surrender. The unit flew its first operations during December 1944 in support of the Ardennes Offensive. Typical missions consisted of pinprick attacks conducted by less than 20 aircraft, each carrying a single 1,100lb (500kg) bomb. The deteriorating war situation,

*Above: **Rocket-Assisted Take-Off (RATO) comprising two Walter HWK 109-500A-1 Starthilfe jettisonable rocket pods could be used to project faster take-off times and shorter runway distances as well as a spectacular (and noisy) initial rate-of-climb.***

*Right: **The finest role of the Ar 234 was in reconnaissance, where, fitted with drop tanks on the wings to extend their range, they could easily fly a 450 mile mission. The quality of its cameras brought the Germans a wealth of intelligence, though little good news!***

coupled with shortages of fuel and spare parts, prevented KG 76 from flying more than a handful of sorties from late March to the end of the war. The unit conducted its last missions against Soviet forces encircling Berlin during the final days of April. During the first week of May the unit's few surviving aircraft were either dispersed to airfields still in German hands or destroyed to prevent their capture.

ARADO Ar 234 | 31

32 | GERMANY

Below: **The four-engined Arado Ar 234C prototype fitted with twin Jumo engines under each wing**

Above: **Allied officers look on as the engines are started on a captured Arado Ar 234 during evaluation of the bomber. Maintenance on the aircraft was extraordinarily high. The brakes burned out quickly given the high landing speeds required and thus had to be replaced after every third mission. The engines each needed to be overhauled or replaced after an average of just ten flight hours.**

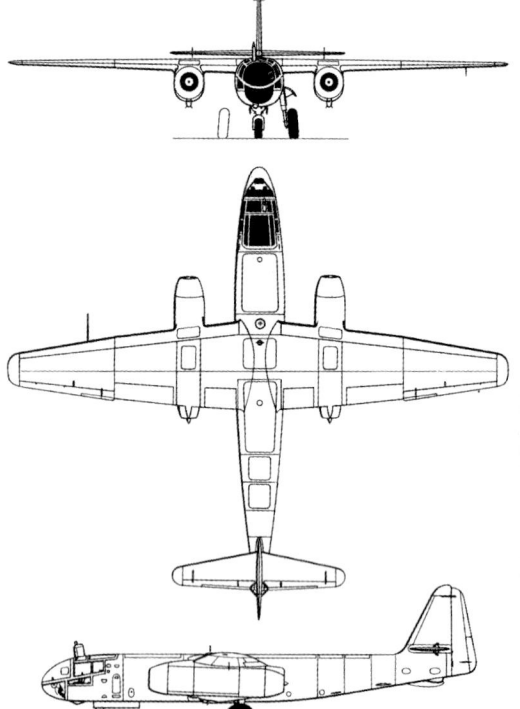

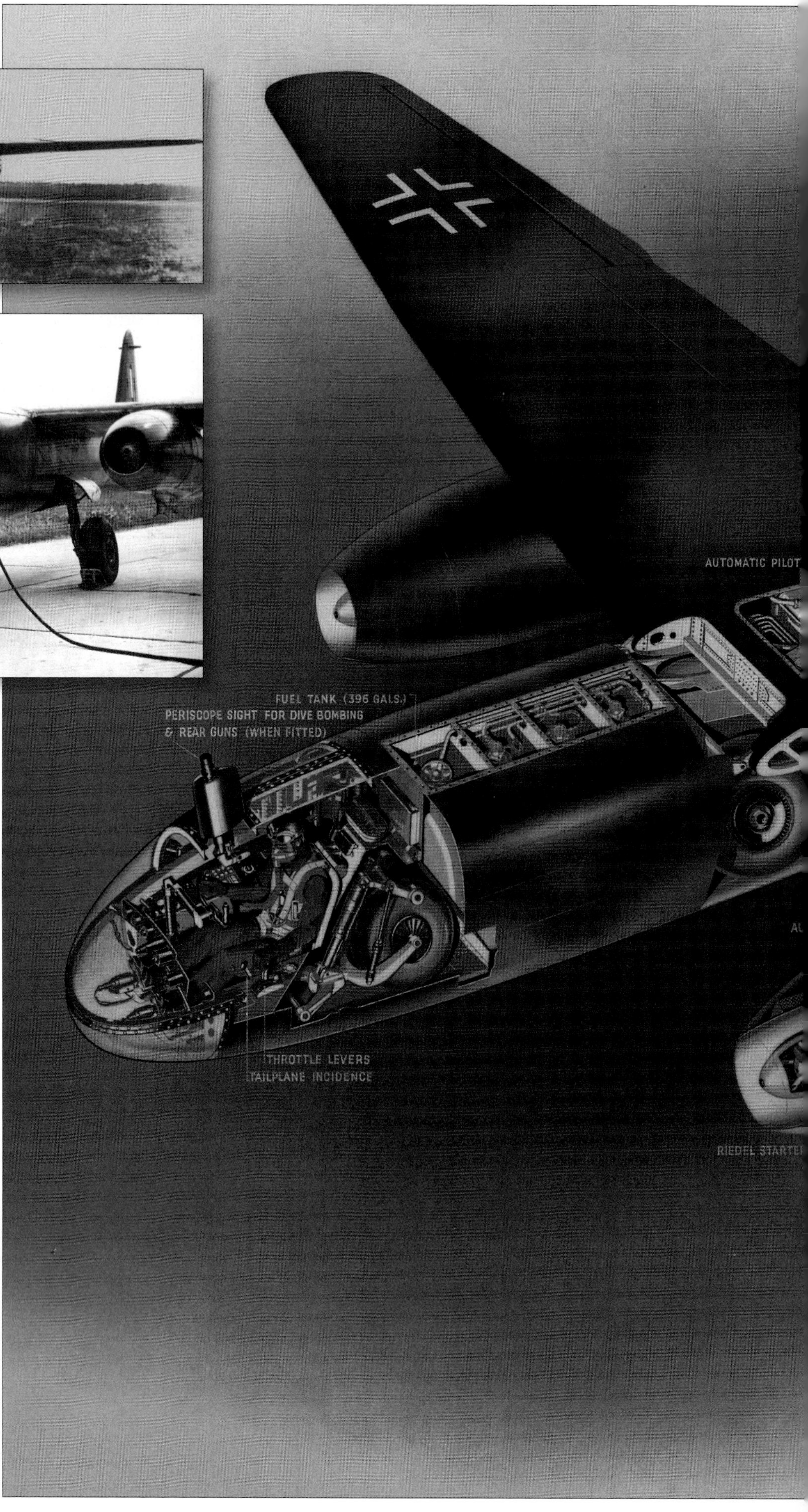

ARADO Ar 234 | 33

Messerschmitt Me 328

Originally conceived in 1941 as a parasite fighter to protect German bomber formations, the small Me 328 was powered by a pair of pulsejets, but the unsuitability of these engines effectively doomed it from the start.

The Me 328 began life as project P.1073, a cheap and simple escort fighter to either be towed aloft by a Heinkel He 177 or Junkers Ju 388, or carried on a Me 264 in a 'Mistel'-type configuration. To keep production costs down, the design was to be constructed of wood wherever possible. The Me 328 was of a standard mid-wing configuration with a circular sectioned fuselage. The cockpit was raised with the rear of the canopy moulding into the fairing that tapered back to the tail section. The initial design placed the engines either side of the rear fuselage behind the cockpit with the tailpipes extending beyond the tail, but on production aircraft it was decided to mount them below the wings. The single fin of the tailplane fitted halfway up. The undercarriage consisted of a retractable skid, to which a dolly could be fixed for take-off. Armament was to be in the form of two 20mm MG 151/20 cannon, which in the event was never fitted. Three major base forms were conceived with the first expected to be a powerless glider. The second was to feature a pair of pulsejet engines for its propulsion, while the third proposed the use of Junkers Jumo 004 series turbojet engines.

Famed pilot Hanna Reitsch carried out a test programme on the two prototypes of the glider version, releasing from its carrier aircraft at altitudes of 9,800-19,700ft (3,000-6,000m). Ground launches, using both cable-type catapults and rocket-assisted carriages on rails were also successful.

Progress was deemed promising and seven prototypes were each fitted with a pair of Argus As 014 series pulsejet engines. However, during static testing it soon became apparent that the same problems which were to plague the early development of the V-1 flying bomb – namely, excessive vibration – made the aircraft almost impossible to fly and the manned flight programme was suspended in mid-1944, after only a few test flights had been made.

Work still progressed to a limited extent. A four-engine, pulsejet-powered bomber variant was proposed but, like the parasite fighter before it, never realised. Other roles envisaged included that of a navalised fighter being launched by a U-Boat submarine, as a defence interceptor and ground attack fighter. None materialised. In a final roll of the dice, moves were made to revive the Me 328 in 1944 as a suicide flying bomb based on the Me 328B, fitted with 2,000lb (900kg) of explosives, but it was dropped in favour of the Fieseler Fi 103R (Reichenberg).

Ultimately, the pulse engine technology was never fully capable for the particular Me 328 airframe, while the parasite concept proved too complicated to ever become operational.

Above: The Messerschmitt Me 328 parasite fighter on the back of a Dornier Do 217.

Messerschmitt Me 328

Engine:	2 x Argus As 014 pulse-jets
Power:	800lb thrust each
Length:	23ft 6in (7.17m)
Wingspan:	22ft 8in (6.9m)
Height:	5ft 3in (1.6m)
Empty weight:	3,527lb (1,600kg)
Max speed:	500mph (805km/h)

Below: The Me 328 was first produced as a glider to test its aerodynamics.

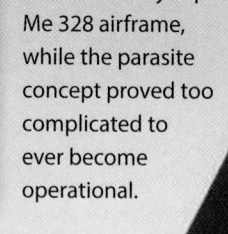

Junkers Ju 287

Left: The swept-forward wing was suggested by the project's head designer, Dr Hans Wocke, as a way of providing extra lift at low airspeeds, then necessary because of the poor responsiveness of early turbojets at the vulnerable times of take-off and landing.

When Junkers was tasked with producing a fast jet bomber for the Luftwaffe, one thing its engineers could not be accused of was lack of forward thinking. The result was one of the strangest and most revolutionary aircraft to take to the skies during World War 2.

German aircraft engineer Hans Wocke worked for Junkers and in 1943, proposed a swept-forward wing concept for a fast jet bomber capable of outrunning any known enemy air defences. During World War 2 it had become apparent that aircraft with straight wings had a built-in speed limit, imposed by air compression at the leading edge. It was known that a swept back wing would reduce compressibility, but Dr Wocke believed that a swept-forward wing would have even more advantages. In most circumstances, it would increase stability in flight, especially at low speeds. It would also mean that the central part of the wings would stall first, so the controls on the outer part of the wings would remain effective for longer. As a side benefit the design also gave more room for the internal bomb bay.

In March 1944 Junkers was given a contract to produce a prototype of the new bomber. The first aircraft, Ju 287 V1, was to be a flying test bed produced from as many existing components as possible. The resulting hybrid aircraft used the fuselage from an He 177A, the tail from a Junkers Ju 388, the main wheels from a Ju 352 transport aircraft and even a nose wheel from an American B-24 Liberator. The revolutionary wings would be the only major new component. Two Jumo 004 engines were hung in nacelles under the wings, with the other two mounted to the sides of the forward fuselage.

This remarkable aircraft made its maiden flight from Brandis airfield on 16 August 1944 in the hands of Siegfried Holzbaur. Initial flight tests were generally successful, although the forward-swept wing caused problems under some flight conditions. The most notable of these being 'wing warping' of the main spar and wing assembly. Tests suggested that the warping problem would be eliminated by concentrating greater engine mass under the wings. The second and third prototypes, V2 and V3, were to have employed six of these engines, in a triple cluster under each wing. Both were to feature an all-new fuselage and tail design intended for the production bomber, the Ju 287A-1. V3 was to have served as the pre-production template, carrying defensive armament, a pressurised cockpit and full operational equipment.

Work on the Ju 287 programme, along with all other pending German bomber projects, came to a halt in July 1944, but Junkers was allowed to go forward with the flight testing regime on the V1 prototype. The wing section for the V2 had been completed by that time. Seventeen test flights were undertaken in total, which passed without notable incident.

In March 1945, as the Allies closed in on Germany, the Ju 287 was belatedly ordered into production. However, within a month the Junkers factory building the V2 and V3 was overrun by the Red Army; at that time, the V2 was 80% complete, and construction of the V3 had just begun.

Junkers Ju 287V1

Engine:	4 x Junkers Jumo 004B-1 turbojets
Power:	1,984lb thrust each
Length:	60ft 0in (18.3m)
Wingspan:	66ft 0in (20.11m)
Height:	5ft 5in (4.7m)
Empty weight:	27,558lb (12,500kg)
Max speed:	347mph (558km/h)

Right: The Ju 287 was intended to provide the Luftwaffe with a bomber that could avoid interception by outrunning enemy fighters. The unfinished second and third prototypes, which far more accurately reflected the design of the eventual production bomber, were captured by the Soviet Union in the closing stages of World War 2.

GERMANY

Horten Ho 229

Horten Ho 229A V3	
Engine:	2 x Junkers Jumo 004B turbojets
Power:	1,956lb thrust each
Length:	24ft 6in (7.47m)
Wingspan:	55ft 0in (16.76m)
Height:	9ft 2in (2.81m)
Loaded weight:	15,238lb (6,912kg)
Max speed:	607mph (977km/h)

Designed and built by the Horton brothers in 1943, the Ho 229 was unlike anything in military aviation at the time. Although the jet-propelled flying wing crashed during its third test flight, it remains one of the most unusual and futuristic combat aircraft tested during World War 2.

In 1943, Hermann Göring issued a requirement for a '3 ×1000' light bomber, ie one that could carry 1,000kg (2,200lb) of bombs a distance of 1,000km (620 miles) with a speed of 1,000km/h (620mph). The Horten brothers, Walter and Reimar, concluded that their low-drag flying wing design could meet all of the goals and put forward their private project, the H.IX.

The H.IX was of mixed construction, with the centre pod made from welded steel tubing and wing spars built from wood. Designer Reimar swept each half of the wing 32 degrees in an unbroken line from the nose to the start of each wingtip, where he turned the leading edge to meet the wing trailing edge in a graceful and gradually tightening curve. There was no fuselage, no vertical or horizontal tail, and with landing gear stowed, the upper and lower surface of the wing stretched smooth from wingtip to wingtip. Horten mounted elevons (control surfaces that combined the actions of elevators and ailerons) to the trailing edge and spoilers at the wingtips for controlling pitch and roll, and he installed drag rudders next to the spoilers to help control the wing about the yaw axis. The pilot sat in a streamlined cockpit at the front of the wing, with the engines embedded either side.

Successful test flights of a glider version, the Ho 229 V1, in early 1944 led to construction of the first powered wing, the Ho 229 V2. Horten first selected the BMW 003 jet engine, but owing to delivery delays switched to the Junkers 004. To accommodate the larger engine, elements of the wing had to be redesigned delaying the first flight until mid-December 1944.

By this time, the design had been taken from the Horten brothers and given to Gothaer Waggonfabrik, and a production order for 40 aircraft placed. Finally, the first powered flight was made in Oranienburg on 2 February 1945 with test pilot Lt Erwin Ziller at the controls. The aircraft reportedly displayed very good handling qualities, with only moderate lateral instability. While the second flight was equally successful, the undercarriage was damaged by a heavy landing. There are unsubstantiated reports that during one of these test flights, the V2 undertook a simulated 'dog-fight' with a Messerschmitt Me 262, and outperformed it.

However, on 18 February 1945, disaster struck during the third test flight. After about 45 minutes, one of the Jumo 004 turbojet engines developed a problem, caught fire and stopped. Ziller was seen to put the aircraft into a dive and pull up several times in an attempt to restart the engine and save the precious prototype. It is believed Ziller became unconscious from the fumes from the burning engine and the aircraft crashed just outside the boundary of the airfield. Ziller was thrown from the aircraft on impact and died from his injuries two weeks later. The aircraft was destroyed.

Development continued with a series of larger prototypes, but none flew before the end of the war.

Top and below: **The third prototype of Horten's flying wing jet bomber was captured by the Americans and shipped to the US for evaluation.**

Fieseler Fi 103R

With the tide of war flowing inextricably against it, Germany became increasingly desperate in its response. Out of this desperation came the Fieseler Fi 103R, a piloted version of the V-1 flying bomb, that was code-named Reichenberg. Its pilot was given a slim chance of survival, but in essence, these were suicide missions.

SS officer Otto Skorzeny is credited with the idea of a piloted version of the V-1 flying bomb able to make precision attacks. The operational model became the Reichenberg IV and its conversion from the standard V-1 flying bomb was extremely simple. Protected by an armoured glass windscreen, the pilot sat on a pywood bucket seat in a small cockpit in front of the engine. The instrument panel comprised of an arming switch, a clock, an air speed indicator, altimeter and a turn and bank indicator. Flight controls were of the conventional stick and rudder bar type. The power of the Fi 103R came from the 770lb thrust pulsejet engine mounted in the upper rear of the fuselage. A powerful 1,870lb (850kg) warhead was packed into the nose assembly, making for one inexpensive and easy-to-produce terror weapon.

The first powered test flight was performed in September 1944, though it crashed after the pilot lost control. Subsequent test flights were carried out by test pilots Heinz Kensche and Hanna Reitsch. Reitsch herself experienced a number of crashes from which she amazingly survived unscathed.

Unlike the similar Japanese 'Ohka', the Reichenberg IV was not intended as a suicide weapon, though in practice the distinction would have been blurred. It was intended to be carried to the operational area beneath an

The Reichenberg was a manned version of the rocket-powered V-1 flying bomb, with its cockpit positioned just forward of the pulse-jet.

Above: Test pilot Hana Reitsch was deeply involved in the Reichenberg programme following her early testing of the aerodynamics of the V-1 flying bomb.

He 111 bomber. After launch, the pilot was to aim his aircraft at the intended target and then jettison the cockpit canopy and bale out, but it was calculated that his chance of survival was less than 1 per cent. Consequently, the 100 volunteers who signed up to fly the bombs were known unofficially as 'Selbstopfermaenner' or 'Self-sacrifice Men'. Although about 70 Reichenberg IVs were built for use by special unit KG 200, none were used operationally and development ended in October 1944.

Fieseler Fi 103R-IV

Engine:	1 x Argus As 014 pulse jet
Power:	770lb thrust
Length:	26ft 3in (8m)
Wingspan:	18ft 9in (5.72m)
Height:	6ft 6in (2m)
Loaded weight:	4,960lb (2,250kg)
Max speed:	500mph (800km/h) in dive

Heinkel He 162

Germany 1944 and with World War 2 drawing to its irrevocable conclusion, the Nazi leadership turned in desperation to so-called 'wonder weapons'. With the first jet engines now available, a new fighter was to be prepared for the Luftwaffe – cheap to build, available in quantity, and able to be flown by even novice pilots. The result was the Heinkel He 162, better known as the Volksjäger, or 'people's fighter'.

As early as spring 1944 there were calls for a new jet fighter, one that could be built rapidly and in quantity, using cheap materials and unskilled labour. The proposal caught the attention of an increasingly desperate Führer, and in June 1944 an Emergency Fighter Programme (Jäger-Notprogramm) was outlined, which was to yield no fewer than 5,000 fighter aircraft each month. An official requirement was subsequently drafted and was issued to a number of manufacturers, including Heinkel. The specification included a single BMW 003 turbojet engine, a loaded weight of no more than 4,400lb (2,000kg), 30mm cannon armament, a maximum speed of at least 466mph (750km/h), an endurance of 30 minutes at sea level, and a take-off run of no more than 1,640ft (500m)… and the fighter was to be taken into combat by Hitler Youth! Heinkel's designers worked around the clock in order to adapt its own lightweight jet fighter to meet the official requirement.

On 30 September 1944 the German air ministry (Reichsluftfahrtministerium – RLM) announced that the Heinkel Project 1073 had won the order. At this stage, the fighter carried the designation He 500. Eager to confound Allied Intelligence, this was soon switched to He 162, 'reusing' a designation once applied to a Messerschmitt bomber project.

In keeping with the frantic nature of the 'people's fighter' project, by the end of 1944 the first prototypes were nearing assembly in the Schwechat factory. Cover names assigned early on in the project included Schildkröte (tortoise) and Salamander (as it often called today), although the company referred to the He 162 internally as the Spatz (sparrow).

The He 162's sleek, streamlined fuselage employed light-alloy materials and a semi-monocoque structure. The fuselage cross-section was circular, and the nose was a separate component made from moulded plywood. The single-piece wing was fabricated primarily from wood, with a plywood skin, although it was fitted with flaps of light alloy and the detachable tips were made of metal. The pilot of the He 162 was seated beneath an upward-hinging blown canopy that provided an excellent view forward.

Heinkel He 162A-2

Engine:	1 x BMW 003E-1
Power:	1,760lb thrust
Length:	29ft 8in (9.05m)
Height:	8ft 7in (2.60m)
Wingspan:	23ft 8in (7.20m)
Weight (loaded):	6,184lb (2,805kg)
Max speed	490mph (790km/h)
Range:	385 miles (620km)
Armament:	2 x MG151 cannon

Below and top right: **The first prototype He 162 V1, W.Nr. 200 001, VI+IA in its bare metal finish. The aircraft was completed and ready for take-off at Heidfeld on 1 December 1944.**

Heinkel He 162A-2

1. Pitot tube
2. Moulded plywood nose cap
3. Nosewheel retraction mechanism
4. Spring-loaded nosewheel extension assembly
5. Shock absorber scissor
6. Nosewheel
7. Nosewheel fork
8. Nosewheel leg
9. Nosewheel door
10. Gun trough
11. Nosewheel well
12. Rudder pedal
13. Window panel (visual nosewheel retraction check)
14. Wooden instrument panel
15. One-piece moulded windscreen
16. Revi 16G gunsight (interchangeable with the Revi 16B)
17. Jettisonable hinged clearvision canopy
18. Ventilation disc
19. Heinkel cartridge-operated ejection seat
20. Ejection seat handle grip
21. Throttle control quadrant
22. Retractable entry step
23. Gun barrel shroud in cockpit wall
24. Port 20mm MG 151 cannon
25. Ammunition chute
26. Main oxygen supply bottle (3.5 pint/2 litre capacity)
27. Explosive charge ejector rail
28. Pilot's headrest
29. Canopy hinge
30. Ammunition box behind cockpit (120 rounds per gun)
31. Flexible main tank (153 Imp gal/695 litre capacity)
32. Fuel lines
33. FuG 25a IFF radio compartment
34. Beech plywood wing skinning
35. Jet intake
36. Riedel two-stroke starter motor bullet
37. Oil tank
38. BMW 003E-1 Sturm axial flow turbojet
39. Auxiliary intake
40. Seven-stage axial compressor casing
41. FuG 24 R/T homing loop
42. Annular combustion chamber
43. Exhaust centre body
44. Exhaust outlet
45. Jet efflux fairing
46. Heat-resistant aft dorsal decking
47. Light metal tailplane
48. Starboard fin housing R/T receiver aerial
49. Starboard rudder
50. Rudder tab
51. Elevator
52. Elevator tab
53. Tailcone (movable through +3° to -2°)
54. Port tailfin structure
55. Rudder structure
56. Tailplane/tailfin attachment
57. Port tailfin upper and lower plates (housing R/T transmitter and IFF aerials)
58. Tailskid
59. Dural fuselage skinning
60. Monocoque fuselage construction
61. Control cables
62. Downswept wing root fillet
63. Hydraulically-operated flaps
64. Port aileron
65. Detachable downswept aluminium wingtip
66. Wooden T-section rear spar
67. Wooden wing structure
68. Wooden T-section forward mainspar
69. Impregnated integral wing tank (39.6 Imp gal/180 litre capacity)
70. Vertical wing/fuselage attachment bolts (four stations)
71. Single rear horizontal engine mounting/attachment bolt
72. Two forward vertical engine mounting/attachment bolts
73. Port mainwheel well
74. Mainwheel hydraulic retraction jack
75. Mainwheel extension spring
76. Wooden mainwheel door
77. Mainwheel leg
78. Mainwheel tyre (660mm x 190mm)
79. Shock absorber scissor
80. Narrow-track main undercarriage assembly

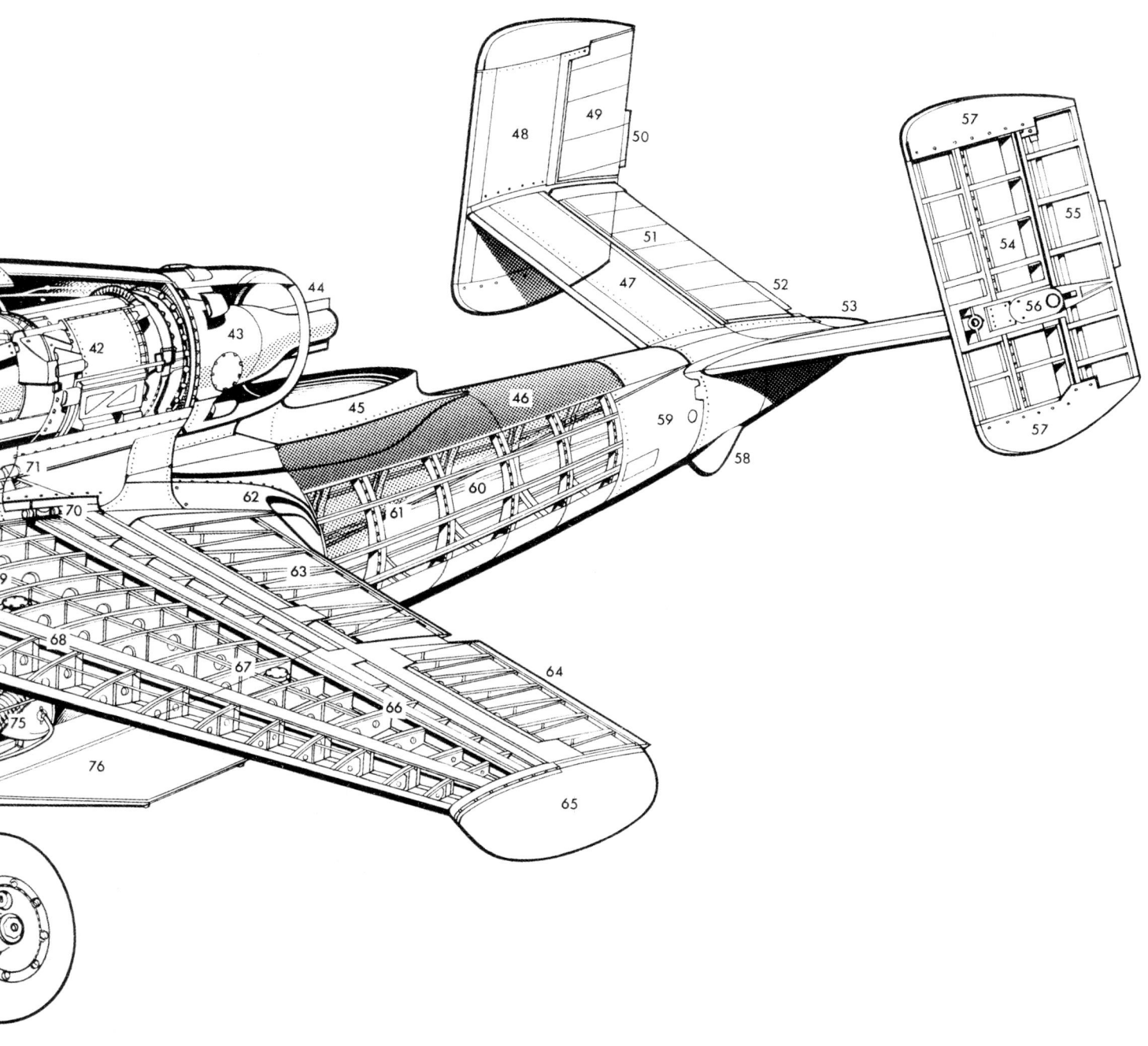

HEINKEL He 162 | 43

Left: Four days after its maiden flight, the dangerously rushed nature of the He 162 project became manifest in tragic circumstances. In front of a large group of Luftwaffe and RLM top brass, as well as high-ranking Nazi officials, the leading edge of the V1's starboard wing was torn off in high-speed flight. Test pilot Gotthold Peter was killed in the subsequent crash.

While the jettisonable 'bubble' canopy was a forward-thinking feature, the use of a cartridge-activated ejection seat was even more radical. The narrow-track tricycle landing gear was fully retractable, with all three units being housed within the fuselage. The original specification for the 'people's fighter' called for an armament of either one or two 30mm cannon, although Heinkel's first design specified 20mm weapons. As a result, the aircraft was revised to

Top left: He 162 W.Nr. 310 078 'White 5', I/JG1 of Hauptmann Heinz Künnecke, 1945.

Bottom left: 'Yellow 11', the He162A-2 flown by Oberleutnant Emil Demuth, the commanding officer of III/JG1, was unusual in that it displayed a tally of no fewer than 16 kill markings on the port tailfin. These were all claimed by Demuth on the Focke-Wulf Fw 190. The aircraft has a red, white and black nose tip and the emblem of I/JG1. Note the red arrow head on this machine, and the small '20' next to the main tactical number.

Below: Too little too late – despite this impressive rank of Heinkel He 162s at Leck, the aircraft saw service too late to have any impact on the war.

accommodate a pair of 30mm MK108 cannon mounted in the sides of the fuselage below the cockpit (as the He 162A-1). Developed under the name Sturm (Storm), the BMW 003 turbojet was mounted above the high-mounted wing, immediately aft of the cockpit, with a direct attachment using an arrangement of three bolts.

By 6 December the first prototype was ready to take to the air, in the hands of Heinkel test pilot Gotthold Peter. With no time to lose, the He 162 V1 attained a speed of 520mph (840km/h) during its maiden flight from Schwechat airfield. Although Peter succeeded in putting the prototype back down safely, he had had to curtail the 20-minute flight after it was discovered that an undercarriage door had torn off during the high-speed run.

The Luftwaffe had always been sceptical of the 'people's fighter', and the first aircraft issued to Jagdgeschwader 1 were not welcomed by the pilots. After a nine-week period of training at Parchim, I/JG1 took its He 162s to nearby Ludwigslust on 8 April, and began final working up for combat. By the middle of April, however, the Red Army was approaching dangerously close to Ludwigslust, and the decision was taken to move I/JG1 once again, this time heading north to Husum, and then to Leck, not far from the border with Denmark. With little in the way of on-site maintenance facilities, I/JG1 was hamstrung. Things were also looking bad for II/JG1, which lost its commander on 24 April, when Hauptmann Dähne crashed his He 162 into the Baltic Sea. With the Soviets pushing ever closer to Marienehe, the training programme at the facility had to be abandoned. Hitler put all jet fighter units into the hands of the SS, and Göring responded by establishing his own 'Jet and Rocket Aircraft Special Plenipotentiary'. The surviving He 162s were reorganised to create the Einsatz-Gruppe I/JG1. The unit had around 50 He 162s available, but with fuel supplies dwindling, there was no opportunity to engage the enemy, other than sporadic encounters during the course of training flights. It was too little, too late. On 4 May, German forces in north-west Germany and Denmark surrendered to the British.

In the event, less than 180 He 162s were produced, and of these, just 116 were delivered to the Luftwaffe – officially, at least. Ultimately, the project was a waste of valuable resources. It was never the 'pilot's aircraft' that was promised, and the dreams of the Allied air forces being held at bay by ranks of jet fighters flown by Hitler Youth never materialised.

Bachem Ba 349 Natter

Desperate times called for desperate measures. The Bachem Natter was designed as a vertical take-off rocket-powered interceptor armed with a nose full of rockets. It was intended to be expendable; by that stage of the war, the Luftwaffe was prepared to think of its pilots the same way.

Dr Erich Bachem's Ba 349 Natter (Viper) was the world's first, manned, vertical-take-off interceptor. The aircraft was an imaginative solution to a desperate problem but World War 2 ended before the weapon saw combat.

During the spring of 1944, the Allied bombing offensive began taking a serious toll on the German war machine. Requirements were issued for an inexpensive fighter made of non-essential materials that could defend important targets. Messerschmitt, Junkers, Heinkel, and Erich Bachem submitted proposals but air ministry officials remained unenthusiastic about Bachem's design. Undaunted, he sought the support of Reichsführer Heinrich Himmler, head of the SS (Nazi Party security forces). Himmler liked Bachem's proposal and signed an order to build 150 Bachem Ba 349 Natters using SS funds.

Bachem's design was simple and easy to build. Semi-skilled labour could construct one in about 1,000 man-hours. The wings were plain rectangular wooden slabs without ailerons, flaps, or other control devices. The cruciform tail consisted of four fins and control surfaces. Deflecting these surfaces in various combinations controlled pitch, yaw, and roll, once the Ba 349 had reached sufficient speed to generate adequate airflow. Aerodynamic control was augmented by guide vanes connected to the four control surfaces. Bachem positioned each vane within the exhaust plume of the main engine, a Walter 109-509A rocket motor, the same basic engine used in the Messerschmitt Me 163 Komet. The Walter motor generated about 3,740lb (1,700kg) of thrust, but a loaded Ba 349A weighed more than 4,000lb (1,818kg) so lift-off required more power. Bachem got the extra thrust from four Schmidding 109-533 solid-fuel rocket motors that he bolted to the aft fuselage, two per side.

The concept of Natter operations was designed to be relatively simple. A tower guided the rocket plane during lift-off. The flight controls remained locked in neutral position until the solid boosters burned out about 10sec into the flight. Then explosive bolts blasted away the boosters, the flight controls unlocked, and the Natter's 3-axis Patin autopilot began receiving steering commands from the ground via radio. The aircraft continued climbing but the pilot could intercede at any time and take full control.

Below: **Constructed primarily of wood, the Natter had wings of just 13ft span, a liquid-fuelled Walter rocket engine in the fuselage and four externally-mounted solid-fuel boosters. Armament was a battery of air-to-air rockets in the nose.**

BACHEM Ba 349 NATTER

Right: **The first Natter launch tests were carried out by unmanned aircraft, which verified that the concept was sound.**

Far right: **Lothar Sieber, a volunteer 22-year-old Luftwaffe pilot, was briefly the bravest man in the world when he climbed the ladder into the cockpit of the Natter. Just seconds after lift-off the aircraft pitched onto its back and nose-dived into the ground. Sieber didn't stand a chance, and was killed.**

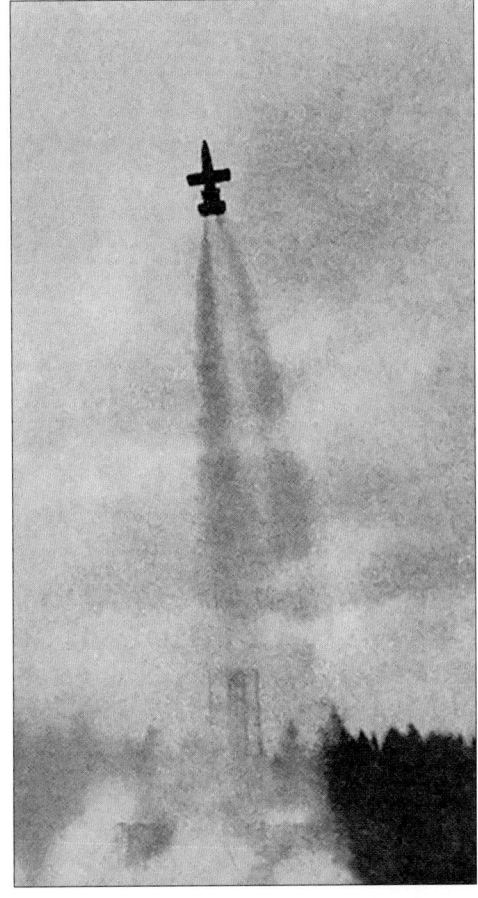

American daylight bomber formations often approached a target at an altitude of 20,000ft (6,250m) to 30,000ft (9,375m). After the Natter had climbed even with the formation, the pilot took control. As he approached the formation the Natter pilot jettisoned the nose cone and fired all 24 Henschel Hs 217 Föhn unguided rockets. Rocket fuel would be nearly exhausted by now, so the pilot began to descend. At about 4,500ft (1,400m), the pilot released his seat harness and fired a ring of explosive bolts to blow off the entire nose section. A parachute simultaneously deployed from the rear fuselage and the sudden deceleration literally threw the pilot from his seat. The pilot activated his own parachute after waiting a safe interval to clear the bits of falling Natter. Groundcrews recovered the Walter motor to use again, but the airframe was now scrap.

Bachem set up a factory to design and build his dream at Waldsee in the Black Forest. By November 1944, the first Natter was ready for tests configured as a motorless glider. A Heinkel He 111 bomber carried one to 18,000ft and released it. The pilot found the aircraft easy to control and the escape sequence worked as designed.

The first manned launch came on 28 February 1945. Oblt Lothar Sieber climbed into a Ba 349A, strapped in, and rocketed off the launch tower. At about 1,600ft (500m), the Natter shed its canopy and headrest and the aircraft veered off and flew into the ground, killing Sieber. Despite the tragedy, more pilots volunteered to fly and the Bachem team launched three test flights in March.

With the end near, the Germans erected a battery of ten Natters at Kircheim near Stuttgart. Pilots stood alert day after day but no US bombers flew into range. Within a matter of weeks the war was over and no Natter was ever launched in anger, probably much to the relief of its pilots.

Right: **US forces captured a number of Bachem Ba 349s as it advanced on Germany. Here a soldier is apparently being given an explanation as to how the Natter operated.**

Bachem Ba 349 Natter

Engine:	1 x Walter HWK 109-509C-1 bi-fuel rocket motor and 4 x Schmidding SG34 solid fuel booster rockets
Power:	3,740lb + thrust
Length:	19ft 8in (6m)
Wingspan:	13ft 1in (4m)
Height:	7ft 5in (2.25m)
Empty weight:	1,940lb (880kg)
Max T/O weight:	4,921lb (2,232kg)
Max speed:	621mph (1,000km/h)

GERMANY

Henschel Hs 132

Developed during World War 2 as a replacement for the outdated Stuka, the Henschel dive-bomber was of unorthodox design and featured a top-mounted jet engine and the pilot in a prone position. The first prototype was close to flight testing when the factory was overrun by Soviet forces.

The genesis for the Hs 132 was an 18 February 1943 specification published by the German air ministry (Reichsluftfahrtministerium – RLM) calling for a single-seat shipping attack aircraft. A piston-engined configuration was originally specified, but the performance requirements soon led to a switch to the emerging availability of jet power. The fuselage was of a circular cross-section, and constructed entirely of metal. The single BMW 003 jet engine was mounted on the fuselage top, as per the Heinkel He 162. Due to the position of the engine, a twin fin and rudder configuration was chosen, to allow the jet to exhaust without interfering with the tail unit. The mid-fuselage mounted wings were mostly of wooden construction, and had a slight taper on the leading and trailing edges. A tricycle landing gear was to be used, with the nose wheel revolving 90 degrees to lie under the cockpit when retracted. The extensively glazed bullet-shaped cockpit was completely faired in with the rest of the fuselage, and the pilot was in a prone position, to withstand the intense G-forces of the fast, steep dive during the bomb run. The Hs 132 was designed to begin its attack in a shallow dive, and after reaching a speed of 570mph (910km/h), the pilot would 'toss' the bomb at the target using a simple computerised sight, and then climb back out of range.

A contract for six prototypes was approved in May 1944, and construction was begun in March 1945. Four versions of the Hs 132 were proposed, including the Hs 132D, which was to have an enlarged wing. The Hs 132V1 was scheduled to make its first flight in June

Above: Although some references refer to this picture as a photo of the completed Hs 132 V1, it is actually an artist's composite impression. The design in terms of engine mounting and tailplane bore a very strong resemblance to the contemporary Heinkel He 162 Spatz.

Henschel Hs 132

Engine:	1 x BMW 003A turbojet
Power:	1,760lb thrust
Length:	29ft 2in (8.9m)
Wingspan:	23ft 7in (7.2m)
Height:	9ft 10in (3m)
Max T/O weight:	7,496lb (3,400kg)
Max speed:	485mph (780km/h)

1945 and it was close to completion (with the fuselage finished at Henschel's Berlin-Schönefeld facility and the wings being finished at Henschel's French subsidiary), when Russian forces captured the intact fuselage in May 1945.

Messerschmitt Me P1101

When American tanks rolled into Oberammergau in Bavaria on 29 April 1945, the soldiers had no idea that they'd found a top secret air test facility that was unknown to Allied intelligence and had never been bombed.

Little attention was paid to the skeletal metal frame of an aircraft that was 80 percent completed but had never taken to the air. It was the Messerschmitt P1101, possibly the most advanced piece of German hardware ever to fall into Allied hands.

The Messerschmitt P1101 was a single-seat, swept-wing jet fighter developed in response to the 15 July 1944 Emergency Fighter Programme which sought the second generation of jet fighters for the Third Reich. Although the Focke-Wulf Ta 183 was preferred by the German air ministry (Reichsluftfahrtministerium – RLM), Messerschmitt was instructed to carry out experimental flights, testing the swept back wing at anticipated speeds up to Mach 1. The worsening war situation led to the building of a full-scale prototype utilising existing components such as the wings (Me 262), landing gear (extended Bf 109), and flight components where possible. Production of the V1 prototype was begun at Messerschmitt's Bavarian Oberammergau Complex with a projected first flight in June 1945.

The P1101 V1 prototype was of duralumin fuselage construction. The fuselage-mounted tandem intakes of preliminary designs were replaced by a single nose intake, and the revised bubble canopy afforded better all-round vision. An operational version would have been powerfully armed with four Mk 108 30mm cannons.

Robert J. Woods, Bell Aircraft Corporation's chief design engineer and a key figure in the exploitation of German technology, became interested in the P1101's variable-sweep wing and tried to have the prototype completed in Germany under US supervision. With the French withholding documents and pieces of the prototype removed by soldiers as souvenirs, the idea of flying the P1101 at Oberammergau failed to materialise. The prototype was later shipped to the US, but damage ruled out any possibility for repair. However many of the Me P1101's design features influenced the Bell X-5, which was the first aircraft capable of varying its wing geometry while in flight.

Messerschmitt Me P1101

Engine:	1 x Heinkel HeS 011A turbojet
Power:	2,866lb thrust
Length:	29ft 2in (9m)
Wingspan:	27ft 1in (8.2m)
Height:	9ft 2in (2.8m)
Max T/O weight:	9,900lb (4,500kg)
Max speed:	612mph (985km/h) estimated

Left: The battered P1101 airframe became a favourite prop for GI souvenir snapshots.

Below: The remains of the Messerschmitt P1101 V1 prototype was shipped to the US for evaluation. Although the aircraft never flew, it strongly influenced subsequent jet fighter designs on both sides of the Iron Curtain.

Caproni Campini N.1

What was the first jet aircraft to fly? If you had been asked that question in 1940, it is likely you would have replied the Italian Caproni Campini N.1… but that was before news emerged of the Heinkel He 178's first flight a year earlier. But while the N.1's place in history might have been denied, some question whether it was even a jet in the purest sense at all!

It was in 1931 that Italian engineer Secondo Campini presented the Italian air ministry with a design for what he called a 'thermojet' engine. Three years later, he was granted approval for the development of two prototypes and a static testbed to demonstrate the principle of his 'jet aircraft'. Lacking the necessary industrial infrastructure, Campini turned to the Caproni aircraft company for the manufacturing of the machines, which were designated Caproni Campini N.1, though they were also referred to as CC.2.

Campini's powerplant was not a true turbojet as it used a conventional 670hp Isotta Fraschini L. 121/R.C. 40 piston engine to drive a compressor, which forced air into a combustion chamber where it was mixed with fuel and ignited. The exhaust produced by this combustion was to drive the aircraft forward. Campini called this configuration a 'thermojet', now more commonly called 'motorjet'. In fact, it could be regarded as an early ducted fan. The intake of this unusual engine was situated at the nose of the aircraft, while exhaust was expelled at the very rear. This left the Campini-Caproni N.1 looking like a long tube with cockpit, wings and tail attached.

Above: The Caproni Campini N.1 was only ever designed as an engine test bed and as such was never developed further or fitted with weapons.

Caproni Campini N.1

Engine:	1 x Isotta-Fraschini L.121/RC40 motorjet
Power:	1,550lb thrust
Length:	43ft 0in (13.10m)
Wingspan:	52ft (15.85m)
Height:	15ft 5in (4.7m)
Max T/O weight:	9,250lb (4,195kg)
Max speed:	233mph (375km/h)

The first flight, from the Caproni factory in Taliedo, near Milan, took place on 27 August 1940, with test pilot Mario De Bernardi at the controls. This was followed by the second prototype over a year later, on 30 November 1941, which was flown from Milan's Linate Airport to Rome's Guidonia Airport, in a highly-publicised event that included a fly-past over Rome and a reception with prime minister Benito Mussolini. This was as good as it got. Although the N.1 was never meant to be more than a test bed, its performance was sorely lacking with a top speed of just 233mph, which dropped off the higher it ascended. Another problem encountered during flight testing was the large amount of engine heat entering the cockpit, which forced the crew to fly with the canopy always open.

It could be said that Campini was ahead of his time and that in 1940 the technology was not available to make his engine designs efficient. However, if nothing else his aircraft proved that the future for military aircraft lay in the raw power offered by the pure turbojet.

Right: The world's second jet aircraft was the Italian Caproni Campini, powered by an innovative motorjet. Although it looked fast, it was slower than the Fiat CR.42 biplane!

Left: Power came from a relatively small piston engine inside the forward fuselage, which turned a variable-pitch compressor in what we would today call a ducted fan. A rudimentary form of afterburner allowed fuel to be burned in a propelling nozzle to give some extra thrust.

CAPRONI CAMPINI N.1 | 49

Yokosuka MXY-7 Ohka

The Ohka (Cherry Blossom) was a Japanese human-guided, rocket-powered missile specifically designed to allow a pilot with rudimentary training to crash himself at high speed into an Allied warship. The idea for this type of attack took shape late in 1944 as Allied air and sea power continued to systematically crush the Japanese war machine.

Below: Yokosuka MXY-7 Ohka Model 11 captured at Yontan in 1945.

It was Vice-Admiral Onishi Takijino who recommended that the Japanese Navy form special groups of men and aircraft and launch them against American warships gathering to conduct amphibious landings in the Philippines. To the Allies, these units became known as Kamikaze, or suicide squads. The Japanese used the word Tokko-tai, meaning Special Attack.

It is estimated that by the end of the war, 5,000 pilots had died making Tokko attacks and the damage they wrought was severe, accounting for seven percent of all US Navy casualties incurred during the entire Pacific war.

Tokko pilots flew almost every type of Japanese military airplane, but initial operations showed the need for an aircraft designed and built specifically for this mission. Ensign Mitsuo Ohta conceived the idea of a small rocket-powered Tokko aircraft. Japanese Navy officials were impressed and the project gathered momentum. The First Naval Air Technical Bureau (abbreviated Kugisho in Japanese) at Yokosuka responded in a few

weeks with the MXY-7 Ohka 11. Essentially a 2,646lb (1,200kg) bomb with wooden wings, powered by three Type 4 Model 1 Mark 20 solid-fuel rocket motors, the single-seat Model 11 achieved great speed, but with limited range. It was carried within striking distance of its target under the belly of a twin-engine Mitsubishi G4M 'Betty' bomber. However, the Ohka's limited range meant that the G4Ms could not make the launch point before they encountered US Navy combat air patrols. Thus the Ohka's combat debut on 21 March 1945 ended disastrously, when Grumman F6F Hellcats intercepted all 16 'Bettys' carrying Ohkas and the entire group was shot down. The Model 11 was the only variant which saw service and 155 were built at Yokosuka, and another 600 at the Kasumigaura Naval Air Arsenal. It is believed that seven US ships were damaged or sunk by Ohkas throughout the war, the USS *Mannert L. Abel* being the first victim near Okinawa on 12 April 1945. Meanwhile, Kugisho developed a new model and boosted its range to about 81 miles (130km). The new version, designated the Ohka Model 22, was modified in two significant ways. Kugisho halved the size of the warhead to 1,323lb (600kg), then installed a new Campini-type hybrid motor-jet engine built by Hitachi called the Tsu-11. Kugisho finished 50 Model 22s while production shifted to underground factories. Only three Tsu-11 engines were built, so most of the airframes remained incomplete and the war ended before any Ohka 22s saw active combat.

Other unbuilt planned variants were the Model 43A with folding wings, to be launched from submarines, and the Model 43B, a catapult/rocket assisted version, also with folding wings so that it could be hidden in caves. Had the proposed Allied invasion of Kyushu Island taken place, the Japanese would likely have employed many hundreds of Ohka aircraft against the attack.

Yokosuka MXY-7 Ohka Model 11

Engine:	3 x Type 4 Mk1 Model 20 rocket motors
Power:	587lb thrust each
Length:	19ft 11in (6.06m)
Wingspan:	16ft 10in (5.12m)
Height:	3ft 9in (1.16m)
Max speed:	576mph (804km/h) in dive
Armament:	2,646lb (1,200kg) warhead

Mitsubishi J8M Shūsui

Appearances can be deceptive, but not so in the case of the Mitsubishi J8M1 Shūsui (Autumn Water). The aircraft was a copy of the Messerschmitt Me 163 Komet, reverse-engineered from a flight operations manual and other limited documentation. A single powered prototype was tested before the end of World War 2.

The Mitsubishi J8M1 Shūsui was a joint Imperial Japanese Navy and Army project using the Messerschmitt Me 163 as a basis for the design. The Japanese were meant to licence-build Me 163 variants, but getting complete airframes and parts to Japan proved problematic, when submarines carrying airframes sub-assemblies and engines were sunk. Therefore, the Japanese decided to attempt to copy the Me 163 using a basic instructional manual on the Komet. The task was handed to Mitsubishi, which would produce both the JNAF version (the J8M1 Shūsui) and the JAAF variant (Ki-200).

A glider version MXY8 Akigusa (Autumn Grass) was built to test the basic aerodynamics of the design and this first flew on 8 December 1944, at the Hyakurigahara Airfield with Lt Cdr Toyohiko Inuzuka at the controls. Inuzuka found the MXY8 almost perfectly emulated the handling characteristics of the Komet.

Meanwhile, Japan was developing its own variant of the German Walter HWK 109-509A rocket motor, known as the Toku-Ro.2 (KR10). The engine still used the German propellants of T-Stoff oxidizer and C-Stoff fuel (hydrogen peroxide/methanol-hydrazine), known in Japan as Ko and Otsu respectively. However, initial tests did not go well when the prototype engine exploded upon start up.

Like the Me 163, the J8M1/Ki-200 had enough fuel for only a short period of powered flight – around 5.5min for the J8M1 and an estimated 7min for the Ki-200 – giving it time to hit the Allied bombers before gliding back to earth to land on its skid. The armament of the J8M1 was to include 2 x 30mm cannons of Japanese origin, while the Japanese Army Ki-200 variant was to be fitted with lighter Ho-105 30mm cannons.

Quite remarkably given the short timescale of development, the J8M took to the air for its first powered flight on 7 July 1945, with Inuzuka once again at the controls. After his rocket-powered take-off, he successfully jettisoned the dolly and began to gain speed, climbing skywards at a 45° angle. However, at an altitude of about 1,300ft (400m), the engine abruptly cut out. Inuzuka managed to glide the aircraft back, but clipped a small building at the edge of the airfield while trying to land, causing the aircraft to burst into flames. Tragically Inuzuka died the next day from his injuries. Following investigation, it was determined that a fuel flow issue caused the rocket motor to cut out. Flight testing was about to resume when Japan surrendered on 15 August 1945 and all work on the J8M ceased. By this time, seven J8M production aircraft had been manufactured (six J8M1 and a Ki-200, with another six J8M1 in various stages of completion).

Mitsubishi J8M

Engine:	1 x Toku-Ro.2 (KR10) rocket motor
Power:	3,307lb thrust
Length:	20ft 0in (6.03m)
Wingspan:	31ft 0in (9.5m)
Height:	9ft 0in (2.68m)
Max T/O weight:	8,532lb (3,870kg)
Max speed:	559mph (900km/h)
Armament:	2 x 30mm Type 5 cannon

*Below: **A pair of Mitsubishi J8M1s from the six completed before the end of the war. Only one flight was ever made, which ended in tragedy.***

Nakajima J1N Kikka

When Germany began to test the jet-propelled Messerschmitt Me 262 fighter in 1942, the Japanese air attaché to Germany witnessed a number of its flight trials. The attaché's enthusiastic reports eventually led the naval staff in Japan to direct the Nakajima firm to develop a twin-jet, single-seat, aircraft similar in layout to the Me 262. The result was the Nakajima Kikka (Orange Blossom).

Nakajima leadership assigned the project to engineers Kazuo Ohno and Kenichi Matsumura who developed an all-metal aircraft, except for the fabric-covered control surfaces. They mounted Ne-20 jet engines in pods slung beneath each wing. Experimentation with turbojet engine technology had begun in Japan as early as the winter of 1941-42 and in 1943 a Japanese technical mission to Germany selected the BMW 003 axial-flow turbojet for development in Japan. The Naval Technical Arsenal at Kugisho developed the Ne-20 turbojet based on this engine.

As the war continued to deteriorate for Japanese forces, its naval pilots launched the first suicide missions using aircraft in October 1944 and this role was now assigned to the Nakajima Kikka. Due to the lack of high-strength alloy metals, the turbine blades inside the jet engine could not last much beyond a few hours, but this was enough time for operational testing and 20 to 30 minute flights for a one-way suicide mission.

The first prototype commenced ground tests at the Nakajima factory on 30 June 1945. The following month it was dismantled and delivered to Kisarazu Naval Airfield where it was re-assembled and prepared for flight testing. The first flight took place on 7 August 1945, with Lt Cdr Susumu Takaoka at the controls. The aircraft performed well during a 20min test flight, with the only concern being the length of the take-off run. For the second test flight, four days later, rocket assisted take off (RATO) units were fitted to the aircraft. The pilot had been uneasy about the angle at which the rocket tubes had been set, and for good reason. Four seconds into take off the RATO was actuated, immediately jolting the aircraft back onto its tail leaving the pilot with no effective tail control. After the nine-second burning time of the RATO ran out the nose came down and the nose wheel contacted the runway, resulting in a sudden deceleration, however both engines were still functioning normally. At this point the pilot opted to abort the take off. Eventually the aircraft ran over a drainage ditch which caught the tricycle landing gear, the aircraft continued to skid forward and stopped short of the water's edge. Development of the Kikka ended four days later when the Japanese surrendered. By this time, another prototype was almost ready for flight. US forces later discovered about 23 Kikka aircraft under construction at the Nakajima main factory building in Koizumi and at a site on Kyushu island.

Nakajima Kikka

Engine:	2 x Ishikawajima Ne-20 turbojets
Power:	1,050lb thrust each
Length:	30ft 4in (9.25m)
Wingspan:	32ft 10in (10m)
Height:	9ft 9in (2.95m)
Max T/O weight:	8,995lb (4,088kg)
Max speed:	432mph (696km/h)
Armament:	Guns: 2 x 30mm Type 5 cannon Bombs: 1 x 1,102lb (500kg)

*Below: **The Nakajima Kikka fitted with JATO rockets and being prepared for its second and final flight.***

Gloster E.28/39

When a diminutive aircraft roared into the sky over RAF Cranwell on 15 May 1941, Frank Whittle had every reason to feel vindicated. As inventor of the gas turbine engine, he had been battling officialdom to support his revolutionary ideas and now here was proof that his concept of jet-powered aircraft worked. However, it will not have been lost on him that Germany had already wrested the lead in this vital technology away from Britain and was closer to deploying it in an operational fighter.

Gloster E.28/39	
Engine:	1 x Power Jets W.1 turbojet
Power:	860lb thrust
Length:	25ft 4in (7.74m)
Wingspan:	29ft 0in (8.84m)
Height:	8ft 10in (2.7m)
Loaded weight:	3,748lb (1,700kg)
Speed:	338mph (544km/h)
Max range:	410 miles (656km)

Britain's first jet aircraft, the experimental Gloster E.28/39, was designed to provide a platform for the flight testing of the new Whittle jet engines and to investigate their potential for use in fighter aircraft. In the absence of official support, Whittle and his colleagues at Power Jets had been forced to carry out development as a private venture. On 28 April 1939, Whittle made a visit to the premises of the Gloster Aircraft Company, where he met chief designer George Carter. Carter took a keen interest in Whittle's project and quickly made several rough proposals of various aircraft designs powered by the engine. Meanwhile, it appeared that the Air Ministry was clearly unconcerned about Britain losing its lead to Germany. When the world's first jet aircraft, the Heinkel He 178, completed its maiden flight on 27 August 1939, the Air Ministry had only just ordered a flyable engine from Power Jets, let alone an aircraft for it to go in. It was September 1939 before the Air Ministry finally issued a specification to Gloster for an aircraft to test one of Frank Whittle's turbojet designs in flight. The resulting E.28/39 designation originates from the aircraft having been developed in conformance with the 28th 'Experimental' specification issued by the Air Ministry in 1939. George Carter worked closely with Whittle, and laid out a small aircraft of conventional configuration. Sometimes referred to as the Gloster Whittle or the Gloster Pioneer, the aircraft was a low-wing monoplane design with tricycle undercarriage and a slightly rotund fuselage to accommodate the single Whittle W.1 engine with its centrifugal compressor. The engine was installed in the centre fuselage and was provided with a nose intake and a tail jet pipe. Two prototypes were built (W4041/G

and W4046/G) and were completed under conditions of high secrecy at Regent Motors, Cheltenham to avoid the risk of bombing at the main Gloster factory.

The E.28/39 (W4041/G) completed taxiing trials on 7-8 April 1941 at Hucclecote (including some initial hops of about 6ft from the grass airfield), before moving to Cranwell for flight test. The historic first 17-minute flight took place on 15 May 1941 in the hands of Flt Lt Gerry Sayer. Handling was reported as being 'light and responsive' although throttle response was said to be sluggish. The aircraft was moved to Edgehill (convenient to both Power Jets and Gloster) and over the following months, tests continued with increasingly refined versions of the engine. Later in the test programme, small auxiliary fins were added near the tips of the tailplanes to provide additional stability in high-speed flight. When Sayer tragically disappeared during a test flight in a Hawker Typhoon in October 1942, his assistant Michael Daunt took over the development programme. After further proving trials, the aircraft was subsequently transferred to Farnborough to allow service pilots to fly and assess the type.

The type was flown with several early jet engines, including the Whittle W.1, W.1A, W.2/500 from Power Jets Ltd and the significantly more powerful Rover W.2B (W4046). The first flight of the second aircraft (W4046) took place on 1 March 1943, although the aircraft was later lost due to 'aileron failure' during flight testing from Farnborough on 30 July 1943. The test pilot, Sqn Ldr Douglas Davie, successfully bailed out from 33,000ft, suffering frostbite on the way down.

Although short lived, the E.28/39 programme achieved its objectives and proved the concept of jet technology, thus paving the way for a new generation of aircraft.

Above: **Head on view of Gloster E.28/39 W4041/G with its large gaping air intake, a feature not seen before on a British aircraft.**

Below: **The diminutive size of Britain's first jet-powered aircraft is given scale by its pilot.**

*Above left: **Stamped 'secret', this is Flt Lt Gerry Sayer's flight test report of his historic flight on 15 May 1941. Of particular significance is his entry under Airscrew type. 'No airscrew fitted with this method of propulsion'.***

*Left: **The Gloster-Whittle E.28/39 W4041/G in its original configuration and before painting. Note the absence of small vertical fins on the tail. The horizontal paint stripe was used as an indication of heating by the turbojet engine***

*Right: **The first Gloster E.28/39 prototype, W4041/G during one of its test flights. By this stage, auxiliary fins had been added near the tips of the tailplanes to provide additional stability in high-speed flight.***

Frank Whittle – father of the jet engine

Frank Whittle was born on 1 June 1907 in Coventry, the son of a mechanic. His first attempts to join the RAF failed as a result of his lack of height, but on his third attempt he was accepted as an apprentice in 1923. He qualified as a pilot officer in 1928. As a cadet Whittle had written a thesis arguing that aircraft would need to fly at high altitudes, where air resistance is much lower, in order to achieve long ranges and high speeds. He concluded that rocket propulsion or gas turbines driving propellers would be required. By October 1929, Whittle had considered using a fan enclosed in the fuselage to generate a fast flow of air to propel an aircraft at high altitude. A piston engine would use too much fuel, so he thought of using a gas turbine. After the Air Ministry turned him down, he patented the idea himself.

In 1935, Whittle secured financial backing and, with Royal Air Force approval, Power Jets Ltd was formed. They began constructing a test engine in July 1936, but it proved inconclusive. Whittle realised that a complete rebuild was required, but lacked the necessary finances. Protracted negotiations with the Air Ministry followed and the project was secured in 1940. By April 1941, the engine was ready for tests. The first flight was made on 15 May 1941. By October the United States had heard of the project and asked for the details and an engine. A Power Jets team and the engine were flown to Washington to enable General Electric to examine it and begin construction. The Americans worked quickly and their XP-59A Airacomet was airborne in October 1942, some time before the British Meteor, which became operational in 1944.

Whittle retired from the RAF in 1948 with the rank of air commodore. He was knighted in the same year and became a research professor at the US Naval Academy at Annapolis. Sir Frank Whittle died on 9 August 1996.

*Above and left: **The Power Jets, Type W.1 turbojet engine, as seen installed in the E.28/39 (above) and from the front (left). Air entered the compressor through barely visible intakes in the sides of the cast aluminium alloy case.***

Gloster Meteor

The Gloster Meteor may have appeared too late to play a major role in World War 2, but as the Royal Air Force's, and indeed the Allies', first operational jet fighter, it trailblazed its way into aviation history. As one of the first of its kind, it was rapidly overtaken by sleek new designs, but its robustness and versatility meant that it would remain in service for over 40 years, a stunning achievement for one of aviation's great pioneers.

Like its German counterpart, the British Air Ministry was initially reluctant to divert valuable resources to unproven jet engine technology during World War 2. However, when Germany eventually forged ahead with development, it was recognised that Britain could not afford to get left behind in this potentially game-changing race.

With the concept of jet-powered flight finally becoming a reality, the next step was to develop an operational fighter. Given its close relationship with Whittle and Power Jets, the Gloster Aircraft Company became the obvious choice to build such a machine. Specification F9/40 was written by the Air Ministry around Gloster's proposals, and an official order for a first production batch of 300 examples of the new fighter was placed on 8 August 1941. By then, work was under way on an initial 12 development aircraft contracted for at the start of the year, even before the diminutive E.28/39 test bed had got air under its wheels. But it was never going to be an easy journey.

Perhaps inevitably it was with the engines that the problems occurred. The first F9/40 prototype was due to use two Power Jets W2Bs, built by Rover, but they were significantly delayed by technical maladies. Rolls-Royce took on the W2B development programme, and work on alternative powerplants was set in train by Frank Halford and Metropolitan Vickers. On 5 July 1942, the first F9/40, serial DG202, was delivered in great secrecy to the chosen testing airfield at RAF Newmarket Heath. Taxiing trials with this W2B-powered machine commenced a few days later, in the hands of Gloster chief test pilot Gerry Sayer, and revealed major shortcomings regarding lack of power. Accordingly Gerry Sayer recommended that the first flight should be postponed until units with a thrust of at least 1,200lb were available. So it was that the Halford H-1, delivering some 2,300lb of thrust, assumed early prominence in the F9/40 programme. In so doing, it staved off the project's complete cancellation even though it would play little part in the Meteor's success. Thus engined, the fifth F9/40 aircraft, serial DG206, turned out to be the first to fly. It finally took to the air at Cranwell on 5 March 1943, with Michael Daunt at the controls. The next two examples to join the flight test programme, DG205 and then DG202, were both fitted with the originally intended powerplants in 1,600lb W2B/23 form when they got airborne in June and July. Despite the superiority of both the H-1 and the Metrovick F2, the Whittle engine, now known as the Rolls-Royce Welland, was selected for production Meteor Is.

Throughout its life, the Meteor remained a very conventional aircraft in terms of its construction, being a simple all-metal airframe typical of the period. It featured a conventional low-mounted straight wing, on which the engine nacelles were positioned about a third of the way across the span. That span was decreased quite early in the Meteor F4 production run, the revised wing now having

Meteor F3

Engine:	2 x Rolls-Royce Derwent I turbojets
Power:	2,000lb thrust each
Length:	41ft 3in (12.57m)
Wingspan:	43ft 0in (13.11m)
Height:	13ft 0in (3.96m)
Loaded weight:	14,460lb (6,559kg)
Speed:	515mph (837km/h)
Max range:	1,350 miles (2,160km) at 10,000ft
Armament:	4 x 20mm Hispano Type 404 cannon

Below: No 74 (Tiger) Squadron, one of the RAF's most illustrious units, became the service's third Meteor F3 squadron in June 1945, forming part of the first all jet fighter wing along with Nos 616 and 504 Squadrons.

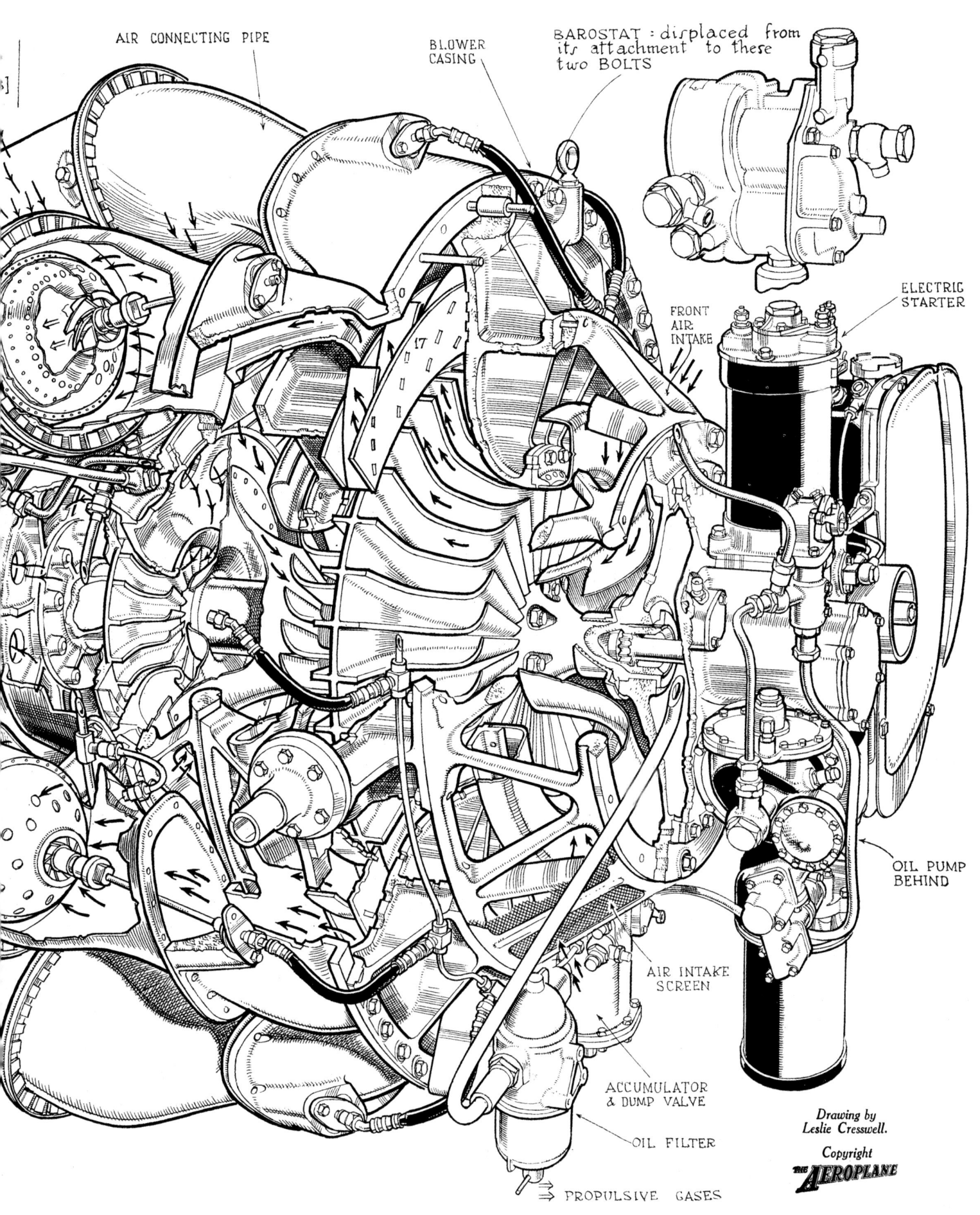

GLOSTER METEOR PROTOTYPE

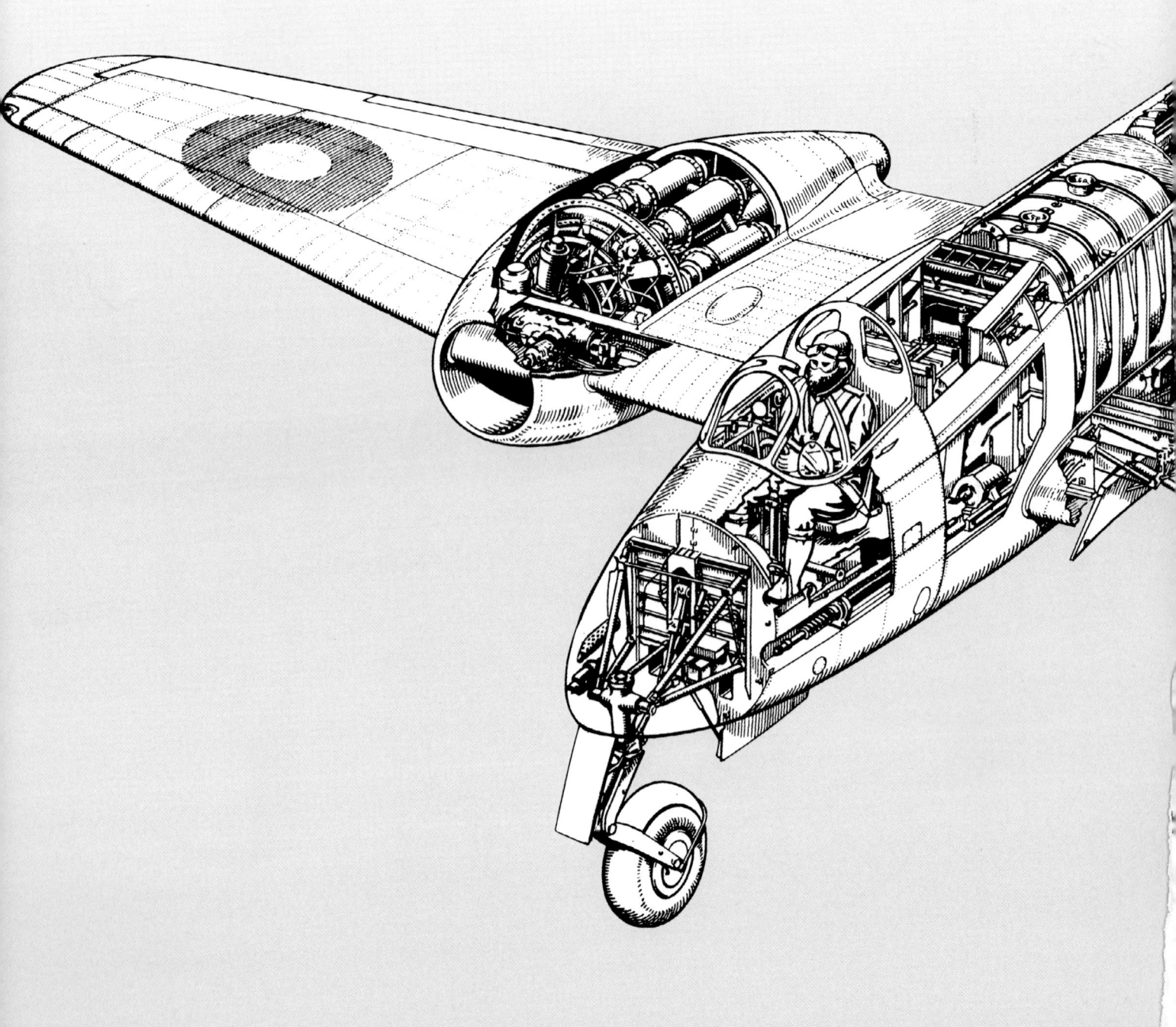

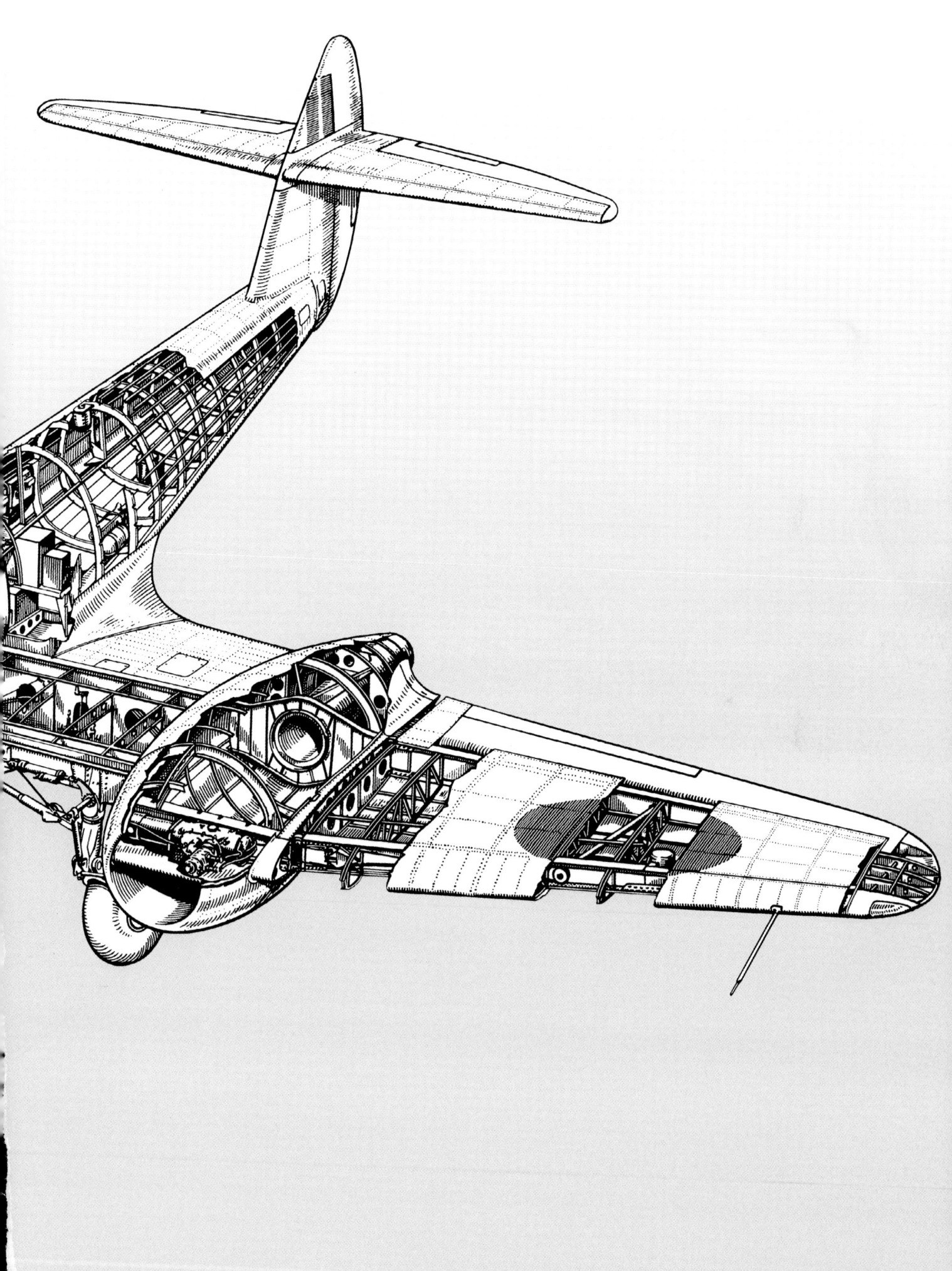

ROLLS-ROYCE RB37 DERWENT I

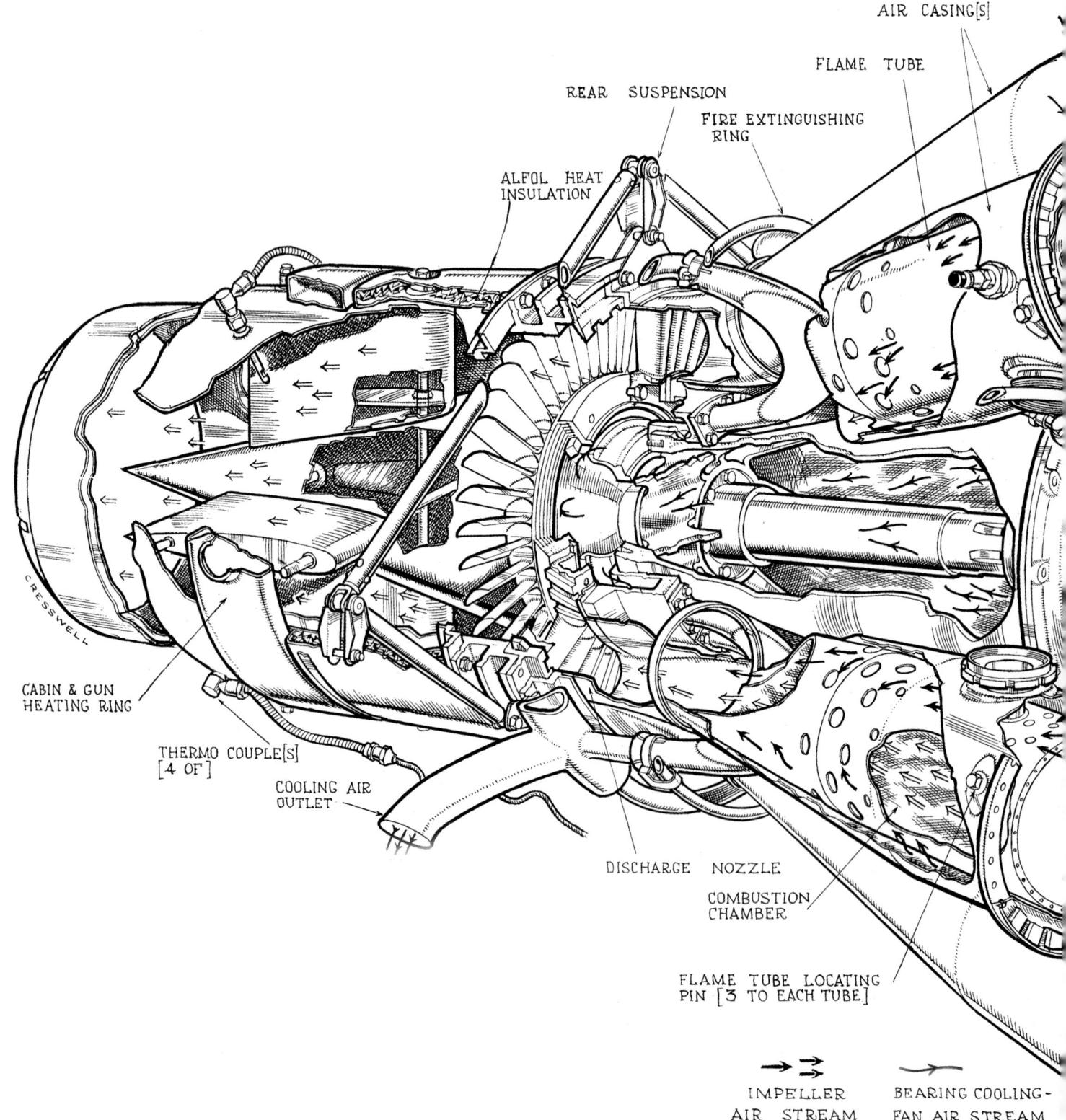

GLOSTER METEOR | 63

Left: RAF pilots enjoyed the increased performance that their new jet fighter gave them, at all heights! None of the early jets could ever truly be described as easy to fly, especially by modern standards. The technology relating to engines and systems was in its infancy, and there was by definition no pool of experience on such machines from which to draw. Meteor pilots soon discovered the type's vices and performance limitations.

more squared-off tips in the name of improving the aircraft's roll rate. The early turbojet engines such as the W2B required large nacelles, and in the case of the Meteor this proved helpful as it rendered it easy to fit different units over the course of the type's development. The nacelles themselves did alter, though, being extended from the Meteor III onwards to help reduce high-speed buffeting. A standard tricycle undercarriage was gradually beefed-up as the Meteor became heavier during the course of development. Typical for fighters of the day, the cockpit was fitted with all-analogue instrumentation. At the outset, the Meteor I had four 20mm Hispano cannon mounted in the nose, and this armament persisted throughout the type's RAF service.

The first production Meteor Is began arriving with No 616 Squadron in July 1944, not long

Below: The first Meteor to take to the air was actually the fifth prototype, DG206/G. The '/G' appended to the aircraft serial denoted that the aircraft was to have an armed guard at all times while it was on the ground.

after the troubled Me 262 had entered Luftwaffe service. By then, the tide of the war in Europe had turned so far in the Allies' favour that it was hard even for this revolutionary new fighter to have much influence on the course of air fighting. Nonetheless, from the end of July 1944, No 616 Squadron's Meteor Is took part in the so-called 'anti-Diver' patrols, the RAF's efforts to combat the menace of the V-1 flying bombs. The unit, and the aircraft's, first two V-1 'kills' were scored on 4 August, one by tipping the 'doodlebug' out of control with the Meteor's wing and the second in a more conventional gun attack. In total, 13 V-1s were destroyed by No 616 Squadron's Meteors before the campaign ended. No 616 Squadron converted to the Meteor III before it was deployed to liberated Europe, initially Melsbroek near Brussels and then Gilze Rijen in the Netherlands. But if there had been any hopes that the RAF's new jets would be able to get to grips with the enemy, they were not to be realised. Initially they were forbidden from operating over territory still held by the Germans and in the

event the only Luftwaffe aircraft destroyed by the Meteors were claimed in the course of strafing runs.

All but the first few Meteor IIIs, soon known as F3s, were powered by the Rolls-Royce Derwent engine, a more potent development of the type's original Welland. It was with the F3 that the large-scale conversion to jets of the RAF's front-line force began. A still greater advance came from May 1945 with the Meteor F4, its Derwent 5 engines each offering a substantial thrust increase to 3,500lb thrust and the short-span clipped wings of most production examples giving superior manoeuvrability. The ranks of RAF day fighter squadrons based in Britain rapidly continued to transition to jets, transforming the air arm forever.

After the war, many years of incremental improvements to the RAF's Meteor force, would see the type being developed way beyond its original design specifications. However, as a front-line day fighter, the Meteor's RAF career was over by April 1957, when No 245 Squadron relinquished its F8s. Night fighter variants soldiered on for a while longer, until No 60 Squadron's final NF14s were phased out in September 1961. Still, though, the RAF wasn't done with the Meteor, as examples of various marks were used for second-line duties right into the mid-1980s. This was a truly remarkable service career by a truly remarkable aircraft.

GLOSTER METEOR | 65

Above: **The business end of the Gloster Meteor F3. Although the aircraft went through many incarnations, one constant was its armament of four 20mm Hispano cannons housed in the nose. The pilot is clearly enjoying bringing his guns to bear on the cameraship!**

Left: **Meteor I EE227, YQ-Y, was one of 15 of the marque delivered to No 616 Squadron during 1944. Following its service with '616', the aircraft was transferred to the Royal Aircraft Establishment and then to Rolls-Royce, where it became the first aircraft to be fitted with turboprops (Rolls-Royce Trents). After a distinguished career EE227 was struck off charge on 27 June 1949.**

De Havilland Vampire

Above: Blood brothers. The historic sight of six Vampire F1s of the RAF's first DH100 unit, No 247 Squadron. Leading the flight is TG/311, coded ZY-O. Initially No 247 Squadron was based at Chilbolton, but later moved to RAF Odiham to become part of the three-squadron Vampire Wing. Early examples featured a fixed cockpit fairing at the rear, which restricted 'over the shoulder' vision. During the production run of the F1, a one-piece sliding hood was introduced.

De Havilland's DH100 Vampire has the distinction of being the second design of jet fighter to enter service with the Royal Air Force. Developed during the war years, its distinctive shape appeared in the skies just too late to see action, with only a few examples delivered by May 1945.

The DH100 Vampire has its origins in Air Ministry specification E6/41 that defined a single-engined jet fighter suitable for operation at great heights, fitted with a pressure cabin for the pilot, and armed with four Hispano 20mm cannon. The requirement went on to state that the aircraft should be as small as possible – jet engines were still in their infancy and certainly not producing huge power outputs – and employ basic constructional techniques. Most importantly, it stated that a de Havilland Halford jet engine would be installed. The aero-engine designer Major Frank Halford had been given access to Frank Whittle's pioneering work on gas turbines; for the projected jet-powered fighter, Halford decided to proceed with the design of a 'straight through' centrifugal engine capable of generating 3,000lb of thrust, which was considered to be high at the time. Halford's engine was developed, and emerged as the Halford H1 (later to be named Goblin I).

Led by Sir Geoffrey de Havilland, the design that emerged at Hatfield was conventional in construction but unconventional in layout, with pilot, guns and jet engine all crammed into a rather small, egg-shaped fuselage, behind which was a twin tail boom. By now designated the DH100, the design was primarily composed of plywood for the forward section and aluminium throughout the aft section. The pilot was positioned ahead of the wing, giving a good all-round field of vision. Air intakes were in the wing roots, with ducting to the compressor of the Halford H1 turbojet, whose exhaust pipe sat neatly in between the booms and below the tailplane. Armament comprised four 20mm Hispano Mk V cannon located underneath the nose.

The first prototype, LZ548/G (where the 'G' signified the need for an armed guard), was designed and constructed by the company in little over a year and made its first flight from Hatfield on 20 September 1943. Completing the 'family firm' image of the aircraft, the pilot was Geoffrey de Havilland Jr. After just a few flights, it was achieving 480mph.

DE HAVILLAND VAMPIRE

It being wartime, development of the Vampire proceeded rapidly. While the first and second prototypes had been primarily involved in proving the new type's flying qualities and were gunless, the third prototype, MP838/G, mounted the intended armament of four 20mm Hispano cannon. MP838 was then sent to the Royal Aircraft Establishment at Farnborough in March 1944 for official evaluation and to be flown by a number

*Below: **The first prototype of the DH100 Vampire. With no need for propeller clearance, the short undercarriage gave the aircraft a very squat appearance on the ground. The Vampire was built too late to see action in World War 2, but its excellent flying qualities gave it a longevity that its designers could never have imagined.***

*Above: **A low wing loading ensured the Vampire exhibited excellent manoeuvrability. Because early jet engines were incapable of giving high thrust levels, the Vampire was intentionally kept small, such that the 3,000lb thrust of the engine was adequate to propel the egg-shaped fighter to speeds edging 550mph in level flight.***

of service pilots. As first flown in prototype form, the Vampire did not exhibit a level of performance that substantially exceeded that of the best piston-engined fighters of the time. Nevertheless, flight testing threw up no great problems and an initial order was placed in May 1944 for 120 Vampire F1 fighters. Compared with the prototypes, these would have shorter, squatter fin/rudder assembles. Production, though, was to be undertaken by English Electric at Preston, to allow de Havilland to continue its all-important wartime work of producing the Mosquito.

It may have missed the war, but the Vampire entered service with No 247 Squadron in March 1946, in time for nine aircraft to take part in the victory celebrations over central London on 8 June that year.

Ultimately, the Vampire was one of those aircraft that just 'worked'. It was highly manoeuvrable, its pilots found it fun to fly and it sold supremely well. Over the next couple of decades, the type would go on to have a successful career with the RAF, the Swiss Air Force (with which it served until 1990) and numerous other countries. Over 4,000 would be produced.

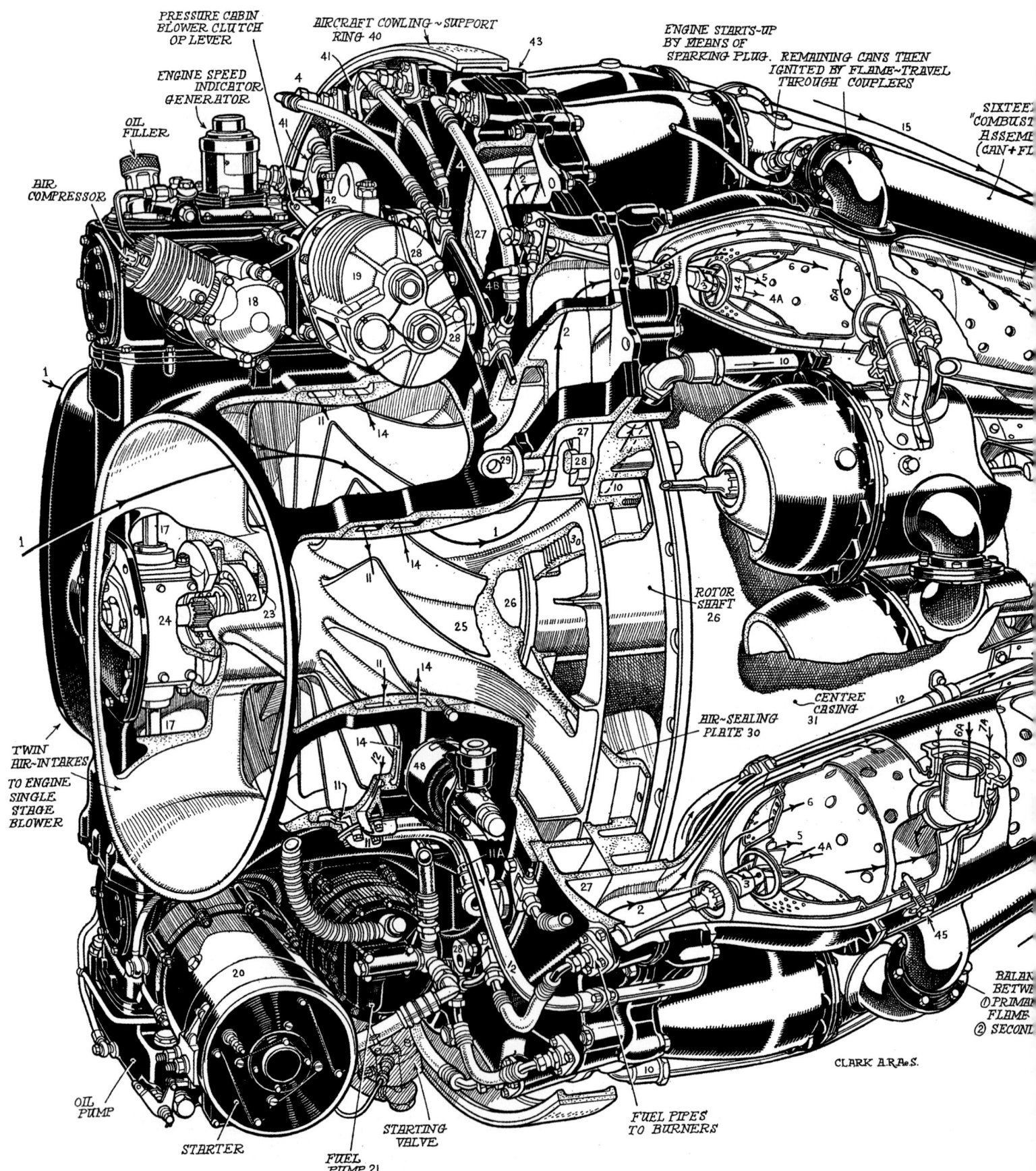

THE DE HAVILLAND GO[BLIN]

The Goblin I develops 2,700 lb. S.T. and the Goblin II 3,000 lb[.]

Flame and Airflows Through Engine

1.—Airflow in through blower and up volutes at 2, around ports and into cans; divides into 3, 5, 6 and 7.
3.—Air into burner mixes with fuel to give flame 4A.
4.—Fuel supply; 4B connection to fuel pressure gauge.
5.—Primary air through swirler to mix with flame.
6.—Primary air through nose cap to mix with flame.
6A.—Primary air and flame between flame tubes via couplers.
7.—Secondary air outside flame tube and entering later to m[ix] with flame.
7A.—Secondary air between cans via couplers.
8.—Secondary air along outside of flame tube to cool junction pip[e]
9.—Primary and secondary air and hot gas drives turbine a[nd] forms jet.
10.—Four streams of air from air behind impellor led to cool ba[ck] face of turbine rotor.

N JET PROPULSION UNIT

using a different combustion chamber, with other minor changes

Drawing by J. H. Clark, A.R.Ae.S.
Copyright *The Aeroplane*

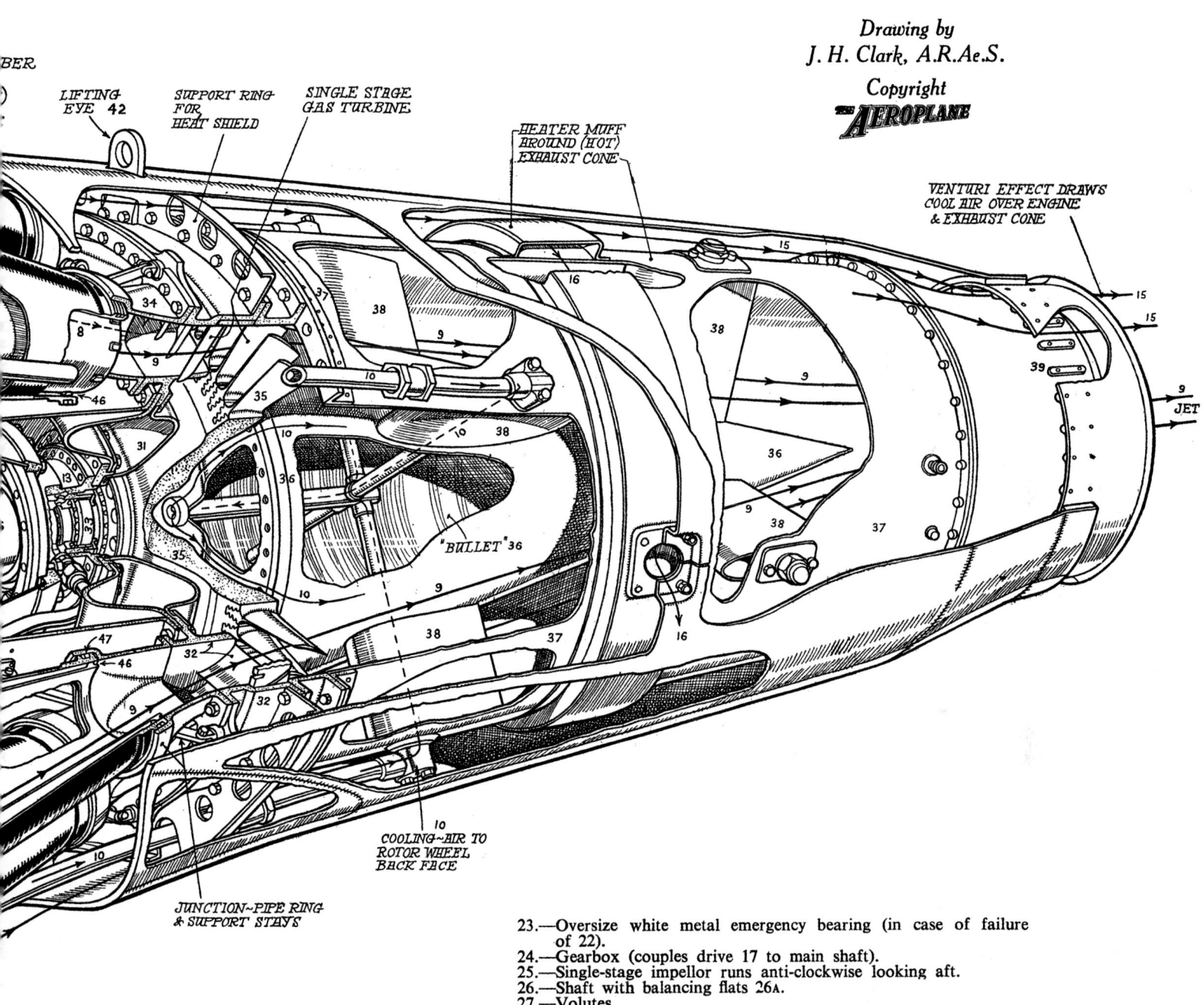

23.—Oversize white metal emergency bearing (in case of failure of 22).
24.—Gearbox (couples drive 17 to main shaft).
25.—Single-stage impellor runs anti-clockwise looking aft.
26.—Shaft with balancing flats 26A.
27.—Volutes.
28.—Through bolts (waisted to thickness of volute blades 27).
29.—Four through bolts 28 also form engine-mounting pickups.
30.—Air sealing plate seals off blower from centre casing (bolted to blower casing).
31.—Centre casing picks up blower, turbine stator 32 and rear bearing 33.
32.—Stator blades and casing.
33.—Air-cooled rear bearing.
34.—Junction pipes direct gases on to turbine blades.
35.—Turbine rotor on shaft 26 and carried in bearing 33.
36.—Bullet behind rotor-wheel forms reaction surface for jet.
37.—Exhaust cone bolted to centre casing 31 via stator casing 32.
38.—Two groups of four streamlined supports hold bullet in exhaust cone (air pipes 10 pass down one group).
39.—Distance pieces between exhaust cone and heat shield provide gap for venturi effect.
40.—Cowling support ring.
41.—Stirrups carry ring 40 off blower casing.
42.—Lifting eye.
43.—Four faces at 90 degrees around blower casing to carry engine-mount trunnions (when required).
44.—Swirler (in flame tube).
45.—Three locating pegs register flame tube in can.
46.—Blisters provide air gap.
47.—Two sealing rings.
48.—Barostat (part cut away to reveal pipes 11 and 12).

UNITED KINGDOM

DE HAVILLAND VAMPIRE

Vampire F1

Engine:	de Havilland Goblin
Power:	2,700lb thrust (in prototype, 3,100lb in production aircraft)
Length:	30ft 9in (9.37m)
Wingspan:	40ft 0in (12.19m)
Height:	8ft 10in (2.69m)
Service ceiling:	40,000ft (12,200m)
Max T/O weight:	10,300lb (4,670kg)
Maximum speed:	540mph (870kph)
Range:	730 miles (1,175km)
Armament:	4 x Hispano 20mm cannon

Top left: Vampire F1 TG/442 coded FMI-H representing its time with No 203 Advanced Flying School at RAF Driffield in 1949.

Left: Scramble, scramble! In time-honoured fashion, pilots of No 501 Squadron run to their waiting Vampires.

*Above: **The Vampire was a pilot's aeroplane. It was generally described as a delight to fly and highly manoeuvrable – and it could reach altitudes that RAF Meteors could not. In a close-in fight, a Vampire could out-turn almost any opponent and it was a good gun platform. However, no pilot would describe the Vampire's performance as 'sparkling', or claim the aircraft to be overpowered. Acceleration of the Goblin engine was painfully slow.***

*Right: **On 3 December 1945, Eric 'Winkle' Brown operated Vampire F1 LZ551/G on HMS Ocean. This was the world's first landing and take-off of a jet aircraft on an aircraft carrier, and was a portent of things to come.***

UNITED STATES

Bell P-59 Airacomet

The Bell XP-59A Airacomet was America's first step into the jet age. Although it did not see combat in World War 2, it gave the US military valuable experience with jet aircraft technology. However, it would not have existed had it not been for a small British aircraft on the other side of the Atlantic…

The United States was slow to enter the field of jet propulsion. Although engineers had considered applying jet turbine technology to aircraft, it was not until early 1941 that Gen Henry H. 'Hap' Arnold, Deputy Chief of Staff for Air (later commanding general of the USAAF), wrote to the chairman of the National Advisory Committee for Aeronautics (NACA), asking him to form a special group to consider jet aircraft propulsion. Two months later Arnold observed the British Gloster E.28/39 powered by Frank Whittle's W.1X turbojet and impressed by what he saw immediately set about exchanging information on this technology. It was decided that the US must begin at once to construct 15 jet turbine aircraft engines based on the new Whittle engine, the W.2B. General Electric was selected to build the engines, while the Bell Aircraft Corporation was chosen to build the aircraft it was to power. The Whittle engine was not overly powerful, so a twin-engined configuration was chosen for the jet fighter. A contract was awarded on 30 September 1941 and the designation XP-59A selected, the latter as a good cover for the true nature of this work because the designation originally referred to a piston engine fighter project proposed earlier by Bell. General Electric used a similar ruse and designated the engine the Type I-A.

During the rest of 1941, Larry Bell and his chief engineer, Harland M. Poyer, assembled a team and began to design the first American jet aircraft. The team was guided only by theory. General Electric would not finish and begin testing the first engine until March 1942, so Bell could only guess at the performance characteristics. In fact, neither the W.1X engine shipped from England nor General Electric's own versions could generate the power levels initially predicted.

Because of the secrecy surrounding the new fighter, the design team had to work within a restricted environment and this produced a rather conventional overall design, complete with straight-wing mainplanes and a traditional tail unit. The cockpit featured a heavily-framed canopy, which gave the pilot somewhat limited vision. The engines were fitted in the wing roots, essentially underslung along the wing mainplanes and separated by the slim fuselage. The engine nacelles featured rounded-rectangular intakes for aspirating the turbojets within and exhausted aft of the wing trailing edges. Overall construction of the aircraft was largely metal with some control surfaces initially completed in fabric. By and large, the

*Left: **With its aggressive armament of one 37mm M-4 cannon and three 0.50in machine guns, the Airacomet certainly had the potential to pack a punch, but sadly its performance did not match its appearance.***

*Below: **When the first XP-59 was being handled on the ground, Bell mounted a dummy propeller on the nose and threw a tarpaulin over the fuselage to disguise it as just another new piston engine aircraft.***

UNITED STATES

XP-59 broke little ground in terms of fighter design. Essentially, it was as basic as possible to house the engines and fly within the specified amount of time.

Thus, on 19 September 1942 Bell shipped the first XP-59A to a remote base in California, Muroc Dry Lake, for the initial flight trials. To maintain secrecy, Bell mounted a dummy propeller on the nose and threw a tarpaulin over the fuselage to give the illusion that the Airacomet was just another piston fighter. On 1 October 1942, Bell test pilot Robert M. Stanley took the XP-59A into the air for the first time. Two General Electric Type I-A centrifugal-flow jet engines drove the unrefined XP-59A airframe to a disappointing maximum speed of just 390mph (628km/h), slower than existing Axis and Allied piston-engined fighters. However, in March 1942, the Bell Company received a follow-on contract for 13 YP-59A test and evaluation aircraft. More powerful General Electric I-16 (J31) turbojet engines powered these and all subsequent production Airacomets. The first of 13 YP-59As arrived for flight-testing at Muroc in June 1943. One of these aircraft set a new unofficial altitude record of 47,600ft (14,512m), but the type was still outclassed by contemporary piston fighters. The third YP-59A (42-22611) was supplied to the RAF (receiving British serial RG362/G), in exchange for the first production Gloster Meteor I, EE210/G. British pilots found that the aircraft compared very unfavourably with the jets that they were already flying.

Although Bell proposed that the USAAF should acquire 300 P-59 Airacomets, an order was placed for 100. Eventually, Bell completed just 50 production Airacomets, 20 P-59As and 30 P-59Bs, with the latter being assigned to the 412th Fighter Group. Each was armed with one 37mm M-4 cannon and three 0.50in machine guns. After the 412th Fighter Group's training squadron was disbanded in 1946, the P-59 slipped into aviation history – none were flying by 1950. Those that were not scrapped or run into the ground during testing became museum showpieces.

While the P-59 was not a great success, the type did give the USAAF experience with the operation of jet aircraft, in preparation for the more advanced types that would shortly become available.

Right: **Tests on the three XP-59As revealed a multitude of problems including poor engine response and reliability (common shortcomings of all early turbojets), insufficient lateral stability, and performance that was far below expectations. Chuck Yeager flew the aircraft and was dissatisfied with its speed, but was amazed at its smooth flying characteristics.**

Bottom right: **Bell XP-59A Airacomet and test pilot Robert M. Stanley. The aircraft first became airborne during high-speed taxiing tests on 1 October 1942 with Stanley at the controls, although the first official flight was made by Col Laurence Craigie the next day.**

Below: **Apart from its engine installation, the basic airframe of the XP-59 was of largely conventional design. In fact, it owed its origins to an original prop-driven, twin-boom design relying on a 'pusher' arrangement that company engineers had been working on before the jet-powered XP-59 programme was envisioned.**

Bell P-59B Airacomet

Engine:	2 x General Electric J31-GE-5 turbojets
Power:	2,000lb thrust each
Length:	38ft 10in (11.84m)
Wingspan:	45ft 6in (13.87m)
Height:	12ft 4in (3.76m)
Loaded weight:	11,040lb (6,214kg)
Speed:	413mph (665km/h)
Max range:	375 miles (604km)
Armament:	1 x 37mm M-4 cannon; 3 x 0.50in machine guns

BELL P-59 AIRACOMET

Above: **An XP-59A Airacomet during a test mission and wearing the short-lived red-outlined National markings, which dates this image as between June to September 1943.**

Right: **Bell YP-59A in flight. X and Y prefixed aircraft had rounded vertical stabilizers and wingtips while the production A and B models had squared surfaces. The YP-59A can be distinguished from the XP-59A because Ys had nose armament.**

Below: **Test pilot Jack Woolams prepares for another test flight in the YP-59A Airacomet. The 13 service test YP-59As had a more powerful engine than their predecessors, but the improvement in performance was negligible, with top speed increased by only 5mph and a reduction in the time they could be used before an overhaul was needed. Two YP-59A Airacomets (42-108778 and 42-100779) were also delivered to the US Navy where they were evaluated as the 'YF2L-1' but were quickly found completely unsuitable for carrier operations.**

Lockheed P-80 Shooting Star

Germany and Great Britain went to war in 1939 with jet aircraft programmes well underway, but the US took longer to appreciate and develop the new technology. The Lockheed P-80 Shooting Star was not the first US jet fighter, but it was the first to be used operationally by the United States Army Air Force (USAAF). Famously designed and built by Lockheed in just 143 days, two pre-production models did see very limited service in Italy just before the end of World War 2.

In 1943, the US Army's Air Tactical Service Command (ATSC) met with Lockheed Aircraft Corporation to express its dire need for a jet fighter to counter a rapidly growing German jet threat. One month later, an engineer by the name of Clarence 'Kelly' L. Johnson and his team of young engineers had delivered the XP-80 Shooting Star jet fighter proposal to the ATSC with the promise that he could deliver a prototype in six months. He was immediately given a letter of intent and told that his 'time starts now'. As the Lockheed factory at Burbank was already running to capacity, Johnson built his own manufacturing site around a small shack on the site, and stole personnel from all over the plant. His team bought out a local machine shop to get the tooling it needed, built walls from a vast supply of wooden packing crates and topped off the ad hoc facility with a big top rented from a local circus. The unsightly hybrid was christened the 'Skunk Works', later the birthplace of the F-104, U-2 and SR-71 Blackbird.

The XP-80 emerged as a conventional all-metal airframe, with a slim low wing and tricycle landing gear. Like most early jets designed during World War 2 – and before the Allies captured German research data that showed the speed advantages of swept-wings

– the XP-80 had straight wings. Nevertheless, it was the first operational jet fighter to have its engine embedded in the fuselage.

Remarkably, on 8 January 1944, day 143 of the contract, a green XP-80 christened *Lulu Belle* was rolled out for its maiden flight at Muroc Army Air Field (now Edwards AFB). Lockheed test pilot Milo Burcham fired up *Lulu Belle's* British Halford H-1 Goblin engine and took off. By the second flight of the day, Burcham was confident enough to alarm spectators by skimming low over the field at 475mph and pulling up into a series of tight aileron rolls.

The second prototype, designated XP-80A, was designed for the larger General Electric I-40 engine. Two aircraft (44-83021 and 44-83022) were built. 44-83021 being nicknamed the 'Gray Ghost' after its pearl gray paint scheme, while 83022, left unpainted, became known as the 'Silver Ghost'. Initial opinions of the XP-80A were not positive, with Burcham commenting that the aircraft had now become a 'dog'. His concerns soon took a tragic turn. Burcham was killed on 20 October 1944 while flying the third pre-production YP-80A, 44-83025. The 'Gray Ghost' was also lost on a test flight on 20 March

*Above: **The XP-80A prototype 44-83021 'Gray Ghost' being test-flown over California in 1944.***

*Right: **Also known as the 'Green Hornet' because of its paint scheme, the XP-80 prototype** Lulu Belle **was powered by the British Halford H-1 Goblin engine. In test flights, the XP-80 eventually reached a top speed of 502mph (808km/h) at 20,480ft (6,240m), making it the first turbojet-powered USAAF aircraft to exceed 500mph in level flight.***

*Below right: **Cutaway of the P-80A featuring the General Electric J33-GE-11 turbojet.***

*Below: **The dark green Lockheed XP-80 prototype** Lulu Belle **being prepared for its maiden flight at Muroc AAF on 8 January 1944.***

1945, following a turbine blade failure, though pilot Tony LeVier survived. The top-scoring USAAF ace, Maj Richard Bong was not so lucky when he was killed on an acceptance flight of a production P-80 in the US on 6 August 1945. Both Burcham and Bong crashed as a result of a main fuel pump failure.

By now dubbed the Shooting Star, in honour of its unparalleled 600mph speed, the fighter

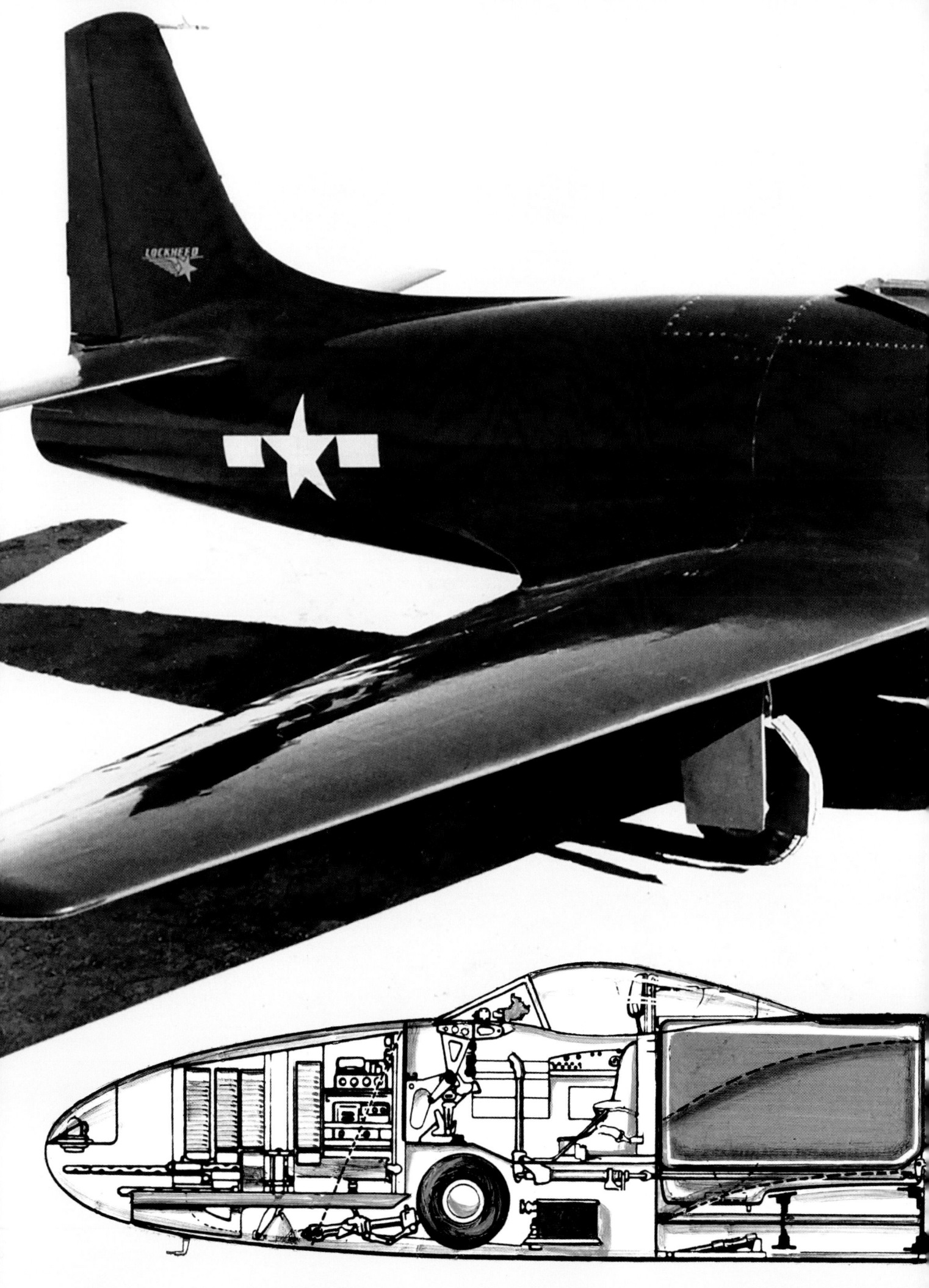

LOCKHEED P-80 SHOOTING STAR | 83

began to enter service in late 1944 with 12 pre-production YP-80As. Four were sent to Europe for operational testing, two to England and two to the 1st Fighter Group at Lesina Airfield, Italy, where they saw limited service flying reconnaissance missions. However, when test pilot Maj Frederic Borsodi was killed demonstrating YP-80A 44-83026 at RAF Burtonwood on 28 January 1945, the YP-80A was temporarily grounded.

Eventually, an initial production order was placed for 344 P-80As and a total of 83 had been delivered by the time World War 2 came to an end, most assigned to the 412th Fighter Group at Muroc Army Air Field. Production continued after the war, although wartime plans for 5,000 were quickly reduced to 2,000. A total of 1,714 single-seat F-80A, F-80B, F-80C, and RF-80s were manufactured by the end of production in 1950.

Although the P-80 did not see air-to-air combat in World War 2, the timely arrival of the Shooting Star by Lockheed set the stage for the aircraft's early dominance during the Korean War as America's front-line fighter. A highlight of the type's service record occurred on 8 November 1950, when Lt Russ Brown, flying an F-80C of the 16th Fighter Interceptor Squadron, shot down a North Korean MiG-15 in the first all-jet air-to-air combat. While the Shooting Star helped usher in the 'jet age' in the USAF, it was soon outclassed by the appearance of the 'next-generation' of swept-wing transonic aircraft. But the story of this ground-breaking jet did not end there… the two-seat TF-80C, first flown on 22 March 1948, became the basis for the T-33 trainer, of which a staggering 6,557 were produced.

*Right: **Left to right: Designer Clarence 'Kelly' Johnson, test pilot Tony LeVier, and an unidentified man with the Lockheed XP-80A prototype 'Gray Ghost'.** This aircraft was lost on a test flight on 20 March 1945, although Tony LeVier escaped. Newly promoted to chief engineering test pilot to replace Burcham, LeVier bailed out when one of the engine's turbine blades broke, causing structural failure in the aircraft's tail. LeVier landed hard and broke his back, but returned to the test programme after six months of recovery.*

*Below: **The straight-wing design of the P-80 meant that it was quickly superseded in front-line service by swept-wing jets, but not before it had played a major role in introducing jet operations to the pilots of the USAF.***

Lockheed P-80 Shooting Star

Engine:	1 x General Electric J33-GE-11 turbojet
Power:	3,850lb thrust
Length:	34ft 6in (10.5m)
Wingspan:	38ft 10in (11.83m)
Height:	11ft 4in (3.45m)
Loaded weight:	14,000lb (6,350kg)
Speed:	558mph (898km/h)
Max range:	1,440 miles (2,317km)
Armament:	6 x 0.50in machine guns

*Left: **With its bullet-shaped fuselage, flush rivets, and smooth skin, the later production P-80 not only looked good but also was an intimidating attack aircraft, boasting six .50-calibre machine guns and underwing shackles for bombs.***

McDonnell FD Phantom

The McDonnell FD Phantom was the first all-jet aircraft to operate from the deck of a US aircraft carrier, and the first jet fighter to serve with both the Navy and Marines. With a top speed of 500mph, according to James S. McDonnell it would 'appear and disappear like an apparition'. He was not entirely wrong, though not necessarily for the reasons he hoped.

On New Year's Eve 1942, the US Navy Bureau of Aeronautics called James S. McDonnell, founder of McDonnell Aircraft Corp, offering the company a contract to design and build the first American jet fighter capable of taking off from and landing on an aircraft carrier. The US Navy wanted a single-seat, jet-propelled, low-wing monoplane. The resulting FD Phantom was very much a 'clean sheet' design by McDonnell, a company that had only been founded in July 1939 and which had little experience of working with the US Navy. The aircraft's concept was conservative, featuring a straight wing, a tailplane with dihedral mounted high to clear the engine exhaust and two Westinghouse turbojets giving just 1,160lb thrust each.

Just over two years later, on 26 January 1945, Woodward 'Woody' Burke piloted the XFD-1

MCDONNELL FD PHANTOM

*Above: **The first of a dynasty. The McDonnell XFD-1 Phantom fighter during early flight trials.***

prototype on its first flight at Lambert Field in St Louis, MO. The XFD-1 was still in development when World War 2 ended, but the US Navy pressed forward with the programme.

The aircraft's greatest moment of fame occurred on the morning of 21 July 1946, when the XFD-1 Phantom roared 400ft (120m) down the deck of the USS *Franklin D. Roosevelt*, a then-recently commissioned US Navy aircraft carrier. The Phantom's pilot, Lt Cdr James T. Davidson, climbed quickly port side, circled the carrier and then landed. It marked the first take-off and landing of a jet-powered aircraft from the deck of a US aircraft carrier.

The XFD-1, later redesignated the FH-1 Phantom, ushered in a new era of naval aviation. McDonnell Aircraft produced 62 FH-1s powered by two Westinghouse J30s offering 1,600lb. VF-17A was chosen as the first Phantom squadron, and received aircraft from the McDonnell line from July 1947. When it completed carrier qualification trials aboard USS *Saipan* in May 1948, VF-17A was unquestionably the first jet fighter-equipped carrier-based squadron in the world. It would

FD-1 Phantom

Engine:	2 x Westinghouse J30
Power:	1,600lb thrust each
Wingspan:	40ft 9in (12.42m)
Length:	38ft 9in (11.81m)
Height:	14ft 2in (4.31m)
Max T/O weight:	12,030lb (5,460kg)
Ceiling:	43,000ft (13,100m)
Max. speed:	480mph (770km/h) at sea level
Armament:	4 x 0.50in machine guns in nose

be the only US Navy operator of the type, although USMC squadron VMF-122 received the Phantom from 1947.

The Phantom proved the concept and developed techniques that would be employed by later US Navy fighter types, but was quickly superseded by newer types.

Bell XP-83

Bell XP-83	
Engine:	2 x General Electric J33-GE-5 turbojets
Power:	4,000lb thrust each
Length:	44ft 10in (13.67m)
Wingspan:	53ft 0in (16.15m)
Height:	15ft 3in (4.65m)
Loaded weight:	24,090lb (10,930kg)
Speed:	522mph (840km/h)
Max range:	2,050 miles (3,300km) with drop tanks
Armament:	6 x 0.6in (15.2mm) machine guns

With the war in Europe signalling the need for long-range escort fighters, the USAAF tasked Bell to build a larger, longer-legged jet fighter. The result was the Bell XP-83, a bulky machine that first flew during World War 2, but did not proceed beyond prototype development.

Owing to their high fuel consumption, early jet fighters suffered from a short range and endurance. In March 1944, the USAAF requested Bell to design a long-range fighter and formally awarded a contract for two prototypes on 31 July 1944. Bell had been working on its 'Model 40' interceptor design since 1943 and engineer Charles Rhodes was tasked with redesigning it as a long-range escort fighter. Retaining the general layout of the earlier P-59 Airacomet, the two General Electric J33-GE-5 turbojet engines were located in each wing root, which left the large fuselage

*Above: **The Bell XP-83 was a prototype escort fighter designed by Bell Aircraft during World War 2. It first flew in 1945 but it was soon eclipsed by more advanced designs.***

free for fuel tanks and armament. The fuselage was of all-metal semi-monocoque design. The armament was to be six 0.5in machine guns in the nose.

Making its maiden flight on 25 February 1945, the first XP-83 proved underpowered and suffered from directional instability. The proximity of the two low-slung powerplants caused hot exhaust gases to buckle the tailplane unless, during run-ups, fire trucks were used to play streams of water over the rear fuselage! The second XP-83 was completed with a slightly different bubble canopy and extended nose to accommodate six 15.2mm guns, the increase in barrel diameter being based on anticipated firepower needs for the planned invasion of Japan. Modified tailpipes, angled outwards, resolved the heat/buckling problem and a revised tailfin was fitted to improve stability. One unique characteristic was the XP-83's refusal to 'slow down' due to its aerodynamic shape and lack of air brakes; test pilots were forced to fly very long and flat landing approaches.

Except with respect to range, which was a formidable 2,050 miles (3,300km) with underwing drop-tanks, the Bell XP-83 offered no improvement over the Lockheed F-80 Shooting Star then already in production. For the post-war fighter-escort role, the newly independent USAF turned to the North American F-82 Twin Mustang and the XP-83 project was cancelled. The redesignated XF-83 soldiered on as a flying testbed for new technology. The first machine was assigned to a ramjet engine test programme. On 4 September 1947 a ramjet caught fire and flames spread to the wing. Pilot Chalmers 'Slick' Goodlin and engineer Charles Fay, bailed out safely but the Bell XF-83 had made its last flight.

Northrop XP-79B

Arguably the most innovative, but deeply flawed, jet aircraft built during World War 2 did not originate in Germany, but the US. Jack Northrop had a penchant for flying wings and when he decided to pair his designs with rocket and then jet technology, the result was always going to be radical. But even more radical, was a proposed method for it to down enemy aircraft. The clue was in its nickname, the 'Flying Ram'.

The fighter that eventually became the Northrop XP-79B had an astonishing parallel development to the Me 163. It began in 1942 when Northrop convinced the US Army Air Force (USAAF) that he could build a fighter that could approach the speed of sound. He proposed a rocket-powered flying wing with a span of only 32ft. The pilot was to fly it in a prone position, the rationale being that such a posture would make him less vulnerable to G-forces and raise his 'blackout threshold' beyond normal limits. Although the resulting MX-334 was eventually viewed as a dead end, much research data had been culled from it, evolving into the far more feasible XP-79.

In January 1943, a contract for three prototypes was issued by the USAAF, each of which was to be powered by an Aerojet rocket engine with 2,000lb of thrust. Developmental problems with the proposed Aerojet engine, and the unlikelihood of its being able to keep the aircraft airborne for more than 30 minutes, led to the cancellation of the rockets and the first two XP-79s that were to be powered by them. The USAAF did, however, consent to completion of the third prototype, which used two Westinghouse 19B axial-flow jet engines with 1,345lb thrust. Like its rocket-powered precursor, the jet-powered version, designated XP-79B, was essentially a wing, with the pilot lying on his stomach between the two jet engines. His head protruded into an acrylic-plastic windshield fitted with an armour glass section. An overhead hatch gave him entry to and, if necessary, a hasty exit from, the cabin. As radical as the XP-79's all-wing configuration looked, its structure was equally unusual. The airframe was made of heavy-gauge magnesium. The leading-edge skin was 0.75in thick; reinforcing steel armour plate of 0.25in

welded at a 45-degree angle just inside the wing's leading edge. The magnesium structure created an extremely sturdy machine, and some thought was given to using the fighter as an aerial battering ram.

Upon receiving reports of approaching enemy bombers, the XP-79B would take off with the aid of JATO (jet-assisted take-off)

*Right: **The Northrop XP-79 was an ambitious design for a flying wing fighter. It had several notable features, including the flying position of the pilot, who operated the aircraft from a prone position, theoretically permitting him to withstand greater G forces. Note also the four-position undercarriage, which caused problems during high-speed taxiing trials. Sadly, the words 'danger' on the air intakes could also be applied to the machine itself.***

*Below: **The sole prototype Northrop XP-79B, one of the most unconventional jets designed during World War 2. Its one and only powered flight was tragically short lived.***

UNITED STATES

packs. Reaching an altitude of 40,000ft, the 'Flying Ram' would then dive into the formation of enemy aircraft at an estimated speed of up to 547mph and clip their wing or tail surfaces with its own reinforced wings. Common sense finally prevailed when the XP-79B order also stipulated that the fighter should accommodate four 0.50in Browning machine guns outboard of the jet engines. Neither the guns nor the cockpit pressurisation system were destined to be installed in the prototype.

Painted white overall and given the serial number 43-32437, the prototype XP-79B was covered with canvas and trucked to the Muroc Dry Lake testing facility. Its first taxiing tests were conducted in June 1945, during which its four-point undercarriage caused tyres to burst on several occasions.

Finally, on 12 September 1945, test pilot Harry Crosby prepared to take the XP-79B up for its maiden flight. After take-off, Crosby climbed to 10,000ft and over the next 15min tested the handling of the revolutionary machine. Things suddenly went wrong during one such turn, and degenerated into a nose-down spin. Crosby finally judged it impossible to regain control of the aircraft and after jettisoning the escape hatch tried to leap clear, only to be struck by the wildly gyrating wing. Crosby fell to his death, his parachute unopened. The XP-79B slammed into the desert floor and exploded in a white-hot flare of magnesium.

Northrop's engineers determined that the control problem that had cost Harry Crosby his life could be corrected, but the USAAF decided to abandon the XP-79B project. By now World War 2 was over, the Lockheed P-80 Shooting Star was entering production, and other more conventional jet designs were showing greater promise than the flying-wing concept.

Northrop XP-79B	
Engine:	2 x Westinghouse 19B turbojets
Power:	1,150lb thrust each
Length:	14ft 0in (4.27m)
Wingspan:	38ft 0in (11.58m)
Height:	7ft 6in (2.29m)
Loaded weight:	8,669lb (3,932kg)
Speed:	547mph (880km/h) projected
Max range:	993 miles (1,598km) projected
Armament:	4 x 0.50in machine guns (never fitted)

Right: **Side-on, the true size of the XP-79B can be appreciated. Despite its large wing, the aircraft was only 14ft (4.27m) long.**

Below: **The flying wing layout of the XP-79B would later be applied to other Northrop types, including of course the B-2 bomber of today.**

Northrop MX-334: First US jet-powered aircraft

The Northrop XP-79 evolved from an experimental flying-wing glider designated MX-324, a simple steel tube and wood affair with faired, fixed landing gear. It was towed into the air behind a Lockheed P-38 Lightning. During an early flight, the MX-324's test pilot, pre-war racing pilot Harry Crosby, encountered trouble when turbulence behind the P-38 flipped the glider upside down. The MX-324 went into a spin. Even when it suddenly came out of the spin, it was still inverted and descending in ever-tightening circles. Crosby managed to exit the aircraft safely. The following jet-powered MX-334 was destined to make history. It first took to the air in October 1943 for some unpowered testing while the Aerojet Corporation completed its XCAL-200 rocket engine, which was to be powered by monoethyaniline fuel, oxidized by red fuming nitric acid. The MX-334 made its first flight with the new engine on 23 June 1944. Although capable of only 3.5min of powered flight, it was America's first rocket-powered aircraft. However, the lack of more powerful rocket engines and a redirection of priorities resulted in termination of the project.

*Below: **Test pilot Harry Crosby demonstrates the small size and two escape hatches of the MX-334.***

Douglas XB-43 Jetmaster

The Douglas XB-43 has the distinction of being America's first jet bomber. It was a development of the XB-42 Mixmaster twin-engined bomber, with turbojet engines replacing the twin inline piston engines. However, delays in the programme and the end of World War 2 effectively killed off the project.

The Douglas XB-42 was a radical design for a long-range twin-engined bomber in which the engines were carried inside the fuselage and powered contra-rotating pusher propellers mounted behind the tail. The first prototype B-42 was ready by May 1942, and performed impressively in its trials, but it was already clear that the new turbojet engines would probably make it obsolete. Therefore, in October of 1943 consideration was given to fitting turbojets to the XB-42. Preliminary studies indicated that the scheme was practical and on 31 March 1944 Douglas received a change order to the original XB-42 contract, which called for the production of two jet-powered versions under the designation XB-43.

Two General Electric TG-180 (later redesignated J35-GE-3) axial-flow turbojets were mounted in the forward fuselage bays that were previously occupied by the Allison piston engines of the XB-42. Flush intakes were incorporated in the upper fuselage sides immediately behind the two-seat pressurised cockpit. The aircraft retained its single dorsal vertical tail fin (the ventral fin was deleted

DOUGLAS XB-43 JETMASTER

*Above: **The prototype of the XB-43. A first flight was finally recorded on 17 May 1946, but by this time it became one of many promising programmes that fell under the axe of the massive military drawdown that followed the end of World War 2.***

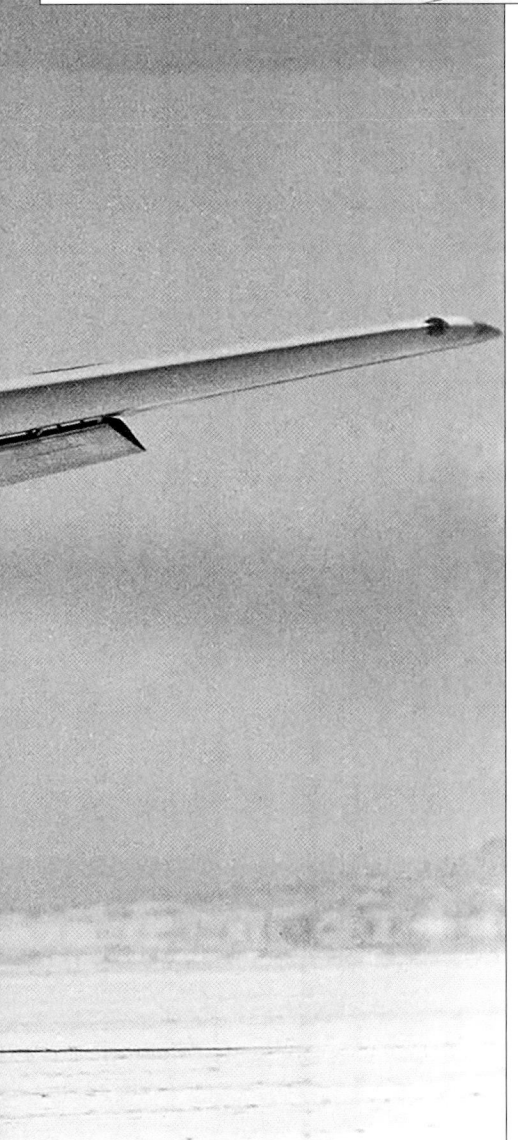

*Left: **The honour of being America's first jet bomber fell to the Douglas XB-43 Jetmaster, a rather awkward aircraft that looked like the compromise that it was. Circumstances meant that it never progressed beyond prototype stage.***

while the dorsal fin was enlarged), retractable tricycle undercarriage, and two-man cockpit arrangement. Two versions were planned, a bomber version with a transparent nose and a maximum bombload of 8,000lb and an attack version with 16 forward-firing 0.50in machine guns and 35 5in rockets. Both versions were to be fitted with a remotely-controlled, radar-directed tail turret with two 0.50in machine guns. However, no bombs were ever carried and the defensive armament was never installed on the XB-43 prototypes.

Assuming tests on the prototypes to be satisfactory, plans were made for an initial production order of 50 B-43s for the USAAF, while Douglas submitted an optimistic proposal for an eventual production rate of as many as 200 per month. However, the end of the war resulted in a slowdown in the B-43 programme, since a jet bomber was no longer urgently needed. The limited availability of the GE J35 engines further delayed the project. Even when the engines were fitted, a failure during ground running caused damage to the airframe that put off the first flight by another seven months. The first XB-43 (44-61508) finally took off on its maiden flight on 17 May 1946, with test pilot Bob Brush and engineer Russell Thaw in the cockpit. Performance was generally satisfactory, but the aircraft was somewhat underpowered. However, by this time, the USAAF had already decided against ordering the B-43 into production as it now favoured a four-engined rather than a twin-engined configuration for its future jet bombers. The XB-43 programme would still continue, but now it would be relegated to the status of a flying testbed. The first prototype was eventually cannibalised for its useful parts to serve the second (s/n 44-61509), which managed a successful test life until December of 1953.

Douglas XB-43 Jetmaster

Engine:	2 x General Electric J35-GE-3 turbojets
Power:	4,000lb thrust each
Length:	51ft 5in (15.7m)
Wingspan:	71ft 2in (21.7m)
Height:	24ft 3in (7.4m)
Loaded weight:	40,000lb (18,000kg)
Speed:	507mph (816km/h)
Max range:	2,500 miles (4,000km)
Armament:	Guns: 2 x 0.50in machine guns. Bombs: 8,000lb (3,629kg)

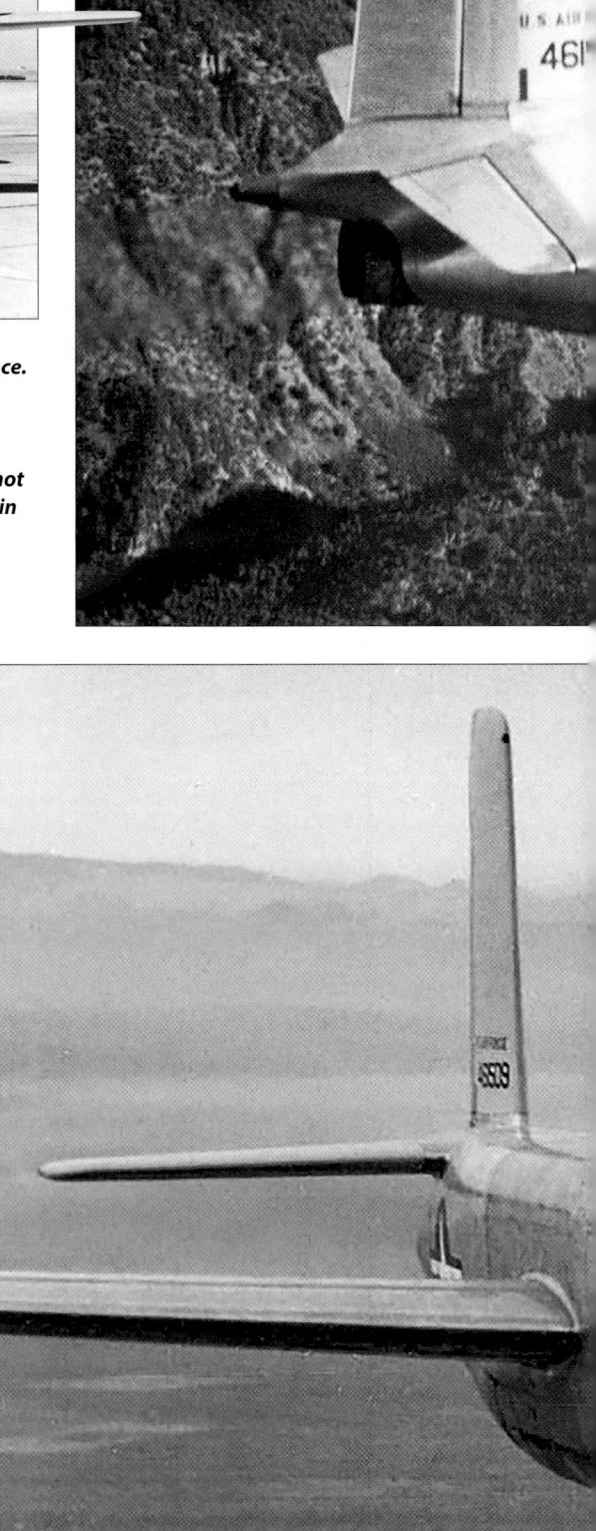

Above: **The Jetmaster featured an unusual twin cockpit arrangement giving it a bug-eyed appearance. A single canopy was planned for production models, but orders were not forthcoming and the programme cancelled.**

Right: **The second XB-43 prototype had a relatively successful career as an engine testbed and was not retired until 1953. It was kept airworthy by cannibalising the first XB-43, which had been damaged in an accident on 1 February 1951.**

Below: **During flight trials, the Plexiglas nose cracked due to temperature changes, and had to be replaced by a plywood cone.**

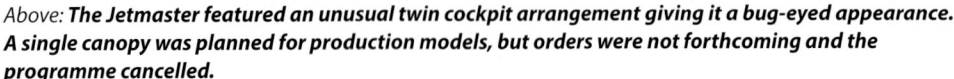

Bereznyak-Isayev BI-1

During World War 2, the Soviet Air Force was concerned that it was lagging behind in the development of rocket and jet powered aircraft. Therefore, in July 1940, work was begun on a high-speed fighter benefitting from rocket or ramjet propulsion. Following the German invasion in June of 1941, the design team, headed by engineers Alexander Bereznyak and Aleksei Isayev, was given just 35 days to come up with a viable platform. Thus was born the the Bereznyak-Isayev BI, a rocket-propelled, short-range defence fighter.

The new design was designated 'BI' for Blizhnii Istrebitel (close-range fighter), but as luck would have it, this also matched the initials of its designers. Although the resulting aircraft was of rather compact proportions, it was to be armed with a battery of four 14.5mm heavy machine guns. Its fuselage would be streamlined and well-rounded for aerodynamic efficiency. The cockpit was fitted forward of amidships and the nose section covered over in a pointed nose assembly. The rocket propulsion system would sit in the aft section of the fuselage which forced a raised fuselage spine. As the propulsion system utilised a liquid propellant, no air intake was required. The tail rudder extended over and under the aft fuselage with the usual horizontal stabiliser mid-mounted. This tailplane also fitted a smaller set of vertical planes at its outboard ends. The undercarriage was of the 'tail-dragger' arrangement and retractable under the aircraft.

As progress on the Dushkin D-1A-1100 liquid-fuelled rocket motor was slow, prototype BI-1 first flew as a glider to test its aerodynamic efficiency, to help prove that the airframe design was sound and to improve on some of its inherent weaknesses.

During October 1941, the development facility was evacuated to the Ural mountains and it was not until April 1942 that BI-1 was

Below: **The bullet-shaped Bereznyak-Isayev BI was the Soviet Union's first rocket-powered aircraft. For testing during the winter period, the standard undercarriage was removed and it was fitted with skids.**

BEREZNYAK-ISAYEV BI-1 | 97

Above: Rear view of the fifth prototype, illustrating well the additional vertical stabilisers fitted to the tips of the tailplane.

Bereznyak-Isayev BI-1

Engine:	1 x Dushkin D-1A-1100 liquid-fuelled rocket motor
Power:	2,430lb thrust
Length:	21ft 0in (6.4m)
Wingspan:	21ft 3in (6.48m)
Height:	6ft 9in (2.06m)
Loaded weight:	3,710lb (1,683kg)
Max speed:	497mph (800km/h)

ready for testing at Koltsove airfield. The aircraft finally made its maiden flight on 15 May 1942 with test pilot Grigory Bakhchivandzhi at the controls. The pilot shut the rocket engine off after about one minute, when a light indicated it was overheating. On landing, the aircraft descended too rapidly because of insufficient forward speed, breaking the main-landing-gear on touchdown. The pilot was unhurt and reported that, aside from the rough landing, the aircraft handled well. The flight lasted only 3 minutes and 9 seconds. Too damaged by its corrosive fuel to fly safely, BI-1 was retired and BI-2 took over the programme, during which it achieved a speed of 419mph (675km/h). Disaster struck on 27 March 1943, when BI-3, piloted by Backchivandzhi, entered a 45-degree dive and crashed into the ground, killing the pilot. The accident put a halt to flight tests, and a lengthy investigation determined that control was lost due to transonic effects on the pitch controls/stabilisers.

Prototypes BI-5, BI-6, BI-7, BI-8, and BI-9 followed into 1944 and the final forms were finished with Merkulov DM-4 ramjets, which required the airframe to be towed into the air prior to launch. Focus then shifted to Isaev's RD-1 rocket engine which covered no more than two flights. But by this time, the BI has reached its technological apex. The Soviet Air Force found little interest in a high-speed fighter with just a 15min endurance window and the programme was terminated.

Below: The maiden flight was eventful with the pilot forced to shut down the rocket engine prematurely. It ended with a heavy landing that broke the main landing gear.

SUBSCRIBE
TO *YOUR* FAVOURITE MAGAZINE
AND SAVE

Aeroplane traces its lineage back to the weekly The Aeroplane launched in June 1911, and is still continuing to provide the best aviation coverage around. Aeroplane magazine is dedicated to offering the most in-depth and entertaining read on all historical aircraft.

www.aeroplanemonthly.com

FREE *GIFT CARD* WITH EVERY SUBSCRIPTION